Wine Myths and Reality

Part 1

Viticulture, Vinification, and the Wine Trade

Also by Benjamin Lewin

Wines of France
Claret & Cabs
The Search for Pinot Noir
What Price Bordeaux

Guides to Top Wines and Vineyards

 1 *Bordeaux*
 2 *Southwest France*
 3 *Burgundy: Chablis & Côte d'Or*
 4 *Southern Burgundy, Beaujolais & Jura*
 5 *Champagne*
 6 *Alsace*
 7 *The Loire*
 8 *The Rhône*
 9 *Languedoc*
10 *Provence and Corsica*
11 *Barolo & Barbaresco*
12 *Tuscany*
13 *Port & the Douro*
14 *Napa Valley & Sonoma*

Wine Myths and Reality

Benjamin Lewin MW

Vendange Press

2010

Copyright © 2016 by Benjamin Lewin

All rights reserved. Published in the United States by Vendange Press.

Library of Congress Cataloging-in-Publication Data
Lewin, Benjamin
Wine Myths and Reality / by
Benjamin Lewin
Includes bibliographical references and index.

ISBN 978-1535396134

Without limiting the rights under copyright reserved above, no part of this publication may be reproduced, stored in or introduced into a retrieval system, or transmitted, in any form or by any means (electronic, mechanical, photocopying, recording or otherwise) without the prior written permission of both the copyright owner and the above publisher of the book. All enquiries should be directed to contact@vendangepress.com.

For my anima figure

Contents

Part 1:

Viticulture, Vinification, and the Wine Trade

I growing grapes

1 The Spread of the Grapevine — 3
A Single Species from the East
The Phylloxera Devastation
Cultivars and Clones
Zones for Grape Growing
Millennia of Innovation

2 Cultivating the Vineyard — 21
The Grapevine Life Cycle
From Deep Roots to Lofty Canopy
The Limits of Yield
The Acid/Sugar Playoff
The Taming of the Tannins
Man versus Machine
Going Green: Organic Viticulture
Phases of the Moon
Modern Trends

3 The Mystique of Terroir — 41
Does the Answer Lie in the Soil?
Licking the Slate
From Pompei to Clos Vougeot
Marketing the Terroir
Is Terroir Immutable?
Draining the Marshes
Terraforming the Mountains
Stress and the Single Grapevine
Garagistes and other Counter-Terroirists
The Far Reaches of Terroir
Does Terroir Matter?

4 Vintage Variation and Global Warming   69
The Origins of Vintage
Vintage Variation
Vintage versus Blending
The Temperature's Rising
Matching the Climate
Harvesting the Vine
Is Global Warming the Enabler?
Convergence of Styles

II making wine

5 Turning Grape Juice into Wine   89
From Vineyard to Fermentation
Good Yeast and Bad Yeast
Chaptalization: Turning Sugar into Alcohol
The Mysteries of Malolactic Fermentation
Heavier than Air
Filtration: Stripping the Wine?
You Can't Taste the Color
In the Pink
Sulfur Dioxide: the Essential Preservative
Residual Sugar
Natural Wine or Unnatural Practices?

6 The Alchemist's Delight   115
Alcohol: Finding the Sweet Spot
Acidity: Essential But Not Too Much
Dry Wine and the Sweet Tooth
Mega Color: Natural Additive or Snake Oil?
Wood v. Steel, Oxidation v. Reduction
Oak: Barrels, Staves, Chips, and Dust
Put a Cork In It
Turning the Screw
God Made the Wine

7 A Thousand Cultivars Bloom   143
Noble Varieties and Commoners
Ancient Origins and Newbies
Cépage Plus Terroir Equals Typicité
The Bitterness of the Super-taster
Aromas of Grapes and Wine
The Bell Peppers of Cabernet
Syrah or Shiraz?
The Ancient Pinot Family
Anything but Chardonnay
Herbaceous Sauvignon Blanc

The Petrol of Riesling
The Grapes of Muscat
Deus ex Machina
Engineering the Grapevine
The End of Evolution?

III the world market

8 Global Wine Trends — 187
From Plonk to Cult Wines
A Faithful Follower of Fashion
The Eggheads of Oenology
Flying Winemakers and Globalization
The Most Powerful Critic in the World
International Brands: Sourcing Wine
Packaging the Product
Taxation: Extortion or Distortion?
The Fanatics of Prohibition
Save your Heart or Sacrifice your Liver?

9 The International Wine Trade — 213
Choose your Tipple
Inequality of Supply And Demand
Crisis in Europe: the Rise of the New World
Boom and Bust in the Vineyards
The Price of Everything
The Supermarket Crunch
The Great Wine Agglomeration
If You Can't Beat 'Em, Join 'Em
The Bootleggers' Heritage
The Unequal Equation of Supply and Demand

10 Fraud and Scandal — 239
Plumbing the Depths
Red, Red Wine
Why Is Antifreeze Delicious?
A Spoonful of Sugar
You Pays Your Money and You Takes Your Choice
The Scandal of the Century
Thomas Jefferson Was Here

Bibliography — 255
Notes — 257
Index — 295

Preface

WINEMAKING IS NOT A MATTER OF CHANCE: the completely natural result of fermenting grapes would be vinegar. Every decision you make (or fail to make) in the vineyard or winery affects the style and quality of the wine that finally emerges in the bottle. Wine does not make itself. Never before has there been so much opportunity for the winemaker to direct viticulture and vinification to shape the wine. Wine has never been technically better, but these new possibilities create the dilemma of whether making better wine narrows differences between places, making wines more similar, so their character is lost. Heated arguments occur wherever there is a history of winemaking as to whether today's wine is better than yesterday's or has lost its soul. Increased opportunity to manipulate the process leads to the question of how far you can go before wine ceases to be natural and becomes an industrial product.

With all these conflicting forces, the question becomes: how and why did the wine in the bottle you buy today come to be like it is. "How" reflects what use the winemaker has made of his ability to influence the process; "why" reflects a mélange of historical, social, and economic forces. The reasons why Bordeaux tastes different from Burgundy, why Barolo is distinct from Rioja, why New World wines are more powerful than European wines, not to mention why wines everywhere have changed so greatly in recent decades, reflect an interplay of factors going far beyond the simple facts of what types of grapes are grown in each place. Never has there been so much experimentation with grape growing or wine making, and so much innovation in wine styles. Yet at the same time, the focus has been sharpening on a small number of varieties at the expense of diversity. Has this led to more or less choice for the consumer?

Many myths stand in the way of understanding why wine is like it is, myths about viticulture, myths about winemaking, myths about the historical verities of wine. I'm interested in the context of each wine, not just how it is made, but also why the winemaker decided to make it like that. "Why" extends beyond the individual winemaker into asking what issues determine the success (or otherwise) of each wine region. The basic question I want to ask in this book is what's really going on when they make wine?

This is not a muckraking book or an exposé, but I do want to debunk myths about wine and to set the record straight by throwing light on issues that have been murky or misunderstood. I believe in the value of transparency. And if the results are not always pleasing, the solution is to change production methods or to educate the consumer, rather than to cover up.

When I mentioned the theme of this book to one of my MW colleagues, he was vaguely horrified. "Oh dear," he said, "you don't want to do that. It will destroy the romantic image." Perhaps it is its ancient origins that give wine its mythic aura. Or perhaps its central role in hospitality. Or the fact that every year is different. Or perhaps it's the halo effect of top wines that have become collectible items. Possibly it's no more than a great marketing success in making wine appear an artisanal product whatever its real origins. For whatever reason, the world of wine has an unusual gap between perception and reality.

When asked if they would like to try an organic wine, many consumers are puzzled. "Isn't all wine organic?" they often ask. Well, no, it isn't. Most of it is an industrial product. Most people think of wine as resulting directly from the fermentation of grapes. But wine production has never been entirely natural. In ancient times, herbs and spices were used for flavoring; in modern times adding sugar before fermentation was introduced to increase alcohol levels, and extraneous notes are introduced by exposure to oak or by other manipulations. In fact, manipulation during and after fermentation is extensive, and wine owes much of its flavor to decisions made by winemakers trying to satisfy the consumer market.

What goes into the bottle, what you actually drink when you open a bottle of wine, is determined not just by the vagaries of vintage and the hazards of winemaking, but also by market forces. Perhaps twenty or thirty years ago, the wine you were offered was what the producer wanted to make, or possibly what he was able to make. The transition to a consumer-driven market has caused a sweeping change, with wines tailored to demand. And of course the wine market is distorted by the iniquities of taxation like any other product, in fact, more than any other product, because alcoholic products are so attractive as targets for taxation. On top of this is the generally hostile attitude of the European Union to any form of alcohol consumption.

The wine you drink depends on the interplay of all these forces. Many of the wines of the Old World have long histories that still significantly impact the wines of today. Most of the wines of the New World are much more recent creations without the same historical constraints. Viticulture and vinification have evolved enormously in the past couple of decades, giving the winemaker far more control over the state of his grapes and what happens to them after harvest. Consumers, especially those who have come recently into wine, are driving a trend towards wines that are fruitier, and that can be drunk sooner than those of the past. Formidable export drives from new wine-producing countries have made new choices in wine widely available. Markets generally have become more open, with wine sold in supermarkets rather than specialist stores. Technological changes in grape growing and winemaking have combined with new sources for production and more open markets to change the face of wine, from plonk sold in 5 liter containers to rare bottles that can be had only on allocation by a happy few.

I begin where it all starts: with the grape. From there we go to how grape juice is turned into wine, to the nature of the international wine trade and its consequences for the consumer, and finally in detail to the wines themselves of the New and Old Worlds, where we look at the effects of contemporary forces in each country on its production of wine. This book makes no attempt to be comprehensive: it is not an encyclopedia, but rather an account of trend setters, driving forces—the factors determining why wine is like it is. At the end of the day, we should see why plonk is different from fine wine, what determines the flavor profiles of different wines, how New World wines differ from Old World wines, what global warming is going to do to wine production, and how all these various forces will impact wine production in the future. Sometimes there are no answers, but the questions are thought-provoking.

This book is intended for anyone interested in why wine tastes as it does. If you don't care about the fine details, it can be read entirely without reference to the charts or notes. (If they look intimidating, just ignore them.) But assertions without support have little conviction, so charts contain supporting information for those who are interested in any particular aspect, and the notes give sources for those who would like to be sure I didn't just make it all up.

One of the pleasures of writing this book has been many fascinating interaction with winemakers and others in many regions, with far too many people to thank individually for interesting discussions, not to mention hospitality and tastings, but I must thank Kip Kumler, Jim Lapsley, Peter Sichel, Helio San Miguel, Liz Thach, and Vincenzo Zampi whose insightful comments on the book helped to improve it greatly. And as always, I was accompanied around the world of wine by my indefatigable traveling and tasting companion, without whom this would scarcely have been possible.

Benjamin Lewin MW

I GROWING GRAPES

MAN HAS GROWN GRAPES since time immemorial. The production of wine can be traced back to 5400 B.C., and cultivation of the grapevine to 4000 B.C. Pictorial representations in frescos and detailed hieroglyphic information on the seals of amphorae show that viticulture and vinification in Egypt had become sophisticated by 2700 B.C. By the time of the Greeks and Romans, viticulture was an important economic activity, as shown by the publication of treatises on the subject. At the start of the Common Era, grapevines began to spread from the Mediterranean across Europe, and in the Middle Ages they were widely propagated under the aegis of the Church. The European wine industry began to take its present form in the eighteenth and nineteenth centuries, and then was drastically reorganized as a result of the phylloxera infestation at the end of the nineteenth century. Wine production started in the New World with colonization, but became a significant part of world production only in the last years of the twentieth century. Major differences in viticulture between Europe and the New World result from their different regulatory systems, the biggest effect being that whereas irrigation is mostly banned in Europe, it is used in most of the New World, resulting in different criteria for choosing vineyard locations.

Development of viticulture and the wine trade over 7500 years.

5400 B.C.	Pottery has traces of tartaric acid, presumed to come from wine.
4000 B.C.	Grapevine is cultivated as an agricultural crop in Mesopotamia.
2700 B.C.	Viticulture and vinification is extensive in Egypt.
300 B.C.	Theophrastus publishes book on Greek viticulture.
1000 B.C.	Phoenicians start extensive export trade in wine.
65 C.E.	Columella publishes manuals for winemaking in Rome.
600 C.E.	Ecclesiastical vineyards spread across Europe.
1880 C.E.	Vineyards reorganized as result of Phylloxera.
2000 C.E.	New World wines become important on world market.

1

The Spread of the Grapevine

IT'S A MYTH THAT VITIS VINIFERA, the grapevine variety from which all fine (and much other) wine is made, is a single species. Vitis vinifera belongs to the Vitis family, which has about 60 members. All form grapes, but only Vitis vinifera is suitable for making wine; the others all have aromas or flavors that become disagreeable in wine. The members of the Vitis family are traditionally referred to as a species, and crosses between them are called "hybrids." But the fact that they can interbreed to form fertile offspring tells you at once that they are not different species. As all of these "species" of Vitis can interbreed, in reality they are distinct subspecies.[1] Although some of the hybrids produced by interbreeding vinifera with other Vitis (sub)species have been used to make wine, to all intents and purposes, all wines ranging from table wines to fine wines today are made from the many varieties of Vitis vinifera.[2] (Some of the hybrids or other members of the family have an important role in providing rootstocks onto which Vitis vinifera can be grafted.)

There are thousands of different varieties of Vitis vinifera from which wine can be made. Some of them have spread over the entire planet; varieties such as Cabernet Sauvignon or Chardonnay are now grown in virtually all wine-producing countries of the world. Some are still restricted to the places where they originated, and are used to produce wine only in one locale. Some have darkly colored skins and are used to make red wine; others have green or yellow skins and are used to make white wine. In a world where diversity is constantly narrowing, the grapevine, and the wine made from its fruit, stands out for its variety.

Where did Vitis vinifera originate? How did it spread worldwide to become the common grapevine used for wine production?

A Single Species from the East

At the end of the Tertiary period, more than 65 million years ago, give or take a few million, there was only a single type of grapevine. Vitis occurs naturally only in the northern hemisphere, and the primitive Vitis developed into different species suited to different environmental niches. Vitis vinifera originated in Eurasia. Almost all of the other species originated in North America.[3]

The original plant that gave rise to Vitis was a hermaphrodite, allowing self-fertilization. Primitive Vitis became dioecious; different plants had male or female flowers, so that both must grow close together for fruit to be formed.[4] (Only the female plants form berries.) Then the plant was domesticated. With domestication, it reverted to a hermaphrodite (possibly because rare naturally occurring hermaphrodites were selected for their ability to form fruit more reliably).[5]

During the Paleolithic era, more than 10,000 years ago, the first wine might have been made from wild grapes.[6] The most ancient traces of wine have been found on fragments of pottery from the Hajii Firuz Neolithic complex in the northern Zagros Mountains of Iran. The pottery dates from about 5400 B.C., and contains traces of tartaric acid, a compound that is produced in this area only by grapes.[7]

Wine probably became important in human culture when the grapevine was cultivated. The big question about domestication is whether it happened only once, so that all existing Vitis vinifera are derived from a single ancestral grapevine. (This is sometimes called the Noah hypothesis.[8]) Alternatively, it could have happened on several different occasions, in which case subgroups of Vitis vinifera should have descended from different ancestral grapevines. One way to distinguish these possibilities is to compare the genetic profiles of Vitis vinifera found in different geographical locations with the profiles of wild grapevines.[9] Different groups of wild grapevines can be distinguished over regions from the Near East to the Western Mediterranean, and judging from their genetic contributions to cultivated grapevines, there may have been at least two different domestication events.[10]

One event most likely took place in Transcaucasia, possibly in the area around the Black Sea, where wild grapevines are still relatively abundant. From there the grapevine may have spread to the Near East, where it may have been cultivated from about 4000 B.C. However, the main alcoholic beverages of the period were beer produced from barley and wine produced from dates, possibly because the major cities of Mesopotamia were close to the southern limits for producing wine from grapes.[11] A second event may have occurred independently on the Iberian Peninsula.

The next important stage in development of winemaking was in Egypt, where hieroglyphs describe sophisticated approaches to viticulture and vinification.[12] The Egyptians grew vines in walled vineyards, developed methods for training the grapevine on an overhead trellis, and may have used irrigation. In making wine, they may have used the addition of chopped up fruit (containing yeast) to

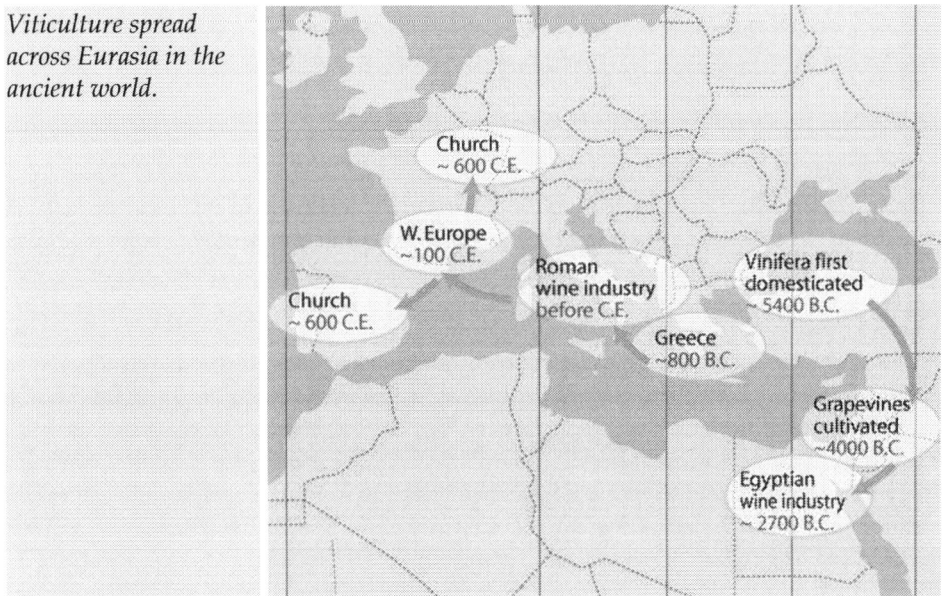

Viticulture spread across Eurasia in the ancient world.

initiate fermentation, and they developed methods for pressing the grapes. The entire wine production process, from viticulture to transport of the finished wine, was illustrated in tomb paintings.

By the time of the Greeks, viticulture was a regular part of farming and trade. Grapevines, together with wheat and olives, were basic agricultural crops. Around 320 B.C., the Greek philosopher Theophrastus (Aristotle's successor) published two series of books, *De causis plantarum* (The Causes of Plants) and *De historia plantarum* (The History of Plants). The Causes of Plants addresses many of the current issues in viticulture, including cultivation of the grapevine, pruning methods, and dealing with pests and diseases. It appears that vines were planted in tidy rows, like those of today, and there was attention to matching varieties to suitable soils.[13]

Cultivation of grapevines and the production of wine was a significant economic interest by Roman times. Around 160 B.C., Cato discussed vineyard management and vines in *de Agri Cultura*, giving a good deal of attention to issues such as pruning methods and the use of wine presses. Around 65 C.E. Lucius Columella published a 12-volume series on agriculture, *de Re Rustica*, including three books on viticulture. In one book he discussed the properties of different grape varieties. In the same century, Pliny also devoted a good part of his writing to descriptions of vines and wines, discussing in some detail the different grape varieties. Unfortunately, none of the names can be equated directly with modern varieties.

By the turn of the Millennium, viticulture was well established all round the Mediterranean. During the first century, the Romans spread the grapevine throughout the empire, extending north in Italy, up from the Mediterranean in France and through Iberia, and across Germany. (The extent of its growth into England at this time is more questionable,[14] although it seems likely that some of

The wine production scene from the tomb of Kha'emweset at Thebes, c. 1450 B.C. shows grapes being harvested, amphorae filled, and wine transported.[17]

the reputed vineyards really did exist.[15]) In 92 C.E., ostensibly to make more economic use of the land by growing more important crops, possibly in reality to protect viticulture closer to home, the emperor Domitian banned new plantings and ordered many of the plantings in the provinces to be uprooted.[16] It's dubious to what extent the edict was obeyed until it was repealed by the emperor Probus in 280 C.E.

With the fall of the Roman Empire, viticulture fell into decline everywhere. In Bordeaux, for example, there is little evidence for much commercial winemaking until the thirteenth century. The role that the Romans had played in spreading viticulture may have been taken over by the Church, which from roughly the fifth to tenth centuries propagated grapevines. "Fecit ecclesias et plantavit vineas,*" said a document of Charlemagne, concerning the foundation of a monastery in the eighth century.[18] Initially the purpose was to ensure the supply of sacramental wine, but production later became a successful commercial activity. The Church was certainly important in developing methods of cultivation, and individual sites, such as Clos Vougeot in Burgundy or Kloster Eberbach in Germany, attest to the success of the monks (especially the Cistercians).[19] Cer-

---

* Build the Church and plant vines.

tainly the Church had a role in spreading varieties and in matching them to local conditions, but it's not entirely clear how the overall economic contribution of the Church compared to that of individual landholders.[20]

By the year 1000, viticulture was well established across Europe, extending north and east of what had been the limits of the Roman Empire. The Loire and Champagne regions of northern France, and the Mosel and Rheingau of Germany were making wine by this time.[22] By 1086, the Domesday Book record-

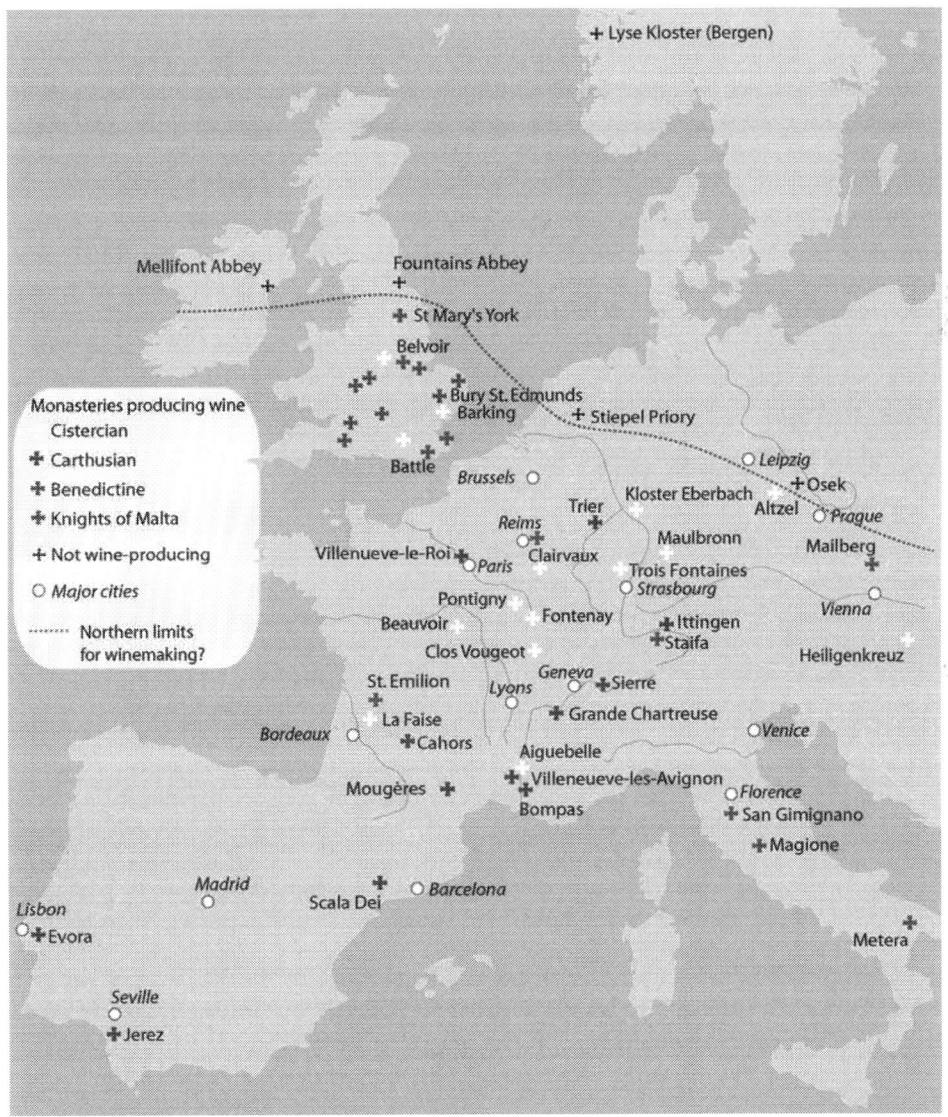

Monasteries of several orders spread across Europe in the middle ages, generally making wine wherever conditions permitted. The northern limits for winemaking must have been to the south of those monasteries that were forced to buy wine because they could not produce it themselves.[21]

ed 42 vineyards in the southern part of England.[23] The wine was not necessarily good, however; when King John tried the wine at Beaulieu Abbey in southern England in 1204, his reaction was to "send ships forthwith to fetch some good French wine for the Abbott."[24] Wine production continued in England until the sixteenth century.[25]

Viticulture extended surprisingly far north in the medieval period, up to Flanders in Belgium, Brandenburg in Germany, and northern Hungary.[26] As imports from the south became more accessible, the more northern vineyards were abandoned and given over to growing grain.[27] The largest areas for commercial wine production were in southwest France, the Rhône, and the Rhine (and some areas around the edges of the Mediterranean). The notable feature of vineyard locations was their concentration along navigable rivers, probably because the cost of water transport was vastly less than the cost of transport over land.[28]

The grape varieties that are predominant today can sometimes be traced back to mediaeval times, but it is hard to go back before that. As one example, Pinot Noir has certainly been grown in Burgundy for a very long time, but the first documented mention of the name occurs only in 1375. It's purely a matter of speculation whether the Romans brought it there or whether it originated later. But by the end of the mediaeval period, the grape varieties of today were being established in the most significant locales.

Vitis vinifera was unknown outside Europe until colonists transported it to the New World. Early colonists started wine production in South Africa in the seventeenth century, and in Australia in the eighteenth century. Cortés brought the first vines to Mexico, where they did so well that wine was exported back to Spain.[29] The vines were then taken down into South America. Vines were taken north to California during the eighteenth century. On the East Coast, after the failure of earlier attempts to produce wine from local grape varieties, Vitis vinifera was brought from Europe during the 17th century. But it did not do well because of the presence of a pest that devoured its roots: Phylloxera.

The Phylloxera Devastation

Phylloxera changed the face of viticulture for ever. This tiny insect, 1-3 mm long, is native to North America. Before human intervention, it extended from the East Coast to the Rockies. Now, of course, its domain is universal.

Its original name was Phylloxera vastatrix, which means phylloxera the destroyer.[30] It has an exceptionally complicated life cycle, with multiple forms, including male and female larvae, and various winged states. It can climb up the plant, it can fly from one plant to the next, and it can burrow down to the roots. It is adaptable: the winged forms are common in its native habitat in North America, but it manages perfectly well without wings in some other environments. Phylloxera is extremely fecund; with a generation time of less than one month, it can run through multiple generations in the course of a year in the vineyard.[31]

The burrowing form of Phylloxera feeds on grapevine roots.

Photograph kindly provided by Kevin Powell.

The burrowing form loves grapevines. It feeds on grapevine roots, using its long proboscis to suck sap out of the vine and to inject toxin. Once phylloxera starts feeding, it is only a matter of time until the vine dies. However, the lethal action is indirect. When damage reduces the pressure of sap below a critical level, phylloxera leave the vine and migrate to a fresh one. But the damaged sites provide entry points for other infections, such as fungal pathogens.[32] Finally the weakened vine dies.

Phylloxera was endemic in the Eastern United States, but the species of Vitis indigenous to North America are all resistant to it. These species are not native to Europe, and the trouble started when they were imported there. One reason was a craze for ornamental grapevines. Another was that some French winegrowers thought it would be interesting to experiment with American varieties. None of the American vines make wine that is particularly good, and some is quite undrinkable, but growers in France thought it was possible that hybrids between these vines and the local Vitis vinifera might give more durable varieties that would make good wine. During the 1830s and 1840s, American vines were imported into France and became widely available.

Phylloxera came as an unwanted visitor with the American vines. Because Vitis vinifera had never been exposed to phylloxera, it had no resistance. Once phylloxera reached Europe, they rapidly migrated to the sensitive local vines. The first traces of phylloxera were found at Kew Gardens in England in 1863, but it was not long before it was omnipresent in Europe. The start of the infection in France has been traced to American vines planted in 1862 by a M. Borty at Roquemaure on the right bank of the Rhône, just north of Avignon (now part of the area where the wine of the Côtes du Rhône is produced). Already by the following year, local vines were infected and dying.[33]

Phylloxera spread amazingly fast through France. During 1870-1871, it traveled up the Rhône forming a triangle of infection with the peak at Tain l'Hermitage. At the same time, small, but isolated, centers of infection appeared around Bordeaux. By 1875, the Rhône triangle had broadened and there was a sizeable area of infection around Bordeaux. These areas widened further by 1880,

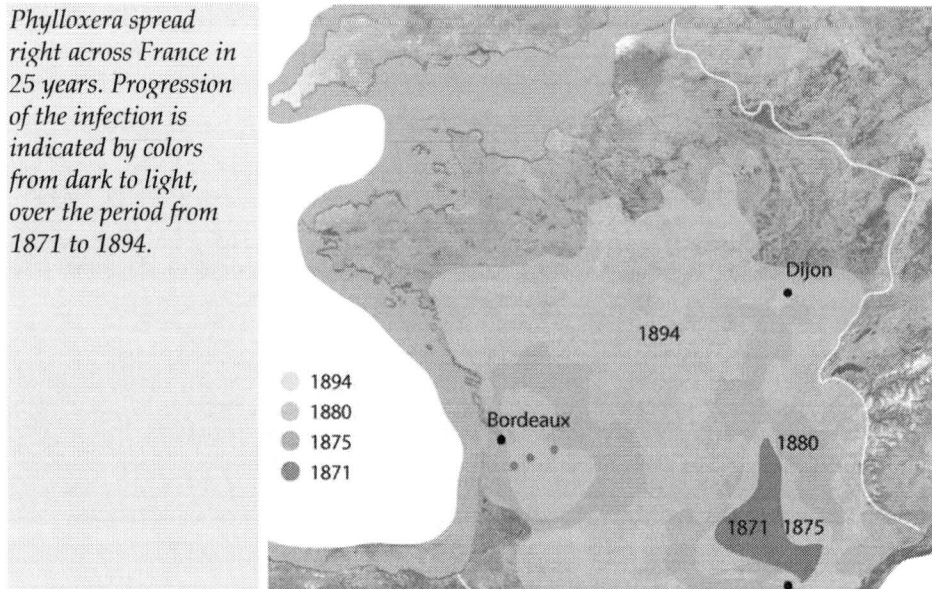

Phylloxera spread right across France in 25 years. Progression of the infection is indicated by colors from dark to light, over the period from 1871 to 1894.

and by 1894 the entire map of winegrowing areas of France had been filled in.[34] The edges of infected areas reported by the Commission on Phylloxéra show a remarkable coincidence with the outlines of the administrative Departéments; it is unlikely that the insect respected the political boundaries, so one might suspect that reporting was less scrupulous in some Departéments than others, possibly understating the extent of the infestation.

Phylloxera was no more likely to respect national boundaries. It spread through Portugal around the same time as in France, wiping out wine production in the Douro by 1895. Its effects became apparent a little later in Italy and Spain, but both were heavily infected within a few years. It was much slower to reach Germany, where major effects did not become apparent until after 1945.[35]

The first reaction was incredulity. "Not in my house," as Lady Macbeth might have said. Denial usually took the form of insisting that well-tended vines would not be susceptible, even though Jules-Émile Planchon, Professor of Botany at Montpellier, quickly established that the cause was an infection with a previously-unknown insect. From the first identification of the insect in 1868, Planchon moved quickly to identify its origins, and in 1873 visited the United States to investigate phylloxera in its native habitat.

There was a scattershot search for solutions. Carbon bisulphide (a primitive neurotoxin) killed the insect, but vast quantities had to be pumped into the ground; the cost was beyond the means of most growers, and effects on the flavor of the wine were uncertain. Drowning the insects was partially effective, but required access to an inexhaustible supply of fresh water. Vineyards in sandy

The commission on phylloxera visiting the vineyards. The two figures at the back in top hats are J. E. Planchon and J. Lichtenstein, and the figure immediately in front of them is the American entomologist C. V. Riley.[38]

soil were relatively resistant, because phylloxera fails to propagate (possibly because it drowns when the soil becomes wet). The protagonists for carbon disulphide became known as *sulfuristes*, those for drowning as *submersionnistes*, but the march of phylloxera was inexorable.

The identification of the source carried the implication that native American vines were resistant to its ravages. By 1875, replanting the Midi (the area of the original infection) with American vines was extensive; more than 7 million cuttings of the Concord grapevine (a variety of Vitis labrusca[36]) were imported.[37] But the vines did not do well in their new environment. And tastings of wines made in France from imported American wines were judged to be fairly disastrous. The *americainistes* who wanted to replant on American vines were soon in a dwindling minority.

The idea of crossing Vitis vinifera with American Vitis was revived, in the hope of producing hybrid varieties that would both be resistant to phylloxera and make palatable wine. Many hybrids were produced, but most showed the "foxy" taste of American Vitis in the wine, although some of the hybrids continued to be planted until the end of the twentieth century. Out of all this, however, emerged the idea that the French Vitis vinifera vines could be protected by grafting onto roots of resistant American Vitis varieties.

Grafting was already well established as a technique for propagating fruit trees.[39] The technique is pretty simple in principle. One plant provides the root that extends below ground. It has a short stem extending just above ground level. A cut is made in the stem, and then a matching cut is made in the stem of the above-ground part of a different plant. The stem is inserted into the root-

Grafting involves fitting the scion into the stem of the rootstock. Two scions have been grafted on to one stem, and then secured with a tape that will be protected with a sealant.

Photograph kindly provided by Dai Crisp.

stock, the grafting site is bound up with tape and protected, and in a relatively short period the two parts seal together to generate a plant with a "rootstock" of one origin and a "scion" of a different origin. In a young plant, you can see a slight bulge in the trunk just above ground level where the graft was made.

In short order, American Vitis species were classified for their relative degrees of resistance to Phylloxera and their compatibility with different soil types. Vitis riparia became the rootstock of choice on clay soils, while Vitis rupestris tended to be used on calcareous soils. One of the main problems in adjusting American rootstocks to European conditions is the much higher content of limestone in Europe; if the rootstock cannot adjust to the low acidity of limestone, the plant develops the disease of chlorosis when the leaves turn yellow and fall off. (Chlorosis results from inability to take up enough iron.) An industry soon grew up in crossing American Vitis species to generate resistant rootstocks that were suited for particular soil conditions with regards to acidity, water retention, and so on. The problem of adaptation to limestone was solved by the discovery of Vitis berlandieri, an American Vitis species from Texas that thrives on chalk.[40] Grafted vines became the norm, and by 1895 more than a third of French vineyards had French vines growing on foreign rootstocks.

The fallout from the phylloxera infection was considerable. The planted area of French vineyards started the long march of decline, falling from 2.5 million hectares in 1875 to 1.5 million in 1914. (It is down to 1 million ha today.) Between 1875 and 1879, production of wine crashed by half; it did not recover until 1900. Some areas, especially those with marginal climates in the north, ceased production altogether. Others changed their grape varieties. The diversity of grape varieties was reduced; we shall probably never know how many simply succumbed to phylloxera and were never propagated on foreign rootstocks.

Phylloxera had a great effect on the way vineyards were planted. Previously, vines had been propagated en foule (literally: in a crowd) simply by sticking a

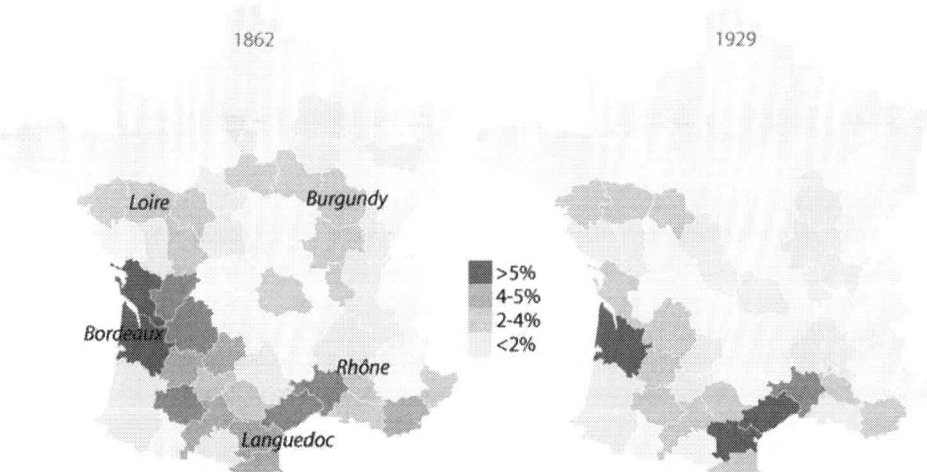

Vineyards retreated from the northern half of France after phylloxera.[41] Color indicates proportion of vineyards from >5% (darkest) to <2% (lightest) relative to total in France.

shoot in the earth. Usually a shoot from an existing vine was bent down into the earth nearby; once it took root, the connection to the mother plant would be cut, leaving a freestanding vine. A vineyard consisted of a haphazard array of vines, each supported by its own wooden stake. By contrast, grafted plants were usually planted in tidy rows (making it easier to work the vines with horse-drawn equipment), but also involving a reduction in the density of vines. This had been as high as 14,000 for vines planted en foule, but is rarely more than 8000 for vines planted on rootstocks. The density can have an effect on the quality of the grapes—at lower planting densities the vines don't have to struggle so hard, and quality is lower.

The major consequence for quality, however, comes from a more direct effect on the yield. Vines planted on rootstocks are usually more productive than those growing on their own roots. By 1914, when the majority of vines were grafted, production had reached the same level as in 1870, but from only 60% of the land area. Greater production is usually associated with lower quality (although tastings to compare the wines made from grafted and ungrafted vines in Burgundy during the period of replanting did not demonstrate any great difference).

Wine production was affected worldwide. During the worst period in France, wine was imported from Spain and Italy. Despairing of producing wine in their native country, some producers left Bordeaux for Spain. Some went to Rioja and revolutionized winemaking there. The boom lasted until phylloxera made it over the Pyrenees in the late 1890s. Then of course the blight followed them. There was no escape in Europe.

Phylloxera has spread worldwide, but it is not completely universal. It spread across the Rockies into California in 1876 and into Australia around the same time. But there are still some holdouts. Most of the grapevines of Oregon are planted on their own roots, Southern Australia is largely free of phylloxera, and Chile is free. A fascinating experiment is ongoing at the Reserva di Caliboro

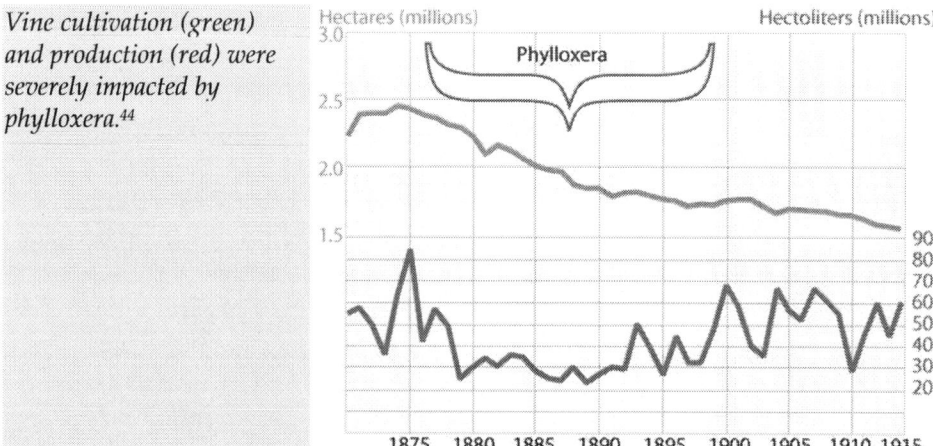

Vine cultivation (green) and production (red) were severely impacted by phylloxera.[44]

estate in Chile's Maule Valley (owned by Francesco Cinzano of Col d'Orcia in Montalcino, Tuscany), where Cabernet Sauvignon and Cabernet Franc have been planted side by side on their own roots and on rootstocks. The vines are managed, grapes are harvested, and wine is made, in exactly the same way for both grafted and ungrafted plantings. The first real harvest was only in 2008, but perhaps soon there will finally be a definitive answer as to the effect of rootstocks on quality of the wine.[42]

Even when you can, it's risky to plant vines on their own roots, because once phylloxera arrives it can spread extremely rapidly. In the late 1980s, California was hit with another phylloxera epidemic. A rootstock called AxR1 had been widely used as the result of advice from the viticulture department at the Davis campus of the University of California. AxR1 is a hybrid between Vitis rupestris and Vitis vinifera; like many hybrids with some vinifera parentage, it is not really very resistant to phylloxera. Like many other viticulture departments, Davis was more concerned with quantity of production (AxR1 is an abundant producer) than with quality or the long term.[43]

During the 1960s and 1970s, about 75% of plantings in Napa and Sonoma were on AxR1.[45] By the late 1980s, phylloxera was enthusiastically feeding on these rootstocks. Initially, there were claims that the epidemic was due to the emergence of a new "biotype" of phylloxera able to chew on rootstocks that had previously been resistant, but it's now clear this had little to do with the problem.[46] AxR1 is not employed at all in Europe because of its known susceptibility to phylloxera, so it was really only a matter of time before it succumbed in California. It was an expensive mistake: replanting on new rootstocks cost the California wine industry more than $1 billion.[47]

In Europe, there are isolated vineyards in several locations where vines have been able to survive on their own roots. The largest single area is the Mosel in Germany, where 55% of vines are still ungrafted. It's thought that phylloxera finds it difficult to propagate on the slate that dominates the region. (However, the German authorities recently banned planting of vines on their own roots. This is controversial. Some growers want to perpetuate ungrafted vines, but others feel it's time to move on; Annagret Reh-Gartner, of von Kesselstatt, told me, "It's irresponsible to plant ungrafted vines, since phylloxera is known to be there."[48])

More puzzling are small vineyards of surviving original vines where the surrounding vineyards have all had to be grafted. Bollinger has a small enclosed vineyard of vines on their own roots from which they produce the Vieilles Vignes Françaises Champagne; Lisini has a small vineyard of Sangiovese in Tuscany. You might wonder whether possibly the vines are rare resistant strains, but this is unlikely to be the case at Quinta do Noval in the Douro of Portugal, where the Nacional Port is made from a vineyard of vines of several varieties all growing on their own roots. As recently as the 1980s, there was still a small plot of ungrafted vines at Château Lafite Rothschild dating from around 1900.[49]

The number of exceptions where ungrafted vines can be found is dwindling. The heritage of phylloxera has made it the norm for vines to be grafted. Growers pay almost as much attention to their choice of rootstocks as to the choice of varieties from which the wine is actually made. Some years ago I was involved in a project to consider genetic engineering of grapevines to see whether it might be possible to introduce phylloxera-resistance into Vitis vinifera to allow it to be propagated on its own roots again.[50] More than one producer looked at me, puzzled, and asked, "Why would we want to do that? We have always grafted."

Old vines growing happily on their own roots in the Bernkasteler Doctor vineyard of the Mosel.

True, the combination of rootstock and scion gives more versatility in matching the grapevine to local conditions, but the basic parameter determining where each variety will grow best is the climate: within the overall zone for grape growing, each variety has a preferred range determined largely by temperature. Here the scion is all important.

Cultivars and Clones

There are more than 10,000 different varieties of Vitis vinifera, and thousands of them are used to make wine.[51] (About 2,000 varieties are characterized as table grapes.[52]) The most famous varieties are distributed around the world, but others are obscure, existing only in highly restricted places, known only to the locals and to the indefatigable cataloguers of the species. The largest diversity among varieties used to produce wine is found in the countries where wine production has been longest established; Italy, France, Greece, Portugal, and Spain have several hundred different varieties each. The term *cultivar*, meaning a *cult*ivated *var*iety of a plant, is often used to describe a distinct grapevine variety.

The differences between cultivars have arisen since Vitis vinifera was domesticated. Most of them have occurred naturally, but in the last century some new cultivars have also been created by crossing (the technical term is hybridizing) existing varieties. Because Vitis vinifera is self-fertilizing, the spontaneous generation of new varieties is an exceptional event, probably happening by cross-fertilization when two different varieties are growing close to each other. It's fair to say that none of the artificial crosses have produced anything as successful as nature itself.[53]

The differences between grapevine varieties are immense. Color is one of the most obvious. The progenitor Vitis was colored, and today's white varieties have lost the ability to produce skin pigmentation. Each cultivar has its own preferred conditions; the temperatures required for growth and ripening are the most critical for determining the zones where it grows best.

It is not always a trivial matter to tell the difference between cultivars. It may be hard to believe, but the traditional way of distinguishing varieties is by *ampelography*—assessing differences in the shapes of their leaves. (The name comes from *ampelos*, the Greek for vine.) Whole books have been written on the ampelography of the grapevine. Personally, I am inclined to view it more as art than science. Ampelography is susceptible to error by confusing varieties with similar appearance and growth characteristics. This has led to some famous mix-ups. Much of the Merlot in Chile was not really Merlot but was another variety that had come from Bordeaux, Carmenère; the two cultivars grow in similar locales and have a similar appearance.

Today we have a more precise method of defining cultivars and relating them to one another. The same technique of DNA fingerprinting used in criminal cases, or to determine human parentage, can be used to distinguish grapevine varieties. Each cultivar has a distinct DNA profile, and comparisons between cultivars can identify parentage. Using DNA fingerprinting has identified the origins of some varieties, such as showing that Zinfandel in California is really the same as the Crljenak grape of Croatia. (It passed through southern Italy, where it is called Primitivo before being brought by immigrants to California where it acquired yet another name.[54])

Each of the popular grapevine varieties has a number of subvarieties. These days, most varieties are propagated as clones. (A clone is a plant whose genetic makeup is exactly the same as a parent plant from which it was regenerated.) Many clones are available for most of the international varieties, and growers can pick those that are best suited to their particular vineyards with regards to the timing of the life cycle or productivity. The process of cloning is actually a bit more complicated than just taking a cutting; in principle, a clone should involve regeneration of the whole plant from a single cell of the parental plant. The advantage of cloning is that the new plant exactly reproduces the properties of its parent; and it can be guaranteed to be free of viruses, which are an ongoing problem in reducing the health of grapevines. (There's a procedure for eliminating viruses during cloning.)

New subvarieties are generated when a mutation occurs in a parent plant and is perpetuated in the cutting that makes the next generation. Some varieties are more prone to mutation than others. Pinot Noir is one of the most prone, and there may be several hundred subvarieties of Pinot Noir in Burgundy, including 200 defined clones. Not everyone uses the clones. Their importance varies with the grape varieties and the region. Usage of clones is much less of an issue in Bordeaux than in Burgundy: "In Bordeaux, you have in the same terroir, some good clones and some lesser ones. It's not a huge thing but it is another factor to consider, but after several others, like terroir. There is less variation between the clones of Cabernet Sauvignon or Merlot than in Burgundy, where clone is more important because there is a wider genetic variation between the clones of Pinot Noir," according to Paul Pontallier, winemaker at Château Margaux.[55]

Some growers believe in propagating the subvarieties that have given good results in their own vineyards. The belief is especially strong in Burgundy, where many feel that not only have the last few hundred years demonstrated the strength of the connection with Pinot Noir, but also that the vines have become adapted to growth in their particular vineyards. When they need to replant a vineyard, they take cuttings from existing vines that have performed especially well. This *selection massale* is the closest equivalent to the way things were before phylloxera. The difference is that now the cuttings have to be grafted on to new rootstocks instead of just sticking a free branch into the ground. The disadvantage is that any viruses or other diseases are likely to be perpetuated by selection massale. In Germany, where it's mandated that only certified clones can be used to replant vineyards, a grower can take his cutting to the institute at Geisenheim to have virus-free clones generated from it.

Selection massale is controversial because of its uncontrolled nature—it's hard to be really sure of the quality of the vines that have been selected. But it does ensure some variety when a vineyard is replanted. The greatest disadvantage of clones is simply that over-reliance on any one clone has a homogenizing effect on the nature of the fruit.

Zones for Grape Growing

The grapevine is amazingly hardy. It will grow anywhere it can get enough (but not too much) water and sunshine. As a practical matter, it grows well enough to make wine between the 50° and 30° latitudes. More precisely, the limits follow the 10 °C and 20 °C isotherms—lines of average annual temperature—which don't exactly coincide with the lines of latitude. In Europe, the grape-growing region extends from the northern limit of Champagne and the most northern wine-growing regions of Germany to the southernmost points of Spain and Italy. In North America, other climatic factors restrict production of fine wines to the West Coast of the United States, although there is also some production farther north in Canada. In the southern hemisphere, the production areas include southern Australia and New Zealand, the southern parts of South Africa, and central regions of Chile and Argentina.

Each variety has a characteristic annual cycle, from the time of flowering to the time of achieving ripeness. The response to temperature is usually characterized in terms of the average daily temperature during the growing season (the period from April to October[56]). Below a certain range, the variety will not ripen. Above the range, it ripens too fast, typically giving muddy or jammy flavors in the wine.

Most varieties have historically been grown in Europe at their northern limits, in regions towards the bottom of their preferred temperature range. The result is that traditionally there have rarely been more than three really good vintages each decade, when temperatures were high enough for full ripening. Poor vin-

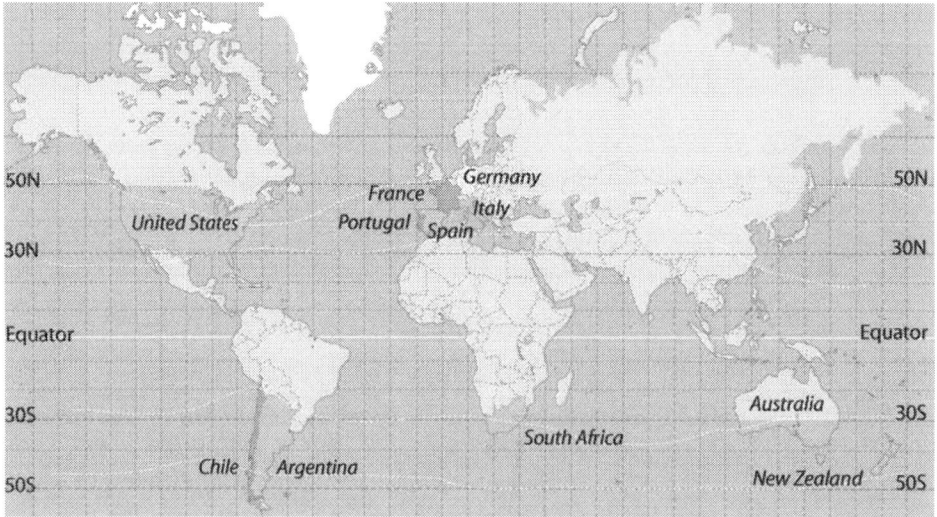

Major sites for grape growing are between the 10° and 20° isotherms in the northern and southern hemispheres. Isotherms are dotted white, the 30° and 50° latitudes are dotted red.

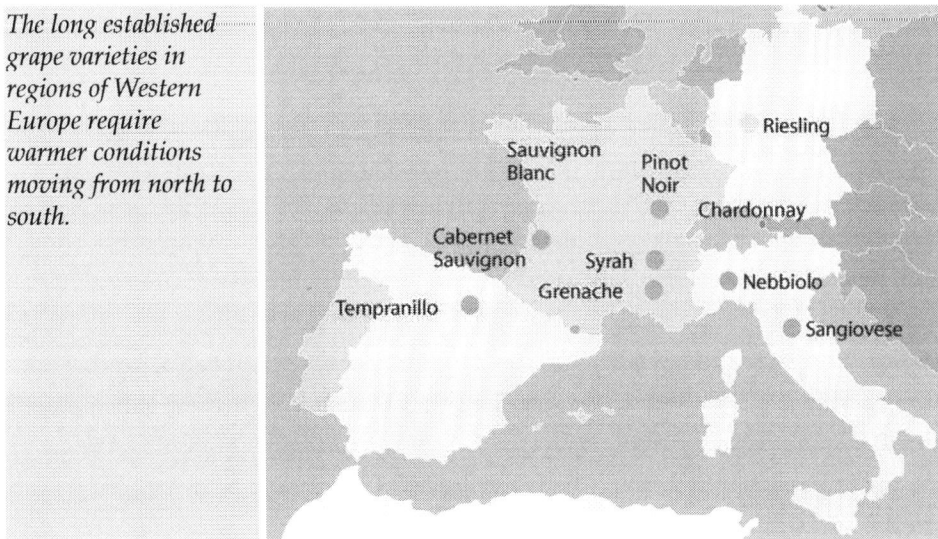

The long established grape varieties in regions of Western Europe require warmer conditions moving from north to south.

tages have resulted when the growing season temperatures were below the minimum for the variety. Of course, the recent warming trend is changing this situation. In the New World, where varieties were chosen more recently, temperatures in each region tend to be more at the upper end for the varieties grown there.

In the northern part of Western Europe, pushing up against the 50° latitude line, where temperatures are relatively cool, the varieties that are most successful are all white. Riesling is grown at the farthest north, in Germany and in Alsace; Sauvignon Blanc and Chenin Blanc are grown in the Loire, the northernmost regions in France for producing still wine. The Champagne region, a little north of the Loire, is an exception in growing Pinot Noir and Chardonnay, but this is due to the genius of making sparkling wine, where addition of a little sugar compensates for pushing ripening to its limits. Beyond the northern limits, England is another exception, where still wine is made mostly from special cold-resistant varieties, but remains marginal for production of fine wine.

Moving towards the south, Burgundy is famous for Pinot Noir, the most delicate of the red varieties, and Chardonnay. Just a couple of degrees warmer and farther south, Bordeaux is the paradigm for Cabernet Sauvignon and Merlot. Moving down to the Rhône, in the north comes Syrah, while the south grows Grenache and other hot climate varieties. The match between latitude and the temperature preference of each variety is not exact, since local temperatures are also affected by other factors, such as the elevation of the vineyards. The famous varieties of Tempranillo (in Rioja), Nebbiolo (in Barolo), and Sangiovese (in Chianti and Brunello) are all found in locales that are a bit cooler than might be suggested by their latitude. In general there's a good correlation between average regional temperatures and the preferred temperature range of the typical variety of the region.

Millennia of Innovation

Man has been improving the grapevine ever since it was first domesticated. New varieties have extended the range of places where it can grow. Specific clones have been selected for ability to ripen later, to produce smaller berries, or to withstand particular climatic conditions. The forced adaptation to grafting on to rootstocks has led to more refined control of productivity. Methods of training have improved the ability to withstand adverse climatic conditions, and management of the canopy has helped to produce riper grapes.

Once the grapevine was domesticated, its pattern of spread was partly due to economic factors, such as trading patterns and the rise and fall of empires, and partly due to more technical developments. It became possible to cultivate grapevines in Bordeaux and Burgundy around the first century C.E., for example, because new varieties developed that would grow and ripen in these cooler climates. These may have been the ancestors of Cabernet Sauvignon and Pinot Noir. In the period up to 1000 C.E., the Church was important in matching varieties to regions. By the late middle ages, the pattern was set in Europe.

There were probably relatively few changes in the way the grapevine was actually grown until the modern era. In ancient Egypt it was grown on a high trellis, a pattern that survives to the present day in the pergola system of Italy. In other places it was grown as a free-standing bush, with a dense array of grapevines perpetuated by rooting plants next to one another. Vineyards were worked exclusively by hand. All this changed with the twin events of the transition to grafting following phylloxera and the mechanization of vineyards, which led to the development of a variety of training systems for cultivating the grapevine, suited to specific climatic conditions. Management of the grapevine, together with developments in mechanization, is now the driving force in adjusting it to each region and climate.

Yet this vastly successful system now is subject to challenge as never before. Impending climate change threatens the established match of varieties to places. And there's a continuing narrowing of the range of varieties, with the same "international" varieties replacing indigenous varieties. Will continuing innovation help to maintain the variety of the grapevine or will it fall victim to homogeneity resulting from globalization?

2

Cultivating the Vineyard

GRAPEVINES ORIGINATED BY GROWING ON TREES in the wild. The shape and height of wild grapevines are constrained only by the limits of the tree providing support. They may be male or female, although both types must grow in the same vicinity if they are successfully to form berries. Today wild grapevines occur only in relatively small, isolated populations around the Mediterranean and towards the Caucasus.

The grapevine is extremely malleable and can be pruned into all sorts of different shapes. Various pruning systems are used to suit different locations. They affect how far the vine can spread out, what height its bunches of grapes hang above the ground, how much shade the grapes get from the canopy of leaves, and so on. The main factors affecting the choice of system are the climate and

Grapevines grow wild on trees. This female Vitis vinifera silvestris is part of a population of 132 vines at Ribera de Huelva river near Seville. Its leaves are brighter green than those of the tree.

Photograph kindly provided by Rafael Ocete.

Grapevines are pruned on to a training system consisting of a trellis with several horizontal wires.

Roses are often planted at the ends of rows to give early warning of pests and diseases.

whether harvesting will be manual or mechanical (mechanical harvesters like the rows of vines to be better separated and the canopy to be relatively high). Other factors can come into play: I remember visiting a vineyard in southern England that had an unusual canopy system, spread out and rather high. Eager to discover the basis behind this new adaptation to climate, I asked the proprietor about the rationale. "Oh," she said, "the previous proprietor had a bad back and trained the vines high so he wouldn't have to bend down."[1]

Vines can be free-standing, trained as a bush, which gives a relatively dense canopy that is suitable for warm dry climates; this is widely used around the Mediterranean. But a common feature in most modern systems is a trellis of horizontal wires, attached to a post at the end of the row of vines. As the vine grows during the season, its shoots are attached to the wires for support.

The type of training system determines the permanent structure of the vine. A "head-trained" system has only a vertical trunk; new shoots emerge from the head of the trunk each year, and are trained along the wires of whatever system is used. A "cordon-trained" system has permanent horizontal extensions along the trellis in one or both directions, and the new shoots grow out from the arms of the cordon.

Whatever system is used, effectively the vine starts out afresh each year. After the harvest, the last year's new growth is pruned off, except for some shoots that are used for the new growth in the next season. New growth is prodigious, and the shoots can easily extend for several feet.

The Grapevine Life Cycle

The grapevine is a sparse looking object at the beginning of the season, all stripped down to bare wood. The vertical trunk may be thin if the grapevine is young, or gnarled and thick if it is old, but will not show much sign of life. It may have a permanent branch extending horizontally in the most common types of pruning, or may stand alone with a barely perceptible bud at the top where a new branch will grow. Some time in March (when the temperature rises above 10 °C), bud break will happen. The first signs of growth are seen as the new shoots push out from the old wood. Shoots and leaves develop over the next couple of months, forming the canopy.

The first critical moment is when flowering occurs in May. Depending on the weather, this may happen relatively evenly or can be prolonged. The shorter the period for flowering, the better, because a more rapid flowering leads to a more uniform ripening of the berries at the end of the season. Typically the period between flowering and the completion of fertilization, called fruit set, is about two weeks. This requires the temperature to rise above 15 °C.

Problems with flowering have a major effect on the size of the crop. Coulure (sometimes called shatter in English) happens when flowers are not fertilized, so they do not develop into berries. Millerandage occurs a bit later, when flowers that were not properly fertilized (actually they were fertilized with dead pollen) fail to expand, giving small berries that ripen irregularly. And, of course, the vine is especially sensitive to a late frost between bud break and flowering, which can kill off the crop.

The size of the grapevine canopy increases over the next few weeks as more shoots and leaves develop, and the next significant moment occurs when the developing berries change color in July. This is called veraison. Until now, the berries have grown rapidly and chlorophyll has been the predominant pigment. At veraison, the skin of the berry becomes translucent for white varieties, and colored for black varieties. This occurs abruptly in any individual berry, but occurs over several days for the plant as a whole, and even for the berries within a bunch.

At the start of the growing season, everything has been pruned off the grapevine except for two of the last season's shoots, extending horizontally from the trunk, from which the new season's growth will come.

Growth slows after veraison, and photosynthesis is directed towards producing sugars for the berries and laying down carbohydrate reserves for the following year. The berries accumulate sugar and lose acidity. Harvest occurs when they are judged ripe. It used to be the case that harvest was generally set a regular 100 days after the flowering, but a trend to harvest riper berries means that the period is now often quite a bit longer.

After harvest, as temperatures drop, the leaves fall off, and then all of the past season's growth is removed by pruning, leaving only the permanent structure of the grapevine, ready to start again next year.

A grapevine does not demand much from the climate: simply more than 1500 hours of sunshine and more than 700 mm of water per year. Then photosynthesis will do the rest, using carbon dioxide from the air to build the structures of the growing plant. The requirement for sunshine translates into a need for the average yearly temperature to be around 14-15 °C. The grapevine is sensitive to cold: it stops growing below 10 °C and is killed by temperatures below −25 °C. It is also sensitive to too much heat: photosynthesis slows down over 30 °C and stops completely above 40 °C. And grapevines need a period of dormancy, a month or two below 10 °C to recover their strength for the next season. These parameters explain the vine's need for the climatic conditions found between the 30° and 50° latitudes.

The success of each particular vintage depends on conditions that year, especially how much sunshine and water (and when the water arrived). This influences the balance between vegetative growth (developing the structure of the plant) and the production of fruit. But it's not quite that simple, because the grapevine actually has a two year cycle. Grapevines start the season with dormant buds, which determine the crop potential for the coming season. These

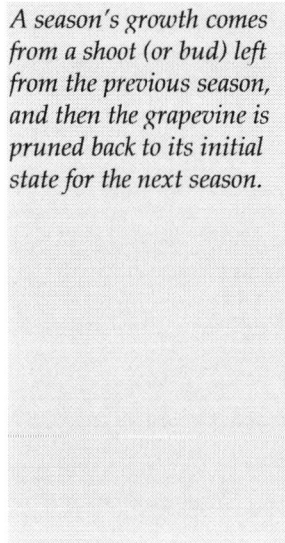

A season's growth comes from a shoot (or bud) left from the previous season, and then the grapevine is pruned back to its initial state for the next season.

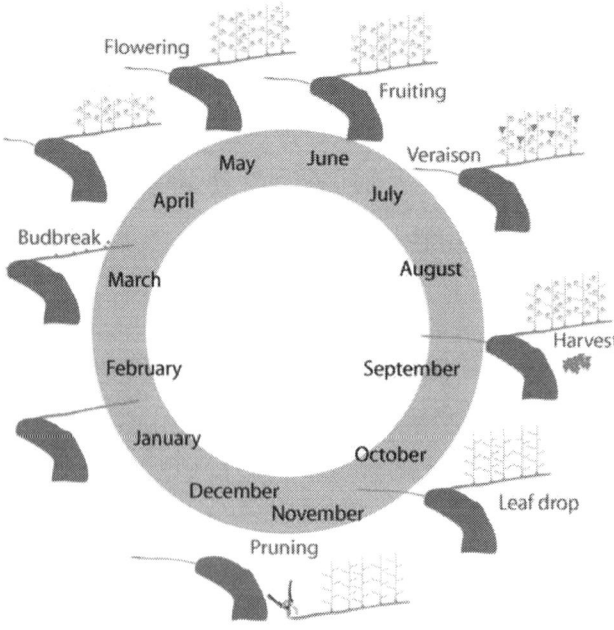

buds can develop into either foliage or fruit; the choice is influenced by exposure to sunlight, which drives development towards fruit. But the dormant buds were in fact formed during the previous year, and the level of budding depends on the amount of light they received that summer. The rationale is probably that the grapevine does not want to commit to producing fruit unless the shoot is in a place where the berries will be exposed to sun. Often the grapevine will compensate in one season for what happened the previous season: so a small crop one year will be followed by a large crop the next year.

From Deep Roots to Lofty Canopy

Well, actually, in a pruned grapevine, the canopy may not be so lofty, but the roots may well be very deep. The root system branches extensively, and it's the root tip that performs many of the most significant functions, including uptake of water and nutrients. If a plant gets the chance, it will follow the path of least resistance and spread its roots out near the surface. If it can't find enough nutrients at the surface, and especially if some stress is imposed by a surface ploughing to remove superficial roots, then it will send its roots down deeper, for several meters if necessary. Conventional wisdom is that grapevines produce the best results in poor soils, often in soils that would not be fertile enough to support any other crop, because this forces them to send their roots deeper.

Left to its own devices, the grapevine would grow as far up as the supporting structure allows. A cultivated grapevine, however, is pruned to form a relatively low canopy, a few feet up at most. (The canopy includes all parts of the grapevine above the root system.) The canopy has a great effect on exposure to sunlight and to wind, and on how much evaporation occurs from the leaves. "Canopy management" has been the focus of viticulture for several years and means that an active tuning of the plant, starting with the pruning system but extending to continual adjustment during the growing season, is used to try to equalize its production of fruit.

Different pruning systems are used in different climates, with cool climates emphasizing the need to expose berries to enough sunshine, and warm climates emphasizing the need to protect them from too much exposure. The canopy needs to be large enough to have a sufficient leaf area to support photosynthesis, but if it becomes too large, the shade can prevent sufficient sunshine from reaching the berries. The objective is to control the number of berries each plant produces and to try to ensure they ripen evenly. This starts with the number of buds that are allowed to develop. After the flowering, when it's possible to estimate the potential yield, further pruning may be used to reduce it. Vendange en vert (or "green pruning") is used to remove excess flowers or immature berries; it's somewhat controversial how much it improves quality, and is a bit undercut by the fact that the plant tends to expand the size of the remaining berries to make up for the forced reduction. Later in the season, leaf-pulling may be used to remove parts of the canopy where they are giving too much shade (actually the leaves can be removed with a machine that burns them off).

One of the critical features of the grapevine is that berries can ripen *only* on the vine. Some plants produce fruit that can be ripened after it has been harvested; it's common with tomatoes, for example, to collect them when still green, but then to ripen them by exposure to the plant hormone, ethylene. Strangely enough, with grapevines we are not really sure which plant hormones are needed for the ripening process, so it is crucial to get the berries to ripeness before the harvest.

The Limits of Yield

Yield is one of the most important (and misunderstood) concepts in viticulture. The amount of wine produced from a given area is usually measured in hectoliters of juice per hectare of land in Europe.[*] It's given in tons of berries per acre in the United States.[†] Yields can be anywhere from 35 to 80 hl/ha for quality wines. (An average production of 50 hl/ha would be equivalent to about 2700 bottles per acre. In a typical Bordeaux vineyard of 8,000 vines per hectare, this is roughly equivalent to producing 1 bottle of wine from every vine.) Yields can be much greater for producing bulk table wine, in the range of 100-150 hl/ha.

Immediately the comparison between quality wine and bulk wine makes the point that better wines are associated with lower yields. Why is this? When a vine produces more grapes, their juice is less concentrated—the vine puts roughly the same total level of energy into producing its fruit, so more fruit means less effort per berry. This is true only up to a point. It is perfectly clear that wine made from grapes at a yield of 50 hl/ha is more concentrated than wine made at 100 hl/ha. But there may come a point, perhaps around the 40 hl/ha level, where further reductions in yield do not have much effect upon perceived quality.

One of the reasons why old vines are highly prized is that the yield naturally goes down as the vine ages. There's no precise measure of when this happens, but French wines may carry the label "Vieilles Vignes" (old vines) as a marker implying higher quality from lower yield. There's no legal definition of the term, and it's left up to the individual producer to decide when the vigne has become vieille. Eventually, of course, production dwindles to uneconomic levels. Generally speaking, vines are replaced at around 25 years of age, as their yield becomes too low to be worthwhile for general production.

The ideal situation for quality is for every vine to have a low, but adequate yield, but it's a myth that measurement of yield in terms of production per unit area of land accurately reflects each vine's activity. A vineyard whose yield has

---

[*] A hectoliter is about 11 cases of wine; a hectare is 2.47 acres.

[†] Very roughly 1 ton/acre is about 16 hl/ha (although the ratio is somewhat different for red wine and white wine).

been reduced because some vines are diseased and are poor producers, while others are churning it out, will not make high quality wine. As a *reductio ad absurdum*, the average yield over the country as a whole is 30 hl/ha for Spain and 57 hl/ha for France;[2] but this is not because Spain routinely makes better and more concentrated wine than France, it is because the plains of Spain are full of diseased vines that reduce the yield without increasing the quality. If you have a significant number of dead or poorly producing vines in your vineyard, the yield per hectare may not correlate with quality at all.

It's the yield per individual plant that impacts quality, but this is something that's difficult to measure en masse. "M. Borie of Ducru Beaucaillou wanted to go from a maximum yield per hectare to a maximum yield per plant. But it's too complicated to survey, the INAO didn't have the means to maintain a file with the density of plantation for each individual grower," according to Jean-Michel Cazes of Château Lynch Bages in Bordeaux.[3] Cazes takes the view that extremely low yields in Bordeaux can be a sign of poor quality rather than the reverse: "It's not that you don't produce fine wines with 20-25 hl/ha, but it's not necessary, at least in Bordeaux... A low yield in a well-maintained vineyard with homogenous production of 40 or 45 hl/ha with old vines is perfect." Really low yields, he believes, mean either low density of planting, bad maintenance, or heterogeneity in the vineyard.[4]

Low yield is not a panacea for all ills. "Surely the predominant myth of the wine industry is that high yields result in low wine quality," says Australian viticulturalist Richard Smart.[5] He believes that low yields are a symptom, not a cause, and that they most commonly result from water stress. Limitations on the water supply, he argues, are the real basis for improving quality. So mimicking low yields, for example by green pruning to remove excess berries early in the season, will not necessarily have the same effect. "Method of yield control is more important than final yield in affecting sensory features," he concludes.

If all the vines are active, other things being equal, a vineyard planted at higher density will produce better quality berries than one planted at lower density. At least in the relatively poor soils of Europe, the extra competition between vines means that each vine produces a smaller number of berries. In Bordeaux, where there is a very wide range of wine qualities, it's noticeable that the best vineyards are planted densely at 8-10,000 vines per hectare, but those of generic Bordeaux are planted at around 4,000 vines per hectare. When yields are restricted, doubling the number of vines effectively halves the production per vine. At a yield of 50 hl/ha, a vineyard planted at 10,000 vines/ha produces 500 ml/vine, but a vineyard planted at 5,000 vines/ha produces 1000 ml/vine.

Vine densities traditionally have been less in the New World, originally because of the lack of tractors that could move along narrow rows, but more recently there's been a move in Napa Valley, for example, towards the narrow rows and high density of Europe. It's not entirely clear this has the same effects on quality in these richer soils as it does in Europe. As Paul Pontallier of Château Margaux says, "The soil is richer in the lesser class Châteaux, therefore the vines are more vigorous which calls for a lower density planting. Higher density works when the vines are very low in vigor."[6]

The Acid/Sugar Playoff

Sugar is at the core of wine production. Without sugar, there would be no alcohol. Fermentation converts sugar from the grape into alcohol in the wine. (Of course, any fruit or vegetable with enough sugar can be fermented to make wine. Unlikely as it may seem, even the cactus has enough sugar for fermentation to give an alcoholic product, which can then be distilled into tequila.) The amount of sugar in the grape is a key factor in determining how vinification occurs and what type of wine is produced.

When sugar levels are low, it may be necessary to help the grapes by adding some sugar before fermentation in order to get enough alcohol to balance the wine. At very high sugar levels, a wine may be brutally alcoholic, and there comes a point at which it is not possible to ferment all the sugar, so the wine is sweet rather than dry.

Grape ripeness is all about increasing sugar and decreasing acidity. In fact, the ratio between sugar and acidity is the most primitive measure of ripeness.[8] In the first few weeks of development, berries become loaded with acidity. Then there is a steady decline. Acidity is diluted as the berry expands, and some of the acids are converted to other compounds. Getting close to the harvest, acidity can drop rapidly. In warm climates, it may be necessary to harvest the grapes before the acidity falls so far that the wine becomes flabby. In cool climates, it may be necessary to wait longer to get rid of excess acidity.

The traditional measure of sugar level is the Brix—this is a number determined by using a refractometer to measure the optical density of the grape juice.[9] The result depends on the amount of dissolved solid matter, but 90% of this is sugar. The potential alcohol, the amount of alcohol that would be generated by converting all the sugar to alcohol, is given by multiplying the Brix by 0.55. Grapes are typically harvested between 21 and 26 Brix, corresponding to 11.5% to 14% alcohol.

Acidity increases sharply after fruit set and then declines. Sugar increases steadily after veraison.[7]

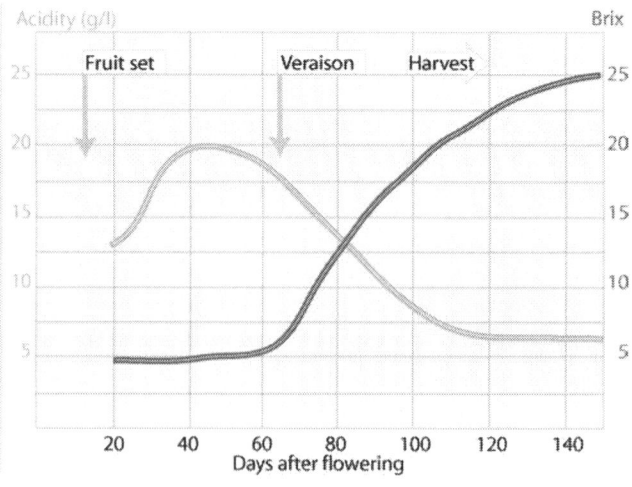

Sugar levels are assessed with a handheld refractometer by putting a drop of juice onto the instrument and reading the result in the eyepiece (the inset shows a view through the eyepiece). More sophisticated refractometers with digital readouts are used in laboratories.

Sugars are synthesized steadily in the berry after veraison until a point about 130-140 days after flowering. Once Brix reaches 25-26, synthesis stops, but the sugar concentration continues to increase as the result of desiccation (as water evaporates through the skin of the grape).

There are two major types of acid in the berry: tartaric acid and malic acid. Their relative proportions have an important effect on taste.

Tartaric acid is synthesized by many plants, including the grapevine. In some geographical areas, the grapevine is the only natural source of tartaric acid, so its residue on ancient pottery leads to the inference that wine was present. It has no distinct taste, but is widely used as an acidifying agent in the food and drinks industry. The berry synthesizes tartaric acid from fruit set until after veraison, and then its level declines in the last few weeks of ripening.[10]

Malic acid is found in all living organisms. It is especially rich in green apples. Indeed, when you smell or taste green apples in a wine, it's due to high malic acid. Its level in grapes peaks around veraison, but then declines sharply. As berries ripen, the total acidity declines, but malic acid declines more sharply than tartaric acid. Loss of malic acid increases with temperature, which is why there is relatively less malic acid in grapes from warmer climates. There's also wide variation in malic acid levels with the grape variety; Chardonnay and Sauvignon Blanc are rich in malic acid, Riesling is intermediate, and Palomino (the grape from which Sherry is made) has almost none.

To make good wine, berries have to have enough sugar to give a decent level of alcohol, and must retain enough acidity to give freshness. There is a strong interplay between sweetness and acidity in the taste of wine: sweetness is much harder to detect as the acidity increases, or viewed the other way round, acidity is much harder to detect as sugar levels increase. At normal levels of acidity, say around 6 g/l (grams/liter), an average person can detect sugar at a level of about 4 g/l. But a wine with high acidity, say 8 g/l, may taste dry even with sugar levels of up to 9 g/l. (In fact, the various taste elements in wine all interact with one another; although alcohol itself tastes sweet, increased alcohol increases the perception of bitterness.[11])

The Taming of the Tannins

They knew some things in the past that have been forgotten today. The Abbé Teinturier of Clos Vougeot explained the advantages of blending from their various terroirs: "We need [grapes that are] cooked, roasted, and green; even this last is necessary; it improves in the cuve by fermenting with the others; it is this that brings liveliness to the wine."[12] Has the need for flavor variety in creating complexity been forgotten today in the stampede to harvest grapes at riper and riper levels?

The moment of truth comes in deciding when to harvest. You have to get this right, because grapes ripen only on the vine. It used to be relatively simple: as soon as the berries reached a reasonable Brix, growers would pick at the first sign of impending bad weather so as not to take any risks. In cool climates, the need to see acidity levels drop would be balanced by concern that rain would dilute the harvest; in warm climates, the risk was more that acidity would decline rapidly, and sugar levels would increase too much. Growers were anxious not to let the level of potential alcohol get too high, because in the days before temperature control, fermentations would become hot, and run a risk of sticking. (Yeast is killed by excess heat, and it can be very difficult to get a stuck fermentation to start up again.) Typically this would lead to picking at a potential alcohol level around 11.5%.

But today sugar levels are only one criterion of ripeness. Berry maturity results from several pathways that may peak at different times. Maturity of grapes can be assessed in several ways depending on which criteria are applied. The size of the berry is important, especially for black grapes, where smaller berries give a higher ratio of skin to pulp. Polyphenols, which include the anthocyanins that give color and the tannins that give structure to a wine, are mostly found in the skin, so berry size influences both the color of the wine and the content of the tannins that are required for aging.

The current buzzword is "phenolic ripeness." As grapes mature, the tannin content increases, but the nature of the tannins also changes from harsher to better rounded. An early measure for phenolic ripeness was simply the appearance and taste of the grape: a ripe berry should come away cleanly when picked, and the color of the seeds should have changed from green to brown. This is not a new idea; around 65 C.E., Columella recommended the color of the pips as the best measure of ripeness.[13] More sophisticated measures now measure the level of tannins in the form of the IPT (Indice des Polyphénols Totaux). The scale for IPT is arbitrary,[14] but increased levels suggest that total phenols have increased from 5 g/l to 6 g/l since 1982, roughly a twenty per cent increase in twenty years.[15]

There's no good measure for the quality of tannins as opposed to quantity, but the concept that tannins mature from being "green" or "stalky" to becoming ripe goes back at least fifty years. Sometimes oenologists talk about "bad" tannins and "good" tannins.[16] At all events, "physiological ripeness" is associated with ripening to a later stage than formerly, and is influenced by color, stem maturity, tannin ripeness, berry shriveling, pulp texture, and seed ripeness. The basic change is that grapes are harvested at much higher sugar levels than previously in order to satisfy the demand for physiological ripeness. The most obvious effect is much higher alcohol in the wine, but prolonged ripening also has a big effect on the aroma and flavor spectrum of the wine, since volatile molecules as well as the phenols change significantly during the extra period on the vine.[17]

One reason why New World wines tend to be higher in alcohol than wines from Europe is that temperature and other climatic conditions lead to slower accumulation of sugar in Europe relative to phenols and other components. Because higher sugar levels are reached more rapidly in the New World, harvesting at the same sugar level as in Europe would mean the grapes had not reached phenolic ripeness.

Man versus Machine

Before phylloxera, when vines were planted on their own roots, they were densely packed. A new vine would be propagated simply by sticking a shoot from an existing vine into the ground close by. This "layering" resulted in a higgledy-piggledy arrangement of vines. Grafting on to rootstocks replaced this disorganization with a neat array of rows. The width of the row was typically set to allow a horse to pull a plough through without wandering to left or to right. Grapes would still be harvested manually by pickers who would work their way along the row, snipping off the ripe berries and placing them in baskets to be carried to the press.

The harvest at Moët et Chandon around 1900 at Le Mesnil-sur-Oger required pickers to collect the grapes by hand from tightly packed vines and place them in large baskets for transport to the press house.

Mechanization replaced the horse after the second world war when tractors were introduced, at first to pull along equipment for ploughing or spraying the vines, then with combined machines that could perform multiple functions. Special tractors were developed in France with a narrow gait that could move along rows with the traditional narrow spacing. Built high, they straddle the row. They were not available in the New World, where conventional farm equipment was used instead, requiring the rows to be more widely spaced. Now, of course, the same equipment is available worldwide, and vineyard work is generally accomplished by machines.

A move to using machines actually to harvest the grapes was driven largely by economics. Picking by hand is labor-intensive and requires a trained workforce to be available specifically for a few weeks per year. It's a relatively slow process, and can be difficult to arrange on short notice if the weather changes unexpectedly. A machine can be fired up at any time, picks the grapes more rapidly, and requires only one trained driver; the overall cost is about a fifth of picking manually. The ability to pick at night, when the grapes are cool, is a great advantage in hot climates. To use mechanical harvesting, the vines have to be organized on a trellis system that suits the harvester.

The big problem with mechanical harvesting is to distinguish between ripe and unripe fruit. The first machines simply beat the vine on the principle that ripe fruit would come off while unripe fruit would stay on. This was not terribly effective, and also resulted in the collection of a fair amount of material other than grapes (known as MOG in the trade). The machines improved when beating was replaced by a shaking mechanism; moving along the trellis, the harvester seizes the vine, moves it sharply in one direction, and then sharply back in the other direction. Mature grapes are released by this action, while immature or rotten grapes are not.

A mechanical harvester straddles the rows as it collects grapes.

Grapes are shaken loose as the machine passes over the vine; they are collected in a container within the machine.

The berries drop on to conveyer belts, and a sorting system removes leaves and other material before they fall into a container. Mechanical harvesters are becoming progressively more automated and sophisticated, for example, with controls to adjust the head for the difficulty of picking each particular variety. They are the norm for large scale producers and are widely used in both the New World and in Europe, accounting for almost all harvesting in Australia, for example, and about 75% of acreage in France.

The highest quality operations continue to use manual picking in the belief that a trained picker can still identify ripe fruit more selectively than a machine. And mechanical harvesters are limited by steep slopes (although they are getting better). Nor are they effective for late harvests when individual berries are selected in each bunch. But with such exceptions, they are now the norm worldwide in all but small-scale operations of the highest quality.

Going Green: Organic Viticulture

By the time you have fertilized with 50 kg/ha of nitrogen, 40 kg/ha of phosphorus, and 100 kg/ha of potassium, sprayed with herbicides to keep the weeds down, sprayed with pesticides to eliminate the insects, and treated with the latest steroids to prevent fungal infection, you may well have poisoned the soil in your vineyard. These are not healthy procedures; indeed they are supposed to stop several weeks before harvest so that the grapes are not contaminated. Remember that pesticides were actually developed from the nerve gases used in trench warfare in the first world war. Conventional viticulture is often encouraged by the authorities because it gives the most reliable results, with the highest yields. But it tends to homogenize the wine, eliminating differences between terroirs, reducing differences between vintages, and altogether turning out a bland product, in the same way that farmed fish never has the same flavor as wild. Of course, you don't have to go to extremes, and there is a growing trend towards "sustainable viticulture," in which use of fertilizers, herbicides, and pesticides is much reduced, although not eliminated. There's no knowing how widely it is practiced.

Organic viticulture goes the whole hog, and uses no chemical fertilizers, with only natural agents to control pests and diseases. Although adopted by many leading producers, it is still a miniscule part of world viticulture. Europe is the leader, but organic vineyards still account for only a measly 100,000 ha (about 2.5%); worldwide they are probably about 1.5%.[18, 19]

An organic vineyard uses natural means of fertilization and weed control. If fertilization is necessary (remember that grapevines give their best results in poor soils), manure is used. Cover crops are used to protect the soil. Instead of the pristine look of rows of vines separated by bare earth, now there is often a ragged cover crop around and between the vines. Sometimes it's a stripped down version of "Nature raw in tooth and claw," where the cover crops compete with the vines. Weeds are removed mechanically. Predatory insects or phero-

A conventional vineyard has bare earth between the vines (top), but an organic vineyard has cover crops (bottom).

mones are used to control pests. (Pheromones are the volatile compounds released into the air that male and female insects use to find one another; saturating the air with pheromones protects the vineyard by causing "sexual confusion," when the insects don't know where to turn.) A vineyard is considered organic only after three years of conforming to the protocol.

A century ago, vineyards could be worked only by horses. In fact, their layout was partially determined by the need to organize the rows so that horses could move through. Ploughing between the rows removed weeds, broke up the soil, and by removing the surface roots forced the vines to put down deeper roots. One of the problems with conventional viticulture is that the weight of the tractors compresses the surface soil, causing problems with drainage. Recently there has been a move towards bringing back horses.

Yields are lower in organic viticulture by about 20%, which contributes to higher quality. Costs are greater by about 20%. It's generally easier for small growers to go organic, because they are not giving up the economies of scale that a large grower gets from conventional viticulture. And they don't have the problem of needing to treat very large areas all at the same time when a problem such as mildew threatens. It's also easier when the vineyard has multiple grape varieties planted, each with different susceptibility to pests and diseases.[20] One problem is that it's hard to be organic if surrounding vineyards are not: pesticides or herbicides may waft across on to your vines. Some organic growers are forced to discard (or bottle separately) the production from the edges of their vineyards to ensure purity of the rest.

One of the biggest problems of organic viticulture is controlling mildew. Modern steroid inhibitors offer an effective control for both types of mildew (powdery and downy), for which there is no organic counterpart. Organic producers are restricted to using copper to treat downy mildew and sulfur to treat oïdium (powdery mildew), or stylet oils (which ironically are derived from petroleum distillate). In fact, concern about accumulation of high copper levels in

As part of the organic viticulture program at Château Pontet Canet, horses have been reintroduced to plough the rows between the vines. The equipment was designed especially and built by the château.

the soil is one of the major drawbacks of organic viticulture.[21] It's perhaps an open question whether it's the lesser evil compared to using steroid fungal inhibitors.

Lack of effective fungal treatments can be critical in humid climates, where mildew can spread rapidly. In Bordeaux, for example, high humidity caused outbreaks of mildew in 2007 that would probably have wiped out the vintage twenty years ago; but the new inhibitors rescued the crop, and the vintage is quite decent. There were some casualties among organic producers, however; at Château Pontet Canet, which had just gone organic, proprietor Alfred Tesseron decided he could not take the risk of losing the entire crop, and the mildew was controlled with modern inhibitors.[22] Pontet Canet is now starting back on the road to organic certification.

The details of what can be described as "organic" vary with the local certifying authority. One of the big issues is use of sulfur. To be labeled as organic wine, no sulfur preservatives can be added. This makes it difficult to safeguard the wine against contamination. Wine made by organic methods, but where sulfur preservatives are used, can be described as "made from organic grapes."

Organic growers tend to harvest sooner than conventional producers; they claim this is because chemical spraying delays ripening. It may also be because the grapevines are simply healthier.

Phases of the Moon

"Some call her sister of the moon
Some say illusions are her game"

These lyrics from Fleetwood Mac perfectly capture the controversy about biodynamics. Biodynamic viticulture sounds off the wall. Treatments are applied to the vineyards according to the phase of the moon. The current model for this is

Maria Thun's annual planting calendar (worked out in the 1970s), which relates ancient elements to organs of the plant (Earth to roots, Water to foliage, Air to flower, Fire to fruit and seeds), and assigns periods for actions according to the zodiac.[23] The biodynamic calendar has four types of days: fruit, flower, leaf, and root, which are defined in terms of four groups of star constellations. Each type of day defines a period when the moon is in one of the constellations. Suitable treatments for plants differ for flower days, fruit days, root days, etc.

Some of the more extreme measures are hard to understand. One of the best known (not to say mocked) procedures involves putting manure in a cow's horn and burying it in the center of the vineyard to make a preparation that is later spread over the vineyard. It is claimed that imitation horns do not have the same effects. Another use of the horn is when horn silica is prepared from finely ground silica buried over the summer in a cow's horn. The powdered preparation or solution is spread on the grapevines in the spring at 4 g/ha. Pests are treated by spreading the ashes of pests on the ground. This is definitely not going to do anything to discourage them. Solutions are made at very dilute levels and are supposed to transmit their effects through "activated water"; this nonsense has no scientific basis. Yet some of the top producers all over the world follow biodynamic practices, and there is absolutely no argument about the quality of their wines.[24] So what's going on?

Biodynamic methods were developed by Rudolph Steiner, a philosopher who created a theory of "spiritual science," which includes biodynamics. All artificial treatments, such as fertilizers or weed killers, are forbidden; compost is generated to replace fertilizers. Compost is based on waste from the vineyard (grape skins, seeds, cuttings from vines) and cow manure. But this is no ordinary compost, such as might be used in an organic vineyard. Steiner prescribed a set of six compost preparations made from plants (valerian, dandelion, oak, bark, nettles, yarrow, chamomile). They are known by numbers 502-507. Used to seed a conventional compost, they convert it into biodynamic compost. "The soil then becomes primed to receive energies streaming down from the cosmos and upward from within the earth itself," according to one modern writer.[25] This is simply beyond all reason.

The concept of the lunatic is a powerful testament to the long existence of beliefs in the effects of the moon. At what point does biodynamic treatment become superstition instead of good care of the land? "The good period for bottling is during the waning moon," says Guy Renvoisé in an otherwise completely serious book debunking nonsense about wine.[26] In fact, it is a common superstition, independent of biodynamics, that wine should not be bottled at the full moon (or, for that matter, during a thunderstorm). Can changes in atmospheric pressure really be significant enough to affect the condition of the wine?

A wide range of superstitions associated with the moon have found their way into wine lore. "Fermentation is quick when the moon is ascendant; if you ferment when the moon is descendant the process is much slower," says Serge Hochar of Lebanon's Château Musar.[27] It is quite widely believed that it is better to prune grapevines (and other plants) during a waning moon. The rationale is that less sap flows out of the cuts because the water table is diminishing.

To be certified as a biodynamic producer,[28] you don't have to follow the phases of moon, merely to apply all the preparations. The original concept for biodynamics envisaged each farm as self-contained, generating its own compost, but these days you can purchase certified preparations. (It's not always straightforward to obtain supplies: for example, cow manure, an essential ingredient for biodynamics, has to be obtained from a source where the cows are not treated with antibiotics.) Wine producers practicing biodynamics vary from those who are certified to those who are basically organic but use some of the biodynamic methods. Certified biodynamic viticulture is a vanishingly small proportion of total wine production.[29, 30]

Irrespective of skepticism about some of the biodynamic methods, the basic question is what effect they have on the soil. Claude Bourguignon is a scientist who has spent the last thirty years studying the soils in France. He is well known for his view that modern farming methods have destroyed the life of the soil. "In the last thirty years, around 90% of the soil life has disappeared... In France, I find soils that have less biological activity than the Sahara," he famously said.[31] He performed a highly quoted comparison showing that a biodynamic vineyard has more trace elements and microbial activity in deep soils than an organic vineyard.[32] Bourguignon believes that biodynamic treatments help support a population of mycorrhizal fungi in the soil that attach to the grapevine roots and transfer trace elements to the vine.

Other studies haven't shown any significant differences in the soil, but it's fair to say that the verdict is out on whether and what difference biodynamic treatments make.[34] It is certainly clear there's a substantial difference between the results of conventional and organic viticulture, but it's not so clear whether going biodynamic makes any further difference. So coming back to the central question: why do producers go to the extra effort and how do we explain the results? Could it be that increased quality is due more to the great care and attention given to the vines? They are not abused with fertilizers or herbicides, the vines are carefully tended, the canopies are adjusted for the conditions of the particular year, yields are kept low—it might be that absolutely identical treatment without the biodynamic additions would give virtually the same effects.

Maria Thun's calendar. The columns show date, constellation of the moon, solar and lunar events, which moon elements dominate the day, and which parts of plants are favored for treatment. A dashed line shows that all treatments should be avoided.[33]

While it's entirely believable that biodynamic treatment of the soil improves grapes and therefore wine, it's much harder to believe that the calendar predicts when bottled wine will taste best. Biodynamic proponents claim that wine tastes best on flower and fruit days.[35] Are consumers likely to respect the biodynamic calendar when deciding whether they want to drink a glass of wine? Yet some major supermarkets in the U.K., not known for a romantic approach to their merchandise, only hold tastings for wine critics on days when the calendar predicts wines will taste best.[36] Jo Ahearne MW of Marks and Spencer tells me that some wines are affected more than others. "The more tannic, the more obvious; if they are very aromatic it's less obvious," she says,[37] and "we now only hold tastings on fruit, flower or (at worst) leaf days." What could be the basis for such an effect? Where is the line that divides unexplained, but plausible, effects from astrology?

Let me state my position explicitly. I am neither a believer nor a skeptic about biodynamic methods. Some of them are puzzling, but one is forced to recognize that there are some great wines made by winemakers who believe that biodynamic practices are an intrinsic part of the quality. However, I do demand that at the end of the day we can find a rational explanation for the effect, or at least that we can see how one may be possible even if we don't have a full explanation right now. So I am prepared to believe that organic methods make stronger grapevines that give better grapes and make better wines. I have a holding position on the various biodynamic treatments while we wait to find out whether they really affect factors such as microbial life in the soil.[38] I find it very difficult to believe that scattering the ashes of pests in the vineyards prevents those pests from returning. And it is completely impossible to believe that passing magnetic forces through water creates a "memory" affecting the way that water is used by the plants: this flies in the face of everything we know about the chemistry and physics of water. I reserve judgment as to whether pruning is better done at certain phases of the moon because it relates to the rate of sap flow while I wait for someone to actually measure that rate of flow; but I refuse to believe that the position of the moon in relation to other astrological bodies has any effect at all on anything other than superstitious behavior. And when I hear that "an important aspect of biodynamics is that we are not dealing with factors, we are dealing with forces, we are harmonizing the forces... [which] are impregnated through water, water has memory,"[39] I begin to wonder whether we are dealing with a rational position or trying to read the entrails as they might have done in ancient Rome.

Modern Trends

So vineyards of today run a gamut of styles, from fully fledged biodynamics where cow's horns filled with manure are planted by the light of the full moon, to industrial agriculture where everything is mechanized, and weed killing, pesticides, fertilizers, and irrigation are used to even out the crop as much as possible from year to year. Good wine is made at all levels: if biodynamic viticulture hits the heights of representing vintage variation in the individual vineyard, mechanized viticulture produces wine of a quality and consistency that was not previously available at this level on this scale.

Is the split widening between the small producer, who is turning more and more to organic viticulture, and the large producer, who takes more and more advantage of the modern techniques available in viticulture and vinification? To what extent (and at what levels of the market) is wine still a natural product?

It's true that we understand more today than ever before about the biology of the grapevine, how to make it productive or to limit its productivity, how to handle the problems of pests and diseases, but it's fair to say that we still do not understand in detail how the effects of different soils and environments (the *terroir*) are represented in the wine. And are the hard-won advances of recent years now threatened by a change in climate that may unsettle the balance between grape varieties and the regions in which they are grown?

3

The Mystique of Terroir

NOTHING IN THE WORLD OF WINE is more controversial than terroir. Opinions vary from belief that great wine comes only from great terroirs to denial that terroir has anything to do with quality. At its simplest, terroir can seem banal: it is not rocket science to suppose that a vine (or for that matter any other plant) grown in sunny, well-drained conditions at the top of a hill will produce different fruit from a vine grown in shady, water-logged conditions at the bottom of the hill. But terroir can be profound if you accept that wines made from even adjacent plots of land show consistent differences in their aroma and flavor profiles; while it is fanciful to suppose you can directly taste the properties of the terroir (Ugh, you might say, do I really want to smell and taste dirt anyway?), there has been a continuing debate as to exactly how its features might influence the fruit and the wine made from it.

Terroir is not in principle a difficult concept, but it occasions a great deal of argument in practice. *Terroir* implies that each vineyard has a unique combination of soil, aspect, and climatic features determining what type and quality of wine it is capable of producing. The basic concept is pretty simple: other conditions being equal, one plot of land will always produce different wine from another, even if it has the same grape varieties cultivated under the same conditions, because its terroir is different. In its purest sense, terroir refers strictly to natural features of the land.

The idea that differences in wine come directly from the land became honed into the concept of terroir in France. When the British philosopher John Locke visited the wine regions of Bordeaux in 1677, he described the basis for the difference between the top vineyards and the adjacent lesser vineyards: "The vine de Pontac [later to become known as Château Haut Brion, the famous first growth], so much esteemed in England, grows on a rising open to the west, in a white sand mixed with a little gravel, which one would think would bear nothing; but there is a such a particularity in the soil, that at Mr. Pontac's, near Bourdeaux the merchants assured me that the wine growing in the very next vineyards, where there was only a ditch between, and the soil, to appearance, perfectly the same, was by no means so good."[1]

Terroir is the pivot of winemaking in France, where the place of origin is found on the label of a quality wine, but the grape variety is not mentioned. Origin is all. The first traces of the modern concept of terroir appear in French literature of the eighteenth century, but the idea developed fully only during the nineteenth and twentieth centuries. In 1777, a French dictionary defined terroir. "On dit, que le vin sent du terroir, qu'il a un gout de terroir..." (it is said that wine smells of its terroir, that it has a taste of terroir... that is, it is has a certain aroma, a certain taste that comes from the quality of the terroir)." The entry distinguished between terroirs appropriate for different types of crops, helpfully adding, "Le terroir de Bourgogne (Burgundy) est bon pour les vins."[2] Actually, the concept that wines might acquire a "gout de terroir" may have preceded the development of the concept that the terroir influences quality of wine.[3] During the early nineteenth century, terroir was generally used in a disparaging sense, implying that the wine was rustic.

Terroir may first have made its way into the wine literature as a factor affecting quality when Dr. Denis Morélot wrote a book on the wines of Burgundy in 1831. Considering the basis for the differences between wines, he said, "I am far from denying this truth: that each of these wines has a particular quality, a taste absolutely different from the others… It is the soil that imprints its native properties on the wines and which creates the differences between them. I am completely convinced that the aspect, the dryness of the soil, the age of the vines, and their variety, powerfully influence the quality of the wine."[4] He went on to discuss in some detail the soils of each commune and their effects upon the wines produced there.

Some geologists are skeptical of the role of soil in the taste of wine. Geologist Jake Hancock commented, "Terroir is a concept which originated in France. It is difficult to think of another country where it could have started, since it has features so characteristic of second-class French thinkers: a combination of the obvious (the quality of a plant depends on where you grow it) and the mystical."[5] Other have been more accepting: James Wilson wrote an award-winning book called simply "Terroir," which attempted in great detail to correlate geology with properties of wine, largely in France.[6]

In the New World, terroir may be denied or disdained as no more than a marketing ploy. One sarcastic modern view sees terroir as a SCAM (Soil + Climate + Aspect = Mystique).[7] Refuting this position, wine critic Matt Kramer says, "A surprising number of winegrowers and wine drinkers— at least in the United States—flatly deny the existence of terroir, like weekend sailors who reject as preposterous that Polynesians could have crossed the Pacific navigating only by sun, stars, wind, smell and taste. Terroir is held to be little more than viticultural voodoo."[8] Kramer regards terroir as a "sense of somewhereness," which is not a bad definition.

One reason why terroir is emphasized far more in Europe is that the typical vineyard size is much smaller than in the New World.[9] Soil properties can change strongly over short distances, so variation in terroir is a feature of relatively small vineyards. But irrespective of whether vineyard size allows terroir to manifest itself in any particular wine, what's the reality here: is terroir a myth or does location of the grapevines determine the intrinsic characteristics of a wine?

And remember that the act of planting a vineyard must impact the terroir: at a minimum, the local ecology will be different when the land is planted with vines instead of whatever was there previously. Often enough, more extensive changes are made: land may be graded, terraces constructed for vineyards on slopes, drainage systems introduced, soil may be brought in—in short, the terroir is created by changes in the vineyard directly affecting the vines or by changes in the surrounding area indirectly affecting the vineyard. When these changes are old and hallowed by time, they are regarded as part of the natural terroir, to be protected from further change. When they are new, they may instead arouse protests about damage to the environment. So what's the balance of terroir: how does it arise and what effect does it have on the vines and wine?

Does the Answer Lie in the Soil?

If terroir exists, if the location where a vine is grown affects the characteristics of its grapes and then of its wine, the answer must lie in the soil.[10] Differences in the physical or chemical properties of the soil between one vineyard and the next must be transmitted to the grapes. This is evidently true at a gross level: differences in the structure of the soil determine how easily and how far down the vine's roots can penetrate, and differences in drainage determine how much water the roots receive. Together with the aspect of the land, which affects exposure to sunshine, it's easy to see how these factors may have an effect on quantity and quality of the berries.[11] Along the same lines, the general nutritive properties of soil, in particular its level of nitrogen and potassium, have a significant effect on growth; indeed, as a general rule, vines produce better wine in poor soil, and it is for this reason that rich soils are not associated with production of fine wine. It's harder to see how the properties of the soil might change the spectrum of aromas and flavors, making one wine "mineral" or another wine "earthy."

The idea that the quality of a wine depends on where it comes from is almost as old as wine production itself. In every civilization going back to the Romans, some wines have been more prized than others. Two millennia ago, the effects of the soil were considered by the Roman Vitruvius, who in a treatise on architecture commented, "These waters are given their different flavors by the properties of the soil, as is also seen in the case of fruits... We find wines of countless varieties and qualities produced in many... places. This could not be the case, were it not that the juice of the soil, introduced with its proper flavors into the roots, feeds the stem, and, mounting along it to the top, imparts a flavor to the fruit which is peculiar to its situation and kind."[12] Here is the very heart of the concept of terroir: the soil directly transmits characteristics to the grapes.

In a famous study of the Bordeaux vineyards, Gerard Seguin of the University of Bordeaux found no connection between wine quality and the chemical composition of soil. "It is impossible," he said, "to establish any correlation between quality of wine and the soil content of any nutritive element."[13] He went on to comment, perhaps a trifle sarcastically, that "if there were such a correlation it would be easy, with the appropriate chemical additives, to produce great wine anywhere." Indeed, Bordeaux alone demonstrates that great wines can be made on a wide variety of soils, acid and gravelly at Château Lafite, iron-rich clay with a limestone base at Châteaux Pétrus and Cheval Blanc, alkaline limestone at Château Ausone. But Seguin found a common feature to the terroirs of the great châteaux: bilan hydrique (hydric balance). The best have well drained soils with water tables just within reach of the vine roots; the consequence is that when the water table drops around veraison (the point at which the berries change color and begin to develop), the supply to the vines is restricted. This is precisely the condition needed to push the vine into giving priority to ripening its berries at the expense of vegetative growth.

Certainly the physical properties of soil may influence choice of grape varieties. The classic example is Bordeaux, where the gravel-based soils of the left bank favor Cabernet Sauvignon, whereas the clay-based soils of the right bank favor Merlot. The reason is that gravel is warmer than clay (stones retain heat from solar radiation, whereas more evaporation, with consequent heat loss, occurs from clay). The difference in temperature is sufficient to allow Cabernet Sauvignon to ripen on the left bank but not on the right bank, but Merlot (which ripens sooner) is successful on both sides of the river.

Rock is pretty solid stuff: vine roots cannot penetrate it directly, and it is important for its physical properties (such as drainage or heat retention) rather than for its chemical constitution. Rock of any sort at the surface has an important effect in reflecting heat back up to the vines. One famous example is the galets—a layer of pebbles at the surface in Châteauneuf-du-Pape—that absorb heat during the day and release it at night. A direct demonstration of the effect of stones comes from Tignanello, the famous super-Tuscan property in the Chianti

The white stones were brought to the surface when the vineyard at Tignanello was replanted.

region. The underlying soil had a high concentration of white stones, and when the vineyard was replanted, these were brought up to the surface. The resulting heat gain brought the harvest forward by one week.[14] And although no one has quantitated the effect, the heat-reflecting properties of slate—whether red, gray, or blue—has an important role in Germany in making it possible for grapes to ripen in marginal conditions.

Limestone is often regarded as favorable for vineyards—especially for white grapes—mostly because of its good drainage. It is also notable for its alkalinity, which is somewhat less advantageous.[15] The acidity of the soil has an important effect on growth of grapevines (and for that matter other plants), especially because it affects uptake of mineral nutrients. Vines prefer slightly acid or neutral soil (pH between 6 and 7); they will not grow in highly acid soils, and in alkaline soils their uptake of iron and other elements is reduced; at its extreme, lack of iron can cause the disease of chlorosis (when the leaves yellow and fall off). Remember also that the effects of the soil are filtered through the rootstock; one of the major issues when grafting was introduced to combat phylloxera was finding American rootstocks able to withstand the more calcareous soils in Europe.

It's a mantra that more alkaline soils give fruit with higher acidity. It's part of the rationale for planting white grapes on limestone, but the reason is not obvious. When I asked an oenologist in Bordeaux to support his assertion that alkaline soils give more acid grapes, he was dismissive: "I don't have any specific work in mind but I am sure you can find that in a good plant physiology book." Surprisingly there appear in fact to be no scientific studies to explain this. Is it another of those myths associated with supposing that terroir has direct effects

Kimmeridgian soil takes its name from Kimmeridge on the south coast of England.

on the grapes.[16] Certainly it's plausible that high calcium concentrations in the soil stress the plant, but we still need evidence that this creates higher acidity in the grapes.[17] With even less support, another stated reason for preferring white to black varieties on limestone is that soils derived from limestone contain less iron (which is true) and that black grapes require more iron[18] (which is a myth).[19]

Various grape varieties are associated with specific soil types, on which they are said to produce their best results. Riesling goes with slate, Chardonnay goes with limestone, and Syrah goes with granite. Does terroir plus cépage add up to that unique combination the French call typicité? To ascribe such specific influence to the terroir may be overstating the strength of the connection. Riesling, for example, is grown in cool climates under conditions that are marginal for ripening; so its best results are produced on the warmest soils, that is, those covered in reflective slate. Other varieties would no doubt also give their best results on the slate, but because Riesling is the top variety in the region, the best soils are reserved for it. So in Austria's Wachau, slate-covered vineyards are planted with Riesling, while the lesser loess-based soils are planted with the less well-regarded Grüner Veltliner; does this mean that Riesling and slate have a unique affinity, or is it simply that the less remunerative variety is not planted on the top soils?

The association of limestone with Chardonnay is often quoted as an example of a terroir-specific effect. In Burgundy's Côte d'Or, Chardonnay tends to be planted on limestone-rich patches, Pinot Noir elsewhere. The best example of specificity comes from a little farther north, in Chablis, where not only is the terroir based on limestone, but a distinction has traditionally been drawn between two types of limestone.

The famous Kimmeridgian soil is a soft mixture of clay and limestone, generally gray in color. It was laid down in the Jurassic period, when the sea retreated, leaving a bed of fossils that give the soil its calcareous nature. It is named for the village of Kimmeridge on the south coast of England, where the fossil beds are exceptionally rich. Kimmeridgian soil occupies about half of the Chablis region;

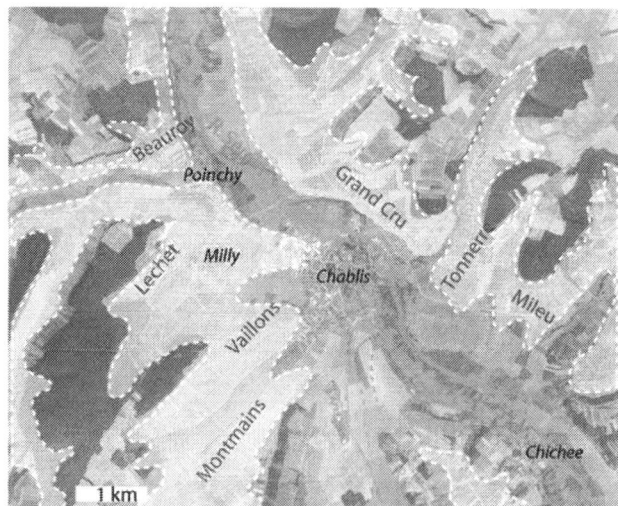

Chablis is divided into Kimmeridgian soil (outlined in white) and Portlandian soil (all other areas except for the alluvial land shown in green, mostly around the river). The grand crus and premier crus (indicated by names in red) are on Kimmeridgian soil.[20]

the rest consists of Portlandian limestone, harder in structure and browner in color (and taking its name from the village of Portland on the English south coast).

Chablis is divided into four quality levels: Petit Chablis, Chablis, Premier Cru, and Grand Cru. The original definition, in 1938 when the total vineyard area of 400 ha was less than 10% of today's 5,000 ha, confined all levels above Petit Chablis to terroirs of Kimmeridgian soil. This remained true as the area expanded: the AOC was described as comprising vineyards in a number of communes around Chablis but "with the exclusion of parcels not situated on Kimmeridgian soil."[21] It was felt that wines produced on the Portlandian limestone never achieved the same quality. But in 1978, when a further expansion occurred, the restriction was dropped.[22]

Was this the abandonment of a futile distinction or a cynical attempt to find a basis for increasing the area of production? Certainly there was a (justified) view that the expansion was associated with areas below the original quality. But was that quality due to the Kimmeridgian soil? The fact is that the Kimmeridgian soil is located on the south and east-facing slopes, where the good exposure helps to compensate for the cool climate, whereas the harder Portlandian soil occupies the plateaus at higher elevations (where the grapes are slower to ripen). So the original distinction was not ill-founded, but it had more to do with aspect and slope than with the underlying geology.[23]

Overt emphasis on terroir is less common in the New World than in Europe, but one of the most famous counter examples is the Terra Rossa soil of

The Terra Rossa soil of Coonawarra is evident in the exposed red bank of earth at the center. Underneath is the limestone ridge.

Coonawarra. This stretch of red loam with a limestone subsoil occupies about half the area of Coonawarra. Coupled with the coolest climate in South Australia, it supports the production of unusually elegant Cabernet Sauvignon (some Shiraz is also grown). The geological features are widely taken to be responsible for the unique quality of the wine, but have been generally misunderstood. It's usually been thought that the Terra Rossa soil, given its bright red color by a high concentration of ferric (iron) oxide, is the crucial feature, but in fact the key is the subsoil.[24] This is an unusually permeable limestone, which gives good drainage of excess water, but retains enough moisture to nourish the vines even in dry periods. Together with a water table that has seeped across from the mountains to the east, this provides a perfect water supply. The water table naturally would be around 1 m, but drains constructed in the region have lowered it to around 6 m, an example of (inadvertent) successful terroir modification.

There's often more than a nugget of truth in the conclusions resulting from generations of experience in matching grape varieties to terroirs, but the explanation may be somewhat different from conventional wisdom. It may owe more to indirect physical effects (such as heat retention or drainage) than to any direct interaction with the soil.

Licking the Slate

The concentration of blue slate covering the famous Bernkasteler Doctor vineyard in the Mosel gives its wines an intense mineral character, it is often said. In fact, from time to time you see people licking the slate to see whether they can detect the mineral taste of the wine. It's all very well to say that Chablis is flinty or that Riesling has a taste of gunflint, but just how would rocks of flint or shale leach flavors into the wine? Imagination plays its role: geologist Alex Maltman points out that the wines of Priorat are often described as tasting or smelling of

The Bernkasteler Doctor vineyard is covered with fragments of blue slate.

graphite (the unusual schist of Priorat is rich in graphite)—but graphite has no taste or smell![25]

Plants synthesize most of their components (almost 90%!) from air and water: the amazing act of photosynthesis enables them to obtain all the carbon, oxygen, and hydrogen they need from carbon dioxide and water. But inorganic components must be obtained from the soil, including macro-elements such as nitrogen, phosphorus, potassium, calcium, magnesium, sulfur, and a series of micro-elements required in lesser amounts.[26] Nutrient uptake is assisted by symbiotic microbes (mycorrhizal fungi) that live on the roots. Soils differ in their concentrations of these elements; deficiencies are manifested in poor growth. But it's a far cry from acknowledging that the soil's provision of nutritional elements influences growth, indeed is essential for it, to supposing that these elements change flavors.

Perhaps the biggest myth about terroir is that wines have a *gout de terroir*, that you can taste the components of the soil in the wine. This is not to say that the soil lacks influence on the chemical composition of wine. Efforts to distinguish the origins of wines by their contents of trace elements show there are differences. One study of 50 trace elements showed consistent differences between three areas of Margaret River in Western Australia.[27] But the levels of the elements are well below taste thresholds. Indeed, it is unlikely that any of the nutrients taken up from the soil reach levels you could taste in the grapes.[28] In fact, if they exceeded the threshold for taste, they would usually be regarded as problems requiring adjustment. The levels allowed by law for mineral salts (such as copper or iron) in wine are well below the threshold at which you could taste them.[29]

Nutrient concentrations may influence vine growth indirectly by their effects on symbiotic fungi that live on the roots, but there's no reason to suppose that any effects on flavor would directly reflect the properties of the mineral. Only some of the inorganic nutrients absorbed by roots find their way into the berries. And wine only partially reflects the constitution of the grapes; after all, wine does not taste like grape juice with some alcohol added, but has a different spectrum of aromas and flavors. Not only are the levels of the elements always well below taste thresholds, but they change significantly between the juice and the wine (many are removed by yeast during fermentation).[30] (And some fining procedures used during vinification, especially the use of bentonite clay, can make significant changes in the mineral composition.)

Flavors in wine are mostly due to complex organic molecules constructed in the grape or during fermentation; they are not ingested from the soil. Certainly wines can be found to have characteristic mineral or earthy flavors, but it is an act of imagination to suppose these come directly from the soil. It's fair to say that the jury is out on whether mineral contents of soil are reflected in any systematic way in berries or in the smell and taste of wine.

Grapevines can have deep roots, and it is generally agreed that the quality of berries increases as the roots go deeper. However, this is not due to differences in uptake of materials from the soil. It's due more to the fact that the vine gets a more even supply of water by using deep rather than superficial roots. It's commonly said that grapevines absorb minerals through more superficial roots, but take up only water from deep roots. Actually, mineral uptake may depend more on topsoil, but not for quite the reason stated. It's not so much that there is a difference in the behavior of deep roots versus shallower roots, but most absorption is done by the mass of the finest roots lying in the top half meter or so,[31] simply because this is where the greatest area of contact with soil occurs. But ascribing minerality to direct uptake from the subsoil is undoubtedly misguided.

Minerality is one of the most difficult qualities to define in wine. Described as flinty, sometimes as smoky, it represents a sort of precise, angular edge, usually associated with good acidity, often with crisp citrus flavors. Certainly it is associated with wines from certain areas, but does that necessarily mean it is a direct reflection of terroir as opposed to representing local winemaking practices or other extraneous influences? The only compound so far identified with minerality is benzene-methanethiol, which gives a smoky quality and has been found in Chardonnay, Sauvignon Blanc, and Sémillon.[32] Since this is a thiol (a sulfur-containing compound that is affected by exposure to oxygen), its involvement implies that smokiness will be enhanced by reductive winemaking (excluding oxygen) and minimized when wine making is more oxidative. Otherwise there's no scientific information on what might be responsible for minerality.

Some varietal characteristics owe as much to viticulture and vinification as to the intrinsic nature of the variety. Sauvignon Blanc has a unique combination of herbaceousness, citrus fruits, and tropical fruits, which display somewhat differently in the classic region of the Loire and the new region of Marlborough, New Zealand. Herbaceousness is due to a methoxypyrazine that forms early during the development of the grapes but declines sharply as they ripen. Tropical fruits result from volatile thiol compounds released during fermentation by the yeasts; their concentration is greatly influenced by choice of yeast and conditions of vinification. The difference between Sauvignon Blanc produced in the Loire and the same variety produced in Marlborough owes little to the difference in soils; it depends more on different regimes for obtaining ripeness, and differences in the styles of vinification which control the concentrations of these thiol compounds.

There is, incidentally, a fine distinction to be drawn between terroir and environmental effects. A classic example was the historical association of extremely earthy aromas and flavors with some red Burgundies. This was not in fact due to terroir, in fact it had nothing to do with the grapevines, but was the result of contamination with the yeast Brettanomyces. Opinion has evolved from regarding it as a corollary of quality to a possible flaw in the wine.[33] What other features of "terroir" might in the future turn out to be due to extraneous factors?

More recently, some Californian and Australian wines have shown a noticeable touch of eucalyptus. While this might be regarded as a feature of terroir, it is in fact due to oil blowing from eucalyptus leaves; sticking to the waxy skins of the berries, some finds its way into the wine.[34] Some might regard this as a feature of terroir, but personally I would regard it as adventitious since you could, after all, cut down the eucalyptus trees. More obviously, in south and west Australia a series of intense forest fires (starting in 2003) created the new phenomenon of "smoke taint" in some wines. Smoky aromas and flavors—which were perceived by tasters as flaws in the wine—were due to specific compounds absorbed by the grapes from the smoke, and the extent of the taint was determined by the timing and duration of exposure of the grapevines to the smoke.[35]

From Pompei to Clos Vougeot

In the century or so before the eruption of Mount Vesuvius in 79 C.E., one of the most renowned wines was Falernian, grown on the slopes of Mount Falernus near Naples. Falernian was a sweet white wine, made from partially dried grapes. Its quality was distinguished according to whether it came from the upper, middle or lower slopes. The middle slope was considered the best, and the wine was reputed to age for 10-20 or more years. The vintage of 121 B.C. was exceptionally fine, and became known as the Opimian wine after the name of the then Emperor. Falernian was in second place when Pliny compiled a list of 80 or so of the best regions for wine production around 70 C.E.[36] Pliny noted that new varieties of vines were becoming available, and commented on their suitability for particular climates, one of the first attempts to match cépages and terroir.[37]

Two millennia later, there was a measure of the value of position on the slope. "The wine, at the summit of the Clos Vougeot, one of the most celebrated vineyards of Burgundy, sells for 600 francs, that of the middle brings 900, and that of the base only 300," according to an Australian observer, James Busby, in 1825.[38] Anticipating concepts of terroir, Busby remarked on the importance of aspect and physical constitution of the ground: "The conclusion may even be drawn, that the intrinsic nature of the soil is of less importance, that it should be porous, free, and light... The soils of the best vineyards are those which contain little nutritious matter."[39]

Why does the middle of the slope give the best wine? The usual explanation is that drainage is most consistent in the middle of the slope. In a dry vintage, the bottom of the slope may do better than the top, in a wet vintage the relationship will be reversed, but from year to year the most consistent supply of water is in the middle.

Often enough, soil composition changes along the slope. A famous example is the rising slope containing the grand crus for white Burgundy, Bâtard Montrachet, Le Monrachet, and Chevalier Montrachet. Going up the slope, the soil changes from 20% clay and 80% pebbles at the bottom to 50% clay and 50% pebbles at the top.[40] Ahah! it is easy to say—the ideal soil composition for great white wine must be that of Le Montrachet (32-36% clay, 64-68% pebbles).

But some suspicion might be occasioned by the fact that mid-slope also gives the best results in many other locations where the underlying soil is different. So it may not be only a matter of drainage or soil composition, but rather due to exposure to the sun. On south-facing slopes (north-facing in the southern hemisphere), the middle of the slope gets the most sunshine. The effect depends on the angle of the sun, so is especially pronounced when the sun is low in the sky, that is, early in the morning and later in the evening.[41] This makes the slope particularly important for avoiding spring frosts and for ripening in the autumn.

Marketing the Terroir

Adam Smith, with his usual keen eye on the market, was the first to acknowledge the economic implications of terroir "The vine is more affected by the difference of soils than any other fruit tree. From some it derives a flavour which no culture or management can equal, it is supposed, upon any other. This flavour, real or imaginary, is sometimes peculiar to the produce of a few vineyards; sometimes it extends through the greater part of a small district, and sometimes through a considerable part of a large province."[42] With his customary skepticism, he went on to question cause and effect: "The whole quantity of such wines that is brought to market falls short of the effectual demand... [and]... therefore can be disposed of to those who are willing to pay more, which necessarily raises the price above that of common wine. The difference is greater or less, according as the fashionableness and scarcity of the wine render the competition of the buyers more or less eager... For though such vineyards are in general more carefully cultivated than most others, the high price of the wine seems to be, not so much the effect, as the cause of this careful cultivation."

The concept of terroir as a distinguishing feature in selling wines is relatively recent. When the appellation contrôlée system was originally conceived in France, it was by no means immediately obvious that it would be based on terroir. In fact, one of its principal protagonists, the politician Joseph Capus, no doubt influenced by the system of wine production in his native Bordeaux, argued in the Revue du Vin de France in 1935 that AOCs should be based on domains rather than terroirs.[43] (Bordeaux is the exception to the dominance of terroir as the defining characteristic of quality in wine; classification here is by the producer.[44]) By 1947, when Capus was President of INAO,* however, he was strongly defending the system of definition by terroir that had by then become entrenched.[45]

Burgundy was the battleground for establishing the importance of terroir. The 1920s and 1930s were a terrible time for Burgundy (as indeed for all of France), with demand for wine suppressed by economic conditions and production impacted by a series of poor vintages through the thirties. Battle was joined in Burgundy between the vins de marque (wines produced by negociants) and the vins de crus (producers' wines identified with particular locations). The producers argued that negociants subjected the wines to undue manipulation.[46] The argument as to whether the producer's label or the origin of the wine was a better guarantee of quality continued until a series of legal cases (collectively known as the Côte-de-Nuits trial) settled the issue in favor of labeling by terroir.[47] In 1935 the AOC system came into effect. The battle was won, but the war for authenticity continued for another fifty years.

The first topographic maps had divided Burgundy into small areas, each with its own name and reputation, falling into a hierarchy of qualities.[48] Following the nineteenth century delineation of vineyards, the AOC system divided Burgundy

---

* Institut National des Appellations d'Origine, the organization controlling the AOCs.

into village land, premier crus, and grand crus. The assignments have scarcely changed since then, and the hierarchy of pricing for each producer's wines faithfully follows the quality levels assigned to each terroir.

Before the AOC system was established, locations (lieu-dits) with different quality levels were defined by the history of the wines they produced: in Gevrey Chambertin, for example, the Chambertin vineyard was well known for producing better wines than the nearby Cazetiers vineyard. However, the boundaries do not reflect any exact definition of the underlying properties of the soil; they were based on the cadastral map, reflecting historical patterns of ownership. There was little thought to making the underlying geology the basis for the delineation of boundaries. A cynical view holds that when INAO began to classify vineyards, a rationalization was required because it was too much of a hot potato to classify the wines themselves.[49] The criteria for distinguishing AOCs are not necessarily well specified (perhaps a certain degree of ambiguity is essential), but some homogeneity of terroir is the unifying concept. This has since been adopted, albeit more in principle than in practice, by other classifications, such as the AVA system of the United States.[50]

Of course, focusing on origin provides a protection against imitation. You can make Cabernet Sauvignon anywhere in the world; but you can produce "Bordeaux" only in Bordeaux. Burgundy, where the concept is the most refined, perhaps has less need of it, because Pinot Noir is less malleable than Cabernet Sauvignon, and it remains difficult for other regions to match what remains (at least at the top end) uniquely elegant and refined. Yet Beaune producer Louis Latour comments, "When you try to analyze in detail the diverse elements of terroir, you find yourself with such uncertainties that it's better not to stick your nose in too far. That said, terroir is an excellent marketing tool, that's why everyone uses it."[51]

Is Terroir Immutable?

Terroir modification is very likely as old as vineyards themselves. Famous vineyards now considered to display the advantages of the terroir where they were planted may in reality owe as much to human reconstruction as to natural features. Among the more ancient of today's top vineyards are Côte Rôtie and Hermitage in the Northern Rhône, where immense efforts reworked the steep hillsides to make them accessible well before 1389, from which the first known descriptions date.[52] The Upper Douro, where Port is produced, is a series of man made terraces, carved out of the schist, after 1700.

Vines grow where not very much else will grow. This is one of the reasons why it so difficult to persuade vignerons to uproot plantings in unsuccessful European vineyards— wine production may be uneconomic, but there is no easy alternative. Sometimes vineyards have strange origins: the small (500 ha) Gimblett Gravels Winegrowing District in New Zealand's Hawke's Bay occupies land so unproductive that it became derelict, and a major part of it was intended for a gravel quarry before it became planted with vines.[53] Here the producers are unabashed about the need for human intervention: they say that "terroir manipulation" is part of the vigneron's art; the soil has no water-holding capacity, so without irrigation the vines would die.[54] They believe soil and climate are perfect, and that irrigation turns this into great terroir. Is that so different from building terraces to manage a slope where instead Nature is providing the rain?

Incidental changes in the local environment sometimes affect terroir. Forster Kirchenstück is the best vineyard in the Pfalz region of Germany. One reason why it stands out from the neighboring vineyards is that a grower constructed a sandstone wall around the 3.2 ha vineyard. Intended simply to emphasize his ownership, even though the wall is not terribly high (varying between 1 and 2 meters) it has two significant effects on the microclimate; it helps to keep wind circulating round the vineyard, so that it dries out well after rain; and some heat is reflected from the wall. Walls can also have the opposite effect; Helenkloster is a tiny vineyard at Mulheim in the Mosel, and a wall on the western edge retains frost, making it possible in most years to produce Eiswein, which requires keeping the grapes on the vine in frozen conditions into the winter.[56]

And in the Pechstein vineyard nearby, the "black basalt stones add a racy minerality to the sandy loam soil," according to famous producer Ernie Loosen, who took over the J. L. Wolf properties in the Pfalz in 1996.[57] In fact, Pechstein means "pitch stone," and the quality of the vineyard is attributed to its black basalt. This no doubt affects drainage and heat retention, but actually it's somewhat unlikely it does anything for minerality in the wine. However, the basalt in reality has two separate origins. A layer at about 3 meters depth resulted from ancient volcanic activity. But the surface layer of small stones, which gives the vineyard its characteristic appearance, comes from a quarry further over in the Pechstein valley. The stones were used in building streets, but those that were too small were thrown away. The closest open field for discarding the stones was the Pechstein vineyard, located at the entrance to the valley![58]

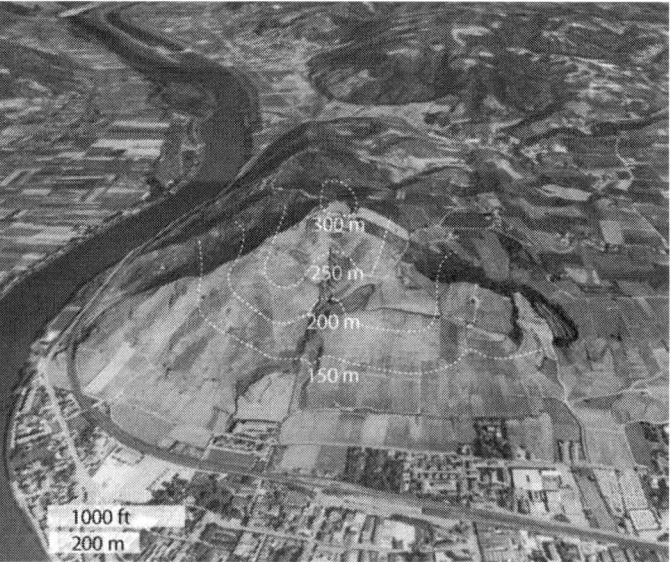

The hill of Hermitage looms over the town of Tain l'Hermitage on the Rhône river. Peak elevation is about 330 m. Vineyards are tenable only because of the construction of terraces and removal of boulders.[55] Extending beyond Hermitage is the lesser appellation of Crozes-Hermitage.

The Kirchenstück vineyard is surrounded by a wall, which has a profound effect on the microclimate within the vineyard.

Photograph kindly provided by VDP Pfalz.

Draining the Marshes

If man cannot influence it, terroir should be immutable, but it's not as simple as that. Historical changes can be hallowed by time as part of the terroir. The Médoc, the area to the north of Bordeaux which produces many world-famous wines, including Châteaux Lafite Rothschild, Mouton Rothschild, Latour, and Margaux, was a hinterland of marshes in the middle ages. (Just a little north of the famous châteaux, the area was regarded as unfit for human habitation.) The classic phrase used to describe the region is "palus and marais," the palus being the waterlogged lands adjacent to the river, and the marais comprising marshy areas farther inland. Starting in 1599, Dutch engineers led by Conrad Gaussen drained the marshes under a mandate from King Henri IV. Basically this involved constructing a dike around each marais with a canal to drain out the water. It's often said that the terroir of the Médoc was created by the drainage of the marais, and that the famous areas for wine production would not otherwise exist. This is not entirely true. Certainly drainage greatly changed the terroir by creating large new areas of cultivable land, but few vineyards were established in the drained areas. Nonetheless, effects on the vineyards in the vicinity could be profound.[59] You rarely see reference to this change of the natural state when the Médoc is described as the perfect terroir for growing Cabernet Sauvignon.

The Médoc is superficially surprising as top terroir for wine because it is so flat and marshy. Most good wine-producing areas are relatively hilly, with slopes and angles that give good drainage. The highest point in the Médoc is only just above sea level (43 meters at Listrac-Médoc). Some areas are in fact below the level of the tide, with immediate consequences for the terrain. As a result of the successive drainage projects, what remain of the marshes in the Haut-Médoc today are mostly the palus extending out immediately from the river. But drainage remains a problem all over the region.

Accordingly, drainage systems are common in the vineyards to stop the accumulation of rainfall near the surface. Several of the top vineyards in the Médoc installed drainage systems following the recognition afforded by the famous 1855 classification. Château d'Yquem to the south of Bordeaux has 100 km of drains under its vineyards. So not only has the entire terrain been changed by major drainage projects, but individual vineyards are drained as necessary. Where does this leave the claim that the terroir of the Médoc should be protected from human intervention because it is uniquely suited to produce the greatest wines?

It has been known since before the eighteenth century that the best terroirs in the Médoc are based on gravel.[60] What are now recognized as the best vineyards were generally among the first to be planted on the famous "gravel mounds."[61] A gravel mound consists of topsoil on compact sand, sitting on top of a gravel bed that can range from a few centimeters to 2 or 3 meters in depth. Below that are alternating layers of compact sand and clay lens. Grapevines can establish deep roots on the gravelly soil, which has good drainage and a low water table. The gravel mounds are ideal terroir for Cabernet Sauvignon.

Because the gravel mounds are slightly elevated, they are not subject to flooding, although in some cases they were surrounded by marais. The second growth of Château Léoville Las Cases provides a famous example: its vineyards sit atop a gravel mound that was surrounded by marshes that flooded at high tide until the marais were drained. This illustrates one of the important effects of draining the marais: not only was the swamped land released for agricultural use, but the lowering of the water table on the adjacent gravel terraces improved their potential for quality wine production. By and large, the effects of the reclamation of the marais on the terroir of the vineyards were indirect rather than direct.

Gravel mounds provide the best terroir in the Médoc, forcing vines to develop deep roots.[62]

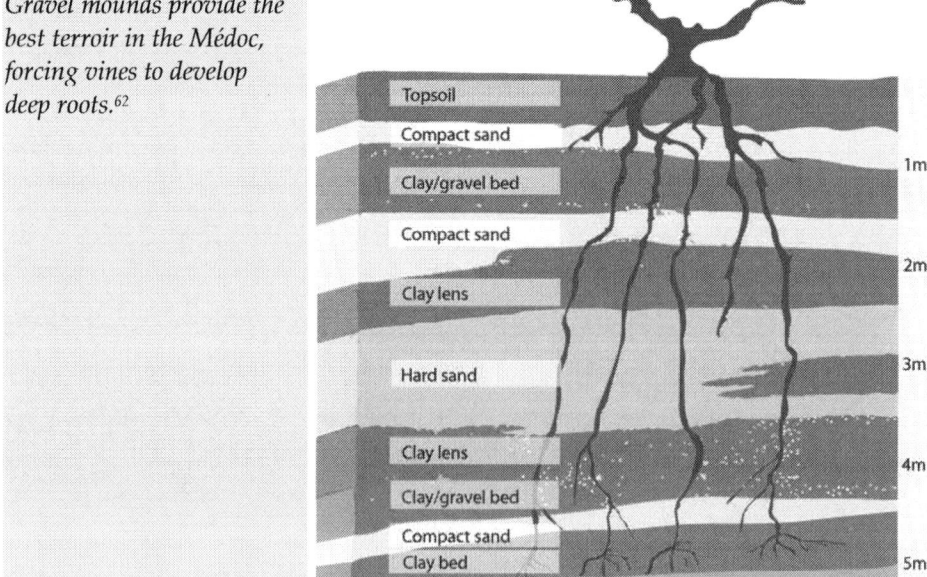

But the gravel mounds do not explain everything. Château Lafite Rothschild is immediately adjacent to three other châteaux. To its south is Château Mouton Rothschild. Both are first growths in Pauillac, but their styles are famously different, Lafite tending to elegance, Mouton more powerful. To the north of Lafite, separated from it only by the stream of the Chenal de Breuil, is Cos d'Estournel. But Lafite and Cos d'Estournel are at different elevations, and Cos d'Estournel has more of the underlying clay typifying St. Estèphe as compared to Pauillac. Although a most distinguished wine, Cos d'Estournel does not aspire to the same breed as Lafite. And to the west, no more than a stream separates Château Lafite from the adjacent fourth growth of Château Duhart Milon (which is actually owned by Lafite Rothschild, but never produces anywhere near the same quality). A little farther over, Château Latour achieves equivalent quality but differs in style from the others. Soils change significantly over short distances, so individual châteaux have variations within their terroirs, making the point that once you reach a size of tens of hectares, you are dealing with terroirs rather than terroir.

Terraforming the Mountains

No vineyard is natural, and the terroir is always influenced by man; just replanting the area with grapevines changes the local environment. But some changes are more extreme than others; indeed, the more extreme the terrain, the more violent is likely to be the effect of planting a vineyard. Mountain vineyards involve the greatest change of all, and nowhere is this clearer than in the plantings of the past two or three decades around Napa Valley.

Vineyards on slopes at elevated altitudes often offer advantageous terroirs. Drainage is good, the soil is not too fertile; often it is mineral or volcanic. There can be more diurnal variation in temperature (this is especially important in warm climates), and in the case of Napa Valley, the vineyards may be high enough to be above the fog line.

Napa Valley is surrounded by steep mountains on both sides, and many of its most famous cult wines come from vineyards on the mountain slopes. Yet constructing vineyards on mountains comes at a high price. It's rarely a matter simply of clearing the land and planting vines; often enough the process is more akin to terraforming, with massive clearance of forests and boulders, extensive reshaping of the terrain, even bringing in new earth by the container load. This can pose serious problems for the local environment, and the propensity to replace mountain tops with vineyards has become a major concern in Napa Valley. Several vineyards at elevated locations on mountains are controversial because of the methods used for their construction.

The Atlas Peak area, to the east of Napa Valley, is one of the most elevated locations for wine production. Only a couple of roads go into the area, and its dozen wineries are mostly at elevations above 1200 feet. When vineyards were first constructed there, no one was especially worried about environmental disruption. As Patrick Elliott-Smith recollected the construction of Elan Vine-

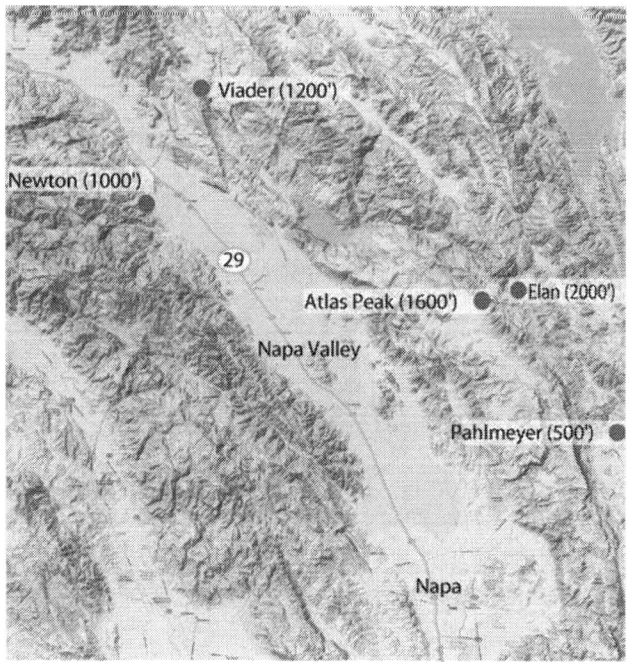

Locations of some of the vineyards at elevated altitudes on the mountains to the west and east of Napa valley.[64] *All involved major changes in the terroir.*

yards: "In 1979, I found my dream parcel of land at the top of Atlas Peak and began clearing the land with a 1953 International bulldozer. We removed boulders the size of cars to make way for the first vineyard."[63] This relatively small scale operation did not cause any particular trouble.

It was a different story when Atlas Peak Vineyards was constructed a few years later. Whitbread, the giant British brewers, purchased a plot of land that William Hill (of the eponymous Napa vineyard) had put together, and tore it apart to construct vineyards. As described by the project manager, Dick Peterson, "There are D10 Cats up there. This is a moonscape, but we're ripping it. We'll put terraces in there...We'll fill that canyon with rocks the size of Volkswagens, then cover it up with some muck from the caves we're digging."[65] This huge project did not pass unobserved. The neighbors sued Whitbread for failing to perform an environmental impact study, but they lost. [66]

Mounting concern about destruction of the environment led to fierce political fights, and ultimately to restrictions on vineyard construction. When Jayson Pahlmeyer constructed a vineyard in Wooden Valley, fifty acres were graded without an erosion control permit, and he was later forced to restore some of the land to its original condition.[67] The Sierra Club, an environmentalist organization, later sued Napa County for issuing permits to Pahlmeyer and others; they argued that erosion control systems on land brought under vineyard cultivation do not eliminate increased delivery of fine sediments to the stream system, which is detrimental to water quality and fish habitat. Construction of more than seventy vineyard projects was placed on hold as a result,[68] an indication of the magnitude of terroir creation in Napa Valley.

One of the most celebrated cases, and a trigger for subsequent regulations, was the construction of Viader Vineyards on Howell Mountain. A 90 acre plot was torn apart to construct vineyards. Boulders were blasted into smaller rocks that were then cleared out by bulldozers. The soil was "ripped" to a depth of 6 feet, by dragging steel rods through the earth. Just as the soil was completely bare, a major rainstorm came through. Sediment and mud ran off into the Bell Canyon Reservoir, a couple of hundred feet directly below the vineyard, polluting the water supply.[69] Subsequent problems with erosion and runoffs led to civil law suits and criminal charges.[70]

Perhaps at the end of the day (environmental issues aside) the question is not whether the terroir is natural or artificial, but whether it is good for wine production. Burgundy is the pre-eminent example of a natural terroir, perfectly suited to the Pinot Noir and Chardonnay cépages. There appears to have been little change in the terroir in several centuries; even the wall around Clos Vougeot, although responsible for maintaining the identity of this rather variable grand cru, has little practical effect. In the Médoc, the best terroirs were being used for wine production before the marshes were drained, but they were improved by drainage of the neighboring areas. In Napa, mountainside vineyards are often the results of wholesale reconstruction, but perhaps we are more conscious of man's efforts because they are so recent.

Viader Vineyards is located on land cleared at elevations of 800-1000 feet on Howell Mountain.[71]

Stress and the Single Grapevine

The grapevine is an extremely useful plant because it does best in poor soils that stress it to push its roots deep to find water and minerals, where other crops can scarcely be grown at all. When it is nutritionally challenged by growth in poor soil, water supply is the key to quality.

One reason why terroir is stressed much more in the Old World than the New is the ban on irrigation in Europe. If drainage is the most important feature distinguishing one terroir from another, as Australian viticulturalist Richard Smart points out, differences will be emphasized when water is provided erratically by rainfall, and reduced when irrigation is permitted, as it is everywhere in the New World.[72] According to California winemaker Randall Grahm, "The pernicious practice of drip irrigation, as routinely practiced here in California, essentially infantilizes plants, turning them into dumb, sterile consumers."[73]

Irrigation is a divisive issue. It is banned all over Europe, except in Spain where it was permitted from 1996, following the drought of the previous two

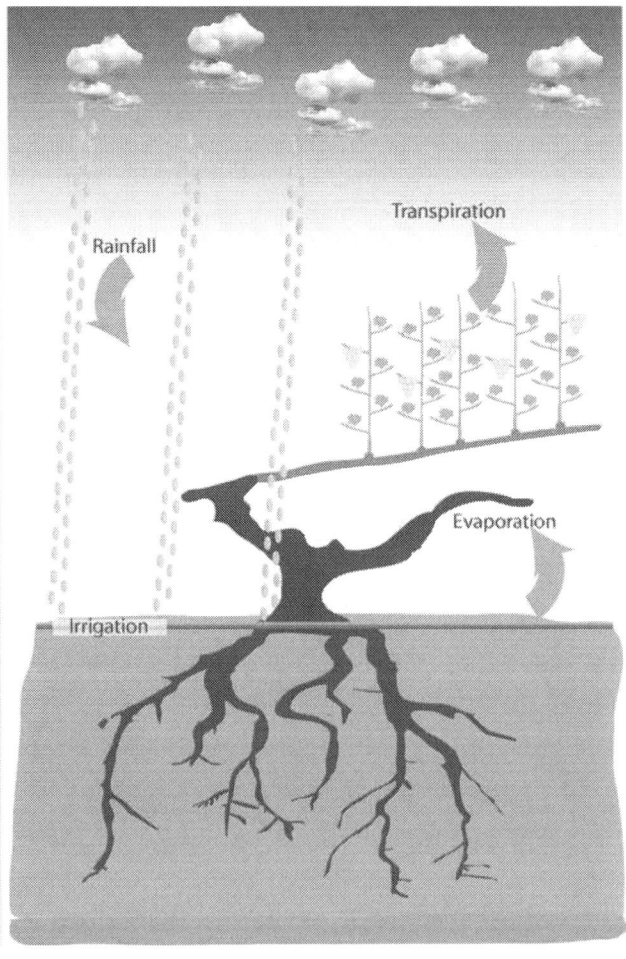

Vines gain water from rainfall or irrigation and lose it by transpiration from the leaves or evaporation from the soil.

years. But much of Europe, especially France which has been a driving force on this issue, is relatively wet; the common problem is too much rainfall rather than too little. The concern is that permitting irrigation would vastly increase yields, and exacerbate the dimensions of the wine lake beyond even its present ridiculous proportions.

In the New World, vineyards are often planted in dry areas. Without irrigation, the vines would wither. Originally irrigation was quite crude, consisting of nothing more than a system of pipes connected to sprinklers that watered the vines from above. Later systems used pipes close to ground level, so the water falls closer to the roots, and the most recent developments use pipes buried underground that release water directly on to the roots. These, however, are expensive to install.

Stress is important for the grapevine because it influences how the plant uses its resources; under stress, it puts more effort into reproducing itself, which means producing fruit. Under good conditions, it just expands itself with vegetative production of more shoots and leaves. Water supply is the major determinant of stress. Water availability is controlled by the balance between provision by rainfall (and/or irrigation) and loss by transpiration from the leaves or evaporation from the soil.

The advantage of the latest irrigation systems is that water supply can be precisely controlled. Humidity meters in the soil make it possible to provide water only when the vine really needs it. Adjustments can be made during the season, so the vine gets more water at the beginning, when it needs to grow, but less towards harvest time, when water causes the berries to swell up. The latest technique is deficit irrigation, which limits the supply of water at critical points in order to stress the grapevine when deprivation is most effective in causing it to adjust its priorities between vegetative growth and fruit production.[74]

Do you make better wine by planting vines in a terroir where water is provided naturally by rainfall, but with erratic variations, and where the level in the soil depends on the balance between rainfall and drainage, or by planting in a dry climate that depends on irrigation, but where the supply can be precisely controlled at each stage of the growing season and adjusted to the soil level? Does modern New World winemaking obliterate terroir? By controlling the water supply through irrigation, and influencing exposure to sunlight through canopy management, are the differences between terroirs minimized so as to achieve more uniform homogeneity in ripe berries?

Garagistes and other Counter-Terroirists

Can you make great wine without great terroir? You can certainly make intense, powerful wines that occupy the commanding heights of the marketplace. But will they age like great wines: that is the question?

The recent phenomenon of garage wines captures the essence of the move to emphasize winemaking over terroir. Garage wines were so named because they are mostly produced under very modest conditions, some literally in basements or garages.[75] Produced mostly on the right bank of Bordeaux, these wines have very limited production (typically less than one thousand cases) from very small vineyards, typically less than 5 hectares. The wines are usually heavily dominated by Merlot (some are 100% Merlot), and generally associated with the new style of super concentration, reflecting very low yields, mature or over-mature grapes, increased extraction during vinification, and a strong emphasis on toasty new oak.

Most garage wines do not come from great terroir. Usually their terroir is quite ordinary. Extreme viticultural and vinification techniques have been used to compensate for the lack of terroir. Some proprietors of larger châteaux have been known to comment sourly that it is easy enough to produce high quality wine on a miniscule scale by using all the tricks of viticulture and vinification, but the real issue is to get quality wine when you have tens of hectares to cultivate.

So what does this tell us about terroir? The garage wines are rich and opulent, intense and powerful, delicious to drink when young, although for some tastes (including my own) really a bit overwhelming as an accompaniment for food. There is perhaps a certain sameness to them—the competition is to out-intensify one another rather than to reflect underlying properties of terroir. The jury is still out on whether they can acquire the complexity with age that used to typify Bordeaux, but personally I am doubtful. However, they remain a forceful demonstration of the effects of extreme winemaking and of the fact that you do not need terroir to make wines that are regarded as reaching the ultimate peak by some segments of the market.

The case against needing terroir for greatness is made better by Grange, the most striking example of a wine universally acknowledged to belong in the pantheon of great wines, but which is associated with no particular terroir.[76] Grange originated as the result of a visit in 1950 to Bordeaux by Max Schubert, the winemaker at Penfolds in South Australia. Impressed by the ageworthiness of Bordeaux, Schubert resolved to produce a wine of equivalent quality in Australia. He settled on Shiraz because it was readily available, whereas the only Bordeaux varietals grown in the region, Cabernet Sauvignon and Malbec, were in too short supply. Unable to blend varietals, he decided to blend Shiraz from two separate vineyards, one at the Penfolds estate in Magill close to Adelaide, and one farther south, which he thought would have complementary properties.[77]

The wine was made using methods comparable to those in Bordeaux, especially with regards to maturation in oak, but did not at first receive a good reception. "A concoction of wild fruits and sundry berries with crushed ants predominating," said one well known critic whom Schubert invited to a tasting of the first vintages (1951 to 1956). Others were less kind. It was the end of the decade before its early aggressive nature resolved to allow the wine to show its true quality. By 1962, it was winning gold medals at Australian wine shows. Since then, it has been internationally recognized as Australia's greatest wine.

Mystique of Terroir

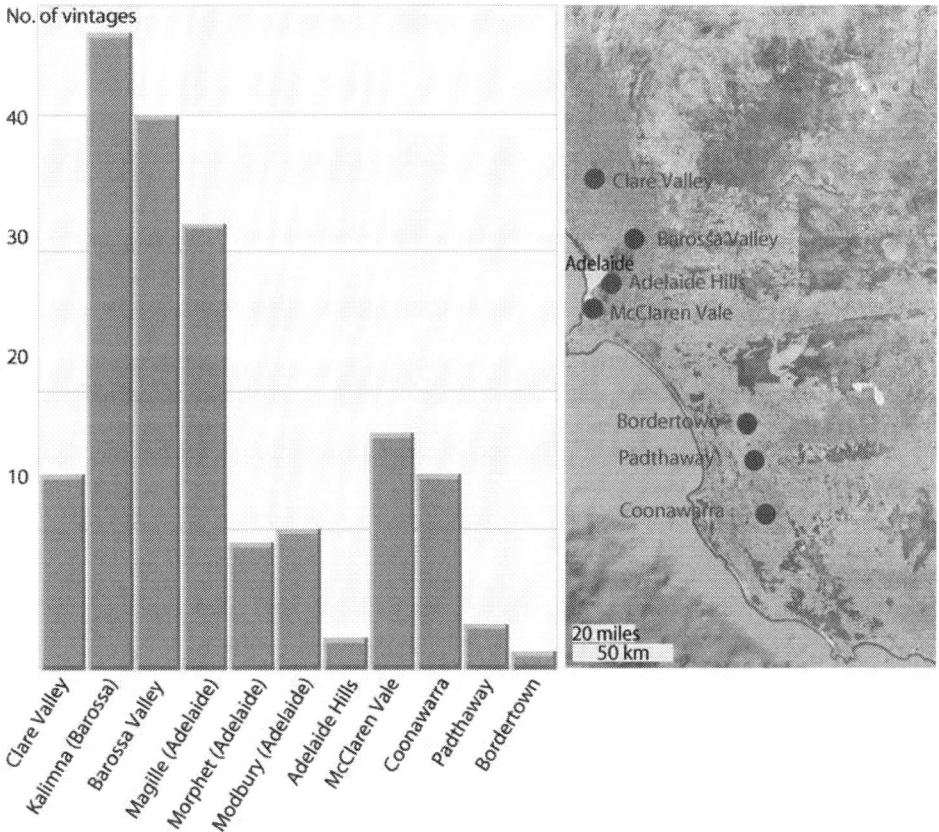

Many different sources were used for the grapes in Grange over a 46 year period. The histogram shows the number of years each source was used.[78] The map shows the varied locations of the vineyards.[79]

Grange started as a terroir wine, with the vineyard sources chosen to provide the same sort of complementary qualities that the Bordelais gain from blending different varietals. After the first couple of vintages, a little Cabernet Sauvignon was added to the Shiraz. However, vineyard sources changed. Grange comes today from a wide variety of vineyards, stretching from Clare Valley to Coonawarra, a distance of 100 miles (160 km), several times the distance across the left and right banks of Bordeaux, for example. Usually it includes wine from the Kalimna vineyard in Barossa, other vineyards in Barossa, and the Magill vineyard in Adelaide, but the other sources vary widely from year to year. On the other hand, in most years the blend is consistent, usually with 90-95% Shiraz and 5-10% Cabernet Sauvignon.[80] This is much less variable than the cépage variation in a typical Bordeaux vineyard over a comparable period. But Grange remains quintessentially itself, in spite of the diversity of sources and their variation from year to year, although you could no longer really call it a terroir wine; it is more a triumph of blending to achieve a consistent style.

The Far Reaches of Terroir

If we have to struggle to explain how the effects of terroir are manifested in grapes and then transmitted across the reaches of vinification to the wine, it becomes even more difficult to explain for wines with extra stages of vinification, such as Sauternes, Champagne, and fortified wines.

The dominant influence on dessert wines such as Sauternes is infection with botrytis, the noble rot. You might consider that terroir extends to the combination of humidity and sunshine that makes for conditions promoting infection, but this is stretching terroir well into the realm of climate.

As a wine relying extensively on blending, and with the flavor profile changed further by the second fermentation in the bottle, Champagne shows less association with terroir than any other fine wine. Yet the vineyards in the Champagne region are classified on the Echelle des Crus; vineyards classified on the bottom of the scale receive only 80% of the price for grapes of those classified at the top. The classification identifies a hierarchy, yet there are very few single vineyard Champagnes. Perhaps this reflects the fact that in a marginal region for wine production, the best sites are simply those that ripen more reliably; but in the context of a production system where the need is essentially for relatively neutral starting material, is it necessarily true that the best Champagnes would be produced from the top-rated vineyards?

There's a similar scale of vineyards in the Douro, top-rated as grade A, going down to the lowest grade of F. Quality of the base wine is more evidently related to the Port that will be produced by stopping fermentation half way; after all, the grapes are good enough to make vintage Port only in a minority of years. Classification is more puzzling in Jerez, where the best vineyards lie on the white chalk Albariza soils. But the grapes will be used to make a neutral white wine that is added to a solera containing wines commingled from the past several decades. What price terroir? The main difference perhaps is between those vineyards that usually give wines directed towards the light Fino style, compared with those that give wines directed towards the richer Oloroso style. Could this all go back to nutrient qualities in the soil?

If it's far from easy to see qualities of the soil reflected first in the grapes and then in the wine, how would we expect to see terroir manifested in spirits after distillation? Brandy's characteristic aromas and flavors are due to volatile compounds, synthesized in the berry or during fermentation, and effectively concentrated and selected during the process of distillation. This seems far distant from any property of the soil.

Yet soil is the basis for distinguishing different regions of Cognac. It all goes back to 1857, when geologist Henri Coquand distinguished six areas for growing grapes for Cognac: in declining order of quality, they form a sort of bull's eye radiating out from the town of Cognac: Grande Champagne, Petite Champagne, Borderies, Fins Bois, Bons Bois, and Bois Ordinaires. The Champagne regions have clayey, chalky thin soils on top of soft chalk from the Cretaceous; the limestone content is very high. "Grande Champagne... produces fine, light Cognacs

How can terroir survive distillation? Base wine is heated in the alambic still and then selected fractions are condensed to make Cognac.

Photo: © BNIC/ Gérard Martron

with a predominantly floral bouquet, requiring long ageing in casks to achieve full maturity," while Petite Champagne, although similar, has less finesse according to the local authority.[81] Borderies has clay and flint soils, producing "fine, round Cognacs, smooth and scented with an aroma of violets." The Fins Bois have more clay in the soil, which is known as "groies," and the cognacs age more rapidly. By the time we get to the Bons Bois, there is more sand in the soil, and the Bois Ordinaires is mostly sandy, although actually not much used for production. Sounds fine, except that it's obviously puzzling how the distinctive soil properties might survive the process of distillation.

But it may all be a mistake. Certainly it would be unusual for geological structures to form concentric circles, and in fact the stratum of chalk runs in a belt from northwest to southeast. Henri Coquand was President of the Geological Society of France; British geologists Jake Hancock and Richard Selley say he "was an experienced geologist and had been working in the Cognac area for several years. He must have known that he was talking nonsense."[82] How could this have happened?

The story goes that Coquand went around the Cognac region together with an expert taster. Coquand assessed the terroir and the taster assessed the brandy. They found that the level of chalk corresponded exactly with quality of cognac assessed by taste. "It's very much worth noting," Coquand wrote in his report, "that taster and geologist never once differed."[83] The very best cognac was produced from grapes grown on soft chalk, while the lowest quality came from soils of clay and sand. At the end of the visit, there was a grand dinner at which Coquand gave a talk describing his results. Selley thinks it was all a joke, based on the humorous suggestion that the quality of Cognac declines in ever increas-

What is the correlation between geology and the Cognac AOCs?[85]

The band of chalk follows a northwest-southeast axis, but appellations are organized as a bull's eye.

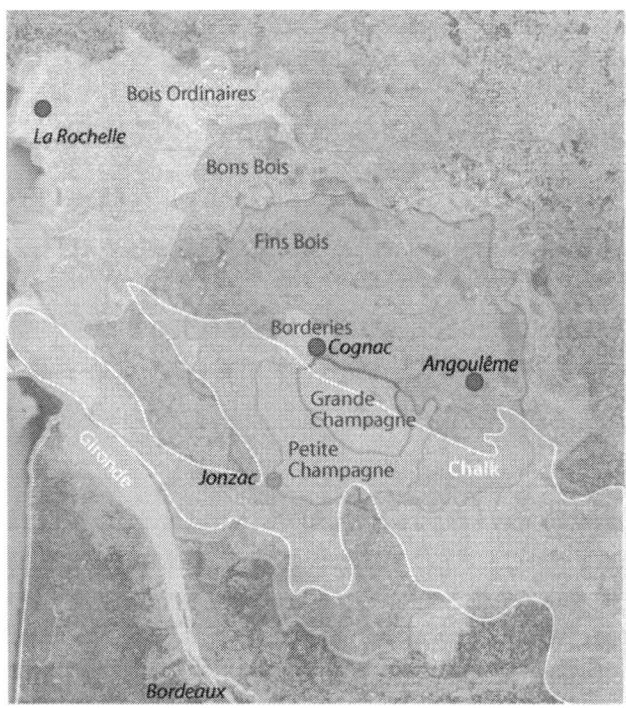

ing circles around the town, although if so, Coquand carried his sense of humor into the report he wrote for the Geological Society.[84]

There is some correlation between the extremes of terroir and the regions defined in the AOC: the best areas, Grande Champagne and Petite Champagne, are mostly on the belt of chalk; and at the other extreme, the Bois Ordinaires are the sandier soils nearer the coast. But there's no geological support for an organization of concentric circles, although the theory has been uncritically accepted ever since Coquand proposed it. Geologist James Wilson commented in his book on terroir, "Concentric bands of lessening quality encircle the bull's eye of Grands Champagne."[86] Yet at the same time he summarized the popular wisdom that "the worse the wine, the better the brandy." Indeed, the ideal wine for distillation should not have too much flavor but should provide a relatively neutral, slightly acidic, base for distillation. But in this case, shouldn't the chalky soils produce better wine that is less good for brandy production?

Does Terroir Matter?

A scientist who was interested in seeing whether terroir determines wine quality would need to have quantitative measures for both terroir and quality. Neither is easy to come by, but sometimes people have tried to devise numerical assessments to ask whether there is a relationship. But there is fatal flaw. To simplify, suppose we can divide wines into two broad groups. In one group, strong intervention in viticulture and vinification produces powerful, alcoholic wines, full of intense aromas and flavors in the "international" style. In the other corner, wine is made with less intervention, and shows less intensity, with more variation reflecting the vintage. It's not unfair to say that the second group is likely to be more representative of terroir than the first group. Now imagine that the critics favor the first group, and that prices follow the critics' acclaim. Any attempt to show an effect of terroir on quality or price will fall down on the fact that the "best" wines are those where grape growing and wine making have been tailored to reduce the effects of terroir; indeed, it may well appear that there is more correlation with some aspect of winemaking, for example, how much new oak is used. Just such a naive analysis indeed yielded the entirely predictable result (and regrettably newsworthy reports) that terroir does not matter.[87] I am afraid this is a demonstration of what computer people would call GIGO (garbage in, garbage out).

There's no doubt that, other things being equal, different plots of land will give different wines. But the differences depend more on physical factors, especially drainage, heat retention, and sun exposure, than on chemical differences. The main effect of these physical differences is on ripening; and the effect is magnified when vines are grown in a marginal climate. So on Burgundy's Côte d'Or, the grapes ripen best in the middle of the slope, creating the line of grand crus. It's hard to doubt that terroir has a significant effect on ripening and therefore in defining relative qualities. But the big question is whether terroir goes beyond changing quantity or quality of the grapes: can the soil change the nature of the wine? Do the grand crus of Chablis make wine that is different in its aroma and flavor spectrum from the premier crus because of their soil; or are all the differences simply the consequences of achieving a better level of ripeness?

Another age old question is whether you make the best wine by concentrating on a single vineyard plot that always gives fine results or by blending the products of plots with different properties. The effects of terroir are most obvious in areas where only a single variety is grown, and the vineyard plot is the only variable. The question is blunted in regions where wines are made by blending different varieties, which is perhaps why Bordeaux (typically made from several varieties) classifies wines, whereas Burgundy (the quintessential single variety wine) classifies terroirs. The debate has been most open, perhaps, in Barolo, where wines are made from a single varietal, Nebbiolo, but over the past two or three decades, production has shifted at most producers from "Barolo," consisting of a multi-vineyard blend, to an array of single vineyard bottlings. The traditional view was that the most complex wine was made by assemblage; the modern view is that the consumer demands the impression of precision given by individual bottlings. This is far from resolving the issue of terroir versus blending, but clearly enough resolves the issue of the dominant force in directing production: it's the market, stupid.

4

Vintage Variation and Global Warming

MOST FOODS HAVE A SELL-BY DATE, but wine has a vintage. As an agricultural product, grapes (and the wine produced from them) inevitably show variation from year to year. But the concept of the vintage is unique to wine. This reflects the fact that wine often is not consumed immediately, but is kept for a period of maturation.

In Roman times, the best wines were commonly kept for ten or twenty years before consumption. Distinctions were made between vintages; the Falernian (made from the slopes of Mount Falernus) was particularly fine in 121 B.C. Even then as now, the distinction was that the best wines were distinguished by vintage, but this was much less important for ordinary wines that were consumed immediately.

The Romans were able to age their wines by using amphorae, which were coated with resins to preserve the wine against oxidation, and sealed with corks. Resinated wines remained common until well into the Common Era. The Allobroges tribe, who occupied the area from Marseilles to Vienne in southern France in the first century C.E., and were admired by the Romans for their skill in wine production, made a wine called "pomatum" (meaning pitch).[1] It took its name from the use of resin to seal the containers, and may have been somewhat comparable to the Greek Retsina (in which pine resin is added to white wine). In fact, the quality of the pitch or resin was regarded as influencing the quality of the wine.[2] Flavoring wine with additional substances ranging from honey or spices to resin was common in both the Roman and Greek cultures. As can be seen from the flavor of Retsina (definitely an acquired taste), this has a profound effect on the nature of the wine.

The origins of the concept that wine is the unadulterated product of the grape are hard to trace, but by the time Europe emerged from the dark ages following the fall of the Roman Empire, wine was no longer being treated with resins or spices. One impetus may have been the belief that sacramental wine must be pure.

The Origins of Vintage

Vintage is a concept both old and new. It has always been important, but its meaning has quite reversed from time to time. The capacity to seal containers in an airtight way was lost after the Romans;[3] cloth or leather was used during the medieval period. This made it important to consume wine quickly, and the importance of vintage was that only the last year's wine was drinkable.

It was not until the late eighteenth century that it again became possible to preserve wine, so that vintage became associated with the ageworthiness of better years.[4] Up this time, wines were produced for immediate consumption. An old French proverb goes "the wine is drawn; it must be drunk," probably referring to the rapidity of spoilage.[5] Young wines were more valuable than older wines.[6] The exported wine was typically the "vin de l'année" of the last vintage. A "vin vieux" would be a wine of the previous vintage, considered less good, and sold off at less than half the price.

At the beginning of the eighteenth century, "New French Clarets" became the rage in the London wine market. These were wines from Bordeaux in a new style of higher quality, and advertisements often emphasized the fact that they were from the latest vintage. The key aspect of vintage in this period may have been the need to demonstrate that the wines were still fresh, effectively requiring that they came from the latest year.

Manufacture of bottles had begun in the early seventeenth century in England, but did not reach the Continent until towards the end of the century. At first, the bottles could be sealed only with ground glass stoppers (an expensive proposition that did not lend itself to mass manufacture). Cork had been rediscovered in the sixteenth century, but became available to seal glass bottles only around 1700.[7] By 1775 the production of bottles was standardized so they could lie flat, enabling the wine to stay in contact with the cork to prevent it from drying out.[8]

Towards the end of the century, distinctions begin to be made between wines on the basis of their potential longevity. Wine brokers in Bordeaux described wines as being "sèveux" (vigorous), meaning that they would age, as opposed to those described as "moins longue garde," which were appropriate for immediate consumption.[9] According to Thomas Jefferson, in his account of his visit to Bordeaux in 1787, at that time the 1783 vintage cost 2,000 livres per tonneau, compared to the 1,800 livres per tonneau of the 1785 and 1786.[10] This may be the first evidence for a premium paid for an older wine.[11]

Jefferson noted that the top wines of Bordeaux did not become ready to drink until after a few years of age. "Château Margau, La Tour de Segur, Hautbrion are not in perfection till four years old; those of De la Fite, being somewhat lighter, are good at three years, that is, the crop of 1786 is good in the spring of 1789."[12] He viewed them as remaining at their peak for a relatively short period. "All red wines decline after a certain age, losing color, flavor, and body. Those of Bordeaux begin to decline after seven years."[13]

By the end of the nineteenth century, a market in old wines had developed in England. Saintsbury, the celebrated author of "Notes on a Cellar-Book," purchased Lafite of the 1878 vintage when it was twenty years old (it had not been properly stored and he was not happy with it!), and mentions the fact that the 1870s were drinkable at 40 years of age.[14] During the twentieth century, the gap between young wines and old wines widened considerably, and by the middle of the century the concept was common that great vintages were marked by developing for many more years than lighter vintages. And the relationship between quality and ageability stretched into the view that great vintages required substantial time before it was appropriate to start drinking them.

Vintage Variation

When vintage was used only to distinguish the most recent year from older wines, variations between vintages were of academic interest, since anyway only one vintage was available. All the same, better vintages sold at higher prices.[15] But once it became possible to age wines for longer periods, and multiple vintages were available at the same time, older vintages became more valuable, better vintages attracted a higher premium, and there were more extreme price fluctuations from year to year.[16]

Vintage is more important in the Old World than the New. Temperature variations are greater from season to season in the traditional growing regions of Europe than in the more recently planted regions of the New World. In Bordeaux, for example, the average temperature over the growing season varies by around 2.5 °C during each decade. In Napa, the typical variation is only around 1.5 °C. On top of this, until 1982, temperatures in Bordeaux penetrated into the preferred range for ripening Cabernet Sauvignon only two or three times per decade. So successful vintages in Bordeaux alternated with poor vintages where the Cabernet could not really ripen. In Napa, by contrast, there was rarely any difficulty in ripening the Cabernet.

Temperature alone does not explain the quality of the vintage. In Bordeaux, rainfall is just as important, for both quantity and timing. Some warm vintages in Bordeaux have been poor, due either to lack of water or (more often) due to too much water, especially at the end of the season. But in the New World, by and large, the heat is reliable—and since water is often provided by irrigation on demand rather than falling from the sky, vintages are much less often spoiled by rain.

But even in Europe, the range of variation is less than it used to be. This is partly due to the warming trend, which has brought many regions up into a range where grapes ripen more regularly, and partly due to advances in viticulture and vinification that have saved vintages that previously might have been lost. In fact, the effects of technology are more significant for poor vintages than for good vintages. During the 2007 vintage in Bordeaux, problems with humidity provided ideal conditions for the spread of mildew; a generation ago, the crop

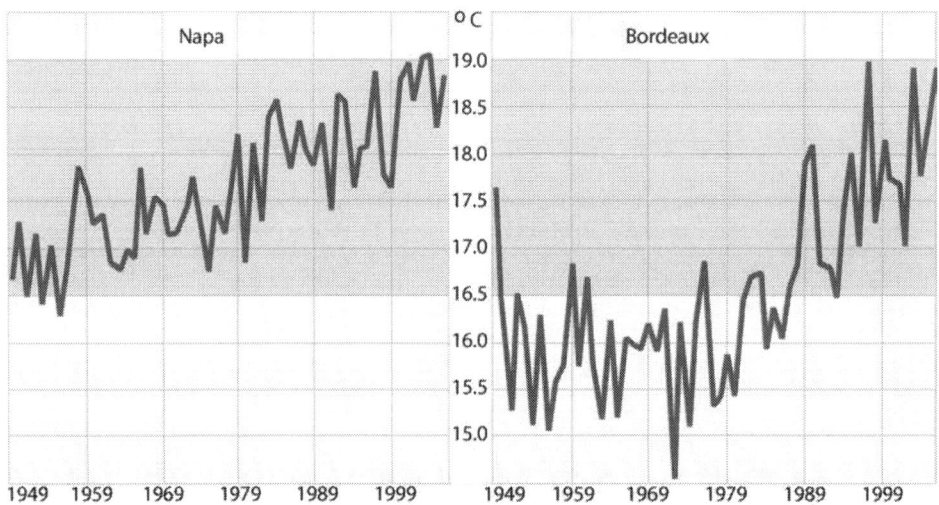

The range of average growing season temperatures is narrower in Napa than in Bordeaux. The shaded purple region shows the preferred temperature range for Cabernet Sauvignon (16.5-19.0 °C).[17]

might have been wiped out, but improvements in the ability to treat mildew rescued the vintage.

If the nature of the vintage depends largely on temperature and rainfall, can its quality be predicted from these factors? If you look at conditions during the year in Bordeaux, where there are records going back for most of the twentieth century, it's clear that the best vintages tend to be relatively hot and dry, and the worst vintages tend to be relatively cool and wet. Not very surprising, although it's certainly not an exact match, because there are vintages that were hot, but spoiled by rain at harvest; however, it's certainly true that it's impossible to get a really good vintage without adequate heat.

Princeton University economics Professor Orley Ashenfelter believes that the quality of a vintage can be predicted from the growing season temperature and the amount and timing of rainfall.[18] His formula for predicting vintage quality in Bordeaux gives about 85% of the importance to temperature, splitting the rest between points added for rain during October to March and points subtracted for rain during August and September.[19] The formula does not do a bad job of rating vintages, although it has some spectacular failures, mostly when the growing season was hot, but the vintage was spoiled for some other reason.[20] The details don't work perfectly, but support the general principle that temperature is good, rain outside of harvest season is good, and rain during harvest season is bad. The formula holds best when the main issue was lack of warmth in the growing season; it breaks down with the recent change in climate to regularly warmer vintages.

Vintage versus Blending

The importance of vintage is accepted without question in the world of fine wine, but it's not appropriate for all wines. The gap between wines intended for immediate consumption and those intended for aging has widened considerably since the late eighteenth century. While vintage is important for the best wines, which take some time to reach their peak, and vintage variation has interest for wines at higher quality levels, for others vintage serves more of its original purpose in ensuring that a wine has not become too old. Vintage dating would be inappropriate for the lowest tier of popular wines, and as a practical matter would make it difficult to move a poor vintage through the marketplace.

The market for short-term wines is dominated by large brands, for which consistency of flavor is all-important: the very antithesis of vintage, where variation is inevitable. In fact, many large brands do not have a vintage at all;[21] wines without vintage account altogether for roughly one third of sales of table wine in the United States.[22] Not only is vintage irrelevant, but a significant feature is the need to obliterate its effects when producing brands. Blending wines from different sources in order to maintain consistency is a much prized skill. The wine moves through the system fast enough that it is always fresh to drink, and like the wines from the early eighteenth century, once a new crop enters the system, the last one should all have been drunk.

The same skill is used at the top end of the market to produce Champagne. This is really making a virtue out of necessity. The Champagne region is marginal for wine production: in most vintages, grapes barely achieve ripeness. They can be turned into palatable wine only by making the transition from table to sparkling wine, and by adding a little sugar (the technical term is *dosage*) at final bottling. Even so, in many years the final product might be a little thin. So more than 90% of Champagne production goes into nonvintage wine, consisting of blends from different years. Only in the best years is a vintage Champagne produced. In fact, the critical measure of a champagne house is not so much the quality of its vintage wine, but its ability to maintain consistency of its nonvintage wine in spite of vintage variation.

A similar solution for handling vintage variation is found in Port. Most Port has no vintage. Vintage Ports are "declared" only in the best years; in a great year, all the shippers may well declare a vintage, in slightly less good years, only some shippers will declare one, depending on how well they feel their wine has turned out. Because vintage Port is produced only in some years, its share of the market fluctuates, but averages about 1%.[23]

Vintage is avoided altogether in Sherry, where wines are blended over a period of many years in the unique solera system. Age is important, but it's the length of time the average wine spends in the solera that determines its quality, not the vintage.

There's a handful of exceptional cases where great wines are blended across vintages. The great producer of Ribera del Duero in Spain, Vega Sicilia, produces a nonvintage Reserva Especiale that in fact sells for about the same price as a current release of its top vintage wine, Unico. But it's hard to break the mantra that great wine must have a vintage, although you might in fact get good results by blending vintages in the same way that blending is performed between wines coming from vineyards with different characters.

Vintage variation is part of the charm and interest of quality wines, but of course represents a range between the wonder of a great vintage and the risks and perils of a poor one.

The Temperature's Rising

Winemakers are in less doubt than anyone about the reality of global warming. A series of unusually warm vintages in Europe over the past couple of decades has increased the ripeness of the berries, leading to a richer, more alcoholic style of wine. So far, this has generally been associated with higher quality because there have been fewer vintages when the grapes failed to ripen properly. The effect in the New World has been less marked so far. There are dire predictions that if this goes much further, it will become impossible to grow the traditional grape varieties in many wine regions.[24]

Increased temperature is the best known effect of global warming, but not the only one that affects plant life; change in the water supply is important for grapevines, as is the increased rate of growth resulting from increased supply of carbon dioxide.[25] Higher temperatures cause the vine to awaken sooner from its winter dormancy, so that bud break occurs earlier; and increased growth shortens the growing season. The entire cycle of the vine is changing: harvest dates have been getting progressively earlier, with winemakers sometimes forced to scurry back from their summer vacations to get the grapes in.

To get a measure of the magnitude of the effect, consider those traditional rivals, Burgundy and Bordeaux. The average temperature difference between them during the growing season is 1.2 °C. The general temperature increase in European wine-producing regions since 1960 has been about the same magnitude. Every degree of warming has the same effect as moving the vineyards 200 km south.

Climate change has previously caused shifts in wine production. Until the sixteenth century, the Champagne region produced still red wines that were exported to Paris; however, the temperature plunge of the mini ice age was followed by sustained cooler temperatures, making it impossible to ripen the grapes fully. Burgundy then became the favored supplier. The change may have been only about 0.2 °C.

The effects of global warming may be most marked at the extremes for grapevine growing (nominally at the limits of the 50° and 30° latitudes). It might become impossible to make wine in southern Europe. Winters may become too warm in some areas, such as southern Spain, to allow vines to achieve dormancy.

By the same measure, regions that are presently marginal, such as England, might actually become attractive for winemaking.[26] The terroir in southern England is not unlike that of Champagne;[27] a small temperature shift could make this an attractive area for producing high quality sparkling wine. A team from leading champagne house Louis Roederer was spotted in England in 2007 hedging their bets by investigating the purchase of vineyards;[28] quite a reversal from the period when the English owned the vineyards of Bordeaux.

Matching the Climate

Average annual temperature has shown wild swings over the past thousand years, with warm or cold trends often lasting for a century. But beware: ten recent reconstructions for historical temperatures showed a serious lack of detailed agreement.[29] However, some general points are clear. It was relatively warm during the Roman period, and then cooled off during the Dark Ages. A warm medieval period started around 1000, but temperature reduced sharply during the Little Ice Age of the late Middle Ages. Vineyards in northern Europe were abandoned during the temperature drop of the mid fourteenth century. Then it stayed cooler from the sixteenth to nineteenth centuries until a generally warming trend culminated in the more exaggerated trend of recent decades.

In regions that have grown wine for centuries, the dominant varieties became established at various times between the Middle Ages and the modern period. These were the available varieties that performed best in the climate of that time. Of course, we can't always trace when varieties first became established in a region, but there are sufficient references to identify the rise to fame of several of the best known black varieties. The important point is that temperatures when these varieties were selected were generally significantly lower than they are today.

Despite large climatic differences between the coolest and warmest regions in Europe, the growing season has roughly the same duration, starting in April and ending between mid-September and mid-October. This is because early-ripening varieties, requiring less heat, have been planted in cooler regions, while late-ripening varieties, requiring more heat, have been chosen for warmer regions. This has an important effect on quality: quick ripening tends to reduce aromatic complexity, and a longer growing season gives the best results. "The best wines are produced with cultivars that just achieve ripeness under the local climatic conditions, as if quick ripening of the grapes burned the essences that make the finesse of great wines," commented Jean Ribéreau-Gayon and Emile Peynaud.[30]

The great expansion of vineyards in the New World over the past two or three decades means that their plantings are more recent. Also, in the absence of any regulations as to what may or may not be planted, there is a greater and more rapid response to market forces and fashion. The climate shows less annual variability, and varieties were chosen for their ability to ripen reliably to match the climate as it is today rather than the climate of past centuries, so the impor-

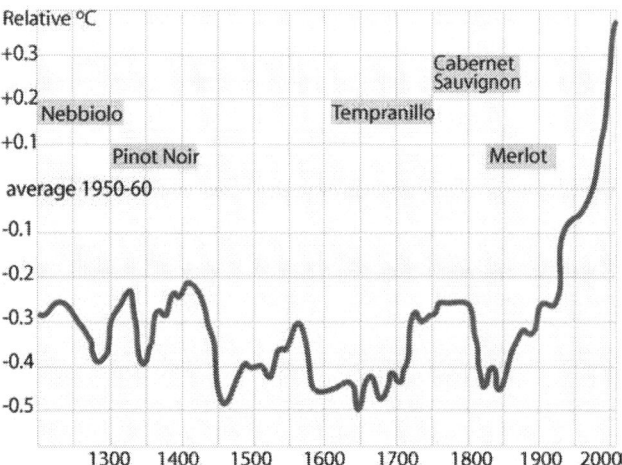

Average temperatures were lower when most of the great varieties were established in their characteristic regions. Nebbiolo and Pinot Noir were established in the Middle Ages; Cabernet Sauvignon, Tempranillo, and Merlot have more recent origins.

Average annual temperatures are relative to 1950-60.[33]

tance of vintage is decreased. The effect is most marked in Australia and New Zealand, where 50% of the vineyards have been planted in the past decade.[31, 32]

Climate is the most important factor in determining which grape varieties are appropriate for each region. The crucial factor is the temperature during the growing season. In the northern hemisphere, this is from April through October; in the southern hemisphere it is October through April.

One way to assess the potential of a wine-producing area by its temperature was invented by Albert Winkler at the University of California in the 1960s. The starting point for calculations is a base of 50 °F (10 °C), which is the temperature at which the vine comes out of dormancy and begins to grow. Each region is characterized by its number of *degree days*—the sum of the average daily temperatures in excess of the base temperature.[34] A day where the average temperature is 60 °F, for example, is worth 10 degree days (i.e., 60 − 50 = 10). To get the total, you add up the score for all days in the growing season.[35] Regions were divided into five zones from zone I (below 2,500 degree days), through zones II-IV at 500 degree day intervals, up to the top category (zone V, over 4,000 degree days).[36] Different grape varieties were recommended for each zone, from the cool climate of zone I to the warm climate of zone IV (zone V is not really suitable for quality wine).[37] Burgundy and Bordeaux fell into zone I at 2,300 and 2,390 degree days, respectively.[38]

The rationale for using degree days is that *only* temperatures above 10 °C contribute to growth, but pretty much the same result can be obtained in a simpler way by taking the average growing season temperature.[39] A change over the growing season of 1.3 °C corresponds to 500 Fahrenheit degree days (that is, one zone). Each variety does best in a characteristic temperature range; below the range it will fail to ripen properly, while above the range it is likely to give jammy wines. Comparing the two best known black varieties, Pinot Noir does best with an average growing season temperature around 16 °C, while Cabernet Sauvignon requires around 17.5 °C.[40] This explains why these varieties were planted in progressively warmer regions, Pinot Noir in Burgundy, Cabernet Sauvignon in Bordeaux.

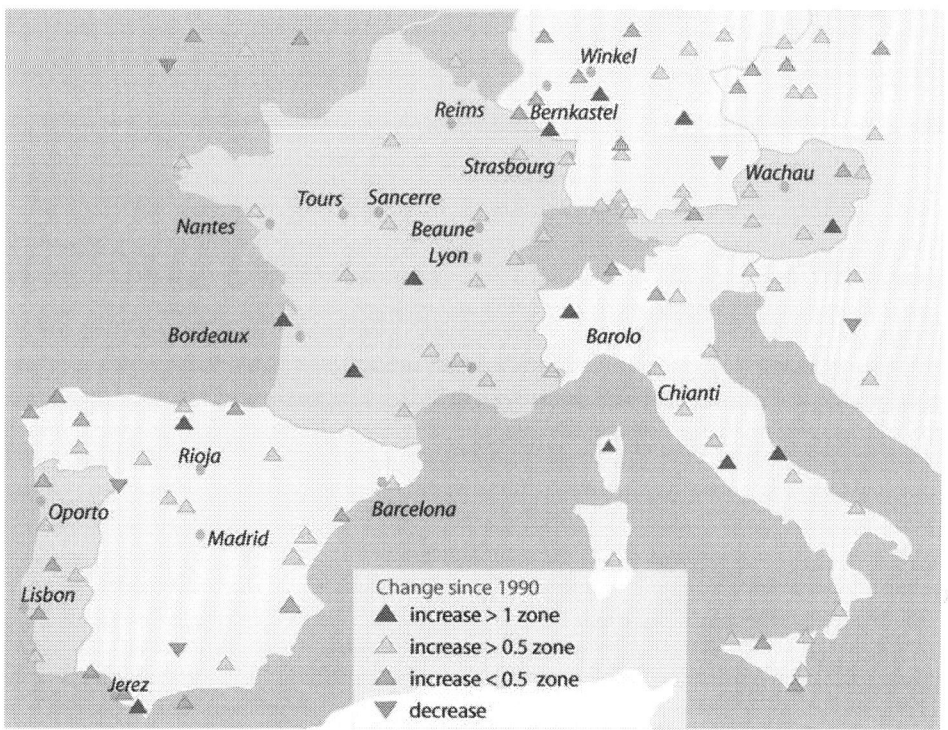

The growing seasons in the wine regions of western Europe have mostly been significantly warmer since 1990.[41] *(A zone is 500 Fahrenheit degree days.)*

The temperature range for best results is only about 2 °C for most varieties.[42] So the recent warming trend has a very significant effect on the match between grape varieties and regions. In most of the classic wine regions of Europe, growing season temperatures have increased by at least half a zone in the past two decades, and several have increased by more than a zone. According to the original concept of degree days, this would mean that different varieties should be planted. And there is every sign the trend will continue.

Average temperature is a relatively crude measurement, because diurnal variation—the difference between daytime and nighttime temperatures—is also an important issue for grapevines. Just like people need to sleep at night, grapevines need to rest. As the temperature goes down, the vine closes its stomata and stops respiration; this conserves water and retains acidity. In warm climates, it's especially important for there to be some respite from photosynthesis, as otherwise acidity is lost too rapidly. By pausing growth at night, the growing season is extended, which allows more time for other flavor components to develop before sugar levels become too high. A warming trend may have different effects depending on whether it increases peak daytime temperatures or reduces the cooling effect at night.

Changes in climate have the potential to alter significantly the effects of terroir. When vineyards are planted on a slope, for example, it is usually the middle of the slope that is the best terroir. Along the escarpment of Burgundy's Côte

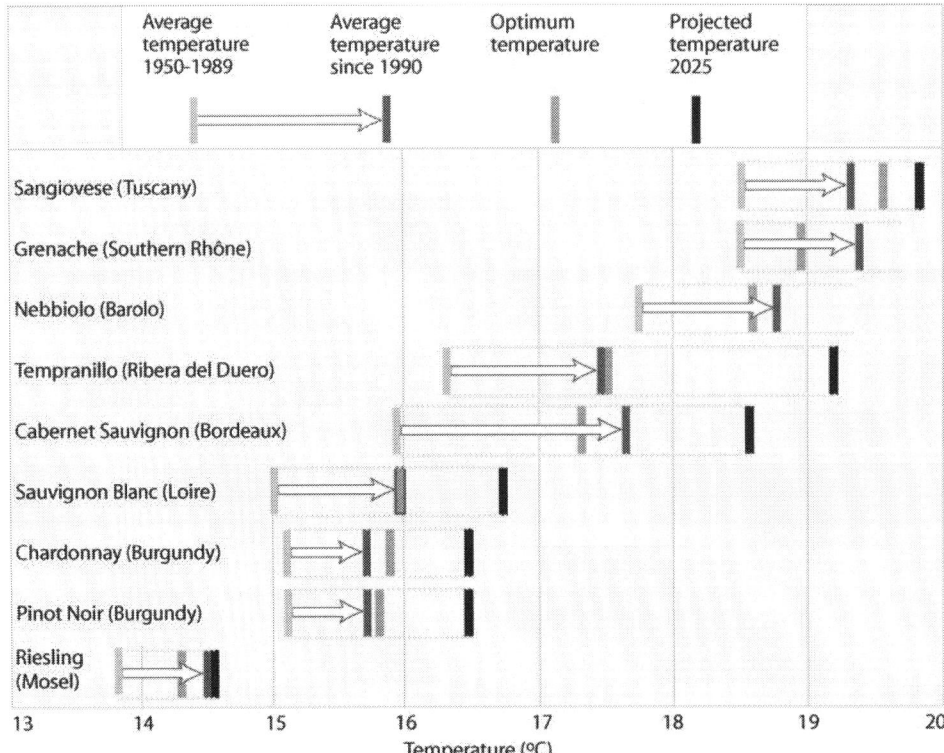

Average growing season temperatures have increased for classic wine regions since 1990.[43] The recent average temperature in most regions is now close to the optimum temperature for the best known varietal.[44] Projections show that by 2025 temperatures will be above the optimum in all regions.[45]

d'Or, the grand crus lie in the middle of the slope, because this is where the grapes reliably ripen best. This could be changed by global warming. And it's also true that terroirs higher up the slope do better in wet seasons, whereas terroirs at the bottom do better in dry seasons, because of drainage patterns, so a general change in rainfall could have a significant effect on relative qualities of terroirs. It would be dangerous to assume that the traditional hierarchy will be immune to change by global warming.

Varieties have traditionally been planted in Europe more at less at the northern limits for achieving full ripeness, with the result that usually there would only be a few really good vintages each decade. Between 1945 and 1990, average growing season temperatures in each classic region were between 0.5 and 1.0 °C lower than the optimum for the predominant variety. About three times every decade, a warmer year than average would bring really good ripening and create an excellent vintage. Global warming has increased the average in all regions since 1990, bringing it close to, or even over, the optimum. If the trend continues for the next decade or two, average temperatures will be well over the optimum, bringing into question whether these regions can continue to grow their traditional varieties.

Harvesting the Vine

Is it a myth that a thousand years of viticulture has enabled the Europeans to match each cépage to the perfect terroir? If you plot lines across Europe where the average temperatures in the growing season were optimal for ripening of the famous varieties, each of these lines (technically they are called isotherms) falls just to the south of the region that is best known for the variety. The Riesling band was to the south of the Mosel (Bernkastel) and Rheingau (Winkel), the Pinot Noir band just to the south of Burgundy (Beaune), and the Cabernet Sauvignon band just to the south of Bordeaux. Of course, temperature isn't the only factor in deciding what variety grows best, but the warming trend of the past twenty years has had a marked effect; the bands for optimum ripening have been pushed to the north, so the proportion of vintages with good ripening has increased significantly in all regions. The match between grape variety and climate is certainly now closer than it has ever been before.

The average increase of roughly 1 °C in growing season temperatures over the past two decades means that today's 16 degree isotherm is located more or less where the 15 degree isotherm was prior to 1990. This has moved each region to the temperature that used to characterize the region to its south. So Burgundy in the past decade has had an average growing season temperature of 15.9 °C, identical to that of Bordeaux in the 1960s.[47] That's a pretty big change given the distinction that is usually drawn between the suitability of Burgundy for Pinot Noir and of Bordeaux for Cabernet. Fortunately, all this has meant so far is better Burgundy and better Bordeaux, but if the trend continues, the temperatures may simply surpass the tolerance of the traditional varieties.

A real warning note was sounded in 2003, when the exceptionally hot conditions were fairly close to the projection for the average for 2050. The Burgundies of that year are too heavy to show the typical delicacy of Pinot Noir; many are more like the wines of the southern Rhône. And personally I don't buy the argument that Bordeaux came out with a great vintage; the wines of the right

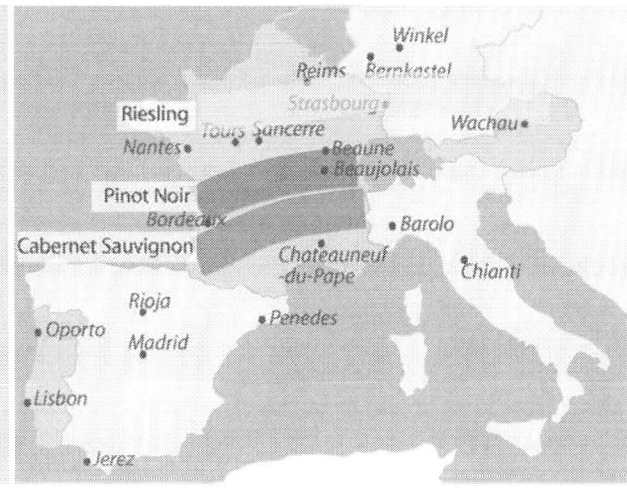

The band providing the ideal temperature for each variety prior to 1990 was just south of where the variety has traditionally been grown.[46]

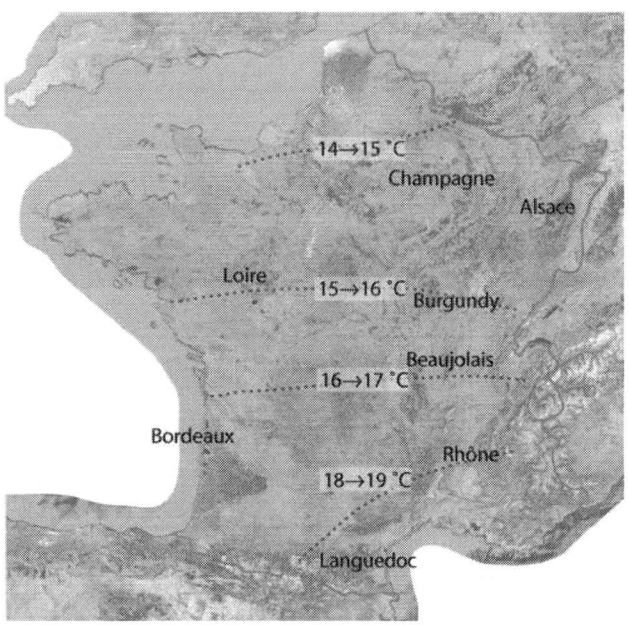

Average growing season temperatures have increased about 1 °C since 1990.[48]

bank are often quite stewed, and those of the left bank seem clumsy by comparison with their traditional elegance. I will bet anyone who bought the propaganda and cellared the wines that they will fall apart in the next few years.

One of the most visible effects of global warming is that harvest dates have become progressively earlier all over Europe. There's a close correlation between higher temperatures and early harvest dates. The harvest in Châteauneuf-du-Pape now usually occurs at the beginning of September instead of the end, virtually a month's advance in half a century.[49] In Burgundy, the average for harvest dates in the past 50 years is earlier than at any time since 1370;[50] and the recent regression in harvest dates shows increasingly early spikes. In the exceptionally hot year of 2003, vignerons who had taken their traditional summer break in August—nothing much usually happens in the vineyard then—had to rush back to Burgundy and organize pickers for the earliest harvest on record (August 23). They started even earlier in the Beaujolais, on August 15.

Winegrowing regions of North America are not suffering as badly as Europe, but projections suggest that Napa Valley and other regions for quality wine production will become too hot for quality grape production in the next fifty years. It will become too hot altogether in the Central Valley to produce wine grapes, wiping out most of California's industry. Warming effects over the past half century have been more pronounced in the winegrowing regions of the northern hemisphere, but similar increases have occurred in the southern hemisphere. Growing season temperatures in Marlborough, New Zealand's best known wine-producing region, have increased about 1 °C since 1970, bringing it from just below the optimum for Sauvignon Blanc to just above it.[51] Climate change has been similar in South Australia.[52] The most striking effects in Australia, which may or may not be related to general climatic change, have been

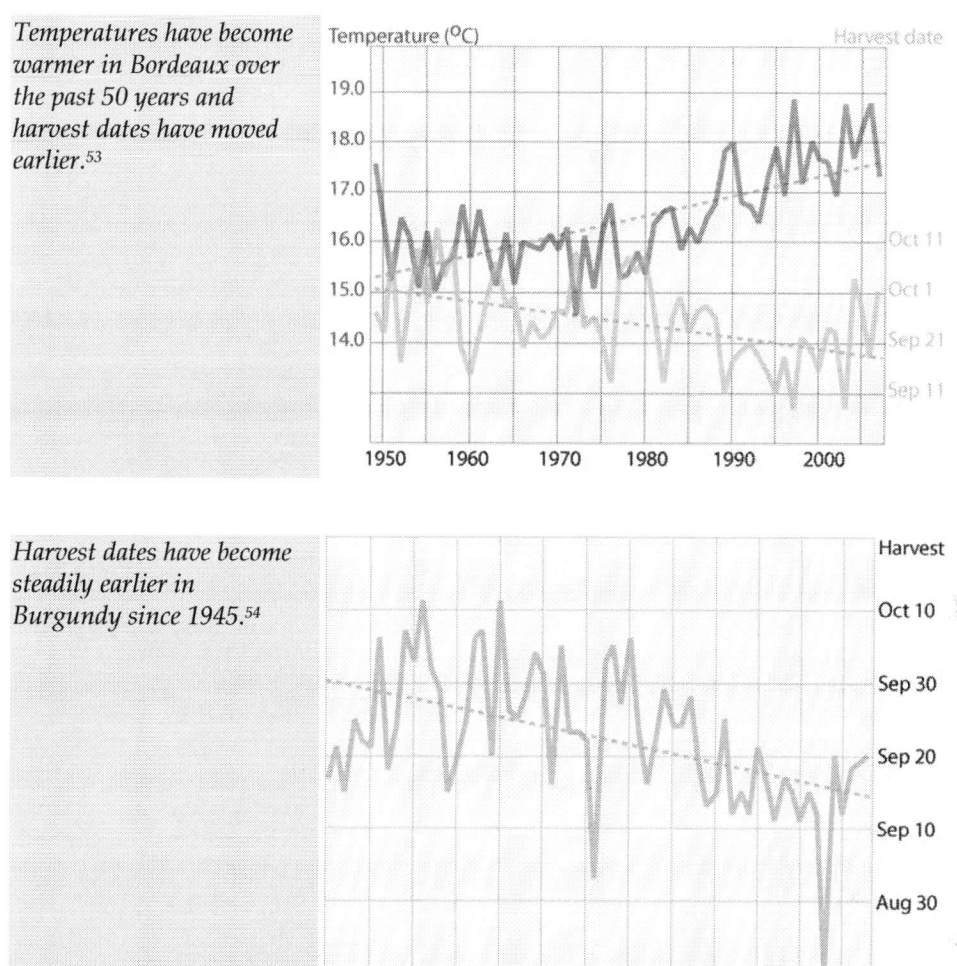

Temperatures have become warmer in Bordeaux over the past 50 years and harvest dates have moved earlier.[53]

Harvest dates have become steadily earlier in Burgundy since 1945.[54]

prolonged longed periods of drought, putting stress on the necessary provision of water by irrigation, and rendering some wine-producing regions potentially infertile.

Is Global Warming the Enabler?

Global warming is by no means solely responsible for the steady increase in alcohol levels and decrease in acidity during recent years, but it has given a powerful push to the trend to harvest grapes at more advanced stages of ripeness. It used to be common for the harvest to occur 100 days after flowering, but now the period is often 110 or 120 days. Sugar rises and acidity falls continuously after veraison (when the grapes change color), and a significant change in the balance occurs with an extra week or two on the vine. Warmer climates enable

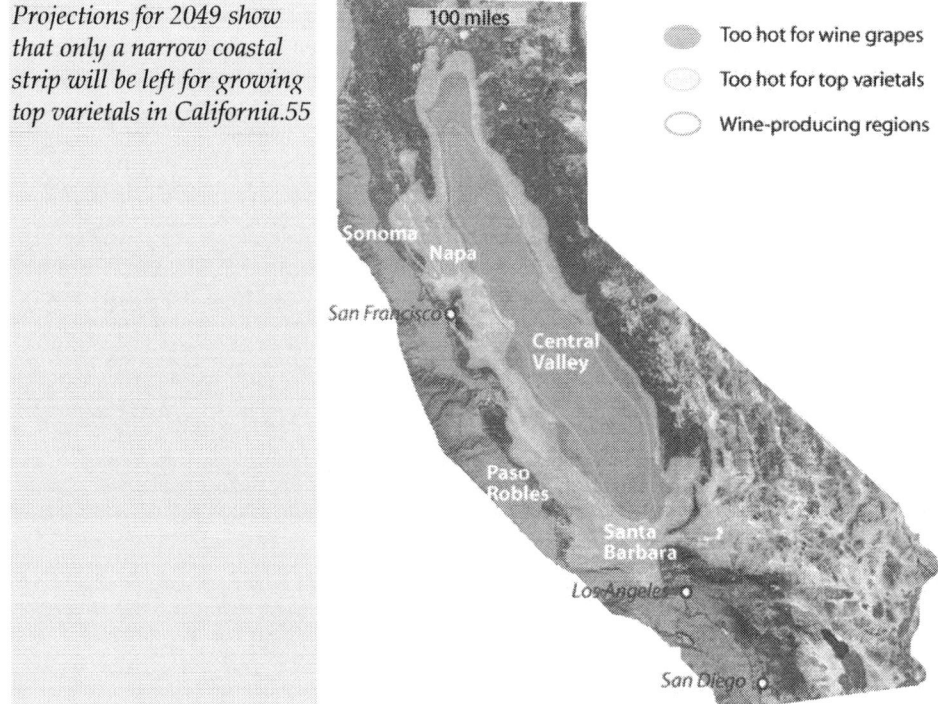

Projections for 2049 show that only a narrow coastal strip will be left for growing top varietals in California.[55]

grapes to reach ripeness more rapidly, and the combination of increased heat with later harvesting makes a powerful trend.

Alcohol levels in Bordeaux have increased about 20% since 1970, and acidity levels have fallen by about one third. Wines in Bordeaux used to be around 12.5% alcohol after chaptalization; now they are more often around 13.5%, in itself quite a difference in style. Higher to begin with, alcohol levels have also been increasing in the New World. Napa Valley has seen an increase in both red and white wines, just outrunning by a little the increase in growing season temperature. Grapes were usually picked at Brix levels of around 22 (potential alcohol about 12.5%) in Napa in the 1970s, but are now typically picked at Brix of 25 or greater (potential alcohol about 14%). While this is more a winemaker's choice than a direct consequence of global warming, it's certainly assisted by the generally warmer temperatures. Similarly, Australian wines increased steadily in alcohol level from 12.4% in 1984 to 14.2% in 2002,[56] although since then the trend has stabilized for reds and been reversed slightly for whites. The cause again is probably due more to seeking phenolic ripeness than to global warming per se.

Change is at its most marked at the limits for wine production. At the northern limits, a study of temperature increase at Geisenheim in Germany shows that already the climate has warmed past the average temperatures required to ripen Riesling and could now ripen Chardonnay; by 2050 it is predicted to be able to ripen Merlot![57] The effects are seen in an increase in the proportion of QmP wine produced each year. This is a direct measure of increased sugar level in the grapes, because for a wine to be classified as QmP it must reach specified sugar levels.[58]

The worldwide trend to harvest riper and riper grapes has pushed up alcohol levels generally. By concentrating on phenolic ripeness, grapes are harvested at much greater sugar levels than previously. But shouldn't the total alcohol level be considered an important criterion of when to harvest grapes? Isn't a wine with too much alcohol just as unbalanced in its way as a wine with insufficiently ripe phenols? Has the concept of phenolic ripeness gone too far and are producers missing the optimum in search of the maximum?

Far from attempting to counteract the trend towards higher alcohol and lower acidity that is promoted by global warming, winemakers seem more and more to be embracing the new "international" style of heavier, richer, fruitier, more deeply colored wines. This may well be rewarded in the marketplace: producers in Bordeaux whose wines today might be mistaken for those of Napa Valley have seen their prices jump over those producers faithful to the old style. How far can this go?

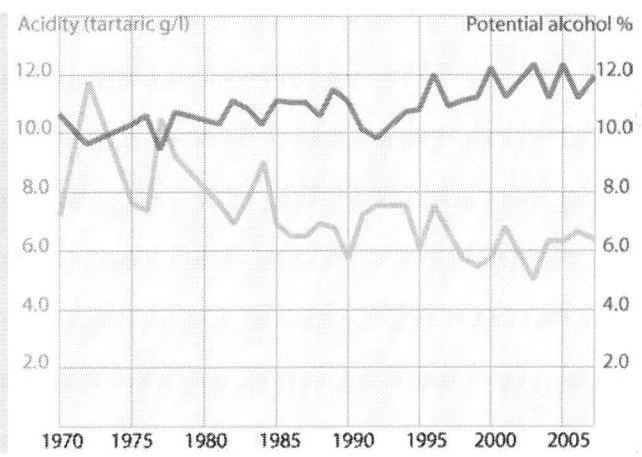

Potential alcohol has increased and acidity has decreased in Bordeaux since 1970.

Alcohol and acidity levels are for Cabernet Sauvignon at harvest.[59]

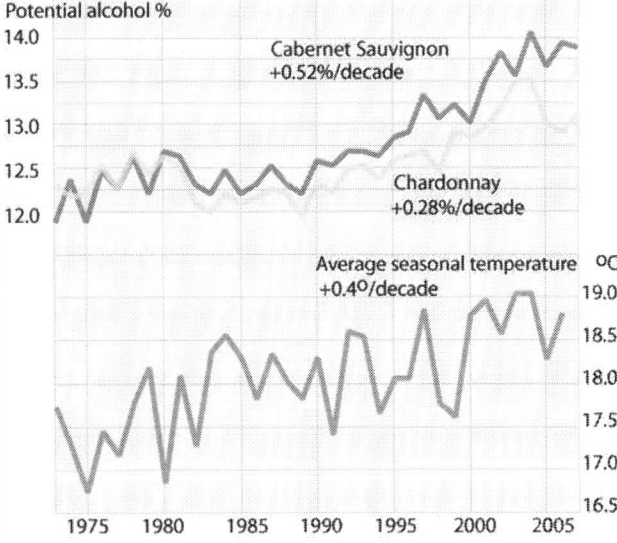

Alcohol levels have increased steadily in Napa Valley in parallel with average seasonal growing temperatures.[60]

High alcohol is not confined solely to the New World or international-style wines. The wines of warm, southern regions in Europe have always been alcoholic. The winemakers can be quite trenchant about the need for high alcohol. "We don't want to give in to the craze for lower alcohol," says Victor de la Serna, who produces wine at Finca Sandoval in central Spain. "The wine would not be balanced, quality would suffer," if artificial methods were used to reduce alcohol. "People should just drink less or split the bottle between three instead of two people," he says.[61]

Convergence of Styles

The issue with early harvests is not just the inconvenience of interrupting summer vacations. The whole cycle of the vine is changed. The warming trend advances the entire cycle of grapevine maturation, from bud break (the start of the growing season), through flowering, veraison, to ripening and harvest. In fact, in France as a whole over the past 50 years, bud break has advanced by 5 days, and harvest has advanced by 17 days. This means that the overall growing season has become shorter. Longer growing seasons are associated with better ripeness (the technical term is the "hang time," meaning how long the grape hangs on the vine before it is harvested). Hang times have usually been longer in Europe than in the New World, and this has been felt to be an advantage in giving the wine more complexity.

Global warming therefore brings some convergence between Europe and the New World. The warming trend has been greater in Bordeaux than in California, so the gap in temperatures between Bordeaux and Napa Valley, one of the major New World competitors to Bordeaux, has narrowed considerably. In the past decade, Bordeaux has warmed up to reach almost the same average temperatures as those of Napa. This is part of the reason for the increased similarity in style between the regions, with Bordeaux now showing more of the riper, richer features associated with Napa valley.

The difference in the seasonal growing temperature has narrowed between Bordeaux and Napa since 1990.[62]

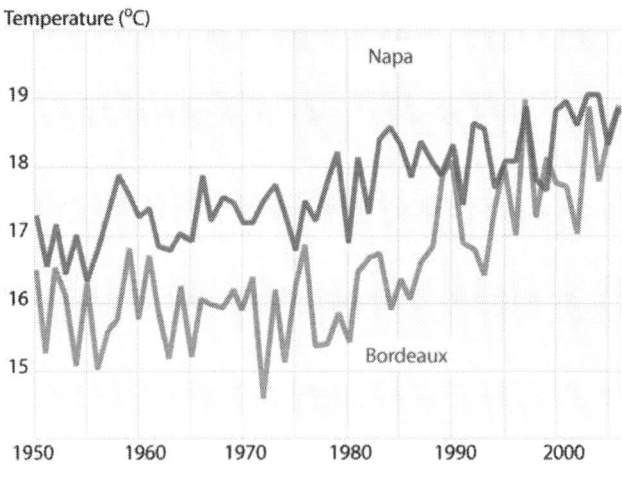

How reliable are the predictions that wine production (not to mention other agriculture) will be threatened by the future warming trend? I was not at all surprised at reports in 2009 that leading researchers had fudged their results in order to exaggerate the global warming trend.[63] Talks and papers on the subject tend to have an air of political commitment, with worst case extrapolations emphasized, although there is little factual basis for supposing we can simply assume the change of the last ten years will be exactly repeated every future ten years.[64] Nonetheless, the fact is that temperatures in wine-producing regions have increased significantly in the past two decades. Of course, this is a relatively short period in terms of environmental change, and there is little direct proof how much might be caused by natural cycles and how much by man-made activities; but the magnitude of the recent increase is greater than any occurring historically, and it would be a remarkable coincidence for this to be unconnected with human actions. The trend is at its most obvious in Europe where the change over the past twenty years has brought several wine regions close to the limits for producing quality wine from their traditional varietals. A blip like 2003 goes well beyond the limits and brings home the dangers if the present trend continues.

II MAKING WINE

THE TASTE OF WINE HAS BEEN CHANGING continuously since ancient times. The major problem with ancient wine was preservation. Because of the lack of inert containers, wine was often treated with wood resins as a preservative. This can have been no more than partially effective, so oxidation as well as the resins themselves must have had a significant effect on the taste. Soon after the start of the Common Era, wood barrels became used for storage; this made it necessary to consume the wine fairly rapidly, before it was spoiled by oxidation. There was a long interregnum before the next stage. During the eighteenth century, two developments made it possible for wine to be aged: the wine was protected by burning a sulfur candle before the barrel was filled (to generate sulfur dioxide as a preservative); and a truly inert container became available in the form of a bottle sealed with cork.

The basis for the process of fermentation that converts sugar in the grapes into alcohol in the wine was not discovered until the mid nineteenth century, and the ability to control malolactic fermentation (which reduces acidity and softens the wine) was not discovered until the second half of the twentieth century. The traditional bottle sealed by cork remained the only available container until the end of the twentieth century, but now is being slowly displaced by the screwcap (not to mention other types of containers such as bag-in-box).

Table II Development of winemaking over 6000 years.

4000 B.C.	Wine is stored in amphorae; resins are added to preserve it.
250 C.E.	Wood barrels used for transport and storage.
18th century	Sulfur is used to sterilize barrels. Corks become available and wine is bottled in glass.
1801	Chaptal introduces addition of sugar before fermentation to increase alcohol levels.
1863	Pasteur discovers that yeast catalyze fermentation of sugar into alcohol.
1939	Peynaud characterizes bacteria involved in malolactic fermentation.
1950s	New oak becomes widely used for red and some white wines.
2000	Screwcaps begin to replace corks, and bag-in-box used for cheaper wines.

5

Turning Grape Juice into Wine

WINE IS NOT A NATURAL PRODUCT, at least not in the form we know it. Wine is a transient stage in the transformation of grape juice to vinegar. Successful winemaking is about making the product as enjoyable as possible while it lasts, and (for fine wines) prolonging the period before the inevitable decay. If you had a completely natural wine, made spontaneously from grape juice without any human intervention, you probably would not like it very much, and it would be rather short lived.

The essential step for all wine production is the alcoholic fermentation, when yeasts attack the grape juice to convert its sugar into alcohol. The same yeasts are involved as those used in making bread, baker's yeast (Saccharomyces cerevisiae; Saccharomyces means "sugar fungus"). But yeast is far more than a mere catalyst for turning sugar into alcohol: it changes many of the compounds present in the grape juice, and creates many of the compounds in wine.

When alcoholic fermentation is over, the grape juice (or *must* as it is called in the trade) has been converted to wine.* But much lies ahead of it. For almost all red wines, as well as for some white wines, another fermentation occurs; catalyzed this time by bacteria, the malolactic fermentation converts malic acid into lactic acid, reducing acidity and generally softening the wine. Like alcoholic fermentation, malolactic fermentation (usually abbreviated MLF and known colloquially in France as "the malo") also has other significant effects on flavor.

We are not finished yet. Only the simplest wines are ready to go to market directly after fermentation. Others go through a period of maturation, and the finest wines may spend months or years in oak barrels before they are ready. If the oak is new, the wine will pick up flavor components from it; even if it is old, the wine will change as the result of exposure to oxygen.

---

* If some sentences seem confusing because they refer to the *must*, remember that it is a noun describing the unfermented or fermenting grape juice, not a verb suggesting an imperative.

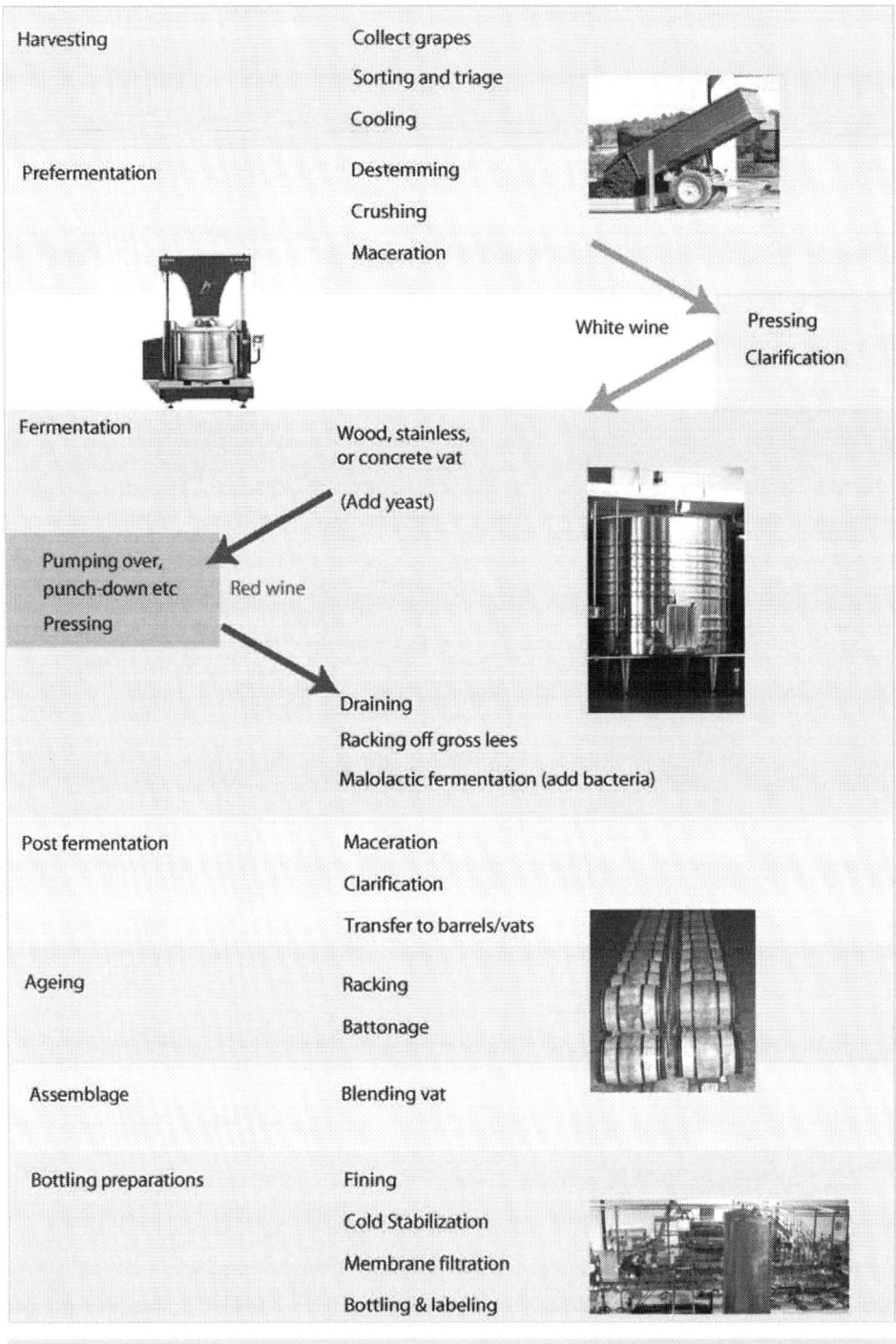

Harvesting	Collect grapes
	Sorting and triage
	Cooling
Prefermentation	Destemming
	Crushing
	Maceration
	→ White wine → Pressing
	Clarification
Fermentation	Wood, stainless, or concrete vat
	(Add yeast)
Pumping over, punch-down etc / Pressing ← Red wine	
	→ Draining
	Racking off gross lees
	Malolactic fermentation (add bacteria)
Post fermentation	Maceration
	Clarification
	Transfer to barrels/vats
Ageing	Racking
	Battonage
Assemblage	Blending vat
Bottling preparations	Fining
	Cold Stabilization
	Membrane filtration
	Bottling & labeling

Winemaking involves the same stages for all types of wine, but they occur in a different order for white wines and red wines.

There's an important difference in winemaking between white wines and red wines, because color for red wine is obtained from the skins. Remember that almost all wine grapes have colorless pulp. (There are a few exceptional varieties, called teinturiers, but they are not generally very important in wine making.[1]) In fact, it's not only color that comes from the skins; other skin components, especially tannins, are important in making red wines different from white wines.

Common stages for all grapes are harvesting, sorting to remove extraneous material or damaged berries, destemming, crushing to release the juice, and (sometimes) maceration to allow the juice to extract compounds from the skins. Then for white wine the grapes are pressed; there are all sorts of presses, but the common principle is that the grapes are squeezed to separate the juice from the skins. The juice is then clarified by removing any large particles (broken bits of skin, and so on) to make it fairly clear and ready to be fermented.

For red wines, the grapes go directly from a destemmer/crusher into the fermentation vat, so the juice ferments in contact with the skins. Release of carbon dioxide pushes the skins to the surface where they form a cap. Various means are used to stop the cap from drying out; depending on the grape variety, the juice may be sprayed over the cap, or the cap may be punched down into the juice. When fermentation is over, the wine is run off into another vat; this is called the free-run wine.

So basically you can make red wine without any pressing at all. In fact, as long ago as the Middle Ages, this was the usual procedure, according to the recommendations of Olivier de Serres in the standard text book of the times (first published in 1600).[2] The grapes may later be pressed to extract whatever liquid has been retained in them; this vin de presse (or press wine) typically contains more extract and is less refined. In the Middle Ages the press wine was usually sold off separately at a lower price; today, a proportion is sometimes added back to the free-run juice to better balance the level of extraction.

At every stage along the way, the winemaker has an opportunity to influence the nature of the wine that will emerge at the end. No decision is without consequences, from the initial stages of deciding how long the juice can be in contact with the grape skins, to the final stage of deciding whether the wine is to be bottled in glass under a cork or screwcap, or is to be sold in some other type of container.

From Vineyard to Fermentation

The key transition from the vineyard to the winery is to keep the grapes in a pristine state. It is all too easy for them to become broken and oxidized en route. They need to be pressed (very gently for white wine) or destemmed/crushed (for red wine) before fermentation starts. Sometimes there will be a period of cold maceration first, when the juice is kept in contact with the skins at low temperature, before fermentation is allowed to start.

Grapes are emptied from containers on to the sorting table; the belt moves under the eagle eyes of the sorters, who remove unripe berries.

Photograph kindly provided by Bodegas Abadia Retuerta.

Whether harvesting is manual or mechanical, grapes are collected at the vineyard in small containers, so the weight of the grapes on top does not crush those in the lower layers. Mechanical harvesters may even have systems to keep the grapes under nitrogen to reduce the risk of oxidation.

One of the major advances of recent years has been increasingly refined sorting of grapes. One common device is a vibrating table, which causes small particles, such as fragments of leaves or insects, to fall through a grid. Other devices include flotation to separate unripe berries (they float on the surface, but ripe berries sink because of their greater specific gravity). Typically the last stage is examination by a keen human eye to pick out anything that is not a fully ripe grape, but the latest invention is an optical scanner that picks out undersized or discolored grapes and directs tweezers to remove them. With all this going on, there should be nothing in the press except nicely ripe berries. It makes you wonder, though, about what contribution the MOG (material other than grapes) made to the wine in the years before this level of sorting became common! Perhaps it contributed to greater variety of flavors.

Before all these developments, grapes were brought directly to the press and just shoveled in. The typical press was a vertical basket, basically a large cylinder that was forced onto the crushed mass of grapes. Control of the pressure on the grapes was fairly crude.

Grapes today are handled much more gently. Wineries are often built in multiple levels, so that the grapes enter at the top level, and then move gently down by gravity, first into the fermentation vats, and then into the maturation vats. Use of pumps to move the juice or wine around is minimized. Pressing is done at very controlled levels. The grapes for white wines are typically pressed in a pneumatic press, where they are squeezed gently against the walls of the container by a bladder that inflates slowly. The latest vertical presses have very delicate controls that allow much higher quality to be obtained when red grapes are pressed after fermentation.

At the start of the twentieth century, grapes were brought from the vineyard in large baskets and shoveled into the press. This view shows the press room at Moët & Chandon in Bouzy.

Once the grapes are in the vat, fermentation can begin. Fermentation converts complex substances to simpler ones. In the case of alcoholic fermentation, the sugars (glucose and fructose) are converted to alcohol. The energy that was stored in the sugars is released in the form of heat. Fermentation is extremely energetic, not to say vigorous. It releases clouds of carbon dioxide, and the must becomes turbulent and hot.

Heat used to be a major problem during fermentation. One of the great advances of recent decades is the introduction everywhere of temperature control.[3] This may take the form of stainless steel vats surrounded by water-cooled jackets, or coils that are inserted into wooden vats (the coils can also be warmed in cases where heat is needed to start fermentation). Before temperature control became common, fermentation could overheat if the weather stayed hot or the juice had a great deal of sugar. This could cause fermentation to become stuck or could result in infection with Acetobacter (bacteria that would convert some of the alcohol to acetic acid). (Fear of stuck fermentation was one of the motives that drove producers to harvest their grapes too soon.) In the old days, producers might even be forced *in extremis* to tip blocks of ice into an over-heated fermentation vat![4] Because it's a slow process to cool the must down, it's still important not to let the grapes get too hot when they are harvested.

Because of the need to extract color and tannins from the skins, red wines are usually fermented at higher temperatures (24-27 °C) than white wines (10-18 °C). High temperature makes the fermentation go faster, so a red wine fermentation is likely to last only a few days, whereas a white wine fermentation may take a

An old basket press (left) has a belt-driven cylinder that is lowered on to the mass of grapes. The latest version of the vertical press (right) employs computer-driven technology for gentle pressing.

couple of weeks. It's a delicate balance with red wines, because although you need extraction, volatile compounds, which are part of the aromatic spectrum, are lost at higher temperatures.

Fermentation temperature can have a significant effect on the aroma and flavor spectrum of a wine, especially in the production of esters. Esters are volatile, fruity substances formed when alcohols react with acids. They are responsible for the characteristic aromas of freshly fermented wines, such as banana, pineapple, or bubblegum, but the esters are rapidly broken down within a few months in bottle. That's why you may find these aromas especially concentrated in wines that are drunk very young. Reducing the fermentation temperature enhances production of esters, and some wines produced by very cool fermentation retain them even after some time in bottle.

Fermentation of red wine is extremely messy. White wine production is somewhat calmer, because the juice has been pressed. This creates another option: the wine can be fermented in barrel instead of in a large vat. (All those skins, seeds, and solid particles floating around would make this difficult with red wine.) Barrel fermentation is used for top-flight white wines that will subsequently be matured in oak, especially Chardonnay. It makes for a better integration between the intrinsic flavors of the wine and the flavors that come from the oak, because tannins inhibit the yeast and slow down fermentation, and the yeast modulates extraction of flavors from the oak.[5]

Bubble, bubble, toil, and trouble. Vigorous red wine fermentation pushes a cap of skin to the top of the vat; must is being pumped back over the cap from the bottom of the tank.[7]

Good Yeast and Bad Yeast

Before Louis Pasteur discovered the cause of fermentation, no one knew how alcohol was produced; it happened spontaneously after fruit was crushed, with varying results.[6] Basically it was known that sugar was converted into alcohol, but not why sometimes it was instead converted to acetic acid or lactic acid.

Pasteur showed that the differing outcomes resulted from infections with different microbes.[8] He demonstrated that infection with certain yeasts converts sugar to alcohol, and that during alcoholic fermentation they also produce many other organic compounds. The discovery that other yeasts (or bacteria) can spoil the wine led to a debate as to whether wine should be protected from further microbial action by pasteurization (heating to kill off any remaining yeast or bacteria).

Pasteur went on to show that fermentation does not require oxygen,[9] and suggested that exposure to oxygen is the cause of aging. His view that "it will be obvious to everyone that air has always been considered the enemy of wine,"[10] has resounded ever since, and indeed remains the subject of active controversy with regards to whether "breathing" occurs through the cork and has any effect on the aging of wine.

If you leave crushed grapes or must in a vat, fermentation will start spontaneously after a while. First the so-called grape yeasts or wild yeasts, which come from the skins of the grapes, will start fermentation. These yeasts are capable of fermenting until an alcohol level of 3-4% is reached, when they die off. Shortly after, the wine yeast *S. cerevisiae* takes over. It's unclear to what extent S. cerevisiae is present on the grapes themselves, but it is widely distributed in the winery, on buildings and equipment (as the result of earlier fermentations); it will continue fermentation until the sugar runs out or until an alcohol level is reached at around 15%.

There's an ongoing debate as to whether fermentation should be allowed to occur by the action of indigenous yeasts (those naturally occurring in the vineyard) or should instead be induced by adding a preparation of cultured yeasts. The process can be controlled by adding a low level of sulfur dioxide to kill the grape yeasts (which are more sensitive than S. cerevisiae) and then by adding a preparation of cultured S. cerevisiae to catalyze the alcoholic fermentation.[11] This gives a great deal of control, since cultured yeasts allow a winemaker to choose what characteristics to emphasize in the wine. Some yeasts bring out aromatic qualities, other suppress them; some help to reduce acidity by consuming more malic acid; specialized yeasts can allow fermentation to continue above the usual limit of 15% alcohol, or may be necessary to ferment juice with very high sugar content.

Traditionalists believe that the indigenous yeast population in the vineyard and winery constitute part of the characteristics of a natural wine; they are wont to refer to cultured yeasts as "industrial yeasts," which contribute to the general homogenization of flavors. This is one of the myths of winemaking. Well, to be more precise, there may be something to the criticism that use of the same yeast everywhere runs counter to diversity, but it is probably not true that indigenous yeasts are part of a vineyard or winery's character. "In a given vineyard, spontaneous fermentation is not systematically carried out by the same strains each year; strain specificity does not exist and therefore does not participate in vineyard characteristics. Ecological observations do not confirm the notion of a vineyard-specific yeast," according to eminent oenologist Pascal Ribéreau-Gayon.[12]

The fact is that a few yeasts become dominant in the course of fermentation; typically only one to three yeasts are present by the end of spontaneous fermentation. But winemakers who practice spontaneous fermentation argue that the variety of successive strains before the dominant strains establish themselves contributes to complexity. The same strain(s) are found for some consecutive years, but over time the dominant pattern changes.

There's a certain risk in relying on indigenous yeasts for fermentation. It's common for spoilage yeasts—yeasts that turn the wine sour or introduce other flaws—to be present among the grape yeasts; if they become established, they can ruin the fermentation.[13] There's also more risk the fermentation will become "stuck"—that it will just stop and be difficult to restart. It's safer to kill the indigenous yeasts with sulfur dioxide and add a culture of reliable yeasts. The cultured yeasts originated, of course, by isolating indigenous yeasts that had produced good results; and there's a fair variety of choice among them. The main criticism made by traditionalists is that the apparent variety is deceptive, because they all tend to have been chosen for vigor and reliability rather than for the quality of wine they produce. Using the same yeasts every year also diminishes vintage variation.

One interesting attempt to have the best of both worlds was tried at Sassicaia, the super-Tuscan winery in Bolgheri. The yeasts that had naturally fermented the wine were collected at the end of one season and cultured. Then they were used to inoculate the must to start the fermentation the next season. But the yeast population changed; the yeasts that were isolated at the end of the season were not the same as those that had been inoculated at the beginning.[14] So much for the consistency of vineyard-specific strains!

Spoilage yeasts can cause all sorts of flaws in wine. Most are simply to be avoided at all costs, but Brettanomyces is highly controversial. This yeast is not usually found on grapes at harvest time, but develops in the winery, often from contaminated wood barrels.[15] It generates a variety of compounds affecting flavor and aromas of wines, the most offensive being barnyard and mousiness.[16] The characteristic collection of aromas is usually known as Brett.[17] Some winemakers believe that no level of Brett is acceptable, and that its presence is simply a flaw. Others hold that a (very low) level is a part of the complexity of wines fermented naturally. Château Beaucastel in Châteauneuf-du-Pape is famous for showing Brett in some vintages, and a survey of Syrah-based wines from the Rhône showed that many have Brettanomyces levels above the detection threshold.[18] Brettanomyces may have been responsible for the barnyard aromas once famously thought to be part of Burgundian terroir.[19] It's not always easy to determine whether a slightly earthy aroma is natural to the wine or results from Brettanomyces infection.

Chaptalization: Turning Sugar into Alcohol

Until the early nineteenth century, the alcohol level of a wine was determined solely by the effectiveness of native yeast in converting the sugar in the must into alcohol. Give or take a little, every 17 g/l of sugar in the grape juice gives 1% of alcohol in the wine.[20] But the yeast don't care where the sugar comes from. It's all the same to them whether it accumulated naturally in the grape or was extracted from beetroots and added to the must before the start of fermentation. It's all going to be turned into alcohol.

Jean-Antoine Chaptal was a chemist who rose to become Napoleon's Minister of the Interior in 1801. He had a strong interest in winemaking; in fact, you might very well call him the first oenologue. He believed that "alcohol is the essential characteristic of wine," and correspondingly that the problem with current wines was their low alcohol levels. His book on wine production went through several editions,[21] and introduced the concept that adding sugar before fermentation would increase the level of alcohol in the wine.[22] He recommended addition of sugar to a level of 5-10% of the weight of the must.[23]

Chaptalization, as it became known, slowly spread through winemaking from northern France to the south. It was not without controversy. Dr. Morélot, a well known contemporary critic on the wines of Burgundy, commented in 1831 that "one makes better wine, with a good taste; but this wine, I do not know if I am fooling myself, is no longer a true wine of Burgundy. Stronger, more alcoholic, and darker in color, it has lost its bouquet, and become more southern in style."[24] Nonetheless, by the 1850s chaptalization was widespread in France,[25] with Burgundy at the forefront.[26]

Dr. Morélot was undoubtedly right that chaptalization changes the character of the wine. The balance you get by adding sugar to increase the alcohol level is different from the results obtained when the same sugar level is reached naturally in the grape (because other compounds are produced by more extended ripening). The rationale for chaptalization in the nineteenth century was the need for the wine to reach a healthy level of alcohol[27] (a completely natural process typically produced wine at 9-10% alcohol). You might certainly argue that a better result was achieved by using chaptalization than by simply fortifying the wine by adding alcohol.[28]

But it's not at all clear that chaptalization is justified in the modern era. If a wine naturally would have an alcohol level of, let us say, 12%, wouldn't it be in better balance at this natural level than by bumping it up to 14% with chaptalization? The fact that chaptalization makes a heavier, some might say clumsier, wine is acknowledged in the AOC regulations in France, which limit chaptalization to a 2% increase in alcohol. That level, of course, was set many years ago, and if the process is to be allowed at all, it would certainly now be appropriate to significantly lower the permitted limit and to restrict more tightly when chaptalization can be used.[29]

A broader name for the procedure is "enrichment," which takes in other ways to provide the sugar, including preparations made from unfermented grape must. Enrichment, or *enrichissement* in French, is an interesting term, because what is enriched is more the grower than the wine. The economics of chaptalization are *very* advantageous. Producing wine from grapes might cost €9 per liter, but adding sugar costs only about €1.25 per liter of product.[30] And chaptalization increases the volume of the product, so you have more to sell.[31]

Producers who use chaptalization have to purchase the sugar through official channels and complete a form reporting the amount of sugar added to each volume of wine. But there are widespread suspicions that the rule has been honored as much in the breach as the observance. One producer in the Loire commented to me darkly that it was amazing how the supermarkets became full of large bags of sugar around harvest time. In the town of Beziers in the Languedoc (where goodness knows the weather is hot enough for addition of sugar to be unnecessary), the local supermarket used to announce "Le sucre est arrivé" by loudspeaker at harvest time.[32]

The sugar in grapes is a mixture of glucose and fructose, but the sugar in beets or maple syrup is largely sucrose. This doesn't make any difference to the outcome when it is fermented, but sugars from different sources have different characteristic levels of certain radioactive isotopes. Analysis of these isotopes in the wine by NMR (nuclear magnetic resonance) can be used to determine how much sugar was added from different sources, and is becoming a significant tool in combating fraud.

Periodically the authorities make an example: suspicion was aroused when large amounts of sugar were purchased from a supermarket near the Beaujolais wine region during the 2004 harvest season, and fines were later imposed on 53 producers and three branches of the Intermarché supermarket chain.[33] Very high fines (up to $27,000) aroused protest: "We want to make a good product, we didn't take the risk of ending up in court lightly, but we didn't have a choice—no one would have bought an 11% wine," said one of the winemakers, bowing to the God of high alcohol.

Even within the legal limits, the extent of chaptalization in France provides a significant proportion of the wine. Although the authorities have the detailed reports of sugar usage that must be completed by producers, they are strangely reluctant to release any information. (When I asked for details, Customs claimed that INAO—the organization responsible for administering the rules for AOC wines—have the information; INAO claimed that Customs have it.) But reports from the sugar producers proudly proclaim chaptalization to be one of the major uses of sugar in France,[34] and from their statistics, I calculate that chaptalization has applied to anywhere from 7% to 23% of the wine produced in France in recent years.[35] Is it comforting to know that at least three quarters of the wine is not chaptalized or disturbing to know that up to a quarter may be treated? If it wasn't for more than a century of tradition, it's entirely possible that chaptalization would be banned today as a swindle to turn sugar into alcohol. And so it should be.

The Mysteries of Malolactic Fermentation

"Malolactic fermentation happens in the wine in the spring by sympathy with the sap rising in the vines," used to be the vigneron's view. After alcoholic fermentation was complete in the autumn, the young wine was usually transferred to barrels to mature for a few months. It would remain quiescent typically until the spring, when another fermentation might (but did not always) occur. Called the malolactic fermentation (MLF), this reduces acidity and softens the wine by converting malic acid to lactic acid; not only is lactic acid weaker than malic acid, but it also offers a more creamy impression on the palate. No one knew why MLF happens, and it was often regarded as undesirable.

By the 1940s it was known that malolactic fermentation happens in the spring because at this point the cellars warm up enough to activate the bacteria that are responsible.[36] By the late 1950s, the great oenologist Emile Peynaud had isolated the bacteria and shown that inoculating wine with them could induce MLF.[37] Before Peynaud, producers tended to view MLF as a problem: after all, the wine had been quiescent for months, and now suddenly it started to bubble and release gas again![38] One of Peynaud's great contributions was to show that MLF could be controlled, and that in fact it usually improves the quality of the wine. Today MLF is regarded as essential for production of almost all red wines and for many white wines (especially non-aromatic, longer-lived wines such as Chardonnay). It is not usually performed with aromatic varieties, such as Riesling or Sauvignon Blanc, where it would interfere with the characteristic aroma spectrum.[39]

There is much more to MLF than simply the conversion of harsh malic acid (with its sharp taste of green apples) to soft lactic acid. It's malolactic fermentation that gives a wine those buttery aromas; this is due to formation of a compound called diacetyl, the same compound that gives buttered popcorn its characteristic smell. At low levels, diacetyl may be considered desirable, for example, in a buttery Chardonnay; but at higher levels it can become overwhelming. The level of diacetyl can be controlled by the duration of malolactic fermentation; it peaks before the end, so to maximize diacetyl, MLF is stopped (by adding sulfur dioxide), whereas to minimize it, wine is kept in contact with the malolactic bacteria as long as possible.

Where and when to perform the malolactic fermentation has become an issue in recent years. After the alcoholic fermentation (and any post-fermentation maceration) has finished, the wine is run off into new containers. In Burgundy, the tradition has been to go straight into barrels, whereas in Bordeaux, at least for the last century, the wine has been transferred to a larger vat.[40] Typically the wine would then rest until the spring before the malolactic fermentation began. More recently, and with much controversy, Bordeaux has been transferring the wine straight into barrel when fermentation is complete, and performing the malolactic conversion shortly after the transfer.[41] This makes the wine more attractive in the short term, especially at the point when the wines are first shown to critics just a few weeks later, but it's not clear that the exact timing or whether it's done in barrel makes any difference in the long term.

Heavier than Air

Carbon dioxide is heavier than air. Bubbling up through the must during fermentation, when one molecule of carbon dioxide is released for every sugar molecule converted to alcohol, it is responsible for the tumultuous appearance of a fermenting vat. After fermentation has been completed and the vat has been emptied out, carbon dioxide can sink into the vat to form a lethal layer devoid of oxygen. From time to time, people have been killed by carbon dioxide poisoning when trying to clean out vats after fermentation.

The release of carbon dioxide has both physical and chemical effects on fermentation. The act of bubbling through the liquid has a purging effect, and can carry volatile compounds along with the gas. This is another reason why it's important to control fermentation temperature; higher temperatures mean faster fermentation, which means a more rapid rate of release of CO_2, and greater loss of aromatic compounds.

Under some circumstances, carbon dioxide forms a layer in the fermentation vat that changes the process of fermentation itself. This process, called carbonic maceration, originated naturally in the custom of putting whole clusters of grapes, uncrushed, into the fermenter. The grapes at the bottom are crushed by the weight of those above, releasing juice that is fermented by yeast in the usual way. The carbon dioxide released by this fermentation excludes oxygen around the intact grapes above them.[42] The lack of oxygen stops respiration, enzymes within the grapes are released, and they ferment the sugar within the grape. Yeast is not involved.

A lagar from the third century B.C. from Spain.

Carbonic maceration produces a wine that is purple, extremely fruity, and lacking tannins. It is suitable for short-term consumption. Malic acid is consumed during carbonic maceration, reducing overall acidity. Wines produced by carbonic maceration have lots of fermentation esters, resulting in aromas of banana, pineapple, bubblegum, and so on.

Beaujolais Nouveau is the classic example of a wine produced by carbonic maceration. These days the process is deliberately controlled. The vat is flushed with CO2 to remove oxygen and filled with whole bunches of grapes—the grapes must be unbroken in order to avoid an ordinary fermentation. The fermenter is kept under a blanket of carbon dioxide while fermentation proceeds. Carbonic maceration is usually just the first stage, and fermentation is not completed. Typically the juice is run off, the residue is pressed, and then the press-run juice and free-run juice are fermented together in the normal way.

Carbonic maceration has ancient origins. It's thought that wine was produced by semi-carbonic maceration in Roman times, when grapes were trodden in large lagares (troughs for holding wine with suitable holes for runoff), and the layer of carbon dioxide caused carbonic maceration in unbroken grapes. Lagares were also used for producing cider and olive oil, and have been excavated all over the wine-producing areas of Spain. Winemaking in Rioja in the nineteenth century used light treading in a lagar, which typically left the majority of grapes unbroken.[43] Similar methods are still used in Navarra, where they are called the método rural (rural method).[44]

Filtration: Stripping the Wine?

"Wine is a living thing." You see this said time and time again.[45] From this comes the concept that if you filter the wine, evisceration is inevitable. But no, wine is not alive: and if it provides a home for living organisms (bacteria or yeast) it will very likely be spoiled in short order. Certainly wine (or at least higher quality wine) is not static but evolves with time; and certainly we can ask what components are removed by filtration, and to what extent they might be necessary for this evolution. But let's base the discussion on a clear understanding that wine is a mixture of water and alcohol containing dissolved components, or perhaps more accurately that it is what chemists would call a colloidal suspension, in which some of its components aren't really dissolved into the liquid but rather are very fine particles suspended in it. If wine is a "thing," it is chemical not biological.

At the end of fermentation, the new wine is a cloudy solution with all sorts of gunk suspended in it. It is not attractive, and is far from the bright, clean appearance that the modern consumer demands. It may be clarified by a natural settling process (débourbage in French) or by the addition of various fining agents that cause suspended matter to precipitate out and fall to the bottom. Fining agents include proteins, siliceous earths, various synthetic polymers, and a clay called bentonite.[46] One current controversy is whether these agents, which don't remain in the wine, should be considered as additives for legal purposes. Also, they can affect whether the wine is considered suitable for specific purposes; for example, some agents would prevent a wine being kosher or being appropriate for vegans.

Before a wine is matured in barrel, the suspended matter (the *gross lees*) is allowed to settle for a day or so. This gives a cloudy solution, but without any large particles. The wine may stay in barrels for up to two years and more material will drop out of suspension to the bottom during this time. This is the *fine lees*, consisting of dead yeast cells and other materials. Fine wines may be kept in contact with the (fine) lees for several months to enable them to absorb compounds from the lees; this increases flavor complexity. The overall result of maturation on the lees is a creamy, richer texture.

The lees also have a protective effect on the wine. They provide a reducing environment, which antagonizes oxidation. Periodically the lees are stirred up (this is called battonage, because originally it used to be performed with a baton

The Oxoline system allows barrels to be stacked in rows and rotated on rollers.

Wine is being racked from the upper barrel to the lower barrel at a Bordeaux château.

The transfer tube is just above the level of the lees in the upper barrel, and transfer is stopped as soon as sediment appears in the tube.

or stick). Battonage prevents reductive flavors from developing in the vicinity of the lees. These days it can be performed more easily by keeping the barrels on a roller system that allows them to be rotated in place (some winemakers call them spinning barrels).

The alchemy of modern winemaking has developed preparations to substitute for aging on the lees. These include various compounds that enhance a round feeling in the wine, interact with tannins to soften red wine, and inhibit browning of white wine.

Maturation in barrel inevitably involves some exposure to oxygen, although it is probably not (as traditionally held) due to seepage of air between the staves of the barrel. Emile Peynaud calculated that oxygen penetration through the wood cask is insignificant.[47] Even though barrels are regularly topped up to compensate for evaporation, there's always some exposure to a headspace of air in the barrel. From time to time (typically every three months) the wine is racked off the lees into a new barrel. The traditional way of doing this is to burn a sulfur candle in the new barrel, and then to siphon the wine into it from a barrel at a higher level; these days there are gentler systems involving compressed gas to push the wine from barrel to barrel. Some oxidative exposure occurs under conventional racking, although it can be minimized by racking under a blanket of inert gas.

When the wine has completed its maturation, it is clarified to give a nice bright appearance. Traditionally for red wines this involves using egg whites, several per barrel. The albumin in the egg white catches suspended material and precipitates it to the bottom of the barrel. Because the albumin is positively charged, it interacts with negatively charged tannins, reducing the overall level and giving a necessary softening to the wine. Of course, it is now possible to use albumin or other preparations rather than egg whites themselves. This is a far cry from the old days: Maria Lopez de Heredia recalls that her bodega in Rioja had a farm with chickens in order to provide a supply of egg whites, and when times were really hard during the war, the chickens provided a source of revenue that kept the company going.[48]

Some treatments are unnecessary technically, but necessary (unfortunately) in order to pacify consumers. All wines contain tartaric acid, and in the form of potassium tartrate, it easily precipitates out in the bottle, forming colorless crystals. The crystals are completely harmless, but can be confused with shards of glass by less knowledgeable consumers. To avoid alarming people and having the bottles returned, producers use cold stabilization, which involves chilling the wine to –4 °C in a cooling tank. A thick layer of ice forms on the outside of the tank, while inside the cold precipitates the tartrate crystals. This prevents any crystallization from happening later.[49]

Cold stabilization largely fixes problems with precipitation for white wines, but red wines are naturally prone to throw sediments. Even after fining, wine is still a colloidal suspension, and tannins or other suspended material can fall out of solution to form a sediment. A whole host of filtration methods are available to treat the wine. This is one of the most controversial stages in wine production. The basic issue is simply how finely the wine is filtered. You will sometimes see a label on quality wines saying "unfiltered," to demonstrate that the wine has been bottled in its natural state.

Wine is a wonderfully receptive host for microorganisms, especially Acetobacter, bacteria that can turn it into vinegar. (The bacteria that like to live on wine are not at all dangerous to people, so there is little danger that a contaminated wine will be harmful, but it is not likely to be pleasant to drink.) The most stringent form of treatment to prevent contamination is a sterile filtration, passing the wine across a membrane with pores that are too small to let bacteria through.[50]

Filtration removes suspended particles from the wine. The question is how this changes the nature of the wine, and whether these particles are needed for the wine to mature. The answer is not straightforward, as different types of filters work in different ways. On the one hand, the holes in a sterile filter that are too small to let bacteria through are still more than a hundred times larger than flavor molecules. On the other hand, filters that work by absorption may not discriminate by size. Industrial production can use pretty brutal filtration methods that take everything out to leave a completely bright, clear wine.

The eminent oenologue Pascal Ribéreau-Gayon expresses the technical view: "Filtration... is intended to eliminate turbidity, foreign bodies, and impurities... It would be ridiculous to suggest that these substances make a positive contribution to flavor. Contrary to a widely held opinion, clear wine always tastes better than the same wine with even slight turbidity."[51] Ribéreau-Gayon believes that the complete absence of filtration is problematic for red wines and that some filtration is essential for white wines.[52]

The problem is probably not so much light filtration to clear the wine, but extensive use of the filters. The critic Robert Parker has been on a campaign against excessive filtration for years: "The effect of excessive manipulation of wine, particularly overly aggressive fining and filtration, is dramatic. It destroys a wine's bouquet as well as its ability to express its *terroir* and varietal character. It also mutes the vintage's character. Fining and filtration can be lightly done, causing only minor damage, but most wines produced in the New World (California, Australia, and South America in particular), and most bulk wines produced in Europe are sterile-filtered. This procedure requires numerous prefiltrations to get the wines clean enough to pass through a micropore membrane filter. This system of wine stability and clarification strips, eviscerates, and denudes a wine of much of its character."[53]

You Can't Taste the Color

Red wine is all about extraction—extraction of color and tannins. Extraction used to be a relatively simple affair. When indigenous yeast were used, there was a lag period before fermentation started, so some exposure of juice to skins was inevitable. During fermentation the skins and other solid matter would rise to the top of the vat, and one technique or another would be used to immerse them periodically in the must. After fermentation, the wine would often be left for a few days before being run off. This would give a decent level of extraction of color and tannins; but anyone who remembers the wines of twenty or thirty years ago knows they were not so deeply colored as today, and measurements show a significant rise in tannin levels since then. The change is due partly to harvesting riper grapes and partly to better methods for extracting color and tannins.

Color and tannins are both in the general class of compounds known as polyphenols.[54] The "poly" in polyphenol indicates that the molecule consists of a chain of phenols linked together. Polyphenols come in a range of sizes, depending on the length of the chain, and one of their important properties is the ability to interact with one another to form longer chains. This softens their effect on the palate. And then as the chains extend (polymerize is the technical term), they reach a point at which they become too large to remain suspended in solution; they precipitate out to form the sediment at the bottom of the bottle. This reduces bitterness and color in the wine. This change in the tannins is an important aspect in the maturation of red wines, and explains why they may start out as bitter, but become softer and gentler with time.

The tannins give structure to a wine—that sense of texture extending beyond mere fruit flavors. More than half of the tannins are in the skin, but stalks and seeds also have a good amount. Tannins are bitter and the sense of a dry mouth you get after drinking a young Cabernet Sauvignon is due to the effect of the tannins in binding to the salivary proteins. In fact, one of the chemical methods for measuring the level of tannin is based upon its ability to interact with the protein serum albumin (found in saliva).

Tannins vary from relatively benign and ripe to astringent and stalky. Tannins in the stalks are somewhat harsher than those in the skin, which is why a noticeable softening occurred in Bordeaux wines when destemming (removing the stems before fermentation) was widely introduced from the 1970s.[55] The tannins in the seeds are the harshest of all, making it important to avoid pressing hard enough to extract tannins from them.[56] The quality of the tannins changes as the berries mature, going from green or stalky character to riper, better rounded

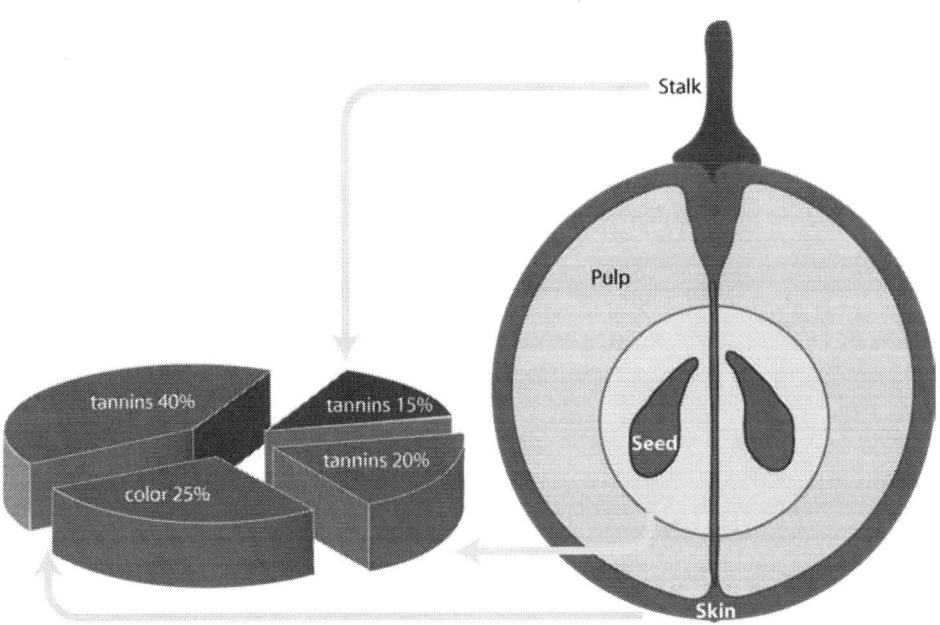

The skin of the berry is the major source of polyphenols, including all of the color and most of the tannins. Seeds and stalks contain harsher tannins than the skin. Per cents in the pie chart indicate the typical proportion of all polyphenols (total color = 25%, total tannins = 75%).

character. The amount of tannins depends on the grape variety, ranging from 1 g/l in a light-bodied red wine to 6 g/l in a heavily extracted full-bodied wine.

It's not straightforward to get a clear measure of the total quantity of tannins—different methods of measurement can give different answers.[57] There is even less agreement on how to assess the quality of tannins. As grapes develop, the total amount of tannins increases, and you can tell by taste that they become less bitter and astringent, but there's no chemical measure of how different tannins affect taste. The general concept that grapes should be harvested only when they reach "phenolic ripeness," is inevitably somewhat imprecise.

Tannins in wine come from the grapes, and are also extracted from the wood if the wine is matured in new oak barrels. Grape tannins are extracted into the juice by contact with the skin. Alcohol affects which tannins are extracted, so a cold maceration (when the juice is held in contact with the skin before fermentation) has different effects from maceration post fermentation (when alcohol is at its peak). During fermentation, extraction of color and tannins occurs as the cap of skins that forms on the top of the tank is pushed into the juice (*pigeage* or *punch-down*) or as juice is sprayed back over the cap (*pumping-over*). Pigeage is usually used for varieties where less overall extraction is wanted (such as Pinot Noir), whereas pumping-over achieves high extraction (and is usually used for Cabernet Sauvignon).[58] Today, enzymes that help to break down cell walls are sometimes added to help increase the level of extraction.[59]

The fact that color and tannins in wine both come from extraction of polyphenols often leads to the completely mistaken assumption that darker wines are better than light colored wines. But you can't taste the color! Subject to the caveat that some varieties are more pigmented than others, you might argue that a wine of some varietal that is darker than another of the same varietal is likely to have a greater level of overall extraction, because color is not extracted in isolation but in combination with other components. But it is not inevitably true that more extracted wines will be better than less extracted wines; and it is certainly not true that the density of coloring matter per se has any effect on the qualities of the wine.

Burgundy has always been a relatively light color, because Pinot Noir is not a heavily pigmented grape, and sometimes the light color is regarded as a disadvantage in the marketplace. Many of the more deeply colored Burgundies that can be found today owe their origins to the introduction of extended cold maceration in the 1980s by the oenologist Guy Accad. A much deeper color and level of extraction was achieved by keeping crushed grapes for up to 10 days before allowing fermentation to start.[60] Accad's techniques are deeply controversial: some believe they bring a modern approach to Burgundy, while to others the approach is an anathema that destroys typical wine qualities.[61]

By contrast with tannins, color can be more precisely measured in terms of both density and hue. Although it has no organoleptic effects, it is useful, as an indication of age and (sometimes) of the condition of a wine. Red wines lose intensity of color with age, and the hue changes from purple to orange. White wines show the reverse effect, and tend to darken with age.

Color is due to polyphenols, including both anthocyanins (purple or red pigments) and tannins (lighter red-brown colors), which are extracted from the skins during fermentation. The dark colors of varieties such as Cabernet Sauvignon and Syrah are due to the high content of anthocyanins. Varieties such as Pinot Noir, Sangiovese, and Nebbiolo give lighter colored wines, because they have less anthocyanins.[62] With age, anthocyanins polymerize (form longer chains) as

Fifty years of Lafite shows how the color changes from purple to red to orange and lightens as it ages.

The purple wine on the left is Château Lafite 2003; the garnet colored wine in the center is the 1978 vintage; the light colored wine on the right is Lafite 1945.

The 1945 was still vibrant and by far the best of the three in 2010.

Young dry white wine is pale, old white wine is darker.

The wine on the left is a Puligny Montrachet from 2005; on the right is the same wine from 1990.

The younger wine was fresh and steely; the older wine tasted somewhat oxidized.

Sweet wines also are deeper in color.

the result of oxidation and fall out of solution, causing both a change in hue (anthocyanins change from blue to red, and tannins change from red to brown) and a general lightening of color intensity.

But there is more to color than simply the concentration or types of anthocyanins. When black grapes are fermented, pigments are extracted from the skin, but this is not of itself enough to ensure good color. Anthocyanins are unstable and have to be "fixed" by conversion to a stable form.[63] The effect of other factors on the color pigments is called copigmentation;[64] it can account for up to half the color of young red wine, and also is responsible for shifting the color spectrum from red towards purple.[65] Low concentrations of cofactors add to the low color profile of varieties such as Pinot Noir.

Sometimes additional color concentration is obtained by cofermenting different varieties together, because one contains cofactors that act on the pigments of another. An especially striking demonstration of this effect is the ability of white grapes to increase color in red wines.[66] The effect depends on the relative proportions of black and white grapes included in the same fermentation vat; probably it peaks at around 10% white grapes, because up to that point, increasing cofactor concentration enhances color; above that point the white juice reduces color overall.[67] It used to be the case that black and white grapevines were intermingled in the vineyard, resulting in cofermentation of both types of grapes in the same vat, increasing color in the wine, whether the winemakers knew it or not.[68]

The basis for color in white wine is more mysterious. The pale yellow-green-straw color of most white wines is due to another class of phenolic compounds found in the skin, called flavonoids.[69] Oxidation of the flavonoids gives wine a golden color as it ages. Since skin contact is limited in white-wine production, the skin color of the grapes has little effect, although some color is gained if there is a cold maceration before fermentation. (Skin contact—called maceration pélliculaire—is used for some white varieties such as Muscat or Sauvignon Blanc, in order to extract aromatic compounds.) Some faint coloration of the pulps of some varieties contributes slightly to color, as in a faint pink in Gewürztraminer. Barrel fermenting or oak-aging produce darker yellow colors by extracting non-flavonoid phenols, principally lignins, from the oak. Deep color in a dry white wine is an indication of possible oxidation.

In the Pink

"Rosés are not wine," the sommelier at a Michelin-starred restaurant in London said to me in disgust when I mentioned that I would be visiting Provence and might try the local wines. True enough, many rosés are made for extraneous reasons—in many cases the main purpose is to improve a red wine rather than to make a good rosé—but rosé production has been increasing lately, with more serious attempts to make good rosé in its own right. So what are the real characteristics of rosé?[70]

How much pink is needed to be rosé and how much is too much? Rosé wines are not well defined, but are made from red grapes with low extraction of color. (Historically, before modern methods for extraction, red wines may have been not so much more deeply colored than the rosés of today.) Several different methods are used for making rosé, with varying results for quality. At its best, a rosé should be delicate, with the freshness of a light white wine, but with just that very faint touch of additional structure, a barely perceptible taint of austerity, coming from skin extraction.

The color intensity of a rosé wine depends on how much skin contact is allowed before the juice is separated. Using white winemaking methods with red grapes produces the lightest colored rosés; the grapes are pressed immediately, and the juice is kept in contact with the skins in the press for only a very short time, while the crushed grapes are being drained. Deeper colors are produced by allowing skin contact for a few hours, somewhat equivalent to maceration pélliculaire for white wines. As with white wines, this enhances softness and fruit, and reduces acidity.[71]

An alternative method is to use a saignée (literally a "bleeding") from vats used in conventional red winemaking. Most often, the main purpose of saignée is to improve the quality of the red wine, and the rosé is a byproduct. By drawing the first juice out of the vat, concentration is increased in the remaining red wine. This juice is rosé because it has not had much time to absorb compounds from the skins.

A major distinction between the two methods comes from their different purposes. When your main objective is a quality red wine, you are looking for fully ripe grapes. A saignée from the must gives different results from macerating grapes produced specifically for making rosé, where preservation of acidity and freshness is as important as ripeness. Jorge Muga, who produces a fine rosé at Bodegas Muga in Rioja, uses grapes from specific vineyards—"it is not a plan B used to improve the quality of the red wine," he told me, pointing out that the grapes are grown in shadier conditions to obtain the higher acidity and lower color appropriate for rosé.[72] Better results are obtained by using higher yields than you would for a red wine, so there is no green harvest, and by managing the vineyard so as to harvest the grapes a little less ripe than they would be for red wine production.

Of course you can make a rosé wine technically by blending in a little red to give color to a white wine. This is illegal in the European Union, except for Champagne where it's relatively common to put a little dry red wine in the mix to give a rosé its color. (Although some champagnes are made by extracting a little color from the red grapes during winemaking.) It is perfectly legal, and not uncommon, in the New World, however, to blend red and white to make pink wine.

But when E.U. Agriculture Commissioner Mariann Fischer Boel proposed early in 2009 to allow production of rosé-colored wines by mixing red and white wines, there was outrage. Presented as a reform that would allow better competition with the New World, the proposal was easily approved by the member states (including France). The fact that the proposal applied only to Vin de Table (meaning that quality wines would still have to be produced by traditional methods) was lost in the brouhaha. "The battle for rosé's nobility risks being lost with a wave of Europe's magic wand," says Xavier de Volontat, president of the French union of wine producers.[73] The blending option would lead to "economic and social destruction," he adds. First reactions at the E.U. were to dig in, but finally they were forced to retract the proposed rule change.[74]

So what is the difference? A "rosé" made by blending uses 3-4% of red wine to color a white wine, so it is essentially made from white grapes. A traditional rosé is made from a black grape variety; most often Grenache, Cinsault, Carignan, even Syrah, Mourvèdre, Cabernet Franc, and Pinot Noir, so the aromatic spectrum is different (although rosé shows the origin of the variety less clearly than either red or white wine). And carefully making a traditional rosé has a more subtle process of extraction. Also, it is more expensive than simply blending in a little red wine, which is why the change was such a threat to traditional producers. What would very likely have happened is that large quantities of unsellable white wine, stored as part of the wine lake, would have been turned into "rosé" to flood the market.[75] Would this be fraud or would this be fraud? The results of the controversy, however, do somewhat leave begging the question of why it is acceptable to blend in red wine to make rosé Champagne.

Rosés are usually dry in France, but are often off-dry in other winemaking regions. The "blush wines," in particular the white Zinfandels, of California are typical examples of pink wines made in an off-dry style.

Sulfur Dioxide: the Essential Preservative

Sulfur dioxide has been used in winemaking for several hundred years. When the Romans first started using wooden barrels, they discovered that burning a sulfur candle inside the empty barrel had a fumigant effect. Its specific effect in preserving wine was recognized when the use of burning sulfur was authorized for wine production in Prussia in 1487. The technique was introduced into modern winemaking by the Dutch in the eighteenth century.[76] Addition of sulfur dioxide as such (directly as a gas or by addition of potassium metabisulfite powder which releases sulfur dioxide when it dissolves) dates only from the twentieth century.[77]

Sulfur dioxide has two important roles: it is an antimicrobial agent that acts as a preservative by inhibiting growth of undesirable yeasts and bacteria; and it is an anti-oxidant that protects fruit and wine against damage from oxygen. Sulfur dioxide exists in two forms. The form that is most effective as an antimicrobial agent is the free gas (molecular SO_2). When it dissolves in water, it generates sulfites, and this form is the most effective as an anti-oxidant.

Sulfur dioxide is used at all stages from harvesting to bottling. Grapes are often dusted with potassium metabisulfite (which releases SO_2) when they are harvested, to protect them from oxidation before they make it into the vat. A low level of sulfur dioxide may be added at the start of fermentation to inhibit the wild yeasts. Sulfur dioxide is used as a protective agent while wine is maturing in barrels; and it is added at bottling as a sterilizing agent.

It's almost impossible to make wine without sulfur dioxide. Only "almost" because there are a few brave organic producers who do just that:[78] but it's an uphill battle to end up with wine rather than vinegar. And it's impossible to be sure of completely avoiding any sulfites in the wine because very low levels can be produced naturally during fermentation.[79] Any wine containing more than 10 ppm (parts per million) of sulfites has to carry the warning "contains sulfites" in both the E.U. and U.S.A: this means that all wines must be labeled irrespective of whether the level is actually likely to cause any health problems.

Used with a very wide range of foods, sulfur dioxide is probably the most common food preservative in existence. The reason for the warning is that some people are allergic to sulfites. But very few people are allergic to the levels in wine, although a small minority cannot tolerate any level.[80] Sulfur dioxide levels are actually much lower in wines than in foods in general; for example, preserved fruits may have more than 1000 ppm, whereas a wine typically will have somewhat less than 100 ppm.

Because the polyphenols in red wine have an anti-oxidative effect, red wine does not need as much SO_2 as white wine. And because sweet wines have sugar that can provide an excellent medium for yeast to grow, they require much higher levels of SO_2. The levels permitted in bottled wine are regulated everywhere wine is made, although of course the details vary with the country.[81] However, the regulations are a bit of a myth in the European Union, where they apply rigorously only for imported wines. Local producers can bypass them by taking advantage of the exceptions allowing higher limits for sweet wines.

There are simply no good alternatives to sulfur dioxide. Pasteurization by flash-heating the wine has been controversial ever since Pasteur proposed it as a means of sterilization.[82] Most producers feel it damages the organoleptic properties and inhibits the development of complexity. An exception is the Burgundian producer Louis Latour, which has used the technique virtually since it was invented, but some people feel the red wines fail to achieve their full potential as a result.[83] And in any case, pasteurization will not prevent oxidation.

It is, however, a myth that sulfur dioxide actually prevents oxidation from occurring. When wine is exposed to oxygen, alcohol (ethanol) is converted to acetaldehyde. This is a compound found in oxidized styles of wine, such as fino Sherry, where it contributes to the characteristic nutty aromas. What sulfur dioxide really does in wine is to combine with the acetaldehyde, forming an odorless compound that does not change the wine's aroma. (This is why sulfur dioxide is not used in the production of fino Sherry.)

Sulfur dioxide's action in removing acetaldehyde makes attempts to reduce it to absolutely minimal levels in order to reduce allergic reactions not exactly misguided, but possibly futile. Acetaldehyde is an allergen (something that provokes allergic reactions), and there comes a point at which reduction of sulfur dioxide is counterbalanced by the increase in acetaldehyde. Unfortunately, some level of allergens may be inevitable, irrespective of efforts made to reduce sulfur dioxide, histamines, or other components.[84]

The need for SO2 is significantly affected by the type of closure. The thinking about what levels of SO2 are necessary (and the regulations) go back to a time when all wine was bottled under cork. Because corks allow some exchange of air with the outside as they age, more sulfur dioxide is needed to protect the wine than in the case of a wine bottled under screwcap, which can come close to a hermetic seal. So producers are slowly rethinking their protocols for using SO2 as they move to other closures than corks in bottles.

Residual Sugar

Left alone, fermentation will continue until almost all the sugar in the must has been converted to alcohol. But the yeast have their limits. Most yeast cannot function at alcohol levels over 15%. So if the must has so much sugar that there is still some left when fermentation reaches 15% alcohol, the process will stop, leaving a sweet wine. Some of the great dessert wines are made in this way, by harvesting grapes very late, when sugar levels have become very high. Sauternes, the late harvest wines of the Loire and Alsace, and the German and Austrian Beerenausleses, all are made in this way.

In all of these wines, the high sugar levels get some help from natural processes. When grapes are left on the vine after the regular harvest date, a certain amount of dehydration occurs, called passerillage in France; by reducing water content in the grape, this increases the concentration of sugar, and the grapes are said to be passerillé. A more forceful concentration occurs when the fungus Botrytis cinerea infects the grapes. Forming a unpleasant looking mold on the surface of the skin, it extracts water and greatly concentrates sugar. But as well as being more concentrated, botrytized grapes have more intense flavors than berries that are merely passerillé, because the botrytis also adds notes of honey and increases volatile acidity (acetic acid), giving that delicious tang of honeyed piquancy.

Winemakers in warm climates have often developed methods for helping the natural process of dehydration after grapes are harvested. The old method of Vin de Paille (wine of straw) in the south of France consists of allowing the grapes to dry out on straw mats in the sun before they are pressed and fermented. Grapes are dried in warm attics to make the dessert wines Vin Santo and Recioto in Italy. Because the grapes are exposed to air during these processes, the wines usually have a slightly oxidized quality.

It's also possible to retain residual sugar in the wine by stopping fermentation before it is completed. One way to do this is to stop the yeast from working, most commonly by adding sulfur dioxide and/or lowering the temperature. This is how sweet German wines are made; and since fermentation is typically only a bit more than half complete when this happens, the resulting wine has relatively low alcohol, in the range of 8-10%. The result can be a beautifully balanced wine, sweet certainly, but with refreshing and lively acidity.

A more dramatic way of stopping fermentation is simply to add enough alcohol to bring the level over 15%, at which the yeast die, and the wine will be stable. This is the basis for all sweet wines based on fortification, such as Port. The sweetness of the wine is due to the sugar that had not been fermented by the time the brandy was added. Fortified wines have an advantage that they are stable against refermentation, whereas sweet wines with alcohol below 15% need to be protected against any reinfection with yeast, usually by keeping the level of sulfur dioxide high.

Natural Wine or Unnatural Practices?

So you are drinking a glass of wine. It is a clear, limpid red color, the nose shows the characteristics commonly associated with its variety, refreshing acidity supports the typical fruits on the palate, and it has a nice long finish. In short, it has precisely the characteristics you expect of that grape variety and place, and you would be able to identify it as such any day in a blind tasting. But is this typicity the natural and inevitable result of minimalist winemaking allowing the wine to establish its own intrinsic character; or is it the result of multiple small interventions and decisions by the winemaker, directing the wine's development down a path that satisfies the historical expectations and traditions of this variety and place?

Let's just follow the grape juice as it turns into wine. Grapes are crushed or pressed and fermented. Even for a minimalist producer, probably the fermentation will take place at a controlled temperature; the choice of this temperature will have a significant effect on how much color and tannin is extracted into a red wine, and whether a white wine emphasizes fruit or other qualities. And you have to choose whether to let the grapes macerate before and after fermentation; whatever you decide will also have an effect on the level of extraction. Malolactic fermentation can be used as opportunity for further control, although a minimalist producer may let it happen (or not) naturally. If the wine is matured in wood, you have to choose whether to use new oak or old oak, and if new oak is used, what toasting regime it has; this has a great effect on the transmission of flavors to the wine.

Sometimes people talk about winemaking in terms of intervention, the presumption being that less intervention makes a more natural wine. Yet minimalist winemaking may not always be quite what it seems, or at least may not necessary involve the minimal extent of change to the wine after fermentation. Consider this tale of two wines produced by Nikolaus Moser at the Sepp Moser Weingut in Austria's Kremstal valley. Schnabel is a tiny vineyard just north of the Danube in the eastern part of Krems. Sepp Moser grow both Grüner Veltliner and Sauvignon Blanc here, and from the Grüner they make two entirely different wines from the same grapes.

Most of the wine is treated conventionally. It ferments (spontaneously) in stainless steel for about 2 weeks, and then the wine rests on the lees for 7 months and is bottled. It is pale in color, brilliantly clear, light and fresh, with faintly aromatic, spicy primary fruits, a very approachable example of a modern Grüner.

The smaller lot is called MINIMAL to reflect minimalist winemaking, with as little intervention as possible. The wine ferments in 300 liter barrels of old Austrian oak; fermentation takes 3 months to complete and the wine also goes (spontaneously) through malolactic fermentation. No sulfur is added, the wine is left on the lees for a year, then it is racked once with a little sulfur added, and bottled the following May. The wine is a medium golden color, not quite clear, and shows a complex, developed nose in a faintly oxidative style.[85] There's a creamy texture on the palate, and dense layers of flavor, somewhat in the style of gracefully aging old Burgundy.

The question is what's really the "minimal" treatment?[86] There was far less control by the winemaker for the MINIMAL wine, but actually much more happened to it: oxidative exposure during prolonged alcoholic fermentation, malolactic fermentation, and a long exposure to the lees in the oak barrels. So you might quarrel with "minimal" as a description, but call this traditional at least. There's no doubt which wine most consumers would prefer: simple and fruity will fly off the supermarket shelf every time. But there's also no doubt which is by far the most interesting wine in terms of aroma and flavor variety, and for that matter, which will probably still be of interest several years from now. Minimalist or traditionalist, old versus new, it's all choices—and every choice changes the wine.

Even a minimalist can't but help make decisions that affect the nature of the wine. You could leave the wine to ferment with indigenous yeast and without temperature control (and periodically probably lose a vintage to spoilage or stuck fermentation), you can leave malolactic fermentation to chance, but you have to decide how long to leave the wine to macerate after fermentation before you run off the juice; and you have to decide what you are going to put the juice into, and how long it is going to stay there before you bottle it. And these days there is a good case to be made that the decision between cork and screwcap will influence the nature and development of the wine in the bottle.

No: wine does not make itself in the vineyard. The winemaker makes the wine.

6

The Alchemist's Delight

WINE IS BASICALLY A MIXTURE OF ALCOHOL AND WATER with various flavoring compounds dissolved or suspended in it. Its complexity derives from a very large number of compounds, each present in tiny quantities. The intricate relationship between aroma and flavor is explained by the presence of hundreds of small, volatile molecules; so far no one has been able to account for all of the components in any one wine, although we now have a pretty good idea of the principal aroma and flavor components that are characteristic of each major grape variety.

A purist might think that, in a natural wine, these components derive directly from the grapes that were harvested in the vineyard. But hold on a moment! With one or two exceptions, grape juice shows little varietal character; each variety develops its typical aromas and flavors during fermentation.

Yeast work furiously during alcoholic fermentation to modify or synthesize a wide range of compounds in the must. The resulting changes in the aroma and flavor spectrum are why wine smells and tastes different from grape juice. Then malolactic fermentation not only reduces the acidity, but also changes the flavor spectrum yet again. And, of course, when wines are matured in oak barrels, compounds leach into the wine from the oak to change it yet further.

All of these processes—alcoholic fermentation, malolactic fermentation, exposure to oak—can be used by the winemaker to emphasize or de-emphasize particular qualities in the wine. Winemakers like to say wine is made in the vineyard, and it's certainly true that getting healthy, ripe berries is a prerequisite: but it's one of the biggest myths of all that making the best wine requires only minimal intervention. Without intervention, wine is rapidly converted to vinegar.

Since some intervention is essential, and given that some means of intervention are hallowed by tradition, it's not always clear where to draw the line between artisanal winemaking and industrial process. Chaptalization, the addi-

The approach has become more scientific since Brueghel the Elder pictured the alchemist at work in 1558.

tion of sugar to the grape juice in order to increase the alcohol level during fermentation, is a couple of centuries old, and rarely arouses controversy. The use of modern techniques, such as reverse osmosis, evaporation under vacuum, or spinning cone, to remove water or alcohol is viewed with more suspicion. Dunking oak chips in the wine instead of putting the wine into oak barrels is on the edge; and what about the addition of oak flavoring compounds? Removal or addition of the typical volatile flavoring compounds of each grape variety is frowned upon; but addition of artificial coloring compounds, although not acknowledged, is practiced widely in the New World. Where does natural wine turn into an artificial beverage?

Is the winemaker of today the equivalent of the alchemist of the middle ages? The alchemist searched for a means of turning base metal into gold. The winemaker has a huge arsenal of devices for influencing alcohol level, acidity, sweetness, color, volatile aromas, and tannins. But the winemaker is a lot more successful in turning his grape juice into liquid gold than the alchemist ever was.

Alcohol: Finding the Sweet Spot

There wouldn't be much point to wine if it didn't have alcohol, and for one reason and another, the exact level is considered important. The first myth about alcohol levels is that the label accurately represents what is in the bottle. The European Union requires labels to identify alcohol levels within 0.5%; and the level must be stated in terms of an 0.5% interval. A wine labeled at 12.5% could have alcohol between 12% and 13%. The United States and Australia require accuracy only within 1.5%, so a wine labeled 12.5% could be anything between 11% and 14%.[1] Accuracy is further reduced by distortions resulting from the tax laws: tax on wine increases when the level goes over 14% alcohol in the United States, where it's strange how many wines are on the market with stated levels of 13.9%, just squeezing into the lower tax bracket.

When most wine was made from grapes grown under slightly adverse climatic conditions in Europe, more often than not it was a struggle to reach adequate alcohol levels. At least in more northern regions, it was only with the aid of chaptalization that a level approaching 12% or 12.5% was attained. But now far more wine comes from new wine-producing regions that are consistently warmer, and global warming has pushed up sugar levels in grapes from the old regions. It's ironic that alcohol levels in wine have been steadily increasing more or less in parallel with concerns about the effects of excess consumption that have led to more and more stringent regulations on what you can buy and how you can drink it. But whether the potential alcohol in the grapes is too low or too high, the winemaker now has a whole new range of ways to change it.

Chaptalization by tipping sugar into the must before fermentation remains the traditional way to increase alcohol. A modern alternative is to take some water out. Various machines, known generically as concentrators, can remove water. Some producers claim this gives a more natural result. This might be true when there's been rain just before harvest, and the grapes are nicely ripe except for this last minute dilution. But when the growing season has not been so good, and the grapes aren't perfectly ripe, removing water concentrates all components, not just the sugar, and so may intensify anything that's out of balance. And what does pushing it around do to the wine? It's an interesting contrast

This reverse osmosis machine is small and portable. To increase potential alcohol from 11% to 12.5% for 300 hl of must (equivalent to 40,000 bottles) would take about 10 hours.

Photograph kindly provided by Bucher Vaslin.

This evaporation sous vide machine is kept in a locked room at a Bordeaux château.

with the trend to building wineries where the wine moves only by gravity so that it is not disturbed by pumping.

The simplest and least expensive method to remove water is by reverse osmosis. This works on the same principle as osmosis, when water crosses a membrane to equalize the concentrations of substances dissolved in it. In typical osmosis, water crosses from the side of the membrane that has a low concentration of substances to the side that has a high concentration. In reverse osmosis, the direction of flow is reversed by applying pressure, so water can be extracted from must.

Some producers prefer the method of evaporation sous vide (evaporation under vacuum). This uses the principle that water boils at lower temperatures as the pressure is reduced. In a vacuum evaporation machine, the pressure is brought low enough for water to evaporate at 20 °C (68 °F). In Bordeaux, where in spite of global warming the climate still does not produce really ripe grapes every year, and where rain is common around harvest time, reverse osmosis machines and vacuum evaporation appear to be used about equally. They are usually hidden away from visitors.

Going in the other direction, the worldwide trend to harvest increasingly riper grapes has pushed up alcohol levels. For some producers, phenolic ripeness is all, and the wine is bottled with whatever alcohol level results. Others take advantage of new methods that allow alcohol levels to be reduced. The simplest method is actually the oldest: adding water to the must. This is illegal in Europe, where it is regarded as fraudulent. But it is sometimes practiced in California, although it was considered illegal until 2002, when there was a change in interpretation of the regulations (resulting from the need to add water to help stuck fermentations in musts of very high Brix). Nominally this is still the only reason why water can be added, but as a practical matter, water can now be added to dilute must or juice down to a level of 22° Brix to facilitate fermentation. (Watering back is limited to 7% dilution in California.) There are no statistics on how frequently it is employed, but its extension into general winemaking might be regarded as a swindle.

Saignée is the opposite of watering back. Some juice is run off at the start of fermentation of black grapes, increasing the ratio of skin to liquid in order to get a more concentrated red wine. The run-off juice is usually used to make a rosé. Saignée is most commonly used with varieties such as Pinot Noir that have less intense color. Like all techniques that change the balance of wine, this is controversial. Producers who use it believe it is a more natural alternative to other methods of concentration. "It is one of the most natural ways to enhance the flavor profile of a given wine without chemical manipulations," one winemaker told me.[2] "Any winemaker worth his salt will use this on occasion to get the best out of a particular style of wine or grape variety," says another.[3] Almost half the winemakers in California admit to using it routinely or occasionally.[4] The other half view it with disdain. "My rosés are made from pressed grapes because I believe wines should reflect the vintage and the place they were grown. If it was necessary, I would probably make a rosé out of the entire lot rather than manipulate the red wine must!" says one winemaker.[5] "Usually this technique or sleight of hand does not produce wines of elegance (however wines of elegance are not in vogue)," another told me.[6]

The majority of winemakers see saignée as a remedial technique, and like other techniques for concentration, it may be appropriate when there has been dilution from rain at harvest. Some producers in California combine watering back with saignée; and there's a trend in California (legal but not publicized) of adding acid first to high Brix musts; some people call this "the acid whip." When you have a must that is simply too high in Brix, you add some water to bring the sugar level down to a level that will ferment, and then you bleed off some juice as fermentation begins, to mitigate the effects of dilution. Is this manipulation or is this manipulation?

Wine can certainly show a lack of richness at low alcohol levels, but can seem clumsy and out of balance at high levels. The "sweet spot" is a concept developed by Clark Smith at Vinovation, in California's Sonoma Valley, which offers a service for adjusting alcohol levels. Vinovation advertises: "Since even small differences in alcohol content can have a large impact on aroma and texture, Vinovation offers the capability... to examine wine characteristics at 0.1% intervals to choose the wine of the best balance for the desired style. These "sweet spot" tastings remove the guesswork from discovering the best alcohol level for your wine."[7]

Clark Smith is passionate about wine and music. If you look at harmonics, he explained to me, you go suddenly from harmony to dissonance, and wine is the same: an 0.1% change in alcohol can completely reverse the feeling of integration. Sweet spots do not follow a continuous distribution, but occur at sharply delineated, separate levels. He makes his point by asking you to compare the astringency levels of three wines. It turns out that those at 13.7% and 14.2% alcohol taste well rounded (people differ in which they prefer), but a blend of the two that brings the alcohol to just under 14% tastes discernibly awkward (everyone agrees on this). So adjusting alcohol is not simply a matter of reducing (or increasing) it, but is a search to find the exact point at which it best integrates to give the most harmonious impression. Smith calls this "post-modern winemaking."

If you take your wine to Vinovation, they will use their reverse osmosis system to separate it into a permeate and retentate. The permeate is material that crosses the reverse osmosis membrane, containing water, alcohol, and other small substances. It is distilled to remove the alcohol. Then it is added back to the retentate, which contains all the other components of the wine. Typically about 25% of the total batch of wine is treated to denude it of alcohol; then it is recombined with the untreated material. In effect, this is the opposite of using reverse osmosis to remove water from must, because the trick of distillation has been introduced to treat the removed material before it is added back. Smith claims that the increase in alcohol in wines over recent years would be even more marked if it were not for Vinovation, which has taken an average of more than one percent alcohol from almost half of the wines produced in California.[8]

Reverse osmosis is a versatile technique that can be used to adjust components other than alcohol. The size of a molecule determines whether it is included in the permeate. Acetic acid is small enough to be included, and can be removed from the permeate by chemical means, which offers a way to treat wines that have volatile acidity (excess of acetic acid). But this is not legal in many jurisdictions.

The most sophisticated system for manipulating wine is the spinning cone, used to recover volatile aromas during production of tea or coffee, to obtain fruit and vegetable essences, and to remove alcohol from wine. The basic principle is that liquid is fed into the top of the spinning cone column (a vertical cylinder roughly 40" in diameter and 13' in height) and flows down over a series of alternating stationary and rotating metal cones. The liquid drips on to a rotating cone and is pulled by centrifugal force into a thin film on the surface, from where it drips on to the next cone. The thin film of liquid is exposed to a stream of nitrogen gas ascending from the bottom of the cone. By flowing across the surface of the liquid film, the nitrogen extracts volatile aroma and flavor compounds, and carries them up to the top of the column.

For treating wine, the process is split into two stages. The column is used first to extract volatile compounds, which are condensed and saved. The treated wine is collected from the bottom of the column. Then the wine is run through the column again at a slightly higher temperature to remove the alcohol. The compounds removed in the first stage can then be added to the dealcoholized wine.

The spinning cone is a industrial apparatus that can handle large volumes.

Photograph kindly provided by ConeTech.

Proponents of these treatments claim that in warm climates better wine is made by picking the grapes riper and removing the excess alcohol than by harvesting at the desired potential alcohol level. But how far should this be taken? If it's okay to adjust alcohol freely, why shouldn't the winemaker use similar techniques to adjust other aroma or flavor components? If it's okay to preserve volatile components by taking them out while the alcohol is removed, and then adding them back, would it be okay to adjust how much is added back?

Certainly the spinning cone can do a lot more than take out alcohol. By adjusting the conditions, individual volatile flavor compounds can be extracted. Pyrazines are volatile components that give Sauvignon Blanc much of its "grassy" character. Southcorp, the giant Australian producer, experimented at one point with removing pyrazines from a batch of unripe Sauvignon Blanc grapes and adding them to wine made from grapes that lost their pyrazines because they became too ripe.[9] "I regard that as natural," said Linley Schultz, the winemaker at the time. At the KWW in South Africa, winemakers went a step further and added pyrazines that had been purchased directly for use as flavoring compounds. The practice came to light after journalist Michael Fridjhon pointed to suspiciously high pyrazine levels in many South African Sauvignon Blancs.[10] It remains unclear how widespread the practice is.[11] No one would object if two wines were blended together to produce a better balanced product, but tinkering with individual flavor components is usually acknowledged to be another matter. At what point have we crossed the boundary between a natural product and an industrial fabrication?

Acidity: Essential But Not Too Much

The winemaker has quite a range of methods for increasing or decreasing acidity in wine, but by far the best result is obtained by picking berries with the right level of acidity. Acidity varies with the climate (higher in cool climates, lower in warm climates) and with the variety. The most important acids in grapes are tartaric and malic. Most of the acidity is tartaric acid, which has no flavor as such, but malic acid has a distinct flavor of green apples. Malic acid is generally more prominent in cool-climate varieties because it is metabolized during the later stages of development in warm temperatures. Red wines tend to have lower acidity than white wines, partly because they tend to be produced in warmer climates, partly because maceration with the skins extracts potassium (which reduces acidity).

Terms for describing acidity in wines range from "flabby" to "balanced" to "crisp."* Technically speaking, wine needs to have about 4-6 g/l of acidity to be in

---

* Acidity is usually measured as the amount of tartaric acid that would produce the same level of acidity as the mix of acids actually present in a wine. Acidity is expressed either in g/l (e.g., 4-6 g/l) or as a percentage (e.g. 0.4-0.6%). In France, acidity is given in equivalents of sulfuric acid, which must be multiplied by 1.5 to get the tartaric equivalent.

a "balanced" range.[12] Higher levels of acidity are needed to balance the sugar in sweet wines. The level of acidity drops with each fermentation; a little is lost during alcoholic fermentation, and then there is a much larger drop if there is a malolactic fermentation.[13]

All wines also have a small amount of volatile acidity, called VA in the trade. "Volatile" means that you can smell it, and for practical purposes in wine, this means acetic acid, the smell of vinegar. It is produced by oxidation of alcohol. At very low levels, it adds liveliness and piquancy, but if levels become high enough to notice directly on the nose, it's a problem. By contrast, you cannot smell the major acids in wine, tartaric and malic.

The most natural way to reduce acidity is by malolactic fermentation, usually considered appropriate for most reds and for many non-aromatic whites. By replacing malic acid with lactic acid, the wine loses the sharp taste of green apples, and gains more creamy textures.[14] In low acid vintages, by contrast, blocking the malo may be a way to retain more natural acidity. Some producers did this in the very hot 2003 vintage in Burgundy.

Wine can be deacidified chemically, which is legal in the cooler climates of Europe. Adding chalk (calcium carbonate) is an old method to remove tartaric acid, by precipitating out the calcium tartrate. More modern variations of this method use more complex chemicals.[15] (Reduction of acidity can also result from cold stabilization to remove potential tartrate crystals.)

Acidification is much easier—you just chuck tartaric acid into the must (or wine). This is legal only in the hottest parts of Europe but is common in much of the New World—many Australian wines are acidified, for example. When you taste a wine where the acidity seems out of whack with the rest of the palate, because you can taste it separately, it may mean that too much acid was thrown into the mix. You would probably get better results by blending in a high acid wine from a cooler climate, but then of course you may no longer be able to label the wine with the name of a single region.

An exception was made in Europe in the unusually hot conditions of 2003 to allow acidification in regions such as Bordeaux and Germany, where it is usually forbidden, but it's difficult to get the level right if you're not accustomed to doing it. Bordeaux producers who did not acidify felt that their wines came out better than those who did, although claims that the acidity levels miraculously corrected themselves during fermentation are hard to understand in terms of conventional chemistry.

The usual rule in Europe is that you can chaptalize in cool regions, and you can add acidity in warm regions. In some regions, both modifications are possible, but not at the same time. But even that limit is thwarted sometimes: the famous Hospices de Beaune in Burgundy bypassed the rule that a wine can be acidified *or* chaptalized by doing both on its wines from the 1997 vintage. Producer Jean Mongeard of Domaine Mongeard-Mugneret in Vosne Romanée argued that you could chaptalize the must and acidify the wine without breaking the rules.[16] How far can you go in manipulating the flavor profile before wine becomes just another processed product?

Dry Wine and the Sweet Tooth

Acidity and sugar are the yin and yang of wine. As acidity increases, sweetness becomes less evident; conversely, a little sugar can disguise excessive acidity. One of the most subtle playoffs is achieved in Champagne, where the cool climate is marginal for wine production, and a straight dry wine would be too acid to enjoy; but by making the wine sparkling, and by adding a little sugar when it is bottled (technically this is called the *dosage*), you get a perfectly delicious balance.

All wine has a little sugar. Even when a wine is fermented to completion, there will be a tiny residual amount that did not get converted to alcohol. Most people can taste sugar in wine at a level above 4 g/l (0.4%). Most dry red wines have less than 1 g/l of residual sugar, most whites are a little higher at 2-3 g/l. Of course, it's not only sugar that makes a wine seems sweet: alcohol gives a perception of sweetness, so a wine with a high alcohol level can appear misleadingly sweet. Glycerol also gives an impression of sweetness.

The legal definition of a dry wine is that it must have less than 4 g/l of residual sugar, but in recognition of the interplay with acidity, wines with sufficient acidity are allowed to have up to 9 g/l and still be described as dry. This is most often used for the Trocken classification in Germany. This can make "trocken" a somewhat misleading description. Fair enough: in some cases the high acidity will give the impression the wine is really dry, but in others, perhaps where the acidity is at the low limit, and the sugar is at the high limit for the category, you will be disappointed by a perceptible taste of sweetness.[17] The consumer would benefit if the European Union stuck rigorously to the notion that dry means less than 4 g/l of residual sugar; at least this is objective, since very few people can taste sugar below this level. Some other term could be used for wines that are expected to taste dry even though they have some sugar.

Residual sugar doesn't only make a wine sweet, it also makes it feel richer. It's a winemaker's trick to leave just a little residual sugar, right at the level of detection or maybe just a fraction above it, to give a bit of kick to the body and a superficial but misleading impression of richness. This panders to the well known fact that market surveys show consumers always claim to drink dry wines, but in blind tastings prefer wines with just a touch of residual sugar. Many of the leading brands, although billed as dry, have low levels of residual sugar. It would be extremely surprising if the sugar level was achieved by natural means. Indeed, Justin Knock, a winemaker at large Australian producer Fosters, says, "We do not practice arrested fermentation and I'd be amazed if anyone else did. It's far too difficult to control at the levels we are discussing (anywhere from 2–10 g/l)."[18] Adding sugar is just part of the final adjustments made before bottling. The extraordinarily successful Yellow Tail red wines have 5-7 g/l residual sugar, and several large American brands, such as Franzia "Chablis" have even more—at roughly 11 g/l, this would be classified as medium dry in Europe. Anything further from authentic Chablis would be hard to imagine. It would be illegal to represent it as a dry wine in Europe.

The most widespread technique for making sweet wine is simply to add sugar after fermentation has been completed. This is not legal as such in Europe, but can be done in the form of adding süssreserve or RCGM (concentrated and purified grape must).[19] This is merely a fig leaf: süssreserve is basically concentrated grape juice and RCGM is obtained from (unfermented) grape juice by a process of filtration and rectification, in which the solution is passed through decoloring resins and ion exchange columns. In reality, RCGM is a concentrated solution of glucose and fructose sugars. Its only difference from a solution made by dissolving purified sugars (more easily extracted from beets) in water is that it was made by partial dehydration of the must of cheap grapes.[20] These techniques are not used to make sweet dessert wine—the artificial nature of adding enough sugar would unbalance the wine—but are used for off-dry or medium dry wines. Known as back-blending, the technique was developed in Germany in the 1950s, but the results are rarely as satisfactory as causing some of the natural grape sugar to remain unfermented.[21]

In a bureaucratic fantasy, the authorities of the European Union have convinced themselves that using RCGM is natural in a way that raw sugar is not. This is one of the dirty little secrets of winemaking: it has no redeeming feature and should be stopped. It's also the case that chaptalization is used in producing sweet wines in other regions, for example in Sauternes, and it seems singularly pointless to add sugar before fermentation in order to leave some over when fermentation stops or is stopped. Shouldn't sweet wines be made from unsweetened must so that the sugar is entirely natural and in balance with everything else? If the must isn't sweet enough, maybe you shouldn't make a sweet wine.

Mega Color: Natural Additive or Snake Oil?

"Virtually everyone is using it. In just about every wine up to $20 a bottle anyway," says one winemaker in California.[22] "It" is Mega Purple, an additive made from grape juice concentrate, widely known to winemakers but kept as obscure as possible to the consumer. It's not even listed in the product catalogs of its producer.

Mega Purple is an extract made from grapes of Rubired, a hybrid variety developed in 1958 by Dr. Harold Olmo of the University of California, Davis, by crossing Alicante Ganzin and Tinta Cão. Tinta Cão is one of the quality black varietals used to make Port, but Alicante Ganzin is a French hybrid created by crossing Aramon Rupestris Ganzin #4 (a hybrid between the Aramon cultivar of Vitis vinifera and Vitis rupestris) [23] and Alicante Bouschet. Alicante Ganzin is a teinturier, meaning that its juice is colored red, and it's mostly used for breeding other teinturiers.

So Rubired is a hybrid with one eighth parentage from Vitis rupestris. It is not a very distinguished variety. "It produces a dark red blending wine, with little character or body, and is used to increase the color of generic or varietal table and dessert wines," says the University of California.[24] So why is it almost 5% of

8000 purple (right) gives a whole new meaning to a plain wrapper. The container has no identification except the name, but is claimed by its manufacturer, California Concentrate, to be the same as Mega Purple. It is dark, sticky stuff (left).

the total crush in California, making it one of the leading varieties, as important as Pinot Noir or Syrah?[25]

The Rubired extract is very deeply colored, very high in sugar, and because of its hybrid origin, has a slightly foxy aroma. It's most commonly used as an additive to give red wines a bit more color, but it also gives them a touch of residual sugar,[26] and a hint of that nasty foxy quality, known pejoratively to winemakers who use it as "Central Valley Red." It's used to overcome deficiencies in a wine, because it adds enough flavoring to hide vegetal notes or even a touch of the animal aromas introduced by Brettanomyces infection. It's been variously described as having "a sort of jammy taste, but with no fruit to it" or giving the wine "a tutti frutti aroma."[27]

Few winemakers admit to using it themselves, although they'll admit its use is widespread.[28] A little goes a long way; most winemakers who will talk about it say that more than 0.1% is noticeable in the wine. Rubired extracts have other purposes as well as treating wine (as food coloring or in fruit juices, for example), but their potency means that a small part of the entire production would be enough to treat all red wine produced in California.[29] Its homogenizing effect on wine flavor may partly explain the general similarities in style between many lower-priced red wines.

Mega Purple was produced by a subsidiary of the conglomerate Constellation Wines, who got into the business when they acquired Heublein in 1994. Heublein owned a grape juice concentrate factory at Madera, California. When the grape juice concentrate business later got into trouble due to over supply, Constellation closed other plants, but continued to produce specialist products at Madera. Mega Purple had been introduced in 1992 as a natural coloring agent, and in 2007 Anil Shrikhande, Vice President of Research and Development for Constellation Wines, said that twenty percent of the annual production of 200,000 liters is sold to the wine industry,[30] alone roughly enough to treat 10% of the red wine

MegaNatural is a series of products made from grapes (right). The Corporate logo of Polyphenolics is amusingly in purple.

produced in California. It is, of course, a vastly cheaper way to increase color than blending in a proportion of wine from a more deeply colored variety.

Today there is also a business in selling wine extract products to consumers. Polyphenolics is a wholly owned subsidiary of Constellation operating out of the plant at Madera with Anil Shrikhande as its President. It sells a series of products called MegaNatural, made from grapes, some of which are sold directly to consumers as dietary supplements, others to manufacturers (sold in 10 or 20 kg containers of powder for bulk use).

No one really knows exactly how widely grape concentrates are used, but by all accounts, they are commonly employed to bump up color and impression of extract in lower priced wines from California and Australia. Coming from hybrid grapes, these concentrates would be illegal in Europe, but of course the precedent for adding concentrate comes from the techniques developed in Germany for back-blending süssreserve. But whether used to add color or sweetness, grape concentrates should really have no place in modern wine making: any benefit from compensating for deficiencies in the wine is outweighed by that general homogenizing quality. There are simply enough opportunities now to make good wine without needing artificial coloring or sweetening. Elderberries (used to add color) were banned in wine by the nineteenth century: Mega purple is a modern equivalent that should be treated in the same way.

Wood *v.* Steel, Oxidation *v.* Reduction

Unless wine is matured in new oak, the containers it passes through on its way from fermentation to the bottle have little direct effect upon it. Fermentation vats can be made of wood, concrete, or stainless steel,[31] and although some producers believe that one or another gives better results, often enough you see all types at one place, just depending on the fashion at the time when they were bought. Some producers believe that one shape is better than another—conical vats rather than cylindrical, for example—mostly because of the way they dissipate heat through the fermenting must, but there's little objective evidence.[32] The general trend these days is towards stainless steel, with a handful of leading producers returning to oak because they feel it gives better aromatics, although one winemaker justifying the change admitted to me, "Science does not explain all the differences between oak and steel." So long as the containers are kept clean (certainly more difficult to accomplish with wood than with concrete or steel), they are not the most important factor at fermentation. One attempt to have the best of both worlds is to use vats with stainless steel construction at the top (where the cap is located) and at the bottom (where the vat is cleaned out), but with oak to contain the bulk of the must.

The major difference between containers, both at fermentation and during any subsequent maturation, is their impact on exposure to oxygen. How much oxygen a wine encounters en route from grape juice to the bottle has a major effect on its style. At one extreme, the new technique of micro-oxygenation increases exposure by bubbling oxygen through the must during or after fermentation. At the other extreme, reductive winemaking (reduction is the opposite of oxidation) uses closed stainless fermentation vats with a blanket of inert gas to completely exclude oxygen.

Oxidation and reduction are key determinants of wine styles. The properties of many components of wine depend on whether they are in oxidized or reduced states. The most dramatic effects are displayed by sulfur-containing compounds. When they are in a reduced state, they produce pungent smells of cabbage, garlic, burned rubber, or rotten eggs. They are known as thiols (more colloquially) or mercaptans (more formally).[33] Hydrogen sulfide, the smell of rotten eggs, is a pungent example of a sulfurous compound.[34] Excessive thiol concentrations resulting from flaws in winemaking can be removed by treatment with copper (an oxidizing agent); in fact, an old trick for dealing with a slight sulfur problem is to drop a copper penny into a glass of wine. The aromas clear almost instantly. While excess thiols are a problem in any wine, some varietals rely for their char-

Fermentation vats may be cylinders, cones, or cubes, made of stainless steel, wood, or cement.

Vats consisting of oak with steel tops and bases were specially constructed for Castello Banfi.

Photograph kindly provided by Castello Banfi.

acteristic aromas on the production of certain thiols at low levels, so the balance between oxidation and reduction is especially important in their winemaking.

Fermentation can occur in the absence of air, but usually gets off to a better start with a kick of oxygen. The most oxidative conditions for fermentation are provided by traditional open-topped wooden fermenters. This also leads to slightly less alcohol in the wine, as some is released into the atmosphere.[35] Modern stainless steel fermenters are closed, but have a valve to allow carbon dioxide to escape. A risk of performing fermentation anaerobically (in the absence of oxygen) is that reductive aromas (such as hydrogen sulfide) can form, and to counteract this, oxygen is sometimes injected.

Micro-oxygenation is the extreme form of oxidative exposure. It may be used during fermentation, it is usually avoided during malolactic fermentation, and its main use is during maturation. It was invented in Madiran in southwest France in 1991 to help reduce the violent tannins of the Tannat grape, and the technique is most suitable for producing wines for short to medium term consumption from tannic grape varieties. Oxygen is bubbled through the wine by using a sparger that distributes the gas in the form of tiny bubbles. By oxidizing the tannins, it advances the state of maturation, with a generally softening effect on the wine, and is most often used as a (cheaper) alternative to maturation in barrel.[36] It's effective because the oxygen is distributed evenly throughout the wine, instead of being restricted to the surface area of the barrel. There's no detailed theoretical understanding of how it works, and it needs to be used carefully to avoid spoiling the wine.

Reductive winemaking occurs in an oxygen-free environment, eliminating the reactions that occur when must or wine is exposed to oxygen in traditional winemaking. It produces wine with bright fruits, typically suited for earlier consumption. It has become especially well established for aromatic varieties such as Riesling and Sauvignon Blanc, where the aromatics are easily lost on exposure to oxygen. (Some of the characteristic features of Sauvignon Blanc are due to thiols, which react with oxygen but are preserved under reductive conditions.)

Reductive winemaking became popular in Australia and New Zealand under the influence of Brian Croser, a leading Australian winemaker,[37] and the reductive style is associated with the New World, although no longer exclusively practiced there. Fermentation occurs in stainless steel, oxygen may be excluded by using inert gas, and there is no exposure to wood. Dry ice (solid carbon dioxide) is used in the press to generate CO_2, which both avoids oxidizing the grapes and maintains the low temperature of the fruit. After pressing, the juice is transferred to stainless steel tanks where it is fermented at cool temperatures. The style of New Zealand Sauvignon Blanc, bright, steely, and full of sharp fruits, owes more to this treatment than to terroir.

The antithesis of reductive winemaking is a technique called hyperoxidation, which is sometimes used for white wines. Oxygen is bubbled through the must before fermentation, destroying anything that reacts with it. By removing compounds that are susceptible to oxygen (essentially tannins, which are undesirable in white wine because of their bitterness), this results in a wine that is more stable when it encounters oxygen later. In principle this can make a stable fruity wine, but the practical problem is stopping the process before the fruit is destroyed. It's useful only for neutral grape varieties, and cannot be used for those whose aromas depend on sulfur-containing compounds (which would be destroyed by the treatment).

Wood or steel, oxidation or reduction, are all perfectly legitimate ways to handle wine, but each treatment produces its characteristics in the wine. Nowhere is the hand of the winemaker more evident than in making choices among these alternatives. Stylistic preference here is clearly imposed rather than intrinsic to the grape variety or the terroir.

Oak: Barrels, Staves, Chips, and Dust

Oak barrels were originally used simply for storage and transport. Often enough wood was available from forests not too far from the vineyards, and the filled barrels could be rolled along, making transport easy. Barrels were replaced only when they became too decrepit to use any more. There was no thought at the time that oak would come to be a component of wine second in importance only to the grape.

Staves are being heated so they can be bent into a barrel, where they are secured by metal rings.

Photograph kindly provided by Taransaud Tonnellerie.

Use of oak not only ensures a certain degree of oxidative exposure, but when the oak is new, it directly transfers flavors to the wine. The big distinction between new oak and previously used oak, and the attention paid to the proportion of new oak, is a phenomenon of the last half century.[38] You see wine described as "matured in 100% new oak" or as using "50% new oak" (meaning that 50% of the barrels were new), because the transmission of flavors is by far the strongest with new oak; the effect is smaller after one year, and by three or four years, a barrel has become a relatively inert storage medium. However, exposure to oxygen is the same irrespective of the age of the barrel.

Barrels come in all shapes and sizes, but the most common is the 225 liter barrique of Bordeaux. For the best quality, planks of oak are seasoned outside for at least two years, and then cut into staves that are bent into barrels. The staves are heated for about 20 minutes to make them pliable. Once the staves have been secured with metal hoops, the barrel is "toasted." Traditionally this was done with an open flame, but today the process is often more precisely controlled by using a specified period of infrared radiation. Toasting is described as light, medium, or heavy, depending on the duration and temperature.[39]

Aromas and flavors derived from oak include coconut, vanillin, butterscotch, cloves, cinnamon, and smokiness.[40] In addition, tannins are extracted to add to those of the grape itself. (These are called ellagitannins, and they tend to be stronger than the grape tannins.) Extraction depends on the length of time the maturing wine spends in oak barrels. A more powerful wine with intense fruit extraction will benefit from longer time in oak than a less powerful wine, where the oak aromas and flavors could overwhelm the fruits. Extraction is also influenced by the level of toasting, which has quite an effect on transfer of flavors to the wine.[41] Toasting enhances some oak flavors and reduces others. Producers are fussy about specifying whether their barrels should have light, medium, or heavy toast.

The origin of the oak makes a big difference. French oak is usually considered the best, because of its tight grain.[42] American oak is a different species,[43] with larger sized pores, and, more to the point, conveys noticeably stronger flavors to the wine. You can detect its use in some New World wines by strong aromas of vanillin, and also in Rioja, where it has traditionally been used rather than French oak. Oak is expensive; barrels of top French oak run about $800 each (which comes to roughly $32 per case of wine). Back in the nineteenth century, Baltic oak was generally used in Bordeaux; recent economic pressure has renewed interest in oak from eastern Europe, although it tends to be sweeter and spicier than French oak (but not as pronounced as American oak).

A producer can play with a lot of parameters when choosing oak. Not only is French oak different from American, but oak from each French forest has its own characteristics. Even the barrels made by different coopers with oak from the same source with the same toasting can give different results; many producers in fact buy barrels from a variety of coopers, and the blend between the wines matured in the different types of barrels adds further complexity to the wine.

The effects of using expensive oak barrels can be mimicked by a range of cheaper options. It's an ongoing debate whether the results are really as good, but it's a rare producer who admits to using staves, chips, or dust, instead of barrels.

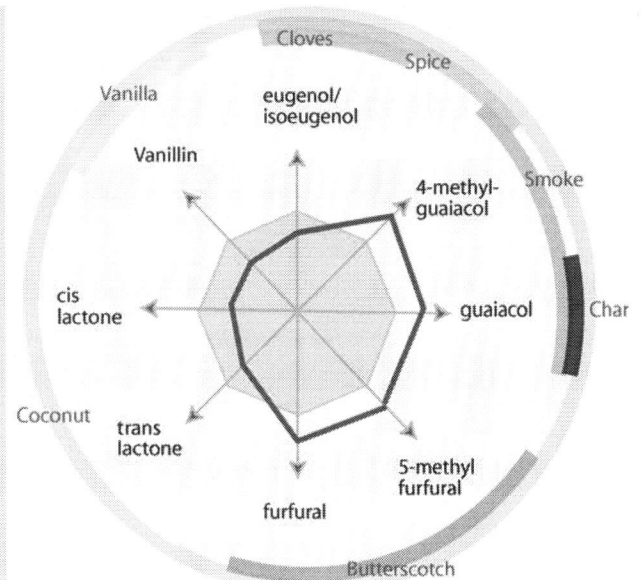

Aromas produced by oak are represented on a spider chart.

The gray octagon at the center shows equal representation of the aroma compounds; the red lines indicate the levels produced by heavy toasting, in which some components have been reduced and others increased.

The aromas associated with each compound are indicated on the circumference.[44]

A barrel room at Château Margaux contains millions of dollars' worth of new oak barriques.

Putting staves of new oak inside vats of stainless steel is the closest to using oak barrels. The planks can be of similar quality to those used in constructing barrels. They can be used to line the tank or simply placed in a matrix at the bottom. A cheaper technique is to suspend cubes of oak or chips (in some sort of bag) inside the fermenting tank. The smaller the format of the oak (chips are smaller than cubes, for example), the quicker the extraction into the wine. Inner staves might need a few months to mimic two years in oak barrels, cubes might need two months, and chips might be effective in only two weeks. Some exposure to air is also necessary to mimic the effects of maturation in barrels; this can be done by micro-oxygenation or other means. There is one possible advantage to the use of alternative oak formats: it's possible to expose red wine to oak during fermentation, thus providing an equivalent to fermenting white wine in barrels.

Just how well do these treatments mimic maturation in oak? The closer you stay to the original, the better you do. One manufacturer of oak beans (cubes) says that "beans, with their barrel-like gradation of color, provide a slow, controlled extraction... Chips offer immediate extraction. However, they usually leave wines with a monochromatic, disjointed flavor profile, along with a harsh and bitter mouth feel."[45] Without going so far, one study by a cooperage firm showed that tasters could detect differences in wines treated with different oak alternatives.[46]

The impetus for using oak alternatives is economic. Inner staves cost the equivalent of $150 per barrel, less than a quarter of the price of the real thing, cubes or chips cost an almost insignificant fraction of that; and of course a further incentive is that the wine can be taken to market much sooner. Going to extremes, you can use oak dust or granules, which are absorbed more or less instantly into the wine; and beyond even that, oak extract, basically a flavoring compound, is available on the market.[47] Indeed, as Michael Broadbent once asked sarcastically in his column in Decanter magazine, why not issue bags of oak with every bottle so that each taster can adjust the wine to his own preference?

Certainly with staves, and perhaps with cubes, good results can be obtained. It's a measure of how much consumers like the taste of oak, and the economics of obtaining it, that the French authorities finally gave way and permitted oak to be used in forms other than barrels. They had no alternative really, given the inroads that New World wines using oak alternatives have made into their traditional markets.[48] But this is a sea change in abandoning traditional values. One reaction was captured by the wine bar owner who said, "[This means] we are going to make wines like we make food at McDonald's."[49]

Why are producers so secretive about use of oak? Wines that are barrel-fermented will say so on the label often enough, back labels will often mention the proportion of new oak or its origins, but producers who use staves, cubes, or chips, will do no more than refer to oak flavors. If the procedure genuinely gives results they consider just as good, if it is nothing to be ashamed of and there is no attempt to trick the consumer, why not state it on the label? Regulations calling for transparency in describing the sources of extraneous flavors would be no bad thing. At least if oak is to be mentioned, the form of application should be stated.

Is it splitting hairs to regard the use of barrels, when some flavors transfer to the wine, as a normal part of maturation, but to raise an eyebrow when oak staves, cubes, chips, or dust are added solely for the purpose of flavoring the wine? If addition of flavoring essences is clearly over the line, where exactly is the line to be drawn?

Put a Cork In It

In most regards, cork is an ideal closure. It is inert, and it retains its elasticity for decades. Granted you have to have a corkscrew to extract it, and it's not always easy to reinsert it, but uncorking offers sommeliers a grand opportunity for pomp and circumstance. The big problem with cork is a contaminant: TCA.

When you open a bottle of wine and you can't detect any fruits on the nose, and then you get a rather musty or moldy, acrid odor of wet cardboard, the reason is most likely that the cork was contaminated with TCA. The wine is *corked*.[50] TCA is one of the most odiferous compounds known to man—most people can smell it at levels of 3 parts per trillion, equivalent to a few drops in a swimming pool—and TCA in the cork rapidly dissolves in the wine underneath it.

Cork is a natural product. It comes from the bark of the cork tree (Quercus suber). The best supplies are in Portugal, which has more than 30% of the world total, and produces more than half of the world's cork. The cork industry is an important economic factor in Portugal; the total value of cork exports is worth more than the value of all Portuguese wine exports![51] The bark can be harvested from a cork tree about once every decade. It comes off in large strips, which are typically seasoned in the forest for about a year and then turned into planks.

They need a fairly extensive cleaning process, which is where some of the problems have occurred.

Natural cork consists of hollow cells containing air, is elastic, and has a non-slip surface that holds it in place in the bottle. Over half the volume of cork is air, which is why it is light and elastic. The cell walls contain suberin, a waxy substance that makes cork water-resistant. The cork is cut into cylinders, the corking machine compresses the cork to fit into the bottleneck, and then after insertion, the cork expands to fill the diameter of the bottleneck.[52] To improve the seal, the cork is coated with paraffin, which repels wine, and with silicone, which acts as a lubricant to ease insertion and extraction.

TCA (2, 4, 6-trichloroanisole) is produced by penicillin fungi that live naturally on cork trees. They act on a group of chlorine-containing compounds (the best known are the chlorophenols) to generate TCA and other compounds related to it.[53] Chlorophenols are used as pesticides and fire retardants, and they can come into contact with cork not only on the trees in the forest but during subsequent processing. One cause of TCA was the use of chlorine to bleach corks during preparation, but now that has been eliminated; even so, there is a certain ineradicable level of natural occurrence. Cork is far and away the most common source of TCA, but the problem can occur in other ways; whole wineries have been infected when penicillin molds have found chlorinated substances in wooden structures, for example. Cork taint typically spoils up to about 6% of bottles at random, but a winery infection can ruin the entire production.

Chlorine cleaning materials are now largely banned in wineries after a series of disasters. Realization of the extent of the problem goes back to the 1980s, when

Cork is harvested from the bark of the tree (left) and then stored as planks (right).

Photographs kindly provided by Amorim.

several French wine producers had large numbers of bottles spoiled by musty odors, too many to be due to individual cases of cork taint. Affected producers were all over the country, including Champagne Roederer, Châteaux Latour, Ducru-Beaucaillou, and Canon in Bordeaux, and producers in Sancerre to the north and Châteauneuf-du-Pape to the south.[54] Pascal Chatonnet, a research scientist at Bordeaux University, who became intrigued when a stainless steel vat at his family winery showed cork-like taint, chased the problem down to contamination of the wineries with chloroanisoles related to TCA.[55] TCA had been identified as the cause of cork taint by a German scientist, Hans Tanner, in 1982,[56] and Chatonnet's work showed that the winery problem was related, but not identical. The cause was usually a persistent contamination of wooden structures in the cellar.

The French producers were not exactly forthcoming about the problem. Critics sometimes pointed to a surprisingly high proportion of spoiled bottles found in tastings, but there was no public acknowledgement, although the châteaux were quietly rebuilding their wineries to eliminate the contaminated material. The full extent of the problem remains unknown, although as many as a quarter of the châteaux of St. Emilion may have had to rebuild their cellars.[57] This was no small undertaking: a contaminated cellar has to be completely destroyed before a new one can be built. It was not until 1998, well after the problem was resolved, that the lid came off in an exposé published jointly in the magazines L'Express and Que Choisir (a consumer review).[58] The authorities seemed to have had no regrets about concealing the problem: "Between a true case of cork taint, concerning 1-2% of bottles, and another taste, [also] described as "corked," more or less serious in individual cases, the consumer could become confused,"[59] says Jean-Louis Trocard, President of the CIVB.* The concern for the consumer is touching, but perhaps it would be better to be confused than to buy bad wine.

A decade later, similar problems surfaced at wineries in Napa Valley. Beaulieu Vineyards had levels of TCA just above the level of detection in its wine from the 1997-1999 vintages, Chalone Vineyards had problems around the same time, and Hanzell Vineyards stopped selling its 2000 Chardonnay because of noticeable TCA levels. The problem at Hanzell turned out to be due to contaminated hoses and drains.[60]

Winery contamination can be a disaster for the individual producer, but cork taint affects a random proportion of every producer's wines. No one knows what the proportion of corked wines was in, say, the first part of the twentieth century, but there is certainly an impression that the proportion has increased in recent decades, presumably due to more widespread use of chlorinated pesticides. Unfortunately, the likelihood of infection has nothing to do with the quality of the cork; the presence of TCA is completely adventitious irrespective of what grade of cork you buy.

---

*Conseil Interprofessionnel du Vin de Bordeaux, the organization representing the producers.

One of the worst aspects is the damage to the producer's reputation, especially when a low level of TCA contamination leaves uncertainty as to the cause of the problem. When TCA is well above the threshold, it's obvious that a bottle is flawed, and even someone who is not knowledgeable about the exact cause will assume that the defect is a one-off. But at TCA levels around the detection threshold, the fruits can be suppressed on the nose and palate without there being overt signs of the characteristic musty odors. Faced with a bottle from an unknown producer, you might easily conclude that this is his style, and he's no good, whereas another bottle might in fact show real quality.

A early as 1982, in his research paper identifying TCA, Hans Tanner proposed a solution: "Replacement of chlorine in the processing of cork should remedy the cork taint problem."[61] You would think the cork producers would be grateful, but not a bit of it. The chairman of Gültig Corks in Portugal reproached Dr. Tanner for giving cork a bad image.[62] The cork industry remained in denial for most of the next two decades. Only after they began to lose significant business to screwcaps did they really try to remedy the problem at source. Progress was partly impeded by the lack of vertical integration in the industry (no firms were involved with all stages of production from forest to cork stopper), making assignment of responsibility difficult, but that has been somewhat counteracted by the growth of Amorim as a leading, vertically-integrated cork producer. Abandoning the use of chlorine in cleaning corks brought the level of TCA contamination down quite a bit, probably to around 2% or so. Some recent techniques allow the corks to be treated to remove volatile compounds, including TCA.[63] Although relatively expensive, this is claimed to have brought the level of contamination below 1%. I am a bit skeptical; it still seems common at tastings to find almost one corked bottle in every other case or so.

In most industries, a rate of 1-2% loss due to poor condition when the goods reach the consumer would be unacceptable, especially when care has been taken to achieve high quality and the damage is due to something completely extraneous, far outside of the producer's control. (Think what would happen to refrigerator manufacturers if 2% of fridges failed, spoiling the food.) The best a wine producer can do with cork is to sample a supply to check that the proportion with TCA is below some limit (most producers use 1%), but there are always some contaminated corks. There are also some losses due to oxidation when a cork seals fails; this does depend on cork quality, and at the lowest levels, oxidation can be just of much of a problem as cork taint.

Cork has its (still) dominant position as the result of history. Imagine the situation if screwcaps had always been used to seal bottles, and a salesman for this new fangled product, cork, tried to sell it to a wine producer.[64] "Cork is a natural product, made from the bark of the tree, by a complicated procedure involving air-drying, washing, and preparation. Every sample is unique because it is slightly different from all the others, and only a small proportion is spoiled by contamination with a highly offensive compound to which people are extraordinarily sensitive. You need a special tool to remove the cork, and this makes it difficult to reseal the bottle" Lots of luck!

Turning the Screw

The screwcap is older than you might think. There are now hundreds of patents for variations of the screwcap used to seal bottles with contents ranging from noxious liquids to water, but the original patent was granted to Dan Rylands in the United Kingdom on August 10, 1889. The first use of screwcaps for alcoholic beverages was for whisky; its introduction by White Horse Distillers in 1926 doubled sales in six months. (Until 1913, whisky bottles were sealed with corks that had to be removed with a corkscrew; the replaceable cork was invented in 1913 by Teacher's, described as 'The Self-Opening Bottle (Patented)," and sold under the slogan "Bury the Corkscrew.")

In the twentieth century, a screwcap was a sign of low quality wine, not necessarily rotgut, but certainly without the pretension of anything bottled under a cork. This changed in 2000, when a group of thirteen winemakers in Australia's Clare Valley, infuriated by damage to their wine, and suspicious (whether justified or not) that they were receiving corks inferior to those available in Europe, started bottling their wines under screwcap.[65] The trend snowballed; still strongest in the New World, where the majority of bottles are closed with screwcaps, it is now being seen more frequently in Europe.

Known in the trade as Stelvins (after the name of the dominant manufacturer), screwcaps got a bad name in the wine industry when early attempts to use them in the 1970s met consumer resistance.[66] Technical trials in Australia, however, produced satisfactory results, so the stage was set for their reintroduction when exasperation with cork taint and oxidation problems passed all bounds. Until the early 2000s, screwcaps remained technically the same as in the 1970s: an outer metal closure that fits on to a thread on the bottle, with an inside liner that fits tight against the top of the bottle to seal the contents.

This matchbox advertising Teacher's whisky shows an early attempt to get rid of the corkscrew.

At first, the wine makers were just relieved to have got away from the problems with cork, and, no doubt, somewhat nervous about consumer acceptance. No one thought much about whether changing the seal on the bottle would have an effect on the wine inside. But it soon became apparent that there can be significant differences between wines bottled under cork or sealed under screwcap.

The main player in investigating the effects of screwcaps has been the AWRI (Australian Wine Research Institute), which started an interesting series of trials when the same wine was bottled in 1997 with different closures. Sample bottles were opened each year to see what differences had developed in taste or chemical composition. It rapidly became clear that the types of closure provide very different levels of seal. Screwcaps are the tightest: less sulfur dioxide gets out of the bottle and less oxygen gets in. They are also very consistent: all screwcaps of the same type give the same result. As you might expect from the old idea that wine "breathes" through the cork, natural corks show more exchange; and individual corks also show somewhat wider variability.[67] As anyone who has bought a case of old wine can attest, that is not a surprise: out of 12 bottles originally all in the same condition, after 10-20 years there will be significant variation in the level of the wine in each bottle. And synthetic corks, made of plastic, showed much the fastest rate of exchange; in fact, by four years after the start of the trial, levels of sulfur dioxide in bottles with synthetic corks were down to the levels at which oxidation becomes overt.

One of the implications of screwcaps' reduced rate of exchange is that you can use less sulfur dioxide at bottling. In fact, it may be essential to do so. A stir was created at the International Wine Challenge in 2006, a competition where more than 9,000 wines were tasted, when many screwcap wines showed rubbery, reductive aromas. (Reductive aromas arise when there is too little oxygen, allowing compounds such as hydrogen sulfide, the smell of rotten eggs, to form.) In fact, 2.2% of the screwcapped wines were spoiled, compared to 4.4% of wine

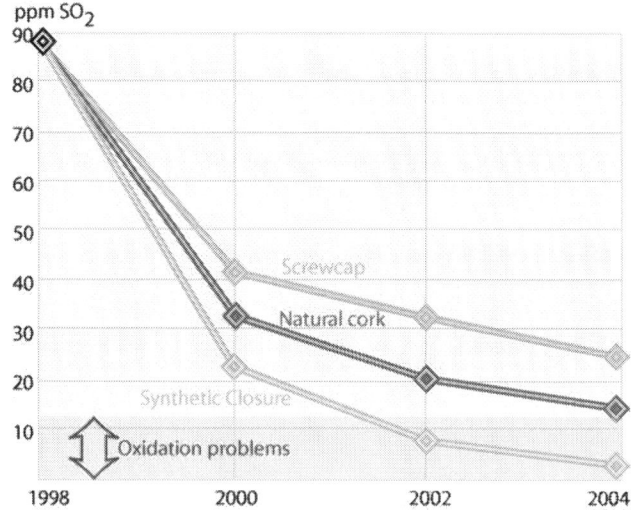

Each type of bottle seal causes the wine to mature at a different rate.[68]

All bottles started with 90 ppm (parts per million) of total sulfur dioxide in December 1997. The level at which oxidation problems start to appear is typically about 12 ppm.

bottled under cork that been tainted or oxidized.[69] However, there's a solution to the problem with screwcaps, which is to use less sulfur dioxide at bottling or to arrange for some subsequent exposure to oxygen.

Tasting comparisons between corks and screwcaps make it perfectly clear that if a wine is going to be consumed within a few months, screwcaps offer a much better chance of drinking it in the original condition that the winemaker intended when he bottled it. There's much less certainty about using screwcaps for wines that are intended for long aging. Part of the concern is that some exposure to oxygen may be necessary for aging—and the recent problems with screwcaps suggest that at a minimum, some oxygen may be needed to avoid reductive problems.

The hot issue of the moment is the OTR—the oxygen transmission rate. This describes the rate at which oxygen gets into the bottle. The variability of natural corks makes this difficult to control. Screwcaps show a level similar to the very tightest corks. The OTR of a screwcap is determined by its liner, the flat cylinder that the metal top compresses against the top of the glass. Research is now taking place to develop new liners that have precisely controlled levels of OTR. The original screwcaps have a layer of metal inside the liner, which makes it basically impermeable. New types of liners are using plastics with defined permeability to oxygen. In the near future, a producer who decides that his Sauvignon Blanc should be kept fresh for rapid consumption will be able to choose a screwcap with a minimal OTR, whereas a producer who is selling a Cabernet Sauvignon intended for long aging would be able to choose a screwcap with an OTR that he thinks is appropriate for development of this wine.

And what of synthetic corks, those molded plastic closures that can be so difficult to get out with an ordinary corkscrew? They certainly did not come out well from the AWRI study. And excessive passage of oxygen is not the only problem. They have a tendency to "scalp" wine, to extract volatile compounds from it that are part of its usual character. Riesling, for example, often shows petrol-like aromas that are due to the presence of a compound called TDN.[70] When TDN levels were measured in bottles two years after the same wine was put under different closures, screwcapped bottles kept all their TDN, corks retained about half—but synthetic corks had less then 5% left.[71] But they are improving all the time, and efforts are being made to develop synthetic corks with controlled OTR, and to make them more neutral to avoid scalping. However, right now they remain suitable only for wine that will be rapidly consumed.

All of which brings us to the question of ageing, and whether oxygen is really necessary. The idea that oxidation is an intrinsic part of ageing goes back to Pasteur, and was widely accepted until the mid-twentieth century. Since then there has been a split. Surveys of winemakers show they continue to believe oxidation is needed for ageing. But most expert technical opinion argues that ageing takes place in reductive conditions. "Reactions in bottled wine do not require oxygen," said Pascal Ribéreau-Gayon.[72] "It is the opposite of oxidation, a process of reduction or asphyxia, by which wine develops in the bottle," according to Emile Peynaud.[73]

Yet there is surprisingly little scientific evidence. The myth here is not that oxygen is, or is not, involved in ageing: the myth it is that we really know what is involved. The AWRI's comparisons between corks and screwcaps opened up the whole issue by demonstrating that the closure is not necessarily inert, and that wine ages differently depending on how much oxygen is available to it. The real question is what's the optimum amount of oxygen for a wine to age to reach its maximum potential? No one has done a definitive experiment. If it were up to me, I would bottle wine under natural cork and under screwcap, and I would keep one set of bottles under normal conditions, and the other set under nitrogen. This would show definitively whether oxygen was needed and whether there is any difference between cork and screwcap aside from oxygen permeability. All of the recent demonstrations of reductive problems in screwcapped wines suggest that a rather small amount of oxygen exposure may be needed for great wines to develop their potential.

Sparkling wine is a completely different case. Bottled under several atmospheres of pressure, with a metal cage to ensure the cork cannot come out, there is no prospect of oxygen seeping into the bottle. (Great Champagne can age in the bottle, but the processes do not depend on oxidation.) Cork isn't completely sacrosanct, because some New World sparkling wines have been bottled under crown caps (the same sort of closure used for beer bottles), but Champagne and all European sparkling wine have stayed resolutely under cork. But now a new alternative threatens this last sanctuary of the cork. Alcan, a major force in screwcaps with their dominant Stelvin closure, spent a million euros developing a new closure for sparkling wine. A lever ejects a plastic cork from the bottle, specially engineered to maintain the satisfactory popping sound of a traditional cork.[74] The lever closure is being tried on Duval-Leroy Champagne on an experimental basis; it remains to be seen whether the original cork will be threatened.

Screwcaps are widely accepted in Australia and New Zealand, but European consumers don't like screwcaps, or at least, when asked about preferences they

In this new Champagne closure, the traditional foil cover extends over the lever at the right, which opens the bottle.

tend to choose natural cork, going back to the old view that screwcaps are associated with lower quality. Resistance remains strongest in Continental Europe, but in the U.K. has slowly given way to the predominance of screwcaps in New World wines, although there is still resistance to using screwcaps for red wines intended for aging. And these days it's not always so easy to tell the difference: screwcap packaging is getting better and better, and the latest version from Stelvin uses a soft insert around the threads under the foil capsule, so at a casual glance there is a little difference from a bottle under cork. Indeed, no one has ever done the critical survey of consumer tastes, which is to ask whether people *knew* whether a bottle was sealed by screwcap or cork when they bought it.

"God Made the Wine"

Some vignerons would lead you to believe that they are merely the agent of the Almighty in converting grape juice to wine. But wine is a human invention. "God made only water, but man made wine," said Victor Hugo.[75]

True enough, if there were no interference, the level of sugar in the grapes would determine the level of alcohol in the wine. But how many wines actually have "natural" alcohol levels between the Scylla of chaptalization and the Charybdis of watering back (or other adjustments)? Except for wines made from exceptionally ripe, late harvest grapes, all wine naturally would be dry; how many sweet wines owe their sweetness entirely to nature? Winemaking more naturally is oxidative than reductive; special precautions are needed to exclude oxygen, but how much oxidation is experienced depends very much on the way the wine is handled. The aromas, flavors, and structural components that wines obtain from oak may meld seamlessly with the product of the grape itself, but you have to recognize that their origin is extrinsic to the grape. Even how you bottle (or otherwise package) the wine will affect how it smells and tastes just a couple of months later. Winemaking is intrinsically an interventionist activity.

7

A Thousand Cultivars Bloom

THERE IS A HUGE DISCREPANCY between the large diversity of Vitis vinifera varieties and the increasing focus in winemaking on a small number of internationally recognized varieties.

Roughly 10,000 distinct varieties of Vitis vinifera are known. About half are found in France or Spain, with most of the rest in Italy, Greece, and Eastern Europe, reflecting their long wine-growing histories and emphasis on domesticating or developing grape varieties. Most of these are varieties that have arisen naturally since Vitis was domesticated. Varieties that have originated in the Americas are more recent, as are many of the varieties in Germany (which have been bred for adaptation to cool-climate conditions).

Several hundred varieties are used to make significant amounts of wine, but fewer than a hundred or so varieties account for half of all plantings. Among these leading varieties, fewer than twenty account for a quarter of the world's vineyards. The concentration of plantings into the leading international varieties has intensified over the past two decades, but this does not necessarily represent a significant loss of diversity in wine since the varieties that have declined are by no means high quality. The top positions on the world planting list are now split between quality varieties and the remnants of the old bulk plantings.

Cabernet Sauvignon now is the most widely planted black varietal in the world, followed closely by Merlot and Grenache (although this latter is far from being uniformly treated as a quality variety). The most striking change in the past twenty years is an almost three-fold increase in Syrah, which was not anywhere near the top ten list in 1990. The area of Carignan, which rarely gives wine of any quality, has halved.

The world's most planted white wine grape remains Airén, a completely nondescript source of white wine in Spain.[1] But its plantings have dropped dramatically since 1990, when it was far and away the most widely planted grape in the world. Chardonnay was not even in the top ten in 1990, but is now

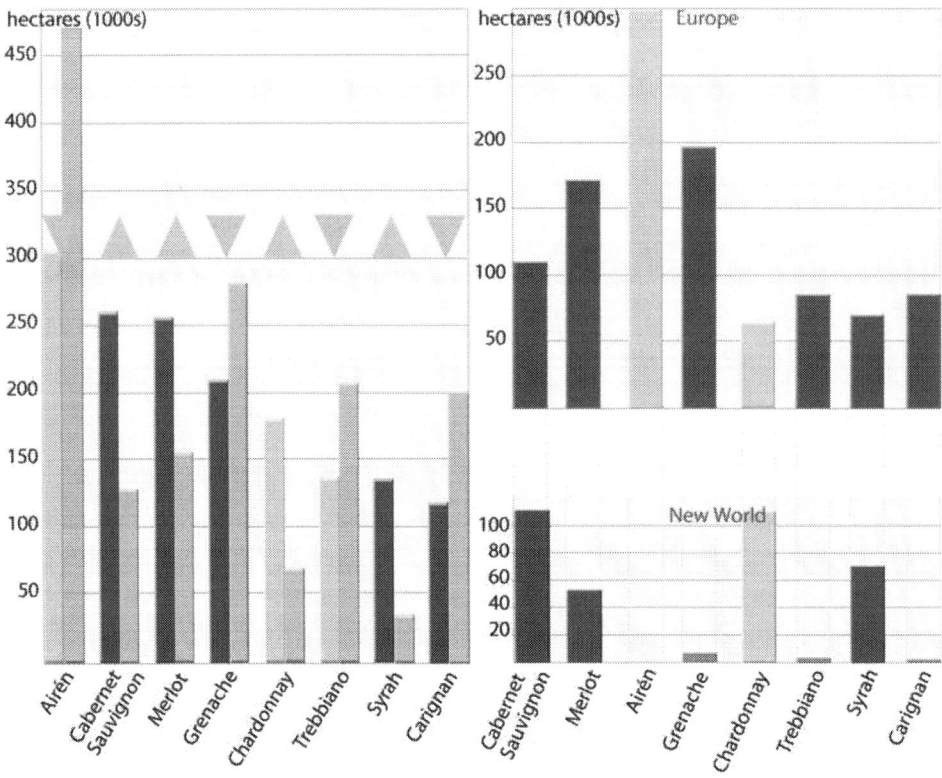

Plantings of the leading varieties changed greatly between 1990 and 2004 (left). Red and yellow show hectares in 2004 and gray shows hectares in 1990. Pink triangles indicate a decrease; green triangles indicate an increase.[2] The top varieties are different in Europe and the New World (right).[3]

the world's leading quality white grape. There is still plenty of Trebbiano (Ugni Blanc), although quite a bit of it is used to make wine for distillation into brandy rather than for drinking.

There's a great difference in distribution of these varieties between the Old World and New World.[4] In spite of attempts at what the French call "cépage amelioration" (improving the types of planted varieties), Europe is still stuck with large quantities of the old bulk production varieties, led by Airén and Trebbiano (Ugni Blanc) in the whites, and Carignan in the blacks. In the New World, where most plantings date from the last two decades, the motto has been "plant the usual suspects." Cabernet Sauvignon production is now split more or less equally between New World and Europe, and there is actually more Chardonnay in the New World than in Europe. The detritus of Airén, Trebbiano, and Carignan is completely missing from the New World. Is this part of the reason why the Old World producers are struggling so hard for market share in the global economy?

Noble Varieties and Commoners

The range of grape varieties is immense, from household names to obscurities known to only a few remaining growers. Going back to the glory days when France *was* wine, its best grapes were called the noble varieties: Cabernet Sauvignon, Merlot, Pinot Noir, basically representing Bordeaux and Burgundy for the reds; and Chardonnay, Riesling, and Sauvignon Blanc for the whites, with more diverse origins.

The criteria for a noble variety are that it should have an international reputation, and that the quality of its top wines can be demonstrated by their aging potential. By this measure, there is no doubt about the position of the first five. Depending on whether your allegiance is to Bordeaux or Burgundy, you might

Grape varieties form a quality tree, with a small group of noble varieties broadening into groups making classic wines, groups that can be interesting (more could be added to this list), a very large number of indifferent varieties (not shown), and the old bulk production varieties right at the bottom.

Noble Varieties

Cabernet Sauvignon	Chardonnay
Merlot	Riesling
Pinot Noir	Sauvignon Blanc

Classic Varieties

Cabernet Franc	Chenin Blanc
Nebbiolo	Gewürztraminer
Sangiovese	Sémillon
Syrah	Viognier
Tempranillo	
Touriga Nacional	

Interesting Varieties

Barbera	Albariño
Carmenère	Aligoté
Dolcetto	Cortese
Gamay	Garganega
Grenache	Grüner Veltliner
Malbec	Marsanne
Montepulciano	Muscadet
Mourvèdre	Pinot Blanc
Pedro Ximénez	Pinot Gris
Petit Verdot	Roussanne
Tannat	Muscat Blanc à Petit Grains
Touriga Franca	Friulano
Zinfandel	Torrontés
	Verdejo

No Name Varieties

Alicante Bouschet	Airén
Aramon	Bourboulenc
Bobal	Chasselas
Carignan	Clairette
Cinsault	Crouchen
Lambrusco	Folle Blanche
	Malvasia
	Trebbiano

regard Cabernet Sauvignon-Merlot blends or Pinot Noir as the epitome of red wine; and although Chardonnay today is far and away the best known quality white grape, a century ago Riesling was held in higher esteem, as judged by auction prices in London. All of these varieties produce very high quality wines in multiple locations. But I would question whether Sauvignon Blanc really belongs in this group. Vinified as a monovarietal, it's a rare Sauvignon Blanc that ages well; blended with Sémillon, it makes some great white wines in Bordeaux, but the number with high aging potential is miniscule—I can count them on my fingers.

Those who feel that this traditional list shows an outdated bias towards France have a point. The most obvious omission from the list of noble black grapes is Syrah, which actually has long made wines of the highest quality in the northern Rhône, but really is if anything more prominent now under its Australian name of Shiraz. Wines from Syrah (or Shiraz) or blends based on it can show as much complexity as the noble black varieties and can age as well. I would certainly include Syrah in the very top group.

Other varieties that can reach equivalent quality, but in a more geographically restricted way, include Cabernet Franc (back to Bordeaux again), Nebbiolo (who can quarrel with the assertion that Barolo can be as great a red wine as any?), Sangiovese (where Brunello di Montalcino has reached its peak in recent years), Tempranillo (the basis for the great Riojas), and Touriga Nacional (perhaps a special case since its greatest role is achieved in Port, which after all is fortified). Among the whites, claims could made for Chenin Blanc, Gewürztraminer, Viognier, although none is quite so convincing.

The existence of some great wines made from these varieties has given them an international reputation. However, all attempts have failed at reproducing the qualities of Nebbiolo, Sangiovese, or Tempranillo outside of their native habitats, preventing them from joining the list of true "international varieties." Some people say the same about Pinot Noir, but that would be to provoke an argument.

There's a sizeable group of interesting varieties, which from time to time make really good wine, although most of the production is at a much lower level, and there's a huge number of fairly indifferent varieties. The joker in the pack is a large number of indigenous grapes that can make interesting wines in their local conditions, although for one reason or another they have failed to penetrate the outside world. A sizeable bunch of no-name varieties make large amounts of wine, but you don't often see these varietal names on the label; it's rare indeed that there's anything of interest.

A handful of varieties make great wines in very special circumstances, but only in those circumstances. Palomino Fino makes great Sherry, but is pretty indifferent as a dry white wine. To quote Jancis Robinson, Palomino makes a potentially great style of wine, but is not inherently a great grape. Malvasia under its synonym of Malmsey has been known to make great Madeira, but otherwise is of little interest. Sémillon achieves greatness principally for its role in the blend of sweet wines such as Sauternes. And I admire the effort, but have been unconvinced by attempts to produce quality wine from old Carignan vines.

Ancient Origins and Newbies

Originally all grapes were black. Color is due to production of the anthocyanin pigments in the skin. Grapevines producing white grapes arose by mutations inactivating the production of anthocyanins. Most major white cultivars have the same mutation, which suggests that the distinction between black and white grapevines must have occurred early in the evolution of the grapevine.[5] Of course, white varieties continue to arise, sometimes by new mutations inactivating the anthocyanin genes.

Today's grapevines can be grouped into sixteen clusters that fall into four general groups. Each group has a geographical bias but there is overlap between the groups, indicating that grapevines were often transported from their sites of origin to new locations. Three of the clusters of the French group contain wild grapevines, suggesting that the traditional French cultivars are closest to the ancestral grapevine (Vitis vinifera silvestris).[7] Two groups contain principally eastern Mediterranean or central European varieties. The group of table grapes is genetically distant from the wine grapes and wild grapes; they probably originated from intense selection during ancient agriculture. Virtually all of the modern grapes with international reputations belong to one of the clusters in the French group.

Grapes have been grown in most of their present locations in Europe for between one and two thousand years. But the names and descriptions of the

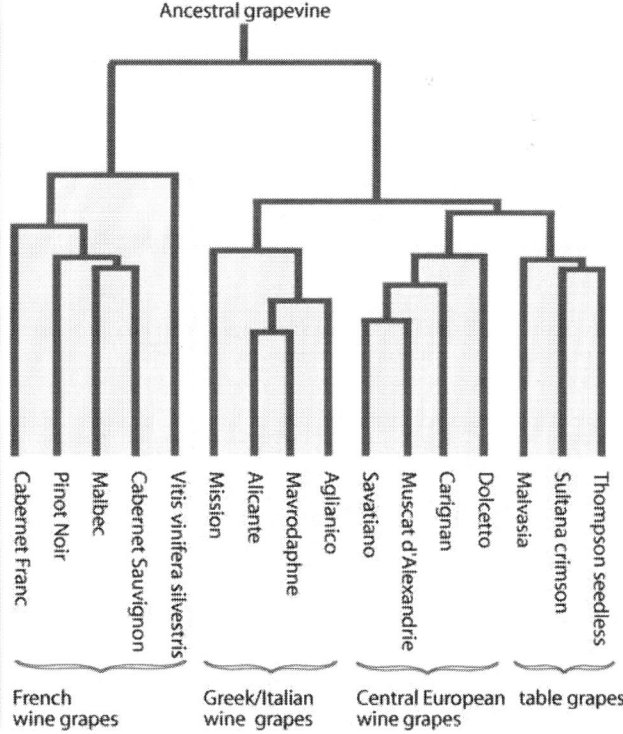

Genetic relationships between cultivars identify four groups: three groups of wine grapes and one group of table grapes.[6]

Branch points show how far back in evolution each cluster diverged.

The 16 individual clusters in the groups vary in size from 4 to 33 cultivars and/or wild grapevines; one representative member of each cluster is named.

varieties grown one or two millennia ago cannot be equated with modern varieties. Indeed, some of the modern varieties, such as Cabernet Sauvignon, Merlot, or Chardonnay are relatively recent arrivals on the scene; they were generated by spontaneous crosses between existing varieties at points in the last five or six hundred years. The oldest of the modern varieties can be traced back to the medieval period. The two most anciently established of the important varieties grown today are Nebbiolo and Pinot Noir. Nebbiolo wins for the oldest known description by a short head (a mere century or so).

It's generally thought that Nebbiolo originated in Piedmont and that its name refers to the nebbia, the local fog forming in the Piedmont hills in the autumn. Several references from the thirteenth century probably identify this variety growing in Piedmont. The Rivoli estate (located in what is now a suburb of Turin) described production of 300 sextaries of wine made from "nibiol" vineyards in 1268.[8] "Neblori" and "nebiolo" are mentioned in documents from 1292 in Alba and 1295 in Asti.[9] There is a continuous stream of subsequent references to the importance of the grape, and it is viewed as the highest quality grape of the region in a famous treatise of 1606.[10]

Pinot Noir is thought to be one of the most ancient varieties, and it is believed that it may have been cultivated in Burgundy from the fourteenth century, although real evidence for its origins is pretty scanty. A grape called Pinot, presumably Pinot Noir, possibly previously known as Noiren, was first mentioned in Burgundy in 1375.[11] In the closely related group of Pinot varieties, Pinot Noir is the ancestral parent, and several different Pinot Blanc clones arose as independent mutants.[12] Indeed, most recently one occurred in the vineyards of Henri Gouges in Nuits St. Georges where it is used to produce a white wine.[13]

Riesling is another old variety, possibly dating back to 1348, to a reference to "Russelinge" in a map in Alsace, but almost certainly known by 1435 when "Riesslingen" grapes were purchased near Hochheim in the Rheingau.[14]

Romantic fancies have wonderfully embroidered the real origins of Syrah. The resemblance between the identity of its alternative name, Shiraz, with the city of the same name in Iran has provoked theories that the grape may have originated in Persia, and was brought to France by the Romans. An early nineteenth century catalog of French grape varieties repeated the local tradition that "Seyras" was originally brought from Shiraz by a hermit who resided in Hermitage.[15] However, DNA fingerprinting shows that it originated in a cross between Dureza (found in the Ardèche region on the west bank of the Rhône) and Mondeuse (a grape of Savoie, well to the east).[16] This places its origins in France, well away from the romance of the East.[17]

Sangiovese is another grape attracting some amusing theories. Translation of the name as "blood of Jove" spawned proposals that it dates from the days of Rome. Soderini mentioned a grape called Sangiogheto in Tuscany in 1590, but there is no proof this was Sangiovese.[18] By the eighteenth century, there are references to Sangiovese as being one of the most planted grapes in Tuscany (together with Malvasia and Trebbiano).[19] DNA mapping identifies the parents of Sangiovese as Ciliegiolo, a Tuscan grape, and Calabrese Montenuovo, a grape from the south.[20] When and where this cross occurred is unknown.

Cépage Plus Terroir Equals Typicité

Or does it? The case for typicity is that each cépage grows best in a specific terroir; the combination brings out unique characteristics of the wine that the French call *typicité*. At its ultimate, the argument supposes that a cépage may be capable of giving its best results in only one place. The case against is that the association of particular qualities with specific combinations of cultivar and place is no more than a historical accident, that the same cultivars can be grown elsewhere; the fact that the wine may be different from historical impressions merely reflects the fact that it produces different results in different conditions.

Certainly some varieties are difficult to grow successfully away from their traditional locales: Pinot Noir is closely associated with Burgundy, Tempranillo with Spain, Nebbiolo and Sangiovese with Piedmont and Tuscany.

Growing Pinot Noir elsewhere to give wines like those of Burgundy has been a holy grail of winemakers; and the quest has yet to be fulfilled. Yet excellent wines are made from Pinot Noir in New Zealand, in Oregon, and more recently in Germany. Do we say they fail to show the typicité of Pinot Noir because they are not easily confused with the wines of Burgundy; or do we say that if history had been different, and Pinot Noir had been grown first in New Zealand, we would regard Burgundian Pinot Noir as failing to achieve New World richness?

There is to date a pretty good case that Nebbiolo gives good results only in Piedmont, at its peak in the regions of Barolo and Barbaresco, and that Sangiovese gives top results only in Tuscany, at its best in Brunello di Montalcino. Efforts to reproduce these wines by growing the varieties elsewhere have so far failed, making a case for saying these cépages have indeed found a unique match with their terroir.

Tempranillo is an ambiguous example. This great grape of Rioja has not been grown successfully outside of Spain, but it has certainly been widely propagated in Spanish regions other than Rioja in the past couple of decades. Is this a case where it has been possible to produce wines with the same typicité in new regions, or one where we have accepted changes in the style of the varietal wine as its boundaries have expanded?

Some varieties are more easily transportable. Cabernet Sauvignon originated in Bordeaux, Syrah originated in the northern Rhône, Chardonnay may have originated in Burgundy. But all now have reputations based on wines made all over the world. New World versions tend to be richer, fuller-bodied, more powerful, more alcoholic than those of Europe, but it is an exceptional taster indeed who can guarantee consistently to distinguish Old and New World wines of these varieties in a blind tasting.

Steven Spurrier's famous "Judgment of Paris" tasting in 1976 makes the case forcefully. This was a blind wine tasting held in Paris when French judges compared Napa Valley Chardonnays and Cabernet Sauvignons with white Burgundy and red Bordeaux. The judges, a distinguished group of top tasters, were confident they could tell the difference, that the contest was not at all serious, and that they had identified the French wines as superior. There was an outcry when the results were tallied and Napa wines came top in both categories; some judges tried to take back their results.[21] The French press ignored or denigrated the results, but journalist George Taber reported the results in Time magazine; not surprisingly, quite a fuss resulted in the United States. The tasting is regarded as a pivotal moment in international acceptance of California wines, but the point is not so much which wines "won" the tasting, but the fact that the judges were completely confused as to which wines originated in France and which in California. What price typicité?

Yet there is a difference. The slightly herbaceous aroma and flavor spectrum of a traditional Bordeaux is distinct from, say, the intense blackcurrant fruits and aromaticity of a Barossa Cabernet Sauvignon. But wait: note that I said a "traditional" Bordeaux. It is not so easy to distinguish today's wines from the left Bank of Bordeaux from those made in California's Napa valley or in South Australia. Warmer climatic conditions and a trend to later harvesting have led to Cabernet Sauvignon in Bordeaux that often more resembles a New World Cabernet Sauvignon than a wine from Bordeaux of fifty years ago. So what's the typicité of Cabernet Sauvignon and has our view of it changed from herbaceous to fruity?

White pepper used to be regarded as part of the typicity of Hermitage, but this is actually a characteristic of Syrah before it reaches full ripeness; today's Hermitage is more often closer to the spectrum of aromatic black fruits found in Shiraz from Barossa Valley. Chardonnay, that most malleable of varieties, takes its character as much from winemaking style as from origin of the grapes; I defy anyone to define typicité for Chardonnay, since even within its traditional Burgundian home there is a great difference between a steely, mineral, unoaked Chablis, and a fat, nutty, buttery Meursault full of new oak from the Côte d'Or.

The aromas and flavor spectrum of each varietal are influenced greatly by ripeness. Perhaps there is a slightly less than ripe typicité for Cabernet Sauvignon (such as traditional Bordeaux) and a fully ripe typicité (as found in the New World). Is the difference between Cabernet Sauvignon and Pinot Noir that we have accepted a change in typicité for the former but are reluctant to do so for the latter?

The Bitterness of the Super-taster

Smell is vastly more complicated than taste. You can distinguish probably around a thousand odors, using hundreds of different types of receptors for odors in the human nose, but there are only five different types of receptors for taste on the tongue.[22] It used to be thought that receptors for different tastes are located in different areas of the tongue, but we now know that a single taste bud contains up to a hundred taste cells and has receptors for all five taste types (sour, salt, bitter, sweet, unami [savory]). Basically the taste of any one of these groups can be distinguished from another, but two tastes in the same group (such as two bitter compounds) cannot be distinguished. More of the complexity of wine is due to its smell than to its taste, although this may not be obvious as the two senses mingle when a wine is tasted. People's abilities to smell and taste vary widely. How far does this bring into question the whole idea of describing wines in a way that is universally meaningful?

We have known for almost a century that individuals' sense of smell differ widely (the first report concerned differences in ability to detect the aroma of verbena).[23] Recent scientific discoveries show that odors are detected by a vast set of receptors with overlapping sensitivities, so a particular odor may be recognized by several different receptors with different sensitivities to it, whereas taste receptors are nonoverlapping (with the sole exception of a partially shared receptor for sweet and unami). Odor receptor genes in the human population vary more widely than taste receptor genes.[24]

Individual capacity to detect specific odorants can vary greatly.[25] Sometimes the same aroma is perceived differently, such as androstenone which some people find unpleasant (urine-like), but others detect as sweet and floral. It's noticeable when people describe wines that their terminology for taste (for example, for sweetness or alcohol levels) is more consistent than their descriptions of aromas, where different people may well use different terms to describe the same odors, often reflecting the fact that the odorant is found in many different sources in nature. When you add these differences in description to differences in detection, it becomes complicated to provide an objective description. But scientific analysis comes to the rescue: many of the characteristic aromas of specific varietals can be identified with particular chemical components, whose concentrations can be measured.

Judging from the number of genes devoted to each type of taste, bitterness may be the most important. There are 25 different genes coding for receptors for bitter compounds, compared with 3 genes responsible for both sweet and unami tastes.[26] (The receptors for salty and sour tastes have not been unequivocally identified.) There is significant variation in ability to taste unami, and generally less variation in sensitivity to sweet, salty, and sour.[27] The widest range comes in sensitivity to bitterness, which is important because bitterness is often associated with toxic compounds.[28]

One of the first insights into taste differences came in the early 1930s when Dupont chemist Arthur Fox accidentally released some PTC (phenylthiourea) in his laboratory. A colleague reacted to the bitter taste, but Fox himself could not detect it.[29] In fact, about 70% of people taste bitterness in the compound. It turns out that this difference is due to a single gene; you can taste PTC as long as you have one active copy of the gene.[30] Although a quarter of the population can't taste PTC, the sensation of bitterness for those who can taste is affected by various factors other than the gene itself, so when tasters are tested, there is a more or less continuous range of sensitivities.

The PTC gene codes for a receptor that binds a set of related chemical compounds, all of which trigger the bitter sensation. Among them is a chemical called PROP,[31] which is now routinely used to test for ability to sense bitterness. Testing with PROP shows that some people are extremely sensitive to it. This sensitivity correlates with a need to add sweetening to counteract the perception of bitterness; in fact, it defines a category of people who have significantly enhanced sensitivity to bitterness. These so-called super-tasters make up about 20%

of the population.[32] The story in the wine world goes that super-tasters can be recognized by taking sugar and cream in their coffee, finding red wine too bitter to enjoy, preferring slightly sweet white or rosé (white Zinfandel is their favorite tipple), finding that artificial sweeteners have a bitter metallic taste, and (where information is available) the occurrence of morning sickness in their mothers.[33]

The larger puzzle for wine drinkers, however, is why enhanced sensitivity to PTC or PROP should imply a difficulty with handling tannins in red wine (or caffeine in coffee), since PTC and PROP are chemically different from tannins or caffeine.[34] No one has systematically tested what range of bitter compounds respond to the PTC receptor, but certainly the super-taster phenomenon seems to have a big influence on tastes in wine.[35]

It's clear that super-tasters have an exaggerated response to bitter compounds, but it's not entirely clear why. They have a higher density than usual of the cells containing taste receptors on the tongue.[38] The usual test for a super-taster is to apply a little blue food coloring to the tongue; the taste buds stand out as bumps in the middle of the blue stain, and you simply count how many there are per square centimeter; roughly speaking, a tolerant taster (not sensitive to bitter taste) has about 50, an average taster has about 100, and a super-taster has about 150. You can apply the test to yourself simply by placing a paper cut-out on the tongue and applying the blue dye to the circle in the center.

But this has never completely made sense, because an increased number of receptors would predict increased sensitivity to all tastes, not just to bitterness. Indeed, it turns out that super-tasters are more sensitive to a range of bitter compounds (not just those recognized by any one bitter receptor) and also to salty, sweet, and sour tastes.[39] In fact, if you define super-tasters as people with

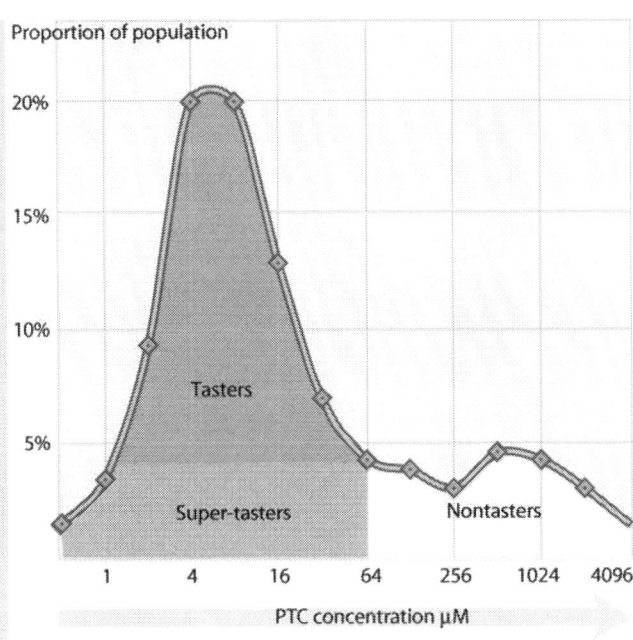

Measuring the threshold level at which people can taste PTC classifies those requiring >64 μM as nontasters.[36]

Super-tasters are defined by their psychological response rather than by the threshold, and comprise about a third of all tasters.[37]

 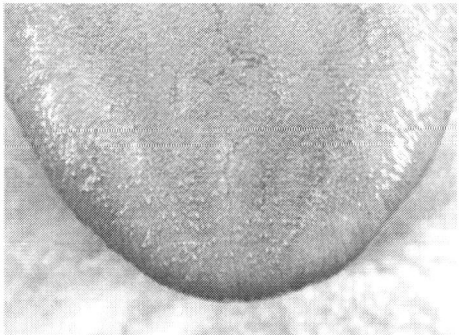

Super-tasters (left) have a much greater density of taste buds, shown by the blue stain, than normal tasters (right). Photographs kindly provided by Tim Hanni MW.

heightened sensitivity to all tastes, PROP isn't the only or best stimulus that reveals them. Super-tasters have been specifically diagnosed from the population of PTC/PROP tasters, but the basis for super-tasting remains undefined. It's possible that the effect depends on the way taste stimuli are interpreted by the brain rather than on the sensitivity of detection. There is in fact no scientific definition of super-tasters: they are basically people who self-diagnose extreme reactions to bitter compounds.[40]

By contrast, differences in detecting sweetness are only about 10-fold (compared with 10,000-fold for bitter), but a major part seems to be due to variation in the amount of a sweet receptor. People who have less of this receptor are less sensitive to sugar.[41]

Most attention is focused on the fact that super-tasters report disagreeable sensations when they drink red wine, but the real implication for wine tasting is that everyone's reaction will be different, depending on exactly where they are along the curves for detecting bitterness and sweetness. Super-tasters are simply the extreme end of the distribution.

Just to add to the puzzle, tannins are usually detected more by astringency than by taste. Astringency is a feeling (not a taste) due to a tactile sensation, created (for example) by tannins when they bind to salivary proteins in the mouth. Super-tasters don't seem to have any increased sensitivity to astringency.[42]

What does all this mean for objectivity in describing the aromas or the bitterness or sweetness of a wine?[43] Should there be a standard for calibrating critics?

Aromas of Grapes and Wine

If you try to classify grape varieties into groups, the criteria owe as much or more to smell as to taste. Certainly acidity and fruit flavors come into it, but the first measure for identifying an unknown wine tends to be its aroma.

Red wines are most often grouped according to whether they convey an impression of red fruit or black fruit. Among the red fruit group, Sangiovese and Nebbiolo usually convey a savory rather than overtly fruity impression, and this can be true also of Pinot Noir and Tempranillo. Among the black fruit group, there's a gradation from herbaceous, to fruity, to overtly aromatic. Some grapes might move from one group to another, depending on their degree of ripeness: Cabernet Sauvignon, for example, tends to be herbaceous when under-ripe but can be jammy when over-ripe.

White wines divide into neutral and aromatic by flavor profile. Some neutral whites have a real affinity for oak, and can be greatly enhanced by time spent in wood, when the oak flavors may come to be as important a part of the profile as the grape flavors themselves. It is less common for aromatic varieties to be exposed to wood. At one extreme, Sauvignon Blanc can be "grassy" or herbaceous; at the other, Muscat (or its relative Torrontés) are rare varieties that actually show grapey aromas.

More than a thousand volatile compounds contributing to aromas have been found in wine.[44] (This compares with a mere fifty volatile aromas in coffee.[45]) The characteristic aroma and flavor spectrum of any wine is due to complex interactions between these components, but as we learn more about smell and taste, often the dominant characteristics of a grape variety can be identified with a few components. The herbaceous qualities of Cabernet Sauvignon or Sauvignon Blanc, those petrol notes of Riesling, the pepper of Syrah, the lychees of

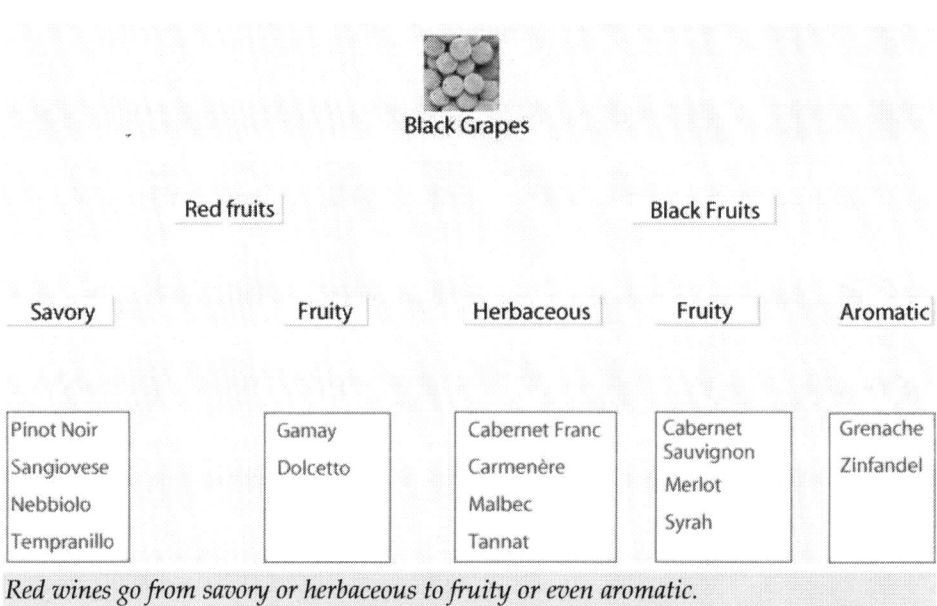

Red wines go from savory or herbaceous to fruity or even aromatic.

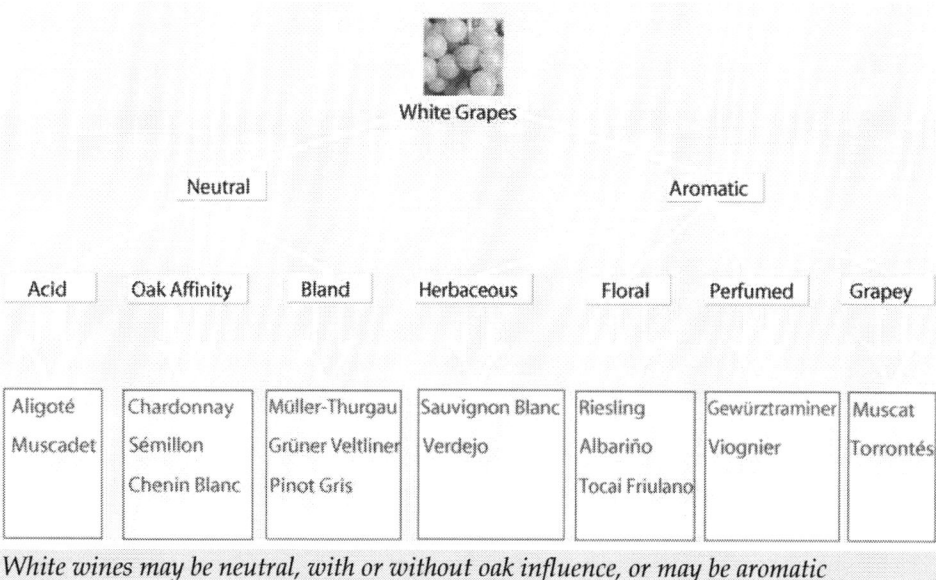

White wines may be neutral, with or without oak influence, or may be aromatic

Gewürztraminer, for example, each resides in particular molecules. Knowing the conditions that favor or disfavor the formation of these components opens up a whole new range of possibilities for influencing wine flavor.

This knowledge reinforces the usefulness of describing wines by their aromas. To the outsider, it may seem fanciful, even pretentious, to say that Cabernet Sauvignon offers an impression of bell peppers, that Sauvignon Blanc shows traces of asparagus and passion fruit, that Pinot Noir is characterized by overtones of earthy strawberries, or to find suggestions of chocolate or coffee in a wine—but finding that the wines have traces of the same chemical components contributing to the characteristics of the fruits or vegetables validates the approach.

The compounds that contribute to flavor and aroma are a dizzying array of chemical types, including thiols (sulfur-containing compounds), esters (formed by reaction between alcohols and acids), and terpenes (hydrocarbons formed by a wide variety of plants, which take their generic name from turpentine). Sometimes the compounds responsible for the characteristic aromas of a grape variety are found in the grape itself (Muscat is a classic example), but more often they are generated during fermentation and maturation, sometimes by directly converting an inactive precursor in the grape into an active odorant, sometimes as the result of a more complex pathway catalyzed by yeast. Some aromas and flavors develop only with bottle aging. And of course some have an extraneous source, the oak of the barrels in which the wine is matured.

Many grape varieties have characteristic aromas of fruits or vegetables that are due to specific identified compounds.

Grape Variety	Aroma	Compounds	Type
Pinot Noir	strawberry	Ethyl acetate, ethyl butyrate, ethyl formate, ethyl hexanoate, furaneol, methyl cinnamate	esters
Cabernet Sauvignon	bell pepper	3-isobutyl-2-methoxy-pyrazine	pyrazine
Syrah	pepper	Rotundone	
	blueberry		
Sauvignon Blanc	gooseberry	4-MMP (4-mercapto-4-methyl-pentan-2-one) (effect depends on concentration)	thiol
	passion fruit, cat's pee		
Riesling	petrol	TDN (1,6 trimethyl-1,2-dihydronaphthalene)	
Gewürztraminer	lychees	*cis*-rose oxide	ester
Muscat	grapes	Geraniol	terpene
Sémillon	figs	ethyl propionate, isobutyl acetate	esters
Carbonic maceration, e.g. Gamay	bananas	isoamyl acetate	esters
Botrytized wines	honey	Sotolon	lactone

It depends a lot on the varietal how much difference yeast make at fermentation. For aromatic varieties such as Sauvignon Blanc, where they play a key role in releasing aromas, the effect is much greater than for neutral varieties. Don't be fooled into thinking yeasts are only machines for converting sugar to alcohol.

Winemaking conditions can therefore have a strong influence on varietal character. For example, thiol compounds are reducing agents, so it follows that their properties are emphasized by winemaking under reductive conditions and minimized under oxidative conditions. This particular aspect of winemaking becomes of prime importance for varieties such as Sauvignon Blanc where a large part of the aroma is provided by thiols.

Aroma and flavors in wine may be generated at any stage of vinification.

Source	Influenced by	Example
Grapes	Berry ripeness	Herbaceousness (bell peppers) in Cabernet Sauvignon
Released from grape precursors during fermentation	Strain of yeast	Gooseberry/passion fruit aromas in Sauvignon Blanc
Created by yeast during fermentation	Strain of yeast	Esters (isoamyl acetate) in carbonic maceration, such as in Beaujolais nouveau.
Created by bacteria during malolactic fermentation	Strain of bacteria	Diacetyl (buttery)
Botrytis cinerea fungus	Extent of botrytis infection	Honey and piquancy in dessert wines
Oak	Type of oak, barrel toasting	Vanillin
Bottle development	Age	Petrol aromas in Riesling

The Bell Peppers of Cabernet

Cabernet Sauvignon may be the most famous black variety in the world, and certainly it is now the most widely planted of the quality black varietals, but its fame originated in the Bordeaux blend rather than as a one hundred percent varietal. On Bordeaux's left bank, it would be thought unsophisticated to make a wine solely from Cabernet Sauvignon; usually it is blended with Merlot, and sometimes Cabernet Franc and Petit Verdot are also added. Cabernet Sauvignon brings structure and austerity to the blend, Merlot contributes fruitiness and fleshiness, Cabernet Franc has leafy notes of tobacco, and Petit Verdot brings a touch of spice. Malbec and Carmenère are varieties that used to be common in Bordeaux, but that today have become rare. On the right bank, Merlot dominates the scene, usually with Cabernet Franc as the subservient variety. Wines labeled

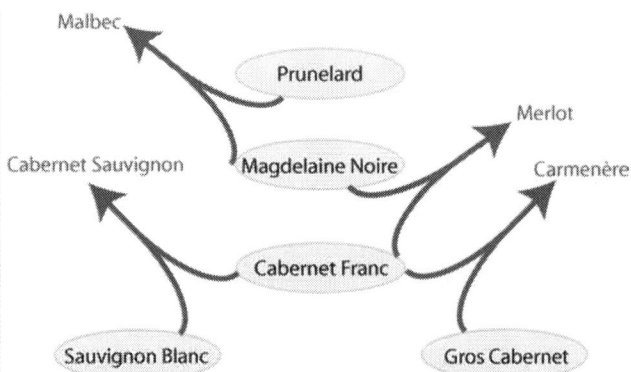

Bordeaux black varietals have incestuous relationships.

Parents are shown in pink ovals; progeny varieties are in red.

as Cabernet Sauvignon are common in the New World, although often they contain a small amount of Merlot (legally limited to 15% if the wine is to carry the varietal label).

The black Bordeaux varieties are relative newcomers to the viticultural scene. They show a tight relationship stemming from several common ancestors. Ironically at the center of the history, since if not exactly marginalized, it has certainly decreased in importance recently, is Cabernet Franc. This turns out to be the common ancestral grape of Bordeaux. A chance cross between Cabernet Franc and Sauvignon Blanc created Cabernet Sauvignon, probably a few hundred years ago.[46] Another cross involving Cabernet Franc, this time with a lost cultivar (examples of which were found in an abandoned vineyard in the Charente region to the north of Bordeaux) created Merlot.[47] The second parent of Merlot, named Magdelaine Noire des Charentes after its rediscovery, was one of the parents of Malbec.[48] Cabernet Franc is also one of the parents of the old Bordeaux variety, Carmenère (now scarcely grown at all).

Cabernet Sauvignon is thought to have been introduced to Bordeaux by Baron Hector de Brane (the proprietor prior to 1830 of Brane Mouton, which was later to become Mouton Rothschild). Armand d'Armailhacq also grew the grape at his château and advocated its use in his book (published in various editions from 1855).[50] It does best on well-drained, gravel soils.

Merlot is a relative newcomer to the list of top varieties. It was a secondary cultivar in Bordeaux in the nineteenth century, increasing in popularity in the

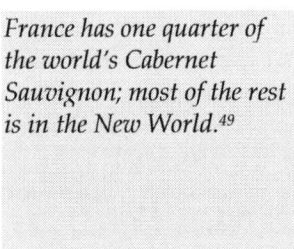

France has one quarter of the world's Cabernet Sauvignon; most of the rest is in the New World.[49]

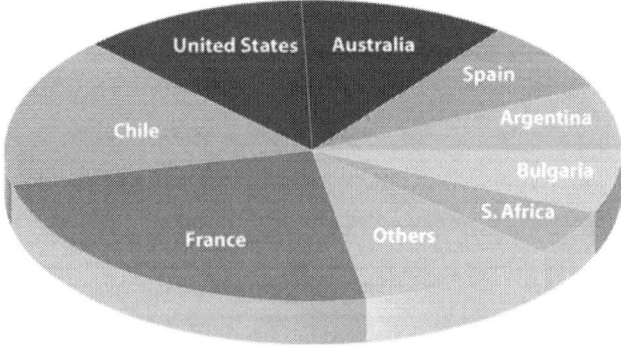

The small, darkly colored berries of Cabernet Sauvignon bring structure to a blend.

second part of the century because of its relatively low susceptibility to powdery mildew, which was becoming a problem. It became significant when it replaced Malbec during the replanting resulting from the phylloxera epidemic.[51] Today it is the major variety in Bordeaux,[52] the most widely planted black variety in France, and close behind Cabernet Sauvignon in worldwide popularity. One of the most famous (and most expensive) wines of the right bank of Bordeaux, Château Pétrus is made almost exclusively (95%) from Merlot, and many of the successful small-production, cult wines are monovarietal Merlots.

Cabernet Sauvignon has spread around the world from its origins in Bordeaux. France remains the country with the most plantings, more than half in Bordeaux, but overall there is now more Cabernet Sauvignon in the New World than the Old. Most of it is grown in climates that are warmer than Bordeaux, and this has had a major effect on our perception of the nature of the variety.

The traditional aroma of Cabernet Sauvignon, as seen in the wines of the left bank of Bordeaux, has a herbaceous note usually described as bell peppers. The fruit aromas and flavors are black, and sometimes young wines, especially from

As Cabernet Sauvignon ripens, its aroma and flavor spectrum changes from bell peppers to blackcurrant to cassis to jam.

Cabernet Sauvignon is usually planted in the gravel soils, as here in the Médoc.

warm vintages, show clear notes of blackcurrants. Wines from the warmer climates of the New World often show blackcurrant aromas, and these can intensify into the more aromatic notes of cassis. In really hot climates, this turns to an impression of jam (as it does with all black varieties). This variation reflects a progression of aromas as the grapes become increasingly riper. Indeed, as Bordeaux has been overtaken by warmer vintages, the traditional herbaceous notes have become unfashionable, and château proprietors may bristle visibly if you describe a wine as showing herbaceousness.

We may now be at the last point in history when one can talk about the bell peppers of Cabernet. The trend is moving so firmly away from the traditional herbaceous flavor spectrum towards the blackcurrant flavors of modern fruit-forward wines that in another twenty years there may be no one left who remembers that Cabernet Sauvignon used to be herbaceous or who does not regard this as a flaw. Yet the blend of very faintly herbaceous Cabernet Sauvignon (on the left bank) or Cabernet Franc (on the right bank) with the fruity Merlot made for some wonderfully complex wines in top vintages. Personally, I believe that something has been lost, and that wines are less complex, when all the fruits are uniformly ripe; it's that very faint (but only very faint) touch of herbaceousness that gives Bordeaux its classic elegance and complexity.

The herbaceous quality of Cabernet Sauvignon is due to its production of a single compound, a pyrazine (3-isobutyl-2-methoxypyrazine, known as IBMP). Not surprisingly, since Sauvignon Blanc is one of the parents of Cabernet Sauvignon, the same compound is also responsible for the characteristic herbaceous notes of Sauvignon Blanc, although in this variety it usually manifests itself more as grassiness or asparagus. Methoxypyrazine synthesis is related to vegetative growth, occurring in the berries between fruit set and the period just prior to veraison. Sunlight triggers its destruction, and its level drops sharply between veraison and harvest. Warmer climatic conditions, coupled with the trend to harvest grapes at greater levels of ripeness, may mean that the level has dropped below detection by the time Cabernet Sauvignon is harvested.

So the aromas and taste of Cabernet Sauvignon from different regions are much influenced by the typical level of ripeness. The transition from herbaceous to blackcurrant reflects how much heat and light the berries have had, and how late they were harvested. Blackcurrants have become more evident than bell peppers as vintages have become warmer in Bordeaux. California Cabernet Sauvignon varies from relatively soft and amorphous black fruits at the generic level to intense blackcurrants from Napa, somewhat leaner from Sonoma. Cabernet Sauvignon from Australia tends to exuberance, with intense aromatics accompanying the blackcurrants from Barossa Valley, less aromaticity from McLaren Vale, and more precise, elegant fruits from Coonawarra. Chile and Argentina produce Cabernet Sauvignon in the style of California, but the fruits tend to be less well focused and less intense.

Syrah or Shiraz?

Syrah, Sirah, Syra, Sirac, Seyras, Schiras, Shiraz are all names by which Syrah has been known in the Rhône. It is the sole red grape of the Northern Rhône, where it is vinified as a monovarietal (the old habit of including some white grapes for softening now being quite rare). The oldest established appellation is Hermitage.

Although wine was being produced in Hermitage in Roman times, there is no knowing what grape varieties were cultivated then, and the modern history of Hermitage starts with a royal visit in 1642, when Louis XIII was offered the wine.[53] Syrah has been grown in the Northern Rhône at least since the seventeenth century, when it became known as Sérine at Côte-Rôtie and as Petite Syrah at Hermitage.[54] Petite Syrah refers specifically to cultivars with small berries,[55] as opposed to those with larger berries, known as Grosse Syrah. The old cultivars now represent less than 10% of modern plantings, however, as they have been replaced by modern clones of varying quality.[56] Current plantings mostly date from clones of Grosse Syrah developed in the 1970s and 1980s, which unfortunately follow the model for higher production at the expense of quality.[57]

Australian Shiraz dates from cuttings taken from Hermitage in 1831 during James Busby's tour of France. Busby (who played a formative role in the early Australian wine industry) referred to it as Ciras or Seyras, and the vines were

France and Australia account for two thirds of the world's Syrah.[59]

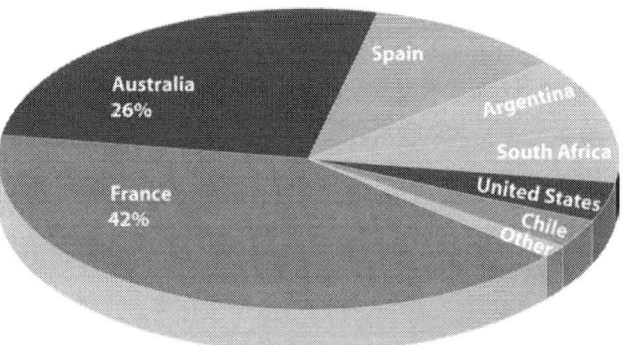

made freely available; by 1860 they had been widely planted in Hunter Valley.[58] The earliest references to the grape in Australia often use "Scyras" as a description, but by the 1860s the wine was generally known as Shiraz or Hermitage. Hermitage ceased to be used in the 1980s to avoid conflict with the wine from France. Australia's most famous example of a Syrah-based wine, Grange Hermitage, changed its name to Grange in 1989.

Syrah is dry, dense, rich, alcoholic, and tannic. It is deeply colored with black hues; perhaps it is not as densely colored as Cabernet Sauvignon. The nose tends towards a mineral blueberry, often with spiciness or peppery overtones, sometimes showing a tarry or burned rubber aroma. Classic notes of white pepper tend to come out in wines made from grapes harvested at lower ripeness levels.

Syrah has spread around the warm climates of the world, with wine styles somewhat indicated by whether it is called Syrah or Shiraz. The wines of the Rhône tend to be relatively backward, often with gamey notes (but these may be due to infection with the yeast Brettanomyces rather than to the variety or terroir). Eventually Hermitage ages toward a similar flavor spectrum as old Bordeaux. The wines of the Languedoc, the other major locus for production in France, tend to be fruitier and richer, but less refined. In hot vintages, Rhône wines can show fruits of black plums, closing the gap quite a bit with the New World style, but they are rarely as full-throated as the Shiraz of Australia or South America. New World Shiraz can be aromatic (more so than Cabernet Sauvignon). Australian Shiraz is often made in an exuberant style, bursting with forward fruits, dominated by notes of aromatic plums, tannins obscured by the fruits, tending to high alcohol of 14% or more. It is at its most forward from Barossa Valley.

Some successes with Syrah are now found in South Africa, where the wines tend to follow the Australian model but with less intensity, more of a halfway house between Australia and the Rhône. Syrah in Chile, often named Shiraz to indicate relationship with the Australian style, can be aromatic, with damsons and black plums showing on nose and palate, with the same high alcohol as Australia, but less weight and lower acidity, sometimes with slightly herbaceous notes reminiscent of the Rhône. Argentina makes Shiraz with soft upfront fruits, usually black plums, in the Australian style but less exuberant, concentrated, and alcoholic.

The Ancient Pinot Family

Burgundy continues to define the essence of Pinot Noir. No other region can reliably aspire to its capture of the delicacy of Pinot, although individual wines from other regions may sometimes be mistaken for Burgundy. France dominates worldwide production of Pinot Noir. However, about 40% of France's Pinot Noir is used for Champagne; in terms of production for red wine, its lead is much smaller. Burgundy's 10,000 ha are roughly twice the area found in any other single region.[60] Germany's position as a significant producer is relatively recent, a result of the trend towards red wine drinking combined with the opportunities opened by warmer climatic conditions. The United States, especially in Oregon and California's Sonoma Valley, and New Zealand are the main New World challengers in Pinot production, although the styles are usually somewhat distinct from Burgundy.

Pinot Noir is definitely a grape for cool climates. All the classic locations for Pinot production in France are in the northern part of the country: Burgundy, Sancerre, Alsace, and Champagne. The regions of Germany are farther to the north yet, Baden just to the north of Alsace, and the tiny region of the Ahr, the most northern region for wine production in Germany, able to ripen Pinot Noir only because of its special properties as a micro climate. In the United States, Oregon might be compared climatically to Burgundy (Sonoma Valley is somewhat warmer), while in New Zealand the move towards Central Otago takes Pinot Noir production into the coolest climate in the country.

There is still generally a distinction between Pinot Noir from the Old World, epitomized by Burgundy, where the wine tends toward a lighter more savory style, and the New World, where it is richer, with more powerful fruits and a fuller body. In France, Burgundy is at its weightiest in the Côte de Nuits, with fruits tending to black cherries, lighter in the Côte de Beaune with fruits tending to earthy strawberries, lighter yet in the surrounding satellite regions. Sancerre in the Loire produces light-colored Pinot Noirs with good acidity and (in a warm year) something approaching the earthy strawberry fruits of the satellite regions around Beaune. Pinot Noir in Alsace can be pale to the point of confusion with rosé, but more intense examples can now be found (although their "typicity" has been questioned), with good acidity and notes of earthy strawberries.

France has almost 30% of the world's Pinot Noir. The rest is distributed between Europe and the New World.[61]

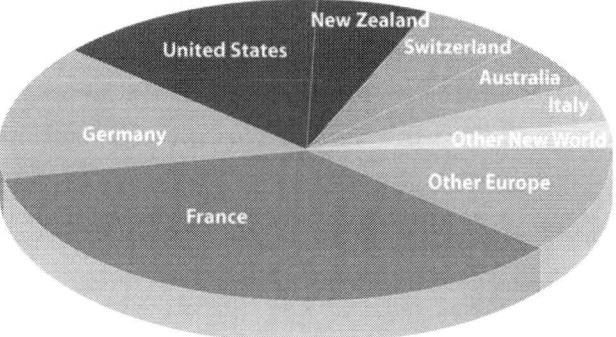

Sweetness of fruits is a marker for all regions from New Zealand. Marlborough shows the bright, forward fruits that typify New Zealand wines, with red and black cherries on the palate, and precise fruit flavors supported by good acidity. The wines often show prominent aromatics. Martinborough (just to the north) is similar to Marlborough, but slightly denser and fuller in style, with more intimations of black fruit, especially cherries. To the south, the cooler climate of Central Otago, a more recent convert to Pinot Noir production, shows earthier aromas and flavors, with more upfront, softer fruit flavors tending to the classic strawberries. Fruits can be lifted by the higher acidity. Winemakers often compare it to Oregon.

South Africa Pinot Noir can be similar in style to New Zealand, but with less bright fruits and less noticeable aromatics. Chile is similar, with a mix of cherries and strawberries, but less fruit intensity and less aromatic than New Zealand, and sometimes a tell tale touch of menthol, often a faintly herbaceous note. Yarra Valley in Australia shows rather soft, earthy flavors, with strawberries predominating, and acidity on the lower side, sometimes marked by a very faint medicinal edge. The wines are lighter than those of New Zealand, the fruits are less lifted. Willamette Valley in Oregon varies more significantly with climate, from wines that can be relatively thin and acid, to those that have palates dominated by earthy strawberries.

Carneros was one of the first regions in California to emphasize Pinot Noir. Its wines have fruits of black cherries, sometimes notes of eucalyptus, and can be lean and spicy. Russian River Valley in Sonoma shows quite weighty fruits in the same spectrum but with more precise delineation of flavors, fuller bodied, and often a little spiciness. Santa Barbara produces Pinots in a softer style, but often too alcoholic. Napa Valley Pinot Noirs tend to be over-ripe, with rather jammy, and sometimes too heavy, fruits.

If there's a single word to describe Pinot Noir, it should be "elegant." Pinot Noir is very easily destroyed by over-extraction, which can be a problem with New World Pinots. Personally, I am somewhat inclined to the view that it becomes difficult for Pinot Noir to retain typicity once the alcohol level goes over 13%. Of course there are exceptions, but the elegance of the aroma and flavor spectrum tends to be lost at high alcohol.

Pinot is an ancient grape family, often thought to have originated fairly closely from wild grapevines. Of course, no one really knows. Speculation about ancient origins is encouraged by Columella's description of a variety resembling Pinot Noir in the first century C.E., although the first clear references to Pinot Noir are not until much later, in the fourteenth century. Pinot is particularly prone to mutation and throws off new variants at a greater rate than most other varieties; there are several hundred clones under cultivation.[62]

Clonal variation affects a wide range of properties, from the size of the berries and overall yield to the time of ripening. All this plays out in the aroma and flavor of the wine. It can be really important to plant the right clone. When they started growing Pinot Noir and Chardonnay in Oregon, producers had a lot of trouble because they planted clones recommended by the University of California at Davis that ripened relatively late. The clones had been chosen for

California in order to get a more extended growing season. The problem was that this required harvesting around the time of the autumn rains in Oregon, with generally disastrous results. In the early 1990s, the so-called Dijon clones were imported to Oregon, giving much better results because they came to ripeness about two weeks earlier. In fact, Dijon clones of Pinot Noir have generally now replaced Oregon's traditional clones (Pommard and Wädensvil). The Dijon clones have acquired an almost mystical significance to the extent that they are sometimes now mentioned on labels, but actually they have nothing much to do with Dijon; the name appears to have arisen simply because the clones are described by D numbers and were imported from Burgundy.

The Pinot family consists of closely related variants: Pinot Noir, Pinot Gris, Pinot Meunier, and Pinot Blanc. The first three are black grapes, the last is white. Their genetic maps are almost indistinguishable, implying they all originate from the same ancestor.[63]

The differences between them are subtle. Pinot Blanc's lack of color is due to the same mutation that prevents anthocyanin production in other white grapes. Pinot Gris has rather variable color, possibly the result of a mutation specifically affecting only the cell layer that produces the skin. Pinot Meunier differs from Pinot Noir in having leaves that are densely covered with fine hairs, whereas the leaves of Pinot Noir are smooth. This gives the underside of the leaves a slightly white appearance, somewhat like dusting with flour, hence the description Meunier (French for miller). The difference between Pinot Noir and Pinot Meunier is due solely to a genetic change affecting only the outer layer of cells. It turns out that this results from a single genetic difference in the pathway for producing giberellic acid, a plant hormone that controls growth.[64] (In fact the mutation is identical to one that has been used to increase production in wheat.)

The relationship between the Pinots is made possible because grapevines are propagated vegetatively, by making cuttings, instead of being grown from seeds.

The Pinot family varies from black/purple (Pinot Noir), red/pink (Pinot Gris) to white (Pinot Blanc). The grapes of Pinot Meunier have the same appearance as Pinot Noir. Photographs kindly provided by the Institut für Rebenzchtung Geilweilerhof, Germany.

When a plant is grown from a seed, all its cells have the same genetic constitution. But when it is propagated by cuttings, each cell layer can inherit the properties of the cell layer of the parental plant. So all Pinot Meuniers are descended from a single plant in which a somatic mutation changed the properties of just the outer cell layer. In fact, if new plants are generated from the cells of this layer (the "true" Pinot Meunier?), they form dwarf grapevines of much reduced size but with increased fruit capacity. If new plants are generated from other cell layers of Pinot Meunier, they are identical to Pinot Noir! So Pinot Meunier is a chimera, with all its cells exactly the same as Pinot Noir, except for the outer layer which is the same as the cells of the dwarf plants. In fact, all the Pinot varieties are chimeras, in which the genetic constitution of the layer of skin cells is different from the constitution of the cells of the inner layer.[65]

Anything but Chardonnay

Anything but Chardonnay, dissenters used to say at the peak of the craze for Chardonnay. A surprising attitude given the enormous variability of Chardonnay. Chardonnay is the most widely propagated white grape in the world; almost every wine-producing country has some. The bulk of production is split between France, the United States, and Australia. The stylistic split between Europe and New World is not always straightforward to define for Chardonnay, because the use of oak can be at least as important as terroir or climate. At one extreme, Chardonnay may be vinified in stainless steel; at the other it may be fermented in new oak barrels and then kept in new oak for months.

Unoaked styles range from the mineral Chablis of northern France to the piercing citrus of New World Chardonnay. Oaked styles range from subtle Burgundies to rich, fat, buttery wines dominated by the aromas of malolactic fermentation from Napa or South Australia. South America and South Africa produce some positively exotic wines with tropical fruits. Perhaps there's an element of caricature in these descriptions, but even if each is an extreme manifestation of match between cépage and locale, certainly the range illustrates the malleability of the variety. Chardonnay is an extraordinary vehicle for displaying the wiles of the winemaker, although it is generally felt that it produces its best results on soils with high chalk content.

Almost three quarters of the world's Chardonnay is in France, the United States, and Australia, but the rest is widely distributed.[66]

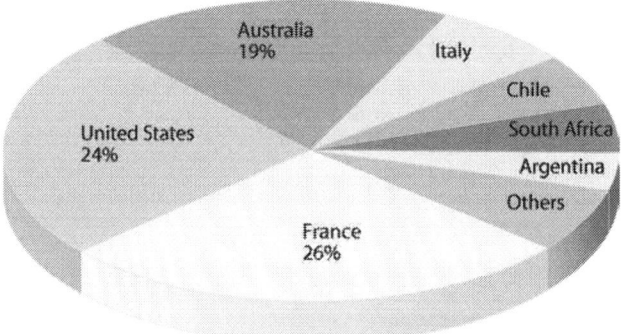

Chardonnay is planted on chalk in Chablis, as can be seen from the white soil on the hill.

Burgundy is the heartland for Chardonnay, producing several classic styles. In the northern outpost of Chablis, reaching full ripeness can be a problem, and the style depends on whether the wine is unoaked (at its best displaying a steely minerality) or oaked (adding hints of smoke and liquorice to the minerality, but not vanillin since the oak is rarely new). Even at grand cru level, Chablis is rarely as full bodied as wines from the Côte d'Or to its south, where use of new oak increases in proportion to the quality of the wine. The style in the Côte d'Or is at its steeliest in Puligny Montrachet, creamier in Chassagne Montrachet, and softer in Meursault, sometimes with a nutty edge. Corton Charlemagne can be fat and opulent. Strength of oak depends on producer style but is not usually obtrusive and tends to be smoky rather than buttery. When you get to the grand crus, with Le Montrachet at the peak, there can be more overt oakiness when the wine is young.

California Chardonnays tend to noticeable oak, with overtones of vanillin and butter even when French oak is used. The style is at its fullest in Napa, similar but a little less rich in Carneros, somewhat leaner in Sonoma, with Russian River Valley providing a more elegant style. Like everything else, Chardonnay from Australia tends simply to be bigger and bolder than the same grape from elsewhere. In the oaked style, Australian Chardonnays are big, oaky, buttery, and alcoholic; in the unoaked style they tend to lime and other citrus flavors. The unoaked style is distinguished from the Old World by the intensity of its bright, forward lemon fruits, absence of minerality, and higher alcohol. A move away from excessive oak in the oaked style leaves citrus flavors noticeable on nose and

Chardonnay clones vary greatly in berry and bunch size. Clone 4 is the most widely planted clone in California, and gives consistently high yields. Clone 15 comes from Washington State and gives smaller berries and much smaller bunches.

Photographs kindly provided by Chalk Hill Estate.

palate, with sweet oak aromas and flavors following on the finish. Tropical notes can be a mark of New World Chardonnays from Australia, New Zealand, or Chile, but not usually California. (Sometimes this is due to fermentation at low temperatures.) Chile and South Africa tend to follow the Australian style, but with less intensity. Northern Italy (Piedmont, Tuscany, and Umbria) produces some heavily oaked Chardonnays, distinguished from the French by a touch of vanillin from the oak, sometimes coming close to a New World style.

Clonal variation of Chardonnay is usually stated to have relatively little effect on flavor.[67] The emphasis on Chardonnay clones is usually placed more on features such as time of ripening, but in fact there are quite noticeable effects on flavor profile when you look for them. The range of difference was shown by an interesting experiment when seventeen different clones were planted at Chalk Hill winery in Sonoma.[68] The clones varied widely in the sizes of the berries, the sizes of the bunches, the overall yield, and the Brix at harvest.[69] Each clone was vinified separately under identical conditions, and when I tasted wine made from six of the clones, the differences were striking. Clone 16 from Rutherglen, Australia was clearly heavier than any of the others, powerful rather than elegant; clone 76, one of the so-called Dijon clones from Burgundy, was more elegant and Burgundian with a better balance of acid to fruit; clone 17, a selection from Robert Young in California, was more mineral than most; clone 22 from Coneglio, Italy, and clone 352 from Espiguette, France were distinctly lighter and fresher than the others, and clone 4 (originating from Stony Hill Vineyard in St. Helena), had distinctly sweeter fruit.[70] You shouldn't expect different clones of any varietal to taste the same any more than you would expect Red Delicious, Granny Smith, Fuji, Gala, or Macoun apples to taste the same.

You can in fact produce Chardonnay in almost any style from any place. The distinctions between Burgundy, Napa, Australia, and so on, owe more to winemaking choices in these locales than to intrinsic qualities of the terroir.

Herbaceous Sauvignon Blanc

Some wines have no character to speak of (the world is full of amorphous white wines with little flavor beyond the basic solution of alcohol in water), some have character thrust upon them by exposure to oak or other means, but some have such powerful intrinsic aromas that, love or loathe them, there is certainly no mistaking their character. The most distinctive white wines have powerful aromas provided by volatile compounds. All wines have volatile compounds, of course, but their presence is an especially strong feature of varieties such as Sauvignon Blanc, Riesling, Gewürztraminer, and the Muscats.

Sauvignon Blanc stands at an intriguing interface between the herbaceous and the fruity. The traditional grape of the eastern part of the Loire, where it is vinified as a single varietal, it is now associated with Marlborough in New Zealand, whose forceful style has come to typify the variety for many people. France remains the largest producer of Sauvignon Blanc, with almost a third of the world's vineyards, but New Zealand is close behind. Other New World countries make up most of the rest, mostly following the bright stainless style of New Zealand.

Sauvignon Blanc from the Loire is classically aromatic with a smell of green unripe fruit. The wines are fresh and soon ready to drink, but typically do not last long. Sancerre and Pouilly Fumé are the best known appellations. Vinified in a neutral manner (old oak or stainless steel), the result is a crisp wine, with high acidity resulting from the cool climate, and mineral overtones. Often failing to achieve full ripeness, the wines can be characterized by the herbaceous aroma known pejoratively as cat's pee.

Sauvignon Blanc's importance extends farther south in France to Bordeaux, where it is one of the two major white varieties. Blended with Sémillon, it is the major component in the dry white wines, but a minor component in the great dessert wines. Typical proportions for the blend are 80:20 for the dry wines and 20:80 for the sweet wines, although some of the most famous dry white wines use 50:50. Most production uses old oak or stainless steel, but the top white wines are matured in new oak, which makes for complexity and age worthiness. The fatter qualities of Sémillon ameliorate the leanness of the Sauvignon Blanc.

France and New Zealand together account for half of the world's production of Sauvignon Blanc.[71]

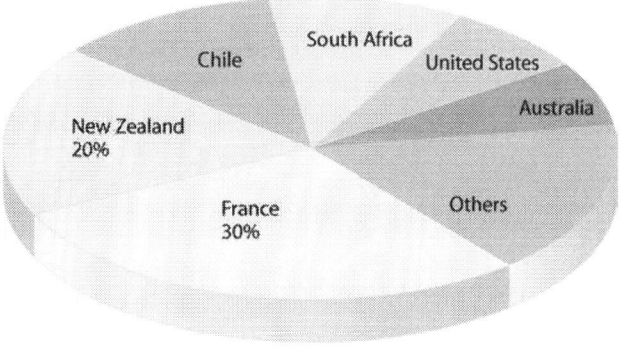

(Sémillon is also important in the sweet wines for its high susceptibility to botrytis.) Today there is a tendency to make pure varietal Sauvignon Blanc using stainless steel like the New World.

The herbaceous qualities of cool climates turn to more perfumed notes in warmer climates. The revolution in Sauvignon Blanc came from New Zealand. Introduced into New Zealand in the 1970s, Sauvignon Blanc became commercially established in the 1980s, and became the paradigm for the modern stainless steel style of production by the 1990s. Made famous by wines from the cool climate of Marlborough, the New Zealand style is achieved by rapidly crushing the grapes, followed by low temperature fermentation (10-14°C) in stainless steel. This gives strong citrus fruit flavors (often showing as grapefruit) and tropical aromas and flavors (typically showing as passion fruit). Accounting for two thirds of Sauvignon Blanc production in New Zealand, the Marlborough region typifies the unoaked New World style of Sauvignon Blanc. Other New World countries follow the style of strong, forward, often piercing fruit, but usually the fruits are not so bright as from New Zealand. In South Africa, acidity tends to be relatively low for the variety, and aromatics of exotic fruits, especially passion fruit, are more noticeable than herbaceous or grassy notes.

Yet another aspect of Sauvignon Blanc is revealed by the Fumé Blanc style pioneered by Robert Mondavi in Napa Valley. The story goes that Mondavi was offered Sauvignon Blanc grapes at a time when the variety was little known in the United States. Reasoning that people were familiar with the Pouilly Fumé wine from the Loire even though they did not know it was made from Sauvignon Blanc, and after experimenting with various styles of production, Mondavi gave the wine the name Fumé Blanc (which also served to distinguish it from those Sauvignon Blancs that were being produced in a sweet style). Half is fermented in oak barrels, to get softness and complexity, and half in stainless steel, to retain freshness; then the wine matures briefly in oak barriques, the result being to introduce creamy and smoky aromas cutting the usual herba-

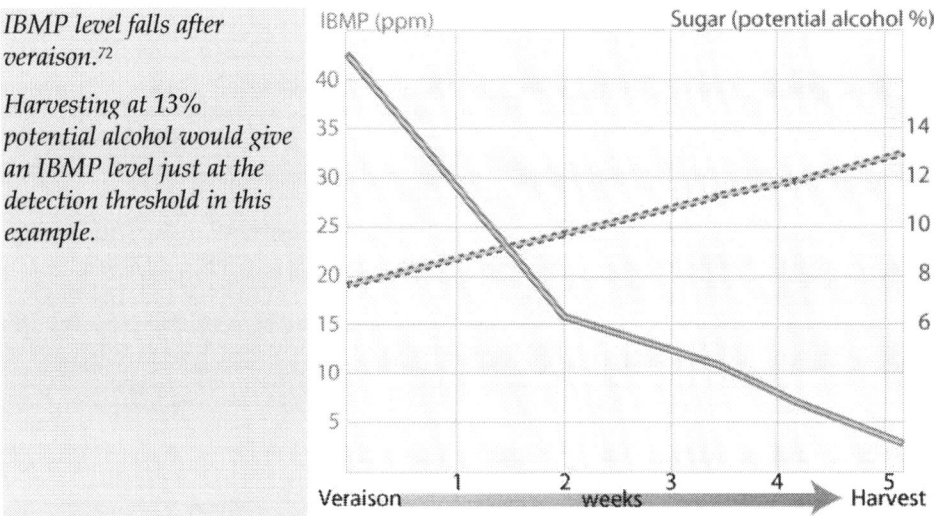

IBMP level falls after veraison.[72]

Harvesting at 13% potential alcohol would give an IBMP level just at the detection threshold in this example.

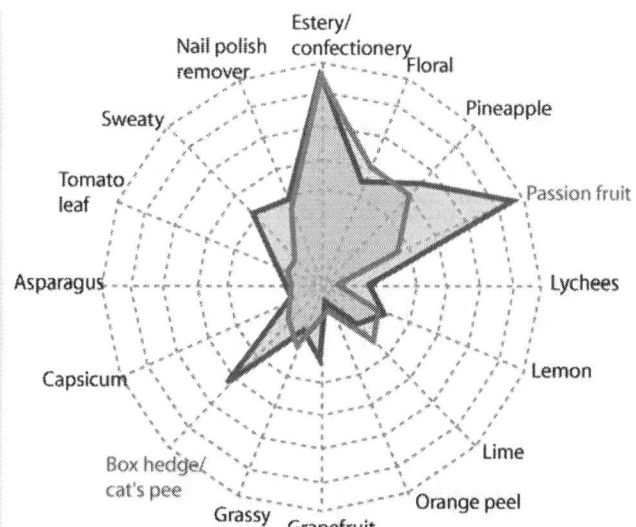

Different aroma profiles result from fermentation with two yeast strains.

The red strain of yeast releases more volatile thiols than the blue strain, resulting in increased concentration of the aromas associated with 4-MMP and the other thiols.[73]

ceousness of Sauvignon Blanc. Imitating Bordeaux, it also has a little Sémillon. First marketed with the 1966 vintage, it remains one of Mondavi's staple wines, and the style has been imitated by other producers in Napa valley and elsewhere. Today most of the grapes come from Mondavi's own vineyards in Napa.

Two types of compounds are responsible for the characteristic aroma and flavor spectrum of Sauvignon Blanc, and their different natures explain the effects of viticulture and vinification on the typicity of the variety.

"Green" characters, variously taking the form of grassy or asparagus-like aromas, result from methoxypyrazines. Synthesized by the plant, they are found in the berry, and the most important is the same IBMP (3-isobutyl-2-methoxypyrazine) found in Cabernet Sauvignon. Humans are very sensitive to methoxypyrazines, and almost all Sauvignon Blancs have a level above detection.[74] (One reason we are so sensitive to methoxypyrazines is that they are an indication of unripeness in fruit.) Exposure to sunlight causes levels to decline, and there is a rapid drop as grapes approach maturity, with losses of 10-fold or more in the last 6 weeks of ripening. The timing of harvest is a key determinant of the level in the grape. Methoxypyrazines are easily extracted from the grapes, so the level in the mature berry essentially determines the level in the wine.

The "tropical" characters in Sauvignon Blanc come from volatile thiols, which are formed during fermentation. The most important is 4-MMP.[75] This is very potent; levels in wine are usually well above the threshold for perception.[76] Its effect is greatly influenced by its concentration; at low concentrations it gives an impression of broom or box, turning to gooseberries, passion fruit and tropical fruits at higher concentrations, and ultimately showing as cat's pee when in large excess.[77] 4-MMP exists in the grape as an odorless precursor. During fermentation, yeast enzymes release it from the precursor form.[78] Different yeasts vary by up to ten fold in their ability to release the volatile thiols, so the strain of yeast used in fermentation makes a significant difference to the aroma of the wine.[79]

The combined effects of IBMP and 4-MMP and their related compounds give Sauvignon Blanc that unique combination of herbaceousness and exotic fruits. How the two types of compounds respond to viticulture and vinification explains the differences between the classical style of the wines from the Loire and the new style of the wines from New Zealand and elsewhere in the New World. High levels of methoxypyrazines are associated with less ripe grapes, so the wines of the cool-climate Loire tend to herbaceousness. Volatile thiols are destroyed by oxidation, so winemaking in traditional conditions, typically using barrels of old oak where exposure to oxygen is high, reduces their levels. The New Zealand style of winemaking in stainless steel, often in deliberately reductive conditions (when a layer of nitrogen is used to exclude oxygen) preserves the thiols, which is why you tend to find notes of passion fruit in Marlborough Sauvignon Blanc.

The Petrol of Riesling

Does a whiff of petrol identify the essential character of Riesling or is it a flaw? It's created in Riesling by TDN (trimethyl-dihydronaphthalene). which is rarely found in grapes but develops in the bottle by slow chemical actions.[80] TDN levels are increased by low yields, warm weather, and high levels of acidity in either fruit or the wines.[81] Petrol develops slowly over some years in French or German Rieslings, but typical growth conditions favor more rapid development of TDN in Australian Riesling, where critic Tom Stevenson comments that, "TDN is typically so precocious that judges are expected to mark down wines showing too much petrol too quickly."[82] When rather young, Riesling can be deceptively simple; the characteristic steely, mineral citrus fruits develop slowly in the bottle. When TDN develops in the same time frame, the result is a dry, perfumed finish perfectly complementing the fruit spectrum; but when it develops first, the impression can be a little raw.

Riesling is the most racy and elegant of grapes, marked by good acidity, with light almost perfumed fruit, showing a range of flavors from green apples to minerals. The focus on sugar made sweetness the major determinant of style in Germany, and indeed, some believe that, because of its very high acidity, the full delicacy of Riesling is only revealed in the presence of at least some residual sugar. Once again the New World has brought a new intensity to bear, with fruit-driven Rieslings from South Australia always showing a completely dry style. Now Germany is following the lead of the New World, with its new emphasis on the trocken (dry) style.

The traditional quality grades of German Riesling are nominally distinguished by the concentration of sugar in the grapes at harvest, but in practice they are also associated with increasing residual sugar in the wines going up the scale through Kabinett, Spätlese, Auslese, and the higher grades of dessert wines. All show soft aromatics, with the fruit spectrum starting with citrus and then showing increasing notes of apricot going through to the highest levels. Even in the trocken style, German Riesling is distinguished from Alsace or the New

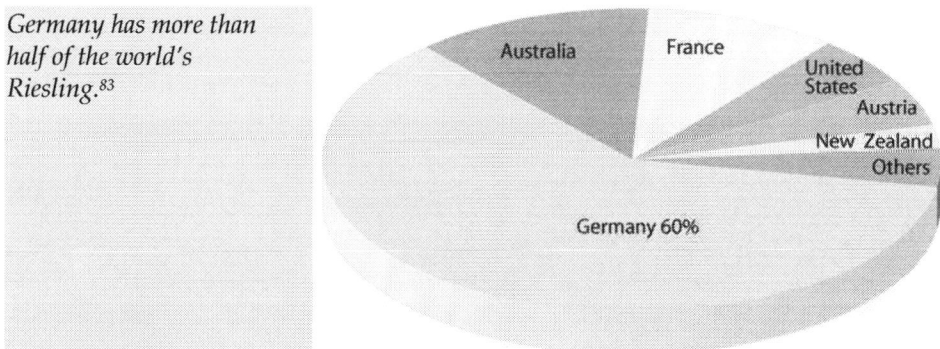

Germany has more than half of the world's Riesling.[83]

World by a certain softness and perfume on the nose, although differences between regions are harder to see in the dry wines. Petrol developing with age increases the sense of minerality.

Riesling shows the playoff between sugar and acidity. When the high acidity has been ameliorated by a little residual sugar, it's an education to taste a series of half-dry Rieslings and try to guess sugar and acidity levels: the interplay is so subtle that it's extremely difficult simply to place the wines in order of ascending residual sugar. The move towards dry wines, better suited to accompany modern food, has seen increasing focus on dry or half-dry styles in German production; indeed, the objective of the new style called Classic in Germany is that the wine should taste dry, even though it may have a little sugar.

Elsewhere in Europe, Riesling is usually dry. Austrian Rieslings tend to have more mineral tones and sometimes higher overt acidity than German (trocken) Rieslings. Alsatian Rieslings have a steely mineral character, lean and austere, with the palate often showing citrus fruits. (But the recent warming trend in Alsace has led to more production of wines with residual sugar.) They are often chaptalized and have higher alcohol than the trocken Rieslings of Germany.

Australian Rieslings usually have those bright, piercing citrus fruits characteristic of the New World. Clare Valley produces high concentration, often with predominant notes of lime as well as lemon. Watervale is the best part of Clare Valley for Riesling. Eden Valley tends to be more floral. Both can have strong notes of petrol or kerosene even when young.

New Zealand Rieslings follow the same style as Australia, but usually have a little residual sugar to soften and balance the acidity. This gives something of a Germanic quality, but without the delicacy or perfume. The generality about New Zealand Riesling is that it has more aromatic complexity but simpler, purer fruits, whereas Australia has more marked fruit complexity.

Beware the Welschriesling! Also known as Riesling Italico, this is widely planted in central Europe, and when labeled as Riesling can fool the unwary buyer. This is a bulk-production grape, giving wine that has little connection with the real Riesling.

Riesling is considered to be a "terroir grape," one that reflects the conditions of viticulture more than most. You see this most clearly in Germany, where wines from the Mosel are the most elegant, with precisely delineated fruits; from the Rheingau there is a little more weight with a delicious sweet/sour balance in the traditional style; and then going farther south the wines become somewhat heavier, with less minerality. The best soils are slate. It is said that the calcareous soils of Alsace give Riesling with more weight and body than the slate soils of Germany; perhaps there is an effect from acidity of the soil, but the difference is more likely to reflect the effects of climate on ripeness, and length of the growing season, than to be due to mineral in the soil. After all, the much larger differences between the styles of German and Australian Rieslings are attributed not to terroir but to winemaking (aided by the climate).

Riesling's characteristic fruit spectrum depends on terpenes, a group of organic compounds that also dominate Gewürztraminer, Muscat, and Albariño.[84] They are also found in Muscadelle, and Sauvignon Blanc, but at levels below the threshold for detection. An overlapping set of terpenes is found in all these aromatic varieties, but relative and overall quantities give each a different aroma spectrum. Muscat is dominated by geraniol (smell of roses), Gewürztraminer by cis-rose oxide (smell of lychees), Albariño has high hotrienol (notes of lime), and Riesling has a complex set of aromas in which no single influence dominates.

Terpenes have their characteristic odors only when they are free volatile molecules. The grape contains a mixture of free terpenes and precursors that are odorless because they are bound to sugars. In most of these varieties, the majority of terpenes are in the inactive bound form.[85] Breaking the chemical bond linking the terpene to the sugar, called a glycoside, releases the odiferous form. This happens to a small degree naturally in the grape itself, and during fermentation, but if you want to increase the concentration, the most effective way is to use cultured yeasts with increased enzyme activities or even directly to treat the must with an enzyme that breaks glycoside bonds.[86] Once again, varietal character is not entirely intrinsic but can be controlled by choices during winemaking. No one has done a systematic tasting test to see whether the results of using

Riesling grows on slate in the Mosel.

Terpenes are major components of the aroma spectrum of Riesling, Gewürztraminer, and Muscat.

Terpene	Riesling	Gewürz-traminer	Muscat	Odor	Other sources
Linalool	✓		✓	Rose	Lavender, bergamot, jasmine, cinnamon, clove, nutmeg, coriander, cardamom, ginger.
Alpha-terpineol	✓	✓		Lily of the Valley	Lilac, pine, bitter orange (Citrus aurantium).
Citronellol	✓			Citronella	Rose, geranium, ginger, black pepper, basil, peppermint, cardamom, lemon eucalyptus
Nerol	✓	✓	✓	Rose, lime	Orange blossom, ginger, basil, cardamom, mint mandarin.
Geraniol	✓	✓	✓✓	Rose	Geranium, lemon, citronella, nutmeg, ginger, grapefruit.
Hotrienol	✓	✓		Hyacinth, linden	Japanese Ho Tree (Cinnamomum camphora), grapefruit peel.
cis-Rose oxide	✓	✓✓		Rose, lychee	Lychee

enzymes produces wines as subtle as those produced by nature, or whether the wines are unbalanced by excessive release of terpenes.

Germany remains the world leader in overall production of Riesling, but Australia has an importance beyond its position in second place for pioneering the New World style of bright, piercing fruits—in the case of Riesling, the fruits can be quite aggressive. Production of Riesling in the traditional sweet styles has been declining steadily in Germany, with trocken or halbtrocken wines now reduced to half of production. Germany remains the leader for producing very sweet dessert wines in the botrytized Beerenauslese and TBA styles, and also for its ice-wine. Botrytized sweet Rieslings are also produced in Alsace and in Austria. The high acidity of Riesling gives it a fantastic ability to age, and the best examples can match any dessert wine in the world for complexity and ageworthiness.

Is Riesling the world's most undervalued grape? At one time, it was the most highly valued white grape in the world; at the end of the nineteenth century, prices for Riesling were higher than for any other white grape at Christie's auctions in London. Today Riesling rarely commands prices comparable to top Burgundies. Yet its versatility is extraordinary, from completely dry wines with the precise delicacy of the Mosel to sweet TBA. The development of complex aromas and flavors over time places it high in the group of wines that become increasingly interesting with age, and it is a perfect match for a surprisingly wide range of foods, with none of the buttery or oaky notes of Chardonnay that can sometimes clash with a meal. What stands between Riesling and wider success?

The Grapes of Muscat

Muscats are thought to be one of the oldest grape varieties, sharing the distinctive feature that the aroma and flavor of the grape comes out directly in the wine. There is no mistaking the perfumed, "grapey" quality of Muscat grapes or wine. The strong aroma makes the grapes especially attractive to bees, leading to suggestions that Muscat was the variety identified by Pliny as Uva apiana (grape of the bees).[87] As might be expected of an ancient grape, there is a huge range of Muscat varieties, from the most refined, Muscat Blanc à Petit Grains to the ordinary Muscat d'Alexandrie (used for both wine and table grape production).

About twenty distinct varieties of Muscat have been identified; most are white, but some are red or pink. Muscat Blanc à Petits Grains is also known as Muscat de Frontignac, and may have been cultivated in southern France by the Romans; it was the dominant grape of Roussillon from the fourteenth until the nineteenth centuries. Muscat d'Alexandrie is widely disseminated around the Mediterranean, its name being sometimes being taken to suggest it may have originated in Egypt.[89] Two varieties that are really only half-Muscats are also widely grown. Muscat Hamburg is principally a table grape, and is the only Muscat that can be classified as a black grape; it may have originated in a cross between Muscat d'Alexandrie and the Black Morocco grape. Muscat Ottonel is the lightest in both color and aroma; the variety is most often used for table

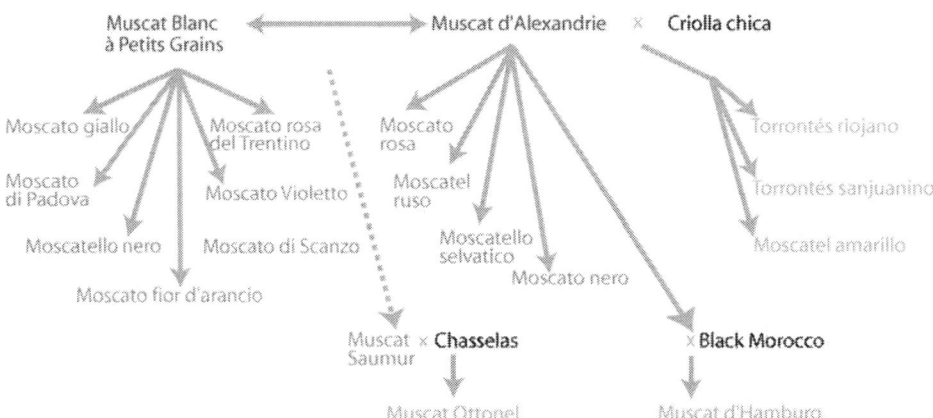

The large Muscat family falls into two main groups, based on Muscat Blanc à Petits Grains and Muscat d'Alexandrie (red). Related members of each group are in gray. Varieties where Muscat is one parent are shown in pink Non-Muscat parents are in black.[88]

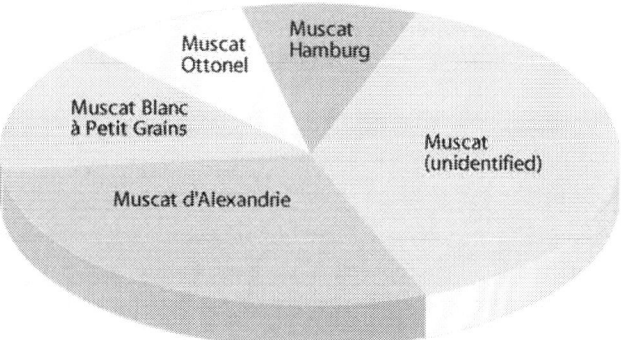

Muscat plantings are not well characterized, but lower quality varieties outnumber Muscat Blanc à Petits Grains.[90]

grape production, but is not always considered to be a full fledged Muscat since it originated in a cross between Muscat of Saumur and Chasselas.

The genetics of the group show that Muscat Blanc à Petit Grains and Muscat d'Alexandrie are related to one another, and each appears to be the progenitor of a large group of subvarieties. Also related to Muscat are the Torrontés varieties of Argentina, which originated in crosses between Muscat d'Alexandrie and the local Criolla chica (a variant of the Mission grape of California). Torrontés have inherited the characteristic grapey aromas of their Muscat parent, although it's not strong as in the original. And the aroma of Muscat d'Alexandrie is less intense than that of Muscat Blanc à Petit Grains.

Muscat Blanc à Petits Grains is of vastly higher quality than the other Muscats, but it is only a small part of worldwide plantings; Muscat d'Alexandrie is about twice as common. Muscat is mostly planted in the warmer areas of Europe; it has not really been taken up in an important way in the New World, with perhaps the exception of the Brown Muscats of Australia (used for sweet, "sticky" wines). The most important plantings of Muscat Blanc à Petits Grains are in southern France, where it is the sole variety permitted in the fortified sweet dessert wine, Beaumes de Venise (from the southern Rhône), and in several appellations for Vin doux Naturel (sweet fortified wines) in the Languedoc, including Frontignac. Being somewhat obscured by the sweetness, varietal character does not usually come through as strongly in dessert wines as in dry wines, but Muscat is an exception, where the strongly perfumed grapes blend beautifully with the sweetness.

The most notable wines made from Muscat d'Alexandrie are at Rivesaltes (in the Languedoc) and at Setúbal in Portugal. Most of the Muscat in Spain is Muscat d'Alexandrie. Red (well, really pink) varieties of Muscat Blanc à Petits Grains are used to make rosé wines in Italy (the variety is called Moscato Rosa or Rosenmuskateller locally) in both sweet and dry styles. The most extreme versions of Muscat are made in Rutherglen, in Victoria, Australia, from a pink variant, Muscat Rouge à Petits Grains, where the must is fortified to block fermentation after only a day, giving a very sweet wine with primary fruit character.

Muscats owe their characteristic aromatics to the same monoterpenes found at lower levels in Riesling and Gewürztraminer. The major terpenes in Muscat are geraniol, linalool and nerol. Geraniol is the most important, with an odor generally described as rose-like, but in high concentrations, as its name suggests, it can give a strong aroma of geraniums, which can become unpleasant in wine. This is one of the reasons why Asti Spumante, made from Muscat Blanc à Petit Grains as a somewhat perfumed sparkling wine, needs to be drunk young; as it ages, it can acquire too strong an aroma of geraniums.

Deus ex Machina

Descriptions of the specific aromas associated with aromatic grape varieties, and their identification with known compounds, make it seem as though it should be possible to identify wines from at least some varietals by their aromas. So if there are objective criteria for assessing wines, could a machine replace the MW (Master of Wine)?

The aroma wheel gives a sense of the complexity of the aromas in wine. It suggests descriptors grouped under topics such as green fruit, tropical fruit, floral, spicy, and so on, with around a hundred individual types of descriptions for either white or red wine. Probably we know the chemical basis (or at least a major part of the chemical basis) for something approaching half of these aromas. They could be measured in a mass spectrometer, which is pretty good at discriminating volatile compounds. In fact, this is what an electronic nose does.

"Electronic nose" is basically a fancy term to describe any piece of scientific equipment that detects volatile aromas. Mostly this is useful for rapidly detecting dangerous compounds, a sort of replacement for the canaries that miners used to take down mines to detect carbon monoxide. Electronic noses have been used by NASA to detect release of ammonia on the space shuttle, there are devices to detect chlorine, nitric acid, or sulfur dioxide when they reach dangerous levels, and there's even one to determine whether meat is safe by detecting volatile compounds released by contaminating bacteria.

An electronic nose has been made to distinguish between espresso coffees on the basis of their aromas.[91] This is somewhat less complex than wine, since 32 volatile compounds represent more than 95% of the total. The machine can distinguish eight different types of coffee (made from beans from different sources)—but it can't tell whether an individual taster will prefer one to another.

A machine could certainly measure visual criteria: it could assess color in terms of density and hue (as measured by the wavelengths). It could objectively analyze some important taste criteria: alcohol level, acidity, residual sugar, all are crucial to any assessment of wine. It might be able to use the ratio of acid to sugar to assess perceptible sweetness. It could measure tannins, but is it possible to give any universal impression of bitterness? It could test for the aroma characteristics of specific varietals: TDN would be an unequivocal marker for Riesling, for example. By assessing relative levels of various volatile components, it could probably do a pretty good job of identifying several aromatic varietals. It would be more difficult to find criteria to identify neutral varieties.

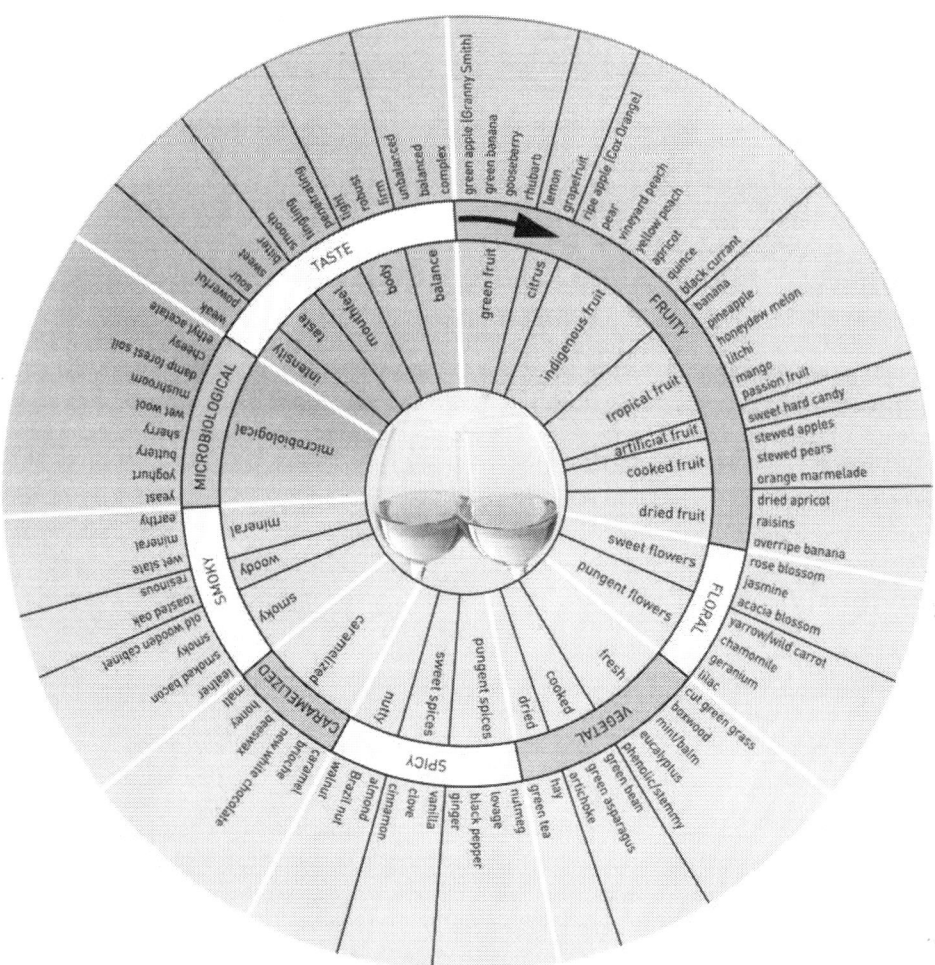

A version of the aroma wheel prepared specially for German white wines has all of the aromas found in Riesling except petrol, which is evidently a sensitive subject. Photograph kindly provided by the German Wine Institute (www.germanwineusa.com).[92]

But could it identify quality? That's a much more nebulous concept, based on assessing the complexity (how many different aromas and flavors contribute to the spectrum), balance (do all the components meld together or does any one stick out), ageworthiness (is there a sense of structure, how will the present aromas and flavors develop over the future). This is essentially a human concept: the best a machine could do would be to try to calibrate the various parameters it can measure against an expert's assessment of quality to see if a pattern could be detected. There are so many different paths to quality—and one of the marks of the highest quality wines is the sheer difficulty of deconstructing their makeup—that success here seems dubious.

Perhaps the measured physical and chemical qualities of wine, from acidity or sweetness to quantities of every volatile compound, could be matched to the taster's descriptions for acid, sweet, floral, perfumed, and so on. At a pinch we might be able to put into software-ese descriptions of tannins ranging from silky and ripe to green and harsh. But how would we describe in terms that a computer could understand qualities such as balance, harmonious, texture, grip—all readily understood but hard to define quantitatively. Personally, I am relieved that I do not have to resolve the conflict behind my scientific training and the value of MWs; I think human tasters are safe from being replaced by an electronic nose.

Engineering the Grapevine

The first genetically engineered crop (a tomato with increased resistance to bruising) went on the market in 1994. Since then, many types of plants have been altered by genetic engineering, and for some crops, genetically engineered plants are now the majority (72% of soybeans worldwide in 2008 were genetically modified).[93] Yet although more than 60 genetically engineered foods have been approved in the United States, not a single case involving vines and wine production has come to fruition.

Suppose you take a cultivar of Vitis vinifera—let's say Chardonnay—and cross it with some other variety. The progeny will have half its genes from Chardonnay and half from its partner. Now let's take those progeny and cross them back to Chardonnay again; the next generation will be 75% Chardonnay and only 25% from the partner. If we keep doing this, with each subsequent cross back to Chardonnay we reduce the proportion of genes from the other variety by 50%. By the time we've done ten generations, only 1 in 1000 genes come from the partner. By 15 generations, virtually all the 30,000 genes should come from Chardonnay.[94] If at each generation we select the plants for some property that comes from the partner cultivar—perhaps this might be resistance to some pathogen—we'll end up in principle with a plant that is basically Chardonnay plus the resistance gene and a handful of others from the partner. No one would object to this process, and in a sense it's what happens naturally as new cultivars develop, but of course it would take several decades to accomplish. In principle, genetic engineering lets us short circuit the process by inserting the foreign gene directly into Chardonnay. So what's the problem?

Scientists are in fact trying the direct approach with powdery mildew, a serious fungal disease that affects Vitis vinifera cultivars. The related grapevine species, Muscadinia rotundifolia, has a single gene that makes it resistant to powdery mildew.[95] Vitis vinifera becomes resistant if the gene is crossed into it by conventional breeding.[96] The Muscadinia gene is now being cloned with the objective of introducing it directly into Vitis vinifera cultivars. People who object to genetic engineering on principle should answer this question: would it better to use grapevines carrying this gene or to continue treating powdery mildew with sulfur or with steroid inhibitors, neither particularly good for human consumption?

Of course, it's relatively rare that a single gene from another grapevine species will be sufficient to confer a specific trait. More often multiple genes will be required. While this could make it even more complicated to construct a resistant strain by conventional breeding, it wouldn't pose any problem in principle for genetic engineering. But there's only a limited number of cases in which the requisite genes will be found in other grapevines; more often it will be necessary to go to other plant species or even to other sources altogether. The same issues apply here that apply to genetic engineering of any crop: will the process lead to reduction of diversity because of increasing reliance on a small number of cultivars that have been engineered? Could it have adverse side effects (such as allowing genes for pesticide resistance to spread to other plants)?

The grapevine is prone to a large number of pests and diseases, and in many cases there are no conventional cures. Nematodes are a perennial problem (in fact, in some areas, rootstocks are chosen just as much for nematode resistance as for resistance to phylloxera). As well as attacking the roots directly, nematodes are vectors carrying diseases such as fanleaf virus. INAO[97] has been testing rootstocks genetically modified to resist the nematode that carries fanleaf virus, against which there is currently no protection, in an experimental plot at Colmar in Alsace. The experiment has been continuing in spite of protests from the Terre et Vin group of producers, who believe that genetic modification will reduce diversity and risk loss of typicity in the wines.[98]

Loss of diversity in rootstocks is not really so much of an issue, but it's a fair point that, since clones have to be modified one by one, the introduction of some desirable gene into a specific clone of some cultivar could lead to its use at the expense of diversity. But is this more than enhancing the trend that is already reducing diversity? The authorities are always pushing clones that are reliable and productive rather than known for their quality.[99] The wine industry is no exception to the trend that commercial production of strains is associated with loss of flavor quality.

The grapevine is a bit different from other plants because of its dependence on grafting. On the one hand, genetic engineering of a scion will be needed to affect resistance to any pests that function above ground or to modify the properties of the cultivar with regards to production of berries. Since the scion cannot survive by itself, it is unlikely any of its traits could be transferred to other plants. On the other hand, it is the rootstock that needs to be modified to affect soil pests such as nematodes; but whatever is done to the rootstock is unlikely to be transmitted to the berries (and therefore to the wine that people consume).

There's a further practical difficulty in genetic engineering scions. Like other plants, grapevines have different cell layers whose lineages separate early in plant development. When a plant is propagated by cuttings, as has been the case for grapevines for thousands of years, these layers are inherited by the progeny. In fact, many grapevines are chimeric—there are genetic differences between their two layers. But genetic engineering is performed with single cells: so the engineered plant can represent the genetic constitution of only one of the layers of the original plant. Any significant differences between the layers of the original (chimeric) plant will be lost.

Personally I am inclined to the view that it's better to perform simple engineering of the grapevine to make it resistant to viruses, bacteria, fungi, and other diseases, than to treat the crop with potentially dangerous inhibitors or pesticides. Although applications are supposed to stop several weeks before harvest, residues can be hard to remove from the grapes; surveys of table grapes sold in European supermarkets have shown significant residues.[100] A grapevine with additional genes coding for natural resistance to pests or diseases would not offer any comparable hazard to human health. However, engineering to "improve" fruit quality is likely to be counter-productive in the same way as other more conventional approaches at breeding; have you ever had a farmed fish with anything resembling the flavor of a wild fish? But in spite of much research, no genetically engineered grapevine has yet been used to produce wine.[101]

Genetic engineering of yeast is a lot simpler than with the grapevine, and it has just as much potential to affect the flavor of wine. Potential targets for modification of yeast are at fermentation (to change features such as how much alcohol is generated), to make the process more resistant to spoilage (by introducing antimicrobial agents), or to affect specific wine properties (such as release or synthesis of aromatic compounds that affect varietal typicity or to increase production of agents such as resveratrol). In contrast with the failure to utilize genetically modified grapevines, there has been more interest in customizing yeasts.[102]

One of the most dramatic developments in genetic engineering has been to produce strains of yeast that can perform both the alcoholic fermentation and the malolactic fermentation. This was done by transferring the genes needed for the process from a bacterium into yeast.[103] Then malolactic fermentation occurs simultaneously with alcoholic fermentation instead of separately.[104] This has major implications for big commercial producers, who can cut time required for production. But it is almost certainly going to result in changes in the aroma and flavor spectrum of the wine in ways that are hard to predict. The ML01 strain is already in commercial use, but its creators are extremely coy about how much and where it is used.[105]

The End of Evolution?

Has evolution of the grapevine come to an end? Well, no, but over the past century it has largely taken a different form from previously. When many different grape varieties grew in close proximity, there were greater opportunities for sexual mating between them to produce new types. Some of the most important modern varieties originated in this way: Cabernet Sauvignon from an adventitious cross between Cabernet Franc and Sauvignon Blanc, Merlot from a cross between Cabernet Franc and a (now lost) variety retrospectively called Magdelaine Noire des Charentes, Chardonnay from a cross between an ancestral Pinot and Gouais Blanc. Some of the parents of the most successful varieties were themselves of no great account—Gouais Blanc produces indifferent white wine. In fact, it was so poorly regarded that several attempts were made to ban its planting in the middle ages;[106] if they had succeeded, we might not have Chardonnay today! Like people, you can never tell how the progeny will turn out.[107]

Opportunities for sexual recombination have been much reduced by the decline in the diversity of planted grapevines and by the modern method of planting each variety in its own separate vineyard block. And if a new variety were to occur, it's unlikely it would noticed or exploited, given the increasing pressure to focus on the tried and tested. There are some minor exceptions: Pinot Gouges (the white strain of Pinot Noir found in Henri Gouges's vineyards in Nuits St. Georges) is used to make white wine, for example. But for the last couple of centuries, new strains of the grapevine have come from breeding programs rather than occurring naturally.

Breeding programs have not done nearly such a good job as Nature. No great varietal has emerged. The most prominent of the man-made crosses is Müller-Thurgau, produced in Germany in 1882 by a cross between Riesling and the table grape Madeleine Royale.[108] The most widely planted grape in Germany, it has the important attributes of growing more easily and offering greater resistance to frost than Riesling. But it's basically good for producing bulk Liebfraumilch rather than quality wine. In fact, breeding programs have generally had their greatest successes in producing new varieties that do well in marginal climates, often because they have greater resistance to cold weather. While useful in allowing the range of viticulture to be extended where natural varieties might not succeed, almost by definition this does not produce great wine.

Selection of clones from existing varieties has had more impact.[109] Whether for good or bad depends on the criteria applied in the selection. There has been too much of a trend for breeding institutes to concentrate on reliability and productivity rather than quality. Often enough this has led to homogeneity and blandness in the wine. But when clones are selected for quality of fruit, or for criteria such as ripening at the most appropriate time for a specific climate, they can improve the wine. There remains, of course, the concern that lack of diversity will offset the advantages gained by having healthy grapevines, and clones cannot do more than allow the best subvarieties to be selected from a cultivar; they will not offer the range of new possibilities created by a sexual cross. If evolution has not ended, then, certainly it is more restricted today.

III THE WORLD MARKET

REGULATION AND TAXATION are as old as wine itself. In ancient Egypt, wine had to be cleared by the authorities as fit for sale, and it was taxed according to its quality level. In Greece, speculation was prevented by refusing to allow wine to be sold before it was bottled and by banning sales on credit. Wine production became a sufficiently important economic factor in the Roman Empire for planting of vines to be regulated. For the next couple of thousand years, regulation was local and sporadic. The modern era started in the first part of the twentieth century with the introduction of legislation in France, culminating in the system of Appellation Contrôlée, to ensure the authenticity of the stated origin of a wine. This evolved into the system that now rules the classification of all wine in the European Union into three categories: table wine, wine with geographical indication, and quality wine. Place names as descriptors for wine remained a free for all outside Europe until recent treaties granting protection to the European place names. In the New World, production of wine is much less regulated, and description focuses on varietals, with less concentration on place of origin, but the marketing of wine is tightly controlled, reaching a ludicrous epitome in the three-tier distribution system of the United States.

Development of regulations.

2500 B.C.	"Inspector of the Wine Test" approves wine for sale in Egypt. Tax determined by quality.
400 B.C.	Laws in Greece prevent watering down wine and require airtight amphorae. Wine cannot be sold as futures.
92 C.E.	Roman Emperor Domitian requires vines to be uprooted in many regions.
~800	Emperor Charlemagne bans treading grapes and introduces other regulations.
1487	Sulfur dioxide authorized as preservative by decree of Prussian Royal Court.
1935	Appellation contrôlée introduced in France.
1962	European Union extends regulations to define quality wines in member countries.
2000	Agreements to protect European place names on wines in New World.

8

Global Wine Trends

INTEREST IN WINE HAS NEVER BEEN SO GREAT AS TODAY. Going back to the ancient world, wine was a focus for the leisured classes. The best wines were treasured, and, much as today, connoisseurs would boast about old wines they had drunk. The Satyricon, a sharp satire of the first century C.E., describes a dinner party at which a rich parvenu, Trimalchio, serves a wine described as real Opimian—the fabled Falernian wine from the year 121 B.C. when Opimius was consul. The wine was supposedly labeled as "one hundred years old," a pointed give-away as to lack of authenticity, but the description emphasizes the social importance of being able to brag about the vintage.[1] Not so much has changed at the top end in the past two millennia.

But in the past half century, the wine market has broadened enormously and quality has improved out of all recognition. "We've converted from being a cottage industry into a competitive consumer luxury-goods industry," says Michael Mondavi, formerly of Robert Mondavi winery in Napa valley.[1] The contrasting directions of two countries at opposite ends of the wine spectrum illustrate worldwide trends. France is the world's largest consumer, with an average annual consumption of roughly 75 bottles per person. In the United States, individual consumption is relatively low, at roughly 11 bottles per person.

"French drinking habits are well known. Essentially they consist of fairly continuous consumption over the course of each day."[1] It took an Anglo-Saxon to make this disapproving comment; it was probably not true even when it was written in 1990, and it is certainly no longer true today. Any French wine producer will tell you that there has been a dramatic fall in consumption over recent decades. Total consumption has almost halved since 1965.[2] But the proportion of wine at the highest quality level (AOC) has increased three-fold over the period. They say, "Les Français boivent moins mais boivent mieux." (The French drink less, but drink better).

By contrast, the United States has slowly been becoming a wine-drinking country, with consumption per person having increased three-fold since 1965.[3] And over that period, there has been a transition from low quality, sweet, fortified wines made from no-name grape varieties to dry wines made largely from quality varietals. With high population compensating for low individual consumption, the United States is set to become the world's largest wine-consuming nation. The decline in France shows the abandonment of wine as an ordinary beverage (much of it was rotgut consumed by workmen on their way to work); while the increase in the United States shows how wine is being embraced as a lifestyle choice.

From Plonk to Cult Wines

Should we measure a country's success on the wine stage in terms of its total volume of production, the value of its sales, or the reputation of its top wines? In most cases, the top wines attract attention, sometimes they create a halo effect helping the others, but if volumes are small their overall sales may make little direct contribution to the health and wealth of the wine region. The volume of lower-priced wines may be more important.[4] There is one major exception to this rule: Bordeaux, where the top wines are the major economic sector.[5]

France still dominates the production of high-end wines. The number of French wines whose price puts them into the category of luxury goods is far higher than for any other country. The United States runs second. Within France, Burgundy outstrips Bordeaux about 2:1 in terms of individual high-end wines—but many of the Bordeaux wines are relatively widely available, while almost all the Burgundian wines are available in only very small amounts. In fact, it is only from Bordeaux that wines at a price level over $100 per bottle make a large contribution to the economics of the region.[7] As you might expect, the Rhône is in third place for high-priced wines from France.

The top regions in the United States are Napa followed closely by Sonoma; in Australia Barossa is followed by McLaren Vale. In Italy the honors are shared between Piedmont and Tuscany; Spain is represented mostly by Rioja.[8] Cham-

Collectors' corner—the number of different wines of recent vintages from each country selling over $100 per bottle at international "s during the 2000s.[6]

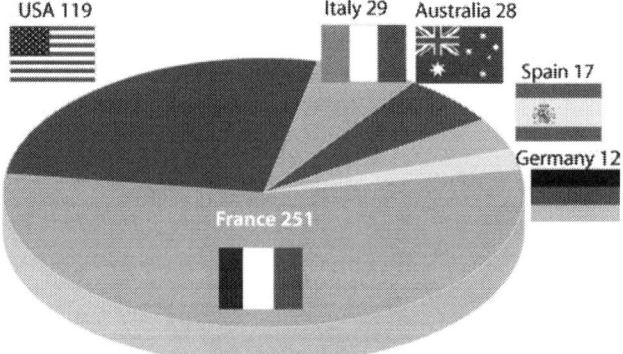

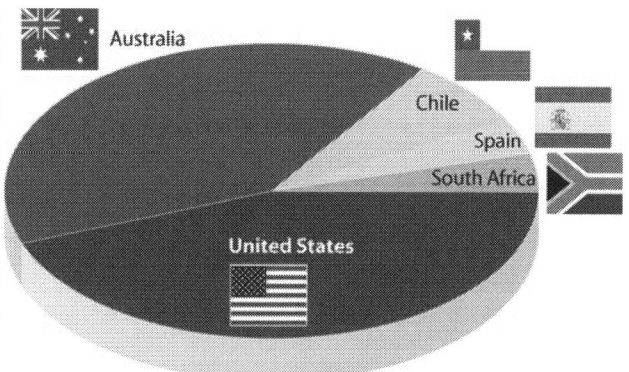

The United States and Australia together account for three quarters of the market share of the most powerful brands.[9]

pagne, Alsace, Madeira, and Port also produce collectible wines. The penetration by the New World is recent; in the 1990s, Australia scarcely figured; in the 1980s Napa was not significant. In fact, it was the legalization of wine auctions in New York in 1995 that really led to the rise of Napa as a prominent region for wine collectibles.

It's a very different picture looking at the distribution of top brands. The United States and Australia dominate by far, each with several brands in the top twenty worldwide. No other country has more than a single brand, and France does not appear at all in the list. Of course, there are wide differences in brand penetration in different countries. In the Anglo-Saxon world, brands dominate the market. In France and Italy, they have a much smaller market share.

Innovations in winemaking technology have had a major effect on the nature of the brands. The introduction of anaerobic methods, in which oxygen is excluded and the wines become brighter with more aggressive, forward fruits, has pretty much led to a new style of wine, as epitomized by New Zealand Sauvignon Blanc. At the other end of the spectrum, the ability to stabilize wine with sterile filtration allows wines with small amounts of residual sugar to avoid spoilage problems, allowing many major brands to make "dry" wines that in reality have low levels of residual sugar. The ability to use oak in cheaper forms than barrels has been responsible for allowing oak-flavored wines to penetrate lower levels of the market.

A Faithful Follower of Fashion

Wine styles are enormously influenced by fashion and limited by the available technology. The deeply colored, intensely extracted, powerful wines of today are made possible by modern methods of viticulture and vinification.

Both red and white wines were made in ancient times. The Egyptians must have made red wines, because most pictures show black grapes and juice. The Greeks prized their sweet wines, made from grapes that had been dried in the sun. The most famous wine of the Romans, Falernian, was white and sweet. In the middle ages in Bordeaux, most wine was white (known as vin clair), but a small amount of red wine was also made. With very short fermentation periods (around two days), the red cannot have been much more colored than a light rosé of today, and presumably the wine was low in alcohol.[10] By the nineteenth century, color and alcohol were prized in many markets; so wines such as those of Bordeaux, which were still relatively light with low alcohol, were habitually strengthened with wines from farther south to give them more color, body, and alcohol.

Auction prices give some idea of the fashion of the moment. Wine was included in the very first Christie's auction in London in 1766, and continued to be sold until the first world war. There were a few sales between the wars, but wine sales then stopped until the department was reopened in 1965. Two centuries of changes in wine fashions can be tracked through the catalogs.

Through the early nineteenth century most sales were of generic wines. Wine was wine. Lots offered in the early 1820s included "Port" and "Sherry" (occasionally the name of a shipper was mentioned), "Madeira" (the best was qualified as East India Madeira), "Champagne" (occasionally named as Sillery), "Hock" (from the Rheingau) was distinguished from "Moselle," and "Claret." Occasionally the name of the bottler was mentioned, but the only producer distinguished by name was "La Fitte." Burgundy was extremely rare. The price range was narrow for all quality wines, roughly £2-5 per dozen bottles.[11] Vintages were mentioned only sporadically.

Things changed little by the middle of the century. The classification of the great châteaux of the Médoc in 1855 had little direct effect on the consumer in London. Not much of a premium was paid even for the first growths; at one auction in 1860, "Claret" sold for £6 6s. per three dozen, whereas "La Fitte Claret" sold for £7 2s. (neither being given the benefit of vintage). The châteaux mostly remained unidentified.[12] Claret continued to sell a bit below Port, Madeira, and Sherry.[13]

By the end of the nineteenth century, the pattern was very different. Wine auctions focused on Champagne, Claret, and to a lesser degree, Port and Sherry. Champagne was by far the most expensive item: at the top, Pommery 1874 was selling for up to £12 per case at Christie's in the 1890s. The most expensive hock was Steinberg Cabinet, usually £5-6 per case. Sales of Burgundy were not common, but Romanée-Conti sold for £6.50 per case and Le Montrachet for £4 per case on the rare occasions they were offered. Lafite Rothschild was generally the most expensive claret, at under £5 per case for the 1870 vintage. Sauternes were even cheaper, with Château d'Yquem at £4-5 per dozen.[14]

Over the past century, a major rearrangement has taken place. Burgundy and Bordeaux hold positions as producers of the most expensive wines; white wines are less in demand than red; and Champagne only rarely rises to the extreme heights. Some wines from new regions make it into the lists of high-priced rarities, including the Rhône and the New World, especially Napa Valley. Hock and fortified wines have dropped off the list.

Today the gap between the top and bottom of the market is far higher in wine than any other beverage. Even aside from scarce cult items, wines at release vary from around $2 per bottle to more than $2000 per bottle.[15] There's nothing like a thousand-fold range of prices for beer or spirits—or soft drinks.

Sweet versus dry, white versus red, fashions come and go. It's a common pattern for wine regions to start by producing sweet wines, and then to move towards production of more sophisticated dry wines. All over the New World, production started with no-name varieties, often fortified to achieve a sweet style, and then made a transition to a dry style with higher quality varietals. The only significant difference in this pattern between the United States, Australia, South America, and South Africa, is the time at which they made the transition. But this is not to sneer at the New World; until the eighteenth century the white wines of Bordeaux were all made as sweet as the vintage allowed.[16]

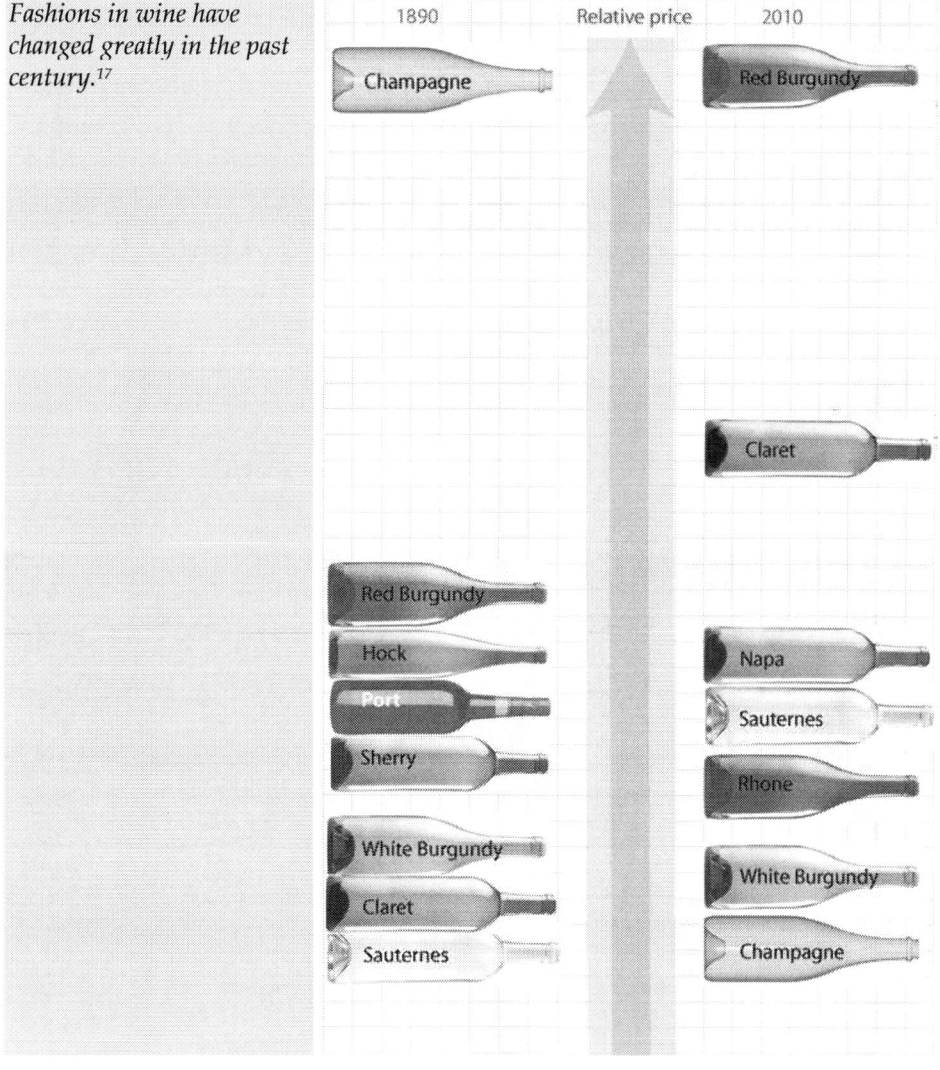

Fashions in wine have changed greatly in the past century.[17]

The Eggheads of Oenology

At the start of the twentieth century, wine production was mostly on a small scale, but by the end of the century most wine was mass produced. As industrial techniques replaced artisanal production, reliability and consistency became more important, creating increased need for technical support. The industry puts relatively little direct effort into research—much less than the food industry, for example—but as wine production has become an economic force in a region, centers for technical support develop at local institutions. Among the best known institutes of oenology today are those at Montpellier in southern France, Geisenheim in the Rheingau of Germany, the Davis campus of the University of California, and the AWRI (Australian Wine Research Institute) in Adelaide.

Oenology departments tend, of course, to specialize in the issues that are important in the vineyards surrounding them. They can be pretty good at solving local problems. The University of Bordeaux was instrumental in rescuing white Bordeaux from the dumps by discovering how to preserve character and freshness. The AWRI has been at the forefront of research into the differences between screwcaps and corks. But while research at the universities can bring helpful insights into viticulture and vinification, there is also more than an element of dead hand coming from the impetus to play it safe rather than to innovate. Oenology departments everywhere tend to favor quantity over quality and to prefer technical sophistication and reliability rather than artisanal variation. One of their most important roles today is to turn out trained oenologists who become winemakers with high levels of technical expertise. The crucial issue here is that the technical expertise should be a means for producing wine of interest rather than an end for homogenization.

University departments tend to place more emphasis on bringing up the general standard from the bottom than diffusing the highest quality down from the top. The institute at Dijon bears some responsibility for the spread of Pinot Droit in Burgundy in the 1960s; this cultivar of Pinot Noir (named for its upright stance) is a reliable producer, but gives quantity rather than quality. Its large berries with thick skins gave a wine that looked better than it tasted. Many of those characterless Burgundies of the period reflect the lack of focus and concentration in Pinot Droit.

Rootstocks might seem to be somewhat less interesting than varietals, but can have a huge effect on viticulture. Witness the debacle of AxR1. This cross between Vitis vinifera and Vitis rupestris is not used as a rootstock in Europe because of its sensitivity to phylloxera, but was recommended by the University of California at Davis for local use because of its reliability in various soils and climates and its high productivity. So widely accepted was the advice, that when AxR1 was duly eaten by an onslaught of phylloxera, almost all of the vineyards in California had to be replanted between 1989 and 1996, an economic devastation for the region.[18]

It's fair to say that the Department of Viticulture and Enology at Davis is no exception to the inclination to favor quantity over quality. Their role has not changed since their reaction in 1964 to the proposal of Fred and Eleanor McCrae to plant a Chardonnay vineyard at Stony Hill. "The professors disapproved of amateurs pretending they were in Burgundy, where Chardonnay was grown, when they were in northern California, where white wine was made out of French Colombard, Chenin Blanc, and other white grapes better able to withstand frost," says historian James Conaway.[19] Stony Hill Chardonnay duly became one of the most famous wines of Napa Valley.

Of course, it's easy to take potshots at academics who rely on the status quo. Many of the most interesting wines of today come from entrepreneurs who took a risk in planting a variety in a location which all conventional wisdom said was designed for failure, from Mas de Daumas Gassac's planting of Cabernet at Aniane in the Languedoc to Cloudy Bay's planting of Sauvignon Blanc in Marlborough, New Zealand. No university department would countenance such risky ventures. To get the best out of the departments, you have to understand where they are coming from, which is reliably raising the general standard. The mistake is to let their influence become so dominant that an entire region follows a single practice.

Flying Winemakers and Globalization

Oenology is almost as old as winemaking. Around 200 B.C., Cato (the Elder) in his book *de Agri Cultura* advised on a whole gamut of activities, from cultivating vineyards to detailing procedures for making wine. Some of his concerns were unique to the period: advice for looking after slaves, for example, including giving them the equivalent of a bottle of wine per day. But many issues have scarcely changed: how to train the vines, what grape varieties might best be cultivated, when to harvest, and how to run the presses.[20] The average vineyard was not so different in size then from a large vineyard today, in the region of 20-40 hectares.[21] Much of the attention given to grape growing and wine production no doubt reflects their economic importance; Cato regarded the business as profitable, although later writers on the subject, such as Columella during the first century C.E., were less convinced.[22] At all events, the tradition of commentary and advice on vineyards and wine production continued for the next millennium or so.

It was only in the second half of the twentieth century that oenology became a hands-on experience in the sense that visiting oenologists would advise wine producers on the spot. This simultaneously brought significant technical improvements to winemaking and generated assertions that all wines were beginning to taste the same.

The first of the great oenologists, who did more than anyone to bring vinification into the modern era based on rational analysis, was Emile Peynaud. He revolutionized winemaking in Bordeaux in the 1950s by introducing methods based on understanding the processes of vinification. Before Peynaud, malolactic fermentation was a mysterious event that might (or might not) happen in the spring. Peynaud demonstrated that malolactic fermentation is caused by bacteria that are sensitive to temperature; they become active as the cellars warm up in the spring.[23]

Peynaud convinced winemakers to replace old barrels, often infected with spoilage bacteria, with clean, new barrels—leading to criticism that he had introduced the taste of oak into wine. The changes that he championed, from using the best grapes to maintaining cellar hygiene, made wine easier to drink sooner. To those accustomed to the view that young wine was tart, tannic, unpleasant, and even undrinkable, this was heresy. Traditionalists distrusted him and claimed that his wines had been homogenized, "Peynaudized," as they put it. "I am not sure of the appellation, I do not recognize the vintage, but I can tell this wine was made by Emile Peynaud," was one famous comment. (Similar comments have been made since, with perhaps more pertinence, about the oenologues of today.) Peynaud's retort was that, "The wines of yesterday were more stereotyped than today's. They were all similar because they shared the same defect. They were oxidized."[24]

Similar accusations reverberate, but with more force, in the present era. Many Bordeaux châteaux are advised by oenologues, of whom Michel Rolland, Stéphan Derenoncourt, Denis Dubourdieu, and Jacques Boissenot are the best known. Each advises a considerable number of château—Michel Rolland more than 50, Stéphan Derenoncourt around 40, Denis Dubourdieu and Jacques Boissenot some 20-30 each. Altogether some 200 of the leading wines of Bordeaux depend on advice from these four oenologues.[25] (And of course they also advise wineries in other regions and countries.)

Michel Rolland in particular is known for producing wines with intense fruit and new oak, very much the modern style of Bordeaux, in some ways more resembling wines of the New World than those of Bordeaux in the past. He is the proprietor of Château Bon Pasteur in Pomerol, and among the châteaux he advises on the right bank are the producers of many of the garage (intense small-production) wines. He is often felt to be the arch apostle of the international style, and was portrayed as a somewhat Mephisthophelean figure in the film Mondovino, which took aim at the globalization of wine.

The "international style" wines depend on changes in both viticulture and vinification. Not only are grapes harvested at increased levels of ripeness, with greater sugar levels (giving higher alcohol levels) and more (and riper) tannins, but the wine is exposed to new oak at an earlier stage. The new style wines tend to be powerful rather than elegant, bursting with fruit, sometimes with jammy rather than savory aromas and flavors. These wines tend to show well at comparative tastings because their intense flavors make it difficult to appreciate wines with more subtle constitutions; even experienced tasters can be fooled. Personally I would question whether these wines are really suitable to accompany food. However, they are much favored by some influential wine critics, including Robert Parker; reflecting the extent of his influence, in France, they sometimes say that a wine made to this prescription has been *parkerisé*.

The Most Powerful Critic in the World

Wine criticism is a relatively new phenomenon. It used to be that critics were essentially the same people who sold you the wine; writing was a subsidiary activity. In the absence of any genuine independence, their corruption was legendary. "Have you received your case of Lafite from the château this year?" one would ask another. Stories used to abound about critics who visited famous châteaux and left the trunks of their cars open, ready for a few complimentary cases of wine.

The absence of genuine critical comment was part of the impetus that led Robert Parker to start *The Wine Advocate* in 1978. Since then The Wine Advocate has become by far the most important newsletter on wine, and Robert Parker so dominates wine criticism that many feel no other critic has any comparable significance. But Parker's importance may perhaps lie not so much in his dominance as in the fact that he really developed the whole idea of independent criticism. Now there are many others earning their living by wine criticism (although it has to be said that many regrettably lack his independence.) Since the 1970s, the transition from a producer-driven to a consumer-driven industry has seen enormous growth of consumer magazines and newsletters focused on assessing and recommending individual wines.[26]

The Wine Advocate established the paradigm for assessing wines with a quantitative score out of 100, much simplifying the process of selection for the consumer. Right from the start, Bordeaux was a major focal point, spurred by the fact virtually no critics had exposed the poor quality of some first growths during the preceding decade. The Wine Advocate was different, starting off by slamming the quality of the 1973 vintage. Château Margaux was described as "a terrible wine… very thin and acidic."

The Wine Advocate reports its ratings in plain text, but Decanter and the Wine Spectator are glossy consumer magazines.

It was with the (then) atypical 1982 vintage in Bordeaux that Parker made his reputation. Relatively warm, prolonged vintage conditions led to a harvest of unusually ripe grapes, giving wines with lower acidity, much riper tannins, and higher alcohol than had previously been common. The low acidity caused many critics to write off the year, at least in terms of a classic long-lived vintage. Among these was Robert Finigan, author of the Private Guide to Wines, then the leading wine newsletter in the United States. This mistake, together with some financial problems, led to the decline and ultimate failure of the Private Guide,[27] opening the way for the Wine Advocate to dominate the market in fine wine assessment.

Robert Parker was one of the first to recognize the quality of the vintage, and his argument that 1982 would be a long-lived great vintage elevated him to become the high priest of wine criticism. From its initial issue of a few hundred copies in the local Washington-Baltimore area, the Wine Advocate has grown to tens of thousands of copies distributed worldwide. In April each year, the Wine Advocate now offers a detailed assessment of the preceding Bordeaux vintage complete with scores out of 100 for most wines.

Its dominance, initially of the market in the United States, later in Europe and Asia, has led to the description of Parker as the world's most influential critic. Indefatigable in his tasting, now supported by a team of writers with responsibilities for particular wine regions, he has built the Wine Advocate into a voice that cannot be ignored by wine producers. Nowhere is this more apparent than in Bordeaux, for which he still takes personal responsibility.

A score of 90 from the Wine Advocate is the tipping point. The saying goes that a wine with a score above 90 cannot be kept on the shelf; but at a score below 90 it cannot be got off the shelf. The Bordelais both rely upon and deplore Parker's influence. One château owner recently said to me, without any perceptible sense of irony, "Nobody pays any attention to the Wine Spectator—it all depends on God's rating." (It goes without saying that God is Parker.) The proprietor said sadly that now the negociants just quote Parker, essentially replacing what used to be their own comments with his ratings.[28] Indeed, Parker scores are commonly appended to wine bottles in wine shops around the world.

The Wine Advocate shows a preference for wines that are dark colored, full bodied, with obvious fruits, and often high in alcohol. This is the modern style pioneered by the New World, and of which the 1982 vintage was a forerunner for Bordeaux. Given this perception, it is ironic that early issues of the Wine Advocate (in common with other commentators of the period) took the view that California wines had alcohol levels that were too high, had too much oak, and were altogether too massive. An early issue commented, "The better Bordeaux are elegant, delicate wines that possess incredible subtlety and complexity, whereas the best California Cabernets are massive, powerful, assertive wines often bordering on coarseness." Parker went on to comment that the California Cabernets did not age well beyond a few years, compared with the much greater longevity of Bordeaux. It is not easy to relate these early views to the wine reviews of the past decade.

Everyone agrees that Parker's scores have a major effect on the price of Bordeaux. There is no doubt that his views affect the general reception of a vintage. The 2008 vintage in Bordeaux is a case in point. This is a decent enough, but not top, vintage, and when the wines first went on the market in April 2009, in rather difficult general financial conditions, prices dropped some 30% from the previous year. Halfway through the campaign, Parker reported that the vintage was much better than had been generally appreciated; prices for those wines that had not come out previously went up sharply. (Many believe this is a fool's paradise.)

The critics' ratings for individual châteaux can swing widely from year to year, but prices show good stability from one year to the next (relative to the overall scale for the vintage). There are certainly exceptions where an extraordinary result by a château may cause a dramatic (but usually transient) spike in its price (corrections in the other direction are much less common), but there is considerable inertia with regards to changing the relative prices of châteaux. Parker's view of a château certainly affects the price of the wine, but he reacts much faster than the market, and it can take some years for a château to change its general position in the rankings. In fact, none of the critics' ratings show close relationships with one another or with release prices of the wines.[29]

Parker's opinions are so important in the world of wine that there is a whole company devoted simply to adjusting wines in order to get better Parker points. Based in California's Sonoma Valley, Enologix was started in 1993 by Leo McCloskey. He's a somewhat controversial figure because his methods are secret, consisting of software that he claims can predict the critical score of a wine from chemical analysis. His database of tens of thousands of wines is used to advise his clients what they need to do in order to bump their score over the magic 90 point level. Few winemakers will acknowledge using his services, but McCloskey claims that tens of wines advised by Enologix score over 90 points in the Wine Advocate.[30]

Whether you agree with Parker's ratings or not, whether it is healthy for any one opinion to be so dominant, there is one thing that can be said with certainty: Parker's ratings reflect his palate. The Wine Advocate takes no advertising and exists solely on its subscription income. That is more than can be said for the vast majority of wine magazines and critics. The leading magazines, the Wine Spectator in the United States, Decanter in Britain, and La Revue du Vin de France, all depend heavily on advertising from wine producers and distributors.

With a circulation of 350,000, the Wine Spectator is by far the largest wine magazine. It's influential in the United States to the extent that retailers rush to stock wines it recommends; it is regarded more or less with indifference elsewhere. Its market position has been captured by Michael Steinberger: "Its content appears tailored to attract two groups of wine drinkers: trophy hunters and people fairly new to oenophilia. For the uninitiated, the Spectator is a superb gateway product: informative, topical, easy on the eyes, mercifully light on the jargon... To appeal to the poseurs, the magazine runs lots of unctuous stories about insta-billionaires and their custom-designed cellars, invariably stocked with a millennium's supply of swank wines. It is partly for this reason that the Spectator is considered a joke by many wine sophisticates; some call it the

"Speculator" after the aforementioned trophy hunters. The magazine is also knocked for its ratings, which are seen as inconsistent and inflated relative to other critics, and for its coverage, which often tends toward the sensational... It's never been proved that advertisers influence scores, but suspicions run deep, especially in wine chat rooms."[31] All too often, the Wine Spectator loses its focus and publishes issues with little to say about wine, but with a lot about lifestyles of the rich and famous.

With articles written mostly by its own staff, the Wine Spectator offers a certain unanimity of opinion in liking bold, fruity, forward wines. This can lead it into error. Barolo had a unprecedented run of wonderful vintages from 1996 to 2001 due to the good weather in Piedmont. But there was general hilarity when the Wine Spectator rated the 2000 vintage. "Italy's jewel box of a wine region produced its greatest vintage ever in 2000—a year I rate a perfect 100 points," James Suckling, their man in Europe, said with characteristic pomposity.[32] True, it was a good, perhaps even a great vintage, but by 2004 when the wines began to appear, cognoscenti were waiting for the wines from 2001, a truly classic vintage. The producers could not believe their luck in having the preceding vintage rated as the best ever, and laughed all the way to the bank as the wines sold out in the United States. The 2001 vintage epitomized the ethereal style of Barolo, but 2000 was just a little too warm to display classic character. The wines showed more obvious fruit than usual, drinking well in their youth; lovely wines, but not classic long-lived Barolo. The Wine Advocate showed much better judgment in rating vintage 2000 at the same 95 points as 1999, and rating 2001 at 96 points.

Among the Wine Spectator's most notable features are its annual publication of the Top 100 wines of the year, released just in time for the Christmas buying season, and the Restaurant Awards issue in August. Both have been tarnished by awards for nonexistent wines or restaurants, and for inexplicable choices. The Top 100 list is a particularly big deal, especially for wines at the very top, which rapidly escalate in price and become scarce, even though the mandate for inclusion on the list is that wines are produced in good quantities and sold at reasonable prices.

In 1999, the top-rated wine on the list was the 1996 Cinq Cépages, a Bordeaux blend made by Chateau St. Jean in Sonoma Country.[33] The magazine commented: "The rise of the 1996 Chateau St. Jean Cabernet Sauvignon Sonoma County Cinq Cépages to our Wine of the Year won't surprise those who've tasted this remarkably rich and polished wine as it has evolved. With its uncommon depth, ripe, juicy flavors and plush, velvety texture, Cépages won votes and admiration from our editors for its quality (a 95-point rating on the Wine Spectator 100-point scale), its $28 price and its availability."

The problem is that the 1996 vintage was only released on to the market in a very small tranche during 1999. It was not generally released until the following year (and at double the price).[34] At the least, it's questionable how supplies could have been adequate to allow people to follow the wine as it evolved. Just to add to the confusion, in replying to criticism, Thomas Matthews of The Wine Spectator referred to the award-winning wine as the 1999 vintage (which certainly could not have been available).[35]

Equally incredible was the Wine Spectator's choice of Guigal's 1999 Châteauneuf-du-Pape as its wine of the year in 2002. There is no doubt that Guigal is a master winemaker: his single-vineyard Côte-Rôties are widely acknowledged to be among the finest wines on the planet. But his wines from the southern Rhône, including Châteauneuf-du-Pape are simply not in the same league. The Châteauneuf is well enough crafted, but it's a middle of the road wine without any particular distinction, and there are any number of other, more interesting wines of the appellation. In response to criticism, the magazine did not provide any further enlightenment about the choice. "This 1999 Châteauneuf-du-Pape is an outstanding effort by an extraordinary winemaker in a difficult vintage," said Thomas Matthews of the Wine Spectator.[36] Fair enough: but does a good result from a "difficult" vintage justify a wine of the year, when other regions may have performed better? There was nothing wrong with this wine, indeed it was commendable, but its choice as wine of the year simply casts doubt on the value of the whole exercise.

But worse was yet to come. Every August, the magazine rates restaurants for their wine lists, placing some 4,000 restaurants in three ascending categories: Award of Excellence (3,249 winners at last count), Best of Award of Excellence (797 winners), and Grand Award (72 winners). The restaurant gets a certificate for the appropriate level of award, which it can display.

An exposé in the New York Times reported that for the basic level of Award of Excellence, all that is required is for the restaurant to send its wine list to the Wine Spectator with a check.[37] The current fee is $250, so the thousands of restaurants on the present list have paid more than a million dollars to the Wine Spectator between them for the year's listing. (You have to reapply every year.) The Wine Spectator makes no claim that it visits restaurants except for those given the Grand Award, but certainly it was not widely appreciated outside of the trade that basically the Award of Excellence is cheap advertising for the restaurant.

Just how easy it is to gain an Award became clear as the result of a spoof application made by writer Robin Goldstein as part of his research. He submitted the wine list from a mythical restaurant, called Osteria l'Intrepido in Milan, created a web site for the restaurant, and obtained a Milan phone number and fax.[38] The rub comes in the wines on the list: they were terrible. The "reserve" list contained three vintages of the great Tuscan wine Sassicaia; but also contained twelve wines that the Wine Spectator had rated poorly, from 58 to 81 points, with comments such as "tasted metallic and odd," "unacceptable, smells like bug spray," "turpentine, hard acidic character."

Certainly Goldstein took some trouble to make the fake restaurant appear real. If it had actually submitted a consistently good wine list, there would be little with which to reproach the magazine, which, as Executive Editor Thomas Matthews pointed out, does not claim to visit the restaurants à la Michelin. "This is a program that recognizes the efforts restaurants put into their wine lists," he said.[39] But when the list includes wines that the Wine Spectator itself has trashed, isn't the wary diner entitled to wonder whether that Award of Excellence certificate on the wall isn't simply a cheap substitute for buying in some good wines? What faith does the Wine Spectator have in its own ratings?

All this is perhaps an illustration of the naïveté with which consumers regard supposedly authoritative magazines. Yet naïveté is not restricted to consumers. An academic study tried to determine whether wine had improved in quality and price by examining the Spectator's Top 100 list.[40] The thesis was that if average scores have increased, wines must have got better; if average prices have decreased, values must have improved. There was no significant variation in average scores over the period, but average price declined 44%. A large part of the price reduction was due to the replacement of French wines by less expensive wines from the New World. The authors concluded that American consumers are getting equally good wine for less money. The study may well be a testament to the power of the Wine Spectator in the market; it suggests that producers have made increasingly successful efforts to provide inexpensive wines made in a style that the Wine Spectator scores well. But unless you believe that Wine Spectator scores represent some objective measure of quality, this sadly proves nothing about value.

Published from London, Decanter magazine modestly bills itself as "quite simply, the world's best wine magazine." It started as a relatively serious, consumer-oriented magazine, with articles from good contributors. Most articles are written by outside contributors, so there is some variety of opinion, and it still retains some heavyweight and knowledgeable writers, but now selling 40,000 copies under the aegis of IPC (International Publishing Corporation, a mass market magazine publisher), it has distinctly more of an LCD tone, personality-driven articles, "promotional supplements" that make it easy to confuse advertising and editorial content, and a host of extra-mural activities including wine tastings, dinners, wine awards, and so on. Its major influence is in Britain, but its impact is not at all comparable to The Wine Advocate or Wine Spectator in the United States.

The Revue du Vin de France really was the world's best wine magazine (granted you had to read it in French), albeit strongly focused on France. Published since 1927, its circulation of more than 40,000 gave it a commanding position. Articles were knowledgeable and wide-ranging, and contributors included two of France's most renowned tasters, Michel Bettane and Thierry Desseauve. But concerned about future policy, Bettane and Desseauve quit the magazine after it was taken over by Marie-Claire (part of the Lagardère publishing group), which had previously purchased a rival magazine in the 1990s, Cuisine et Vins de France, and taken it down market. Unfortunately, their fears were only too well founded.

The increasing diversity of sources for wine, coupled with increasing numbers of new consumers, creates more and more need for informed criticism at all levels from retail to restaurant wine lists. The time when wine was a pursuit of a few, who knew where to obtain reliable advice, is long since past. The problem is the gap between the newsletters, such as the Wine Advocate, whose main readership consists of enthusiasts at some level, and the magazines, now increasingly consumer-oriented, and like all magazines of their type, prone to confuse editorial and advertising content. More of a ladder is needed to enable consumers to climb from dependence on ratings of variable quality to reliance on their own palates.

International Brands: Sourcing Wine

Terroir is irrelevant. The origins and sources of the wine are of relatively little importance. For the majority of today's consumers, the name of the wine brand is the crucial factor. Wines are bought on the same basis as other products: on the reputation of the manufacturer, and on the price.

A wine brand used to be relatively simple. It would typically consist of a single wine, such as Blue Nun Liebfraumilch or Mateus Rosé, the leading brands in Britain during the 1960s and 1970s. Each had its own style and following, and there was none of what today would be called "crossover" to other products of the same company. If you wanted a red wine, rather than a white or a rosé, you wouldn't look to Blue Nun or Mateus to provide it.

Today a brand attempts to provide a complete line offering the consumer a range of options (typically around the same price point). Take Blue Nun, which has been revitalized to provide a range of 20 wines, including red, white, rosé, and sparkling. Most people were probably aware that Blue Nun Liebfraumilch came from Germany (although very few consumers in Britain are aware that Mateus comes from Portugal).[41] But today the only category the brand represents is itself. In the Blue Nun range, the closest to the original Blue Nun is now a Qualitätswein (nominally a step up in grade) that comes from Germany's Rheinhessen region, but the range also includes a Shiraz from Australia, a Cabernet from France, a Zinfandel from the United States, and wines from many other sources. The two important features are the name, Blue Nun, and the varietal.

Some brands add geography as part of their character. The extraordinary success of Yellow Tail started with a single wine in 2001. It became the largest

Blue Nun includes wines from several countries.

imported brand in the United States in 2003, and now is on the list of top ten brands worldwide. Today Yellow Tail includes 13 varietal-labeled wines and also a reserve line (at higher price). But all share the same logo that was associated with the original success: a jumping wallaby, pointing to the origin in Australia, which remains a major selling point. You might view Yellow Tail as a sub-brand of "Brand Australia."

There can be strong reactions when a brand with national origins goes multinational. Lindemans, a well-known brand from major Australian producer Fosters, was accused of "using [a] highly-rated and well-recognized Australian brand with a reputation for quality and integrity and raping it," when they introduced lines from Chile and South Africa.[42] Fosters defended themselves by saying that consumer research indicated that most purchasers recognized Lindemans as a brand but had no idea it originated in Australia.

With their increasingly broad remit,[43] brands are taking over more and more of the market. At the start of the millennium, the top ten global wine brands had 5% of the world market.[44] By the end of the first decade, the list was strengthened by some powerful growing brands from the New World, Jacob's Creek, Lindemans, Blossom Hill, and Yellow Tail.[45] The top brands of still wine have more than achieved parity with sparkling wines, where brands have always dominated the market. Granted that leading brands remain a much smaller share of the wine market than their counterparts in the spirits or beer market, still they are progressing in both market share and increasingly global distribution.

Packaging the Product

As long ago as the 1950s, the giant American producer Gallo used screwcaps, based on the belief that corks were unreliable; unfortunately, however, all this did was to reinforce the general impression that screwcaps were associated with low quality production.[46] It took a while before consumers accepted that a screwcap did not necessarily imply lower quality, but since 2000 there has been a sea change, although there are still big differences between individual countries. Screwcaps are strongest where they started, in Australia (where more than half of the wines use screwcaps) and New Zealand (where virtually all of them do so). Slowly the effect has spread through Europe, led by large supermarkets in Britain that insisted on their suppliers using screwcaps. Germany has been somewhat of a holdout for the traditional view that screwcaps indicate lower quality, but on a recent visit, several producers told me they were now bottling wines for export under screwcap, because corks were not acceptable to their importers in the New World, a complete reversal from how things used to be. Screwcap usage in France is sporadic, but there are examples of important producers in every major region using screwcaps, although the overall proportion remains small.

What would be the ideal container for wine? It would be completely inert, incapable of reacting with water, alcohol, or any of the dissolved components. Glass fits that description better than anything else available. But the ideal con-

Glass bottles with various types of seal account for two thirds of all wine sold; the remaining third is divided between bag-in-box, tetrapak, P.E.T. bottles, and other types of packaging.[47]

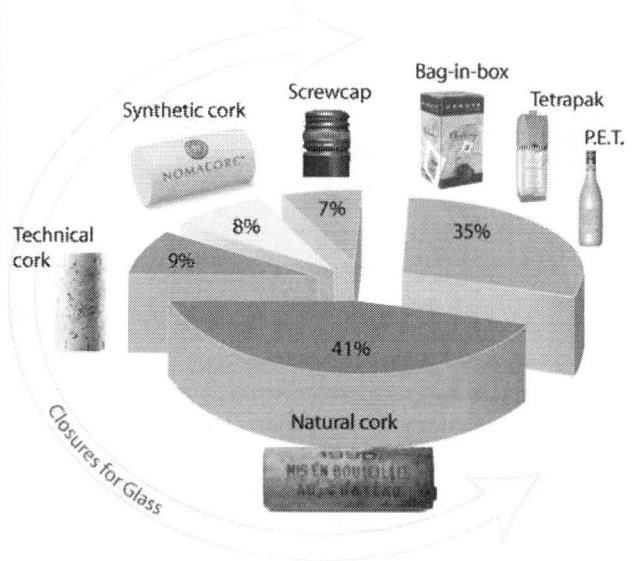

tainer would also be light and easy to transport. Glass is heavy and also (relatively) fragile. The seal for the container would be inert, and preferably reusable: cork has been much improved in the past decade, but there is still an unacceptable level of contamination with TCA, and cork is not easy to reuse. Screwcaps may turn out to be the answer when the issue of oxygen permeability can be resolved.

Another issue is that some wines are aged for long periods, up to several decades, so the container needs to be stable. Glass lasts for ever (although corks sometimes have to be replaced after 25 years or so). Nothing else with the same durability has been found, but there are several alternative packaging media for wines that will be consumed in the short term. Bottles made of aluminum or P.E.T. (a plastic like that used for bottled water) are light, and the tetrapak (adapted from the cardboard cartons for juice or milk) is easily transportable. And the ingenious bag-in-box is well suited for large quantities: it contains a collapsible plastic bag inside a cardboard carton, with a tap. As wine is drawn out, the bag collapses to exclude oxygen, so the wine stays fresh. Bag-in-box is the most rapidly growing segment of the market among the alternatives for cheaper, short-lived wines.

All these new possibilities have significantly changed the way wine is delivered. Glass now accounts for only two thirds of the market, although admittedly it's the more expensive two thirds. Natural cork, which sealed virtually all glass wine bottles two decades ago, is now used in about two thirds of bottles. Technical corks (consisting of agglomerated particles of natural cork) and synthetic corks (made of molded plastic, sometimes colored like real cork, sometimes brightly colored like children's toys) come next in importance. Screwcap is the most rapidly growing segment, increasing roughly five-fold in the five years since 2003. It's probably going to be second after natural cork in the not too distant future.

Winemaking is a natural enough activity, but is it "green?" Obviously enough, organic viticulture makes fewer demands on the environment than conventional agriculture, but the difference hasn't been quantitated. Running a winery is an expensive proposition in terms of energy consumption, but if you calculate how much energy goes into a bottle of wine, the result is a bit surprising. The energy cost of producing bulk wine is just a bit less than half the energy cost of producing bottled wine: the difference is due not only to the materials involved, but also because of the high costs involved in transporting the bottled product.[48] Bottles may be colored green, but they have a high carbon footprint, affected somewhat by the type of closure.

The cork producers have been feeling themselves under attack lately, with problems of cork taint leading more and more producers to switch to screwcaps, and they have gone to some pains to try to show that cork is environmentally the most friendly closure.[49] If a bottle has a carbon footprint of 180 tons of CO_2/million units, a natural cork adds another 10, a synthetic cork another 16, a technical cork another 21-25, and a screwcap another 35-50 depending on exactly how it's made. There's been quite a bit of fuss as to whether corks or screwcaps are better for the environment, but it's obvious that if you really want to make an impact, eliminating or improving the glass is the way to go.

Taxation: Extortion or Distortion?

Alcohol has been a favorite target for taxation even well before it became attractive as a sin tax. In early agricultural economies, wine (and beer) were simply targets among many for possible taxation. In situations where wine became a significant part of the economy, its importance for taxation increased. The Romans received considerable revenues from taxes on wine imports (recorded by stamp marks on the amphorae).[50] Colbert, the great finance minister of France in 1670, commented that the state needed to know how much wine people would buy each year in order to assess the level of revenue.[51] At the peak of production before the phylloxera epidemic, in 1875, taxes on wine and spirits were the largest single item of state revenue in France.[52] But from ancient times until the last century, wine (and other alcoholic beverages) were assessed on the basis of the ease of tax collection and the extent to which taxes could feasibly be raised.

Taxation of wine was used in the same way as other fiscal measures, as part of general policy. During the seventeenth century, for example, English policy was to tax wine imports at rates intended to encourage trade with territories owned by the Crown and to discourage trade with countries with which England was at war.[53] Certainly wine was regarded as a luxury rather than necessity, and therefore appropriate for increases in indirect taxation, but it attracted no particular hostility. One of the first signs of the transition to use taxation of wine to influence social policy was the attempt to reduce alcohol consumption in Britain during the first world war by increasing taxes on alcohol. Yet this was pragmatic, based on concern to increase industrial productivity, rather than representing a moral stance.

The temperance movement of the nineteenth century agitated against consumption of alcohol, but its extreme position, that any form of alcoholic drink was dangerous, caused its efforts to be directed towards prohibition rather than increased taxation. The collapse of Prohibition in the United States dealt a blow to the movement; but the concept that alcohol consumption is a problem for society that should be addressed by fiscal and social policies developed as part and parcel of the politically correct movement in recent decades.[54]

Tax rates on wine vary widely in Europe, but the general rule is that the farther away you are from the producing countries, the less value you will get in a bottle of wine. The countries of the north, ranging from Scandinavia to Britain have very high excise duties, basically a flat tax per bottle. This means that the value of the wine in an inexpensive bottle can become vanishingly small—when you buy a cheap bottle of wine, you are paying tax and getting remarkably little product. In the producing countries of the warm south, excise taxes are much lower, so the overall tax bite depends on local sales tax and is more proportionate to the value of the bottle. Maybe that's why you can get a delicious bottle of wine more cheaply when on holiday.

Whatever the reasons for the variation in tax rates, attempts to use them for social policy are rarely successful. Countries with punishingly high tax rates (Sweden, Britain, and Ireland) have widely varying consumptions. Countries with high consumption (Portugal, Spain, France, Austria, Germany, Ireland) have a huge range of tax rates. Ireland, with the highest tax rate, has one of the

Although Europe is supposed to be a Community, tax rates on alcohol vary enormously. Low tax rate countries are typically less than €1.5, high tax rates are more than €3 for an average bottle.[55]

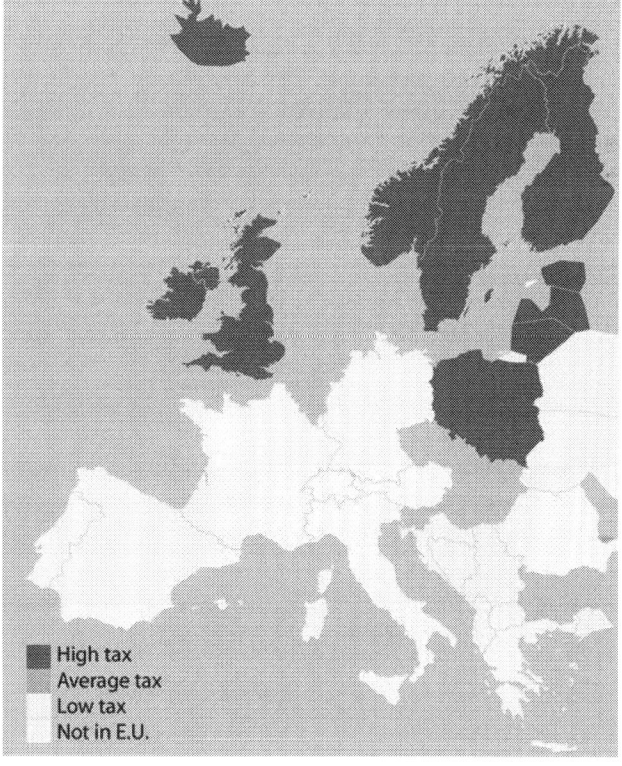

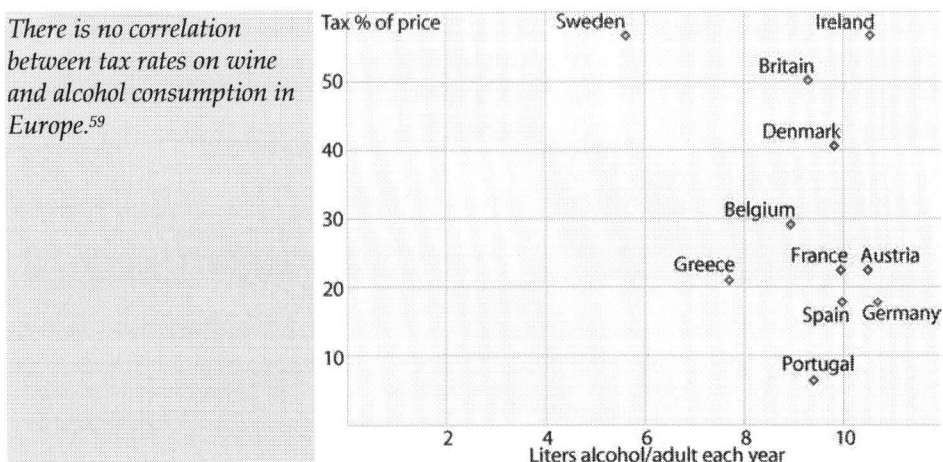

There is no correlation between tax rates on wine and alcohol consumption in Europe.[59]

highest consumptions. Statistics show that people do generally drink less when the cost of alcohol is raised, but it's really a futile endeavor to use taxation to try to stop people drinking.[56] Probably the major consequence for wine drinkers is that people who buy cheap wine get increasingly poor value for money, partly because of the tax bite, partly because quality is compromised by the intense pressure on price. And binge drinking among adults is greatest in countries with high tax rates (Britain and Finland are at the top of the list) and lowest in countries with low tax rates (Spain and Italy are at the bottom).[57]

The consumer who buys an average bottle of wine is ripped off everywhere in the Anglo-Saxon world, although it varies a bit as to who is ripping him off. In Britain, the combination of a standard excise tax with a swingeing rate of VAT means that less than a third of the cost of a £3.99 bottle actually reflects its content. The situation is even worse for someone who buys a bottle at the next price point down, say at £2.99—the wine will be worth only about 50p. In the United States, the stranglehold of the three tier system means that the distributor takes a major share before the wine even gets into the retail chain; the average profit to the winery on the bottle is only about 60¢, so the producer is actually getting the smallest share of the pie of anyone in the chain.[58]

There's not much doubt about extortion with regards to taxation on wine—things haven't changed much since the English were forced to pay Danegelt to head off Viking invaders in the middle ages. And market distortion almost inevitably results from the tax authorities' perpetual attempts to find clever ways to maximize revenues. It's common for different rates to apply, for example, depending on the alcoholic strength. After this was introduced in Britain in the 1860s, merchants began importing wines at different strengths and then blending them to avoid paying the higher tax on the whole lot. You might say that the more intricate the forms of taxation, the more intricate the tricks that are practiced to bypass them.

The distortion of the market affects producers more than consumers. In Britain, for example, the supermarkets try at all costs to keep their wines to crisp price points, £3.99 and £4.99 being the most common. When the tax is increased,

Wine is only a small part of the value of an average bottle in Britain (left) or the United States (right).[60]

their efforts to keep below the price point require the producers to cut prices—but even though the tax increase may only be a few pennies relative to the total cost of the bottle, this can be a major proportion of the producers' profits. The pressure this puts on the system distorts the whole market.

The Fanatics of Prohibition

Where on earth could a newspaper be prosecuted and fined for an article reviewing recent releases from Champagne? Some part of the world where religious beliefs have been enshrined into laws banning alcohol? A dictatorship where free speech has been abolished? Incredible though it may seem, the answer is France. In December 2005, the weekly magazine Le Parisien published an article, "The Triumph of Champagne," a normal enough event in the run-up to Christmas, you might think. But a fanatical anti-alcohol society (AMPAA)[61] sued the newspaper on the grounds that the article was not editorial but constituted advertising—which would be illegal under French law. Le Parisien was fined €5,000.[62]

Perhaps only Kafka could understand the extreme irrationality of the law in France, which after all is one of the great wine (and spirits) producers of the world. "There are three countries in the world which ban the discussion of alcohol: Iran, Afghanistan and France," says Frédéric Delesque, marketing director of Camus Cognac.[63] The French Ministry of Health has published guidelines saying, "The consumption of alcohol, and especially wine, is discouraged." One wonders about the rationality of "especially wine."[64] In another report, alcohol was placed in the same category as heroin and cocaine (very dangerous).[65]

It started with the Loi Evin, a law passed in France in 1991 to control advertising of alcohol and tobacco. The law completely bans all advertising on television, or sponsorship of cultural or sports events; and advertising in the press allows only a very limited description of the product. (It was this restriction that was supposedly breached by Le Parisien.) It's illegal to show people drinking in advertisements. In a context where consumption was falling anyway, the law has had a dramatic effect in further exacerbating the ills of the industry, and it's no exaggeration to say that wine producers feel they are being demonized.

But worse was yet to come. The fanatics of AMPAA sued Heineken for maintaining a web site about its beer in France. In February 2008 the court duly ruled that it was illegal to provide information to users in France; Heineken was given three weeks to close down.[66] Access from computers in France is now blocked not only to local sites, but also (for example) to Orlando wines in South Australia because they are owned by the French company, Pernod-Ricard. Outside of France, you may think it's pretty stupid when you click on the web site of a wine producer and get a message asking you to certify you are over the legal drinking age when the site does not sell wine but provides information; but the inconvenience is as nothing compared with the very real possibility that wine producers will be banned entirely from maintaining web sites in France. The effect on free speech is chilling; there's about as much Liberté, Egalité, Fraternité on the internet in France as in Tiananmen Square in China.

The famous French statesman Talleyrand said sarcastically of the Bourbon kings of France, "They have learned nothing, and forgotten nothing." The same could be said of the fanatics who make laws about wine in Europe, and even (perhaps especially!) in France. Their arrogance surpasses even that of the ignoramuses responsible for the disaster of Prohibition in the United States. The rationale for Prohibition was based on a mistaken moralistic view of the evils of alcohol; such naïveté is understandable in the context of the early twentieth century, but one would hope to see a more sophisticated understanding in the present era.

Today the pressure comes mostly from Europe, but also from some international bodies. WHO has the objective of classifying the danger of consuming alcohol on the same level as tobacco. Back to the same McCarthy-like objective of tarring all with the same brush; it worked at Prohibition, when wine was lumped with spirits, so why shouldn't it work now by lumping wine with tobacco? But there is a difference. Tobacco is harmful not only to the smoker, but also to those subjected to passive inhalation; there is no safe dose. Alcohol is harmful to an individual only in excess; and only to others as a result of inebriated behavior. Truly the lunatics are running the asylum in the European Union.

Indeed, free speech goes out of the window everywhere that alcohol is regulated. If I go into the tasting room of a winery in California, ask for a glass of red wine, and comment that I've heard this has health benefits, the winery can lose its license to produce and sell wine if it responds positively. What happened to the First Amendment?

Certainly there is no question but that alcohol abuse can have serious consequences not only for the individual but others. But that does not make the quiet enjoyment of a drink a criminal offense, although sometimes we seem to be getting close to such a position. And it's curious how binge drinking is a problem in countries where it's illegal or strongly discouraged for the young to have any exposure to alcohol (especially Britain),[67] whereas it's far less of a problem in countries where children are encouraged from an early age to treat wine as part of a normal meal (such as Italy).

Save your Heart or Sacrifice your Liver?

There is no doubt about the damage caused by excess alcohol consumption. Death rates from cirrhosis of the liver correlate with overall consumption of alcohol for countries worldwide.[68] And the decline in alcohol consumption in France since the 1960s has been followed by a decline in liver cirrhosis.[69] The big question is always to what extent you can extrapolate an extreme situation like this to normal levels of consumption.[70] Also, wine consumption has beneficial as well as harmful effects, and it's not clear that there is any simple answer as to the balance at moderate levels of consumption. Unfortunately, commentary, if not the literature itself, is so politically motivated as to make it anything but reliable.

Before clean drinking water became available, wine was undoubtedly a beneficial alternative. In fact, diluting the contaminated water with wine had a significant effect in reducing bacterial infection. And even as recently as the eighteenth century, wine was prescribed as a cure for illness. When the great philosopher David Hume became ill in 1730 with what sounds like a nervous breakdown, his physician diagnosed "the Disease of the Learned;" the prescription for recovery included claret.[71] It would be a bold doctor who would make such a recommendation today.

Health benefits have long been claimed for wine drinking. In 1926, Raymond Pearl, a researcher at Johns Hopkins University, published *Alcohol and Longevity*, a book in which he reported that moderate drinkers had increased life expectancy.[72] He studied death rates in a population of 5,000 people; since the study extended into Prohibition, the sources of alcohol must have been somewhat rough and ready! Heavy drinkers had clearly reduced longevity, but moderate drinkers had a small advantage over abstainers.[73] Subsequent studies confirmed the effect but were largely ignored: rationality had little place in this discussion.

The direct benefits of drinking wine first came to public attention with the report of the French Paradox. The CBS news program "60 Minutes" in the United States reported in 1991 that rates of heart disease in France are lower than those in the United States although the diet in France has relatively more fat. A protective effect was attributed to the high consumption of red wine, and started a move towards drinking red rather than white wine. Actually, the association goes back a long way, starting with a paper in the medical journal Lancet in 1979 showing a strong negative association when wine consumption was plotted against coronary disease. Subsequent studies confirmed that there is a U- or J-shaped curve with a 10-40% reduction in heart disease at levels of moderate consumption. The bottom of the curve is reached at 2-3 drinks per day for males, 1-2 drinks per day for females. The effects are specific to wine: consumption of spirits shows no effects, and beer is less effective than wine.

This type of information is notoriously difficult to interpret because of confounding factors, ranging from smoking to socio-economic status. But allowing for these complications as best as possible, it seems that low levels of wine consumption have a protective effect against diseases with an oxidative component. Red wine is more effective than white because of its content of polyphenols such

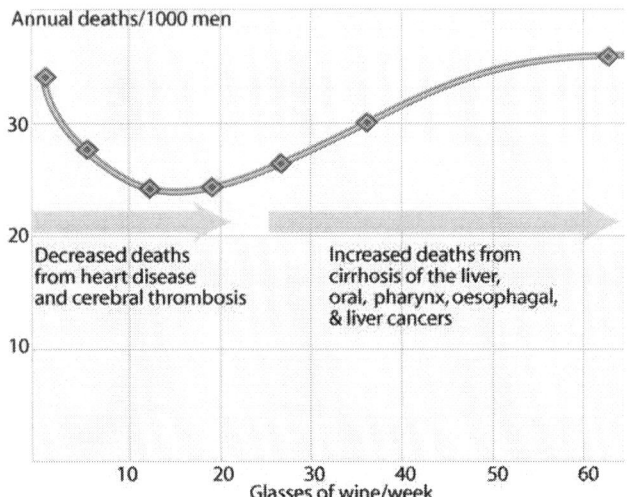

The famous J-shaped curve shows that minimum mortality is associated with moderate drinking.[78]

as tannins, which are anti-oxidants. Among the polyphenols is resveratrol, which has been implicated as an anti-aging agent. You would have to drink so much red wine to get a benefit from resveratrol, however, that you would probably develop cirrhosis of the liver first.[74]

Cancer risks associated with alcohol appear to be determined by cumulative exposure, with both level and duration of consumption playing a role in development of cancers in tissues exposed to alcohol.[75] It's probably true that the balance of benefit to harm is more dubious for women than for men, partly because the curve turns upward sooner,[76] partly because there is probably a connection between alcohol consumption and breast cancer.[77]

Whether pregnant women should drink is another, and more difficult, matter. Fetal alcohol syndrome affects babies whose mothers have consumed alcohol during pregnancy: the syndrome takes the form of some or all of the symptoms of short stature, facial disorder, and neurocognitive defects.[79] There's no cure for this lifelong affliction. FAS was diagnosed as a consequence of chronic alcohol consumption, originally found in specific high risk populations such as the native Americans. Now, but without any further evidence being presented, there has been an elision to concluding that there is no safe level of consumption.[80, 81] This is more the behavior of a witch doctor than a scientist or physician.[82]

There is no evidence for supposing that the risk is directly proportional to total consumption, as opposed to arising over a threshold. If the risk factor is the peak alcohol blood level, a pregnant woman who goes in for binge drinking a bottle of wine at one sitting may be at risk, even if it is the only alcohol she drinks during a week, whereas a women who drinks that same bottle one glass at a time with dinner over a week probably has little risk.[83] Given that alcohol may be a teratogen (an agent that causes birth defects), it is certainly appropriate for pregnant women to be cautious about alcohol consumption; whether abstinence is required is something reasonable people might discuss, rather than be subject to government edicts based on ill-founded extrapolations.

None of the factual information about the balance of risks and benefits appears to have had much effect on expert opinion. After the Royal College of Physicians in London published its recommendations in 1987 that weekly intake of wine should be limited to around 3 bottles per week for men and 2 bottles for women, a member of the working party described the process: "Those limits were really plucked out of the air. They were not based on any firm evidence at all."[84] Yet these unsubstantiated recommendations became the basis for government policy. "More than 10 million people, 31% of men and 20% of women, are now regularly drinking above the guidelines set by Government, and many of these are likely to suffer ill-health or injury as a result," stated a parliamentary report in 2009.[85] Surely if as many as a third of the population are ignoring your recommendations, you might at least question the connection of those recommendations to reality?

Unfortunately, extreme positions have taken over the argument about alcohol consumption, and the "experts" who have extrapolated from their data to the real world have done no favors to the cause of logic.[86] The authorities, who after all tend to be politicians lacking scientific expertise, find it all too easy to take the demagogic course of targeting anyone who enjoys a glass of wine. We all pay the price, literally in higher taxation, and metaphorically by loss of liberty.

9

The International Wine Trade

EXCEPT WHERE BANNED BY RELIGIOUS BELIEFS, alcoholic beverages provide the most common form of relaxation in cultures worldwide. The most popular form of beverage depends on the culture. Wine may be common or may be restricted to the rich or upper classes. In ancient Egypt, for example, wine was a privilege of the rich, and beer was the drink of the poor; whereas in Greece, advances in viticulture made wine available as the preferred drink at all levels of society (although the wine given to slaves was certainly inferior to that drunk by their owners).[1]

The international wine trade has been vigorous for several thousand years. In ancient times, Egypt produced only some of its own wine and imported a considerable proportion. The Phoenicians were notable traders in wine. By the time of the Roman Empire, trade in wine was a significant economic factor. Much of this ceased during the collapse of the dark ages. As the Church extended its tentacles through mediaeval Europe, one of the mandates for priests was to produce locally the wine that was needed for sacramental purposes. This led to the planting of grapevines in most unsuitable places, apparently as far north as Scandinavia, but also provided one of the spurs for developing viticulture.

As commerce picked up, vineyards tended to be planted in locations that made it possible to transport the product, typically along rivers. Improvements in transport, such as the construction of canals, changed the economics, so that vineyards succeeded where the best wine could be made, rather than where locations offered the easiest transport options. Within France, vineyards were all over the country until the eighteenth century, when the railways put the kibosh on outlying areas, and vineyards retreated to areas where wine could be more reliably produced.[2] As wine became more available on the international market, ability to transport well became more of an issue; the relatively light wines of France were at a disadvantage compared to the more alcoholic wines of Spain and the Mediterranean, which traveled better.[3]

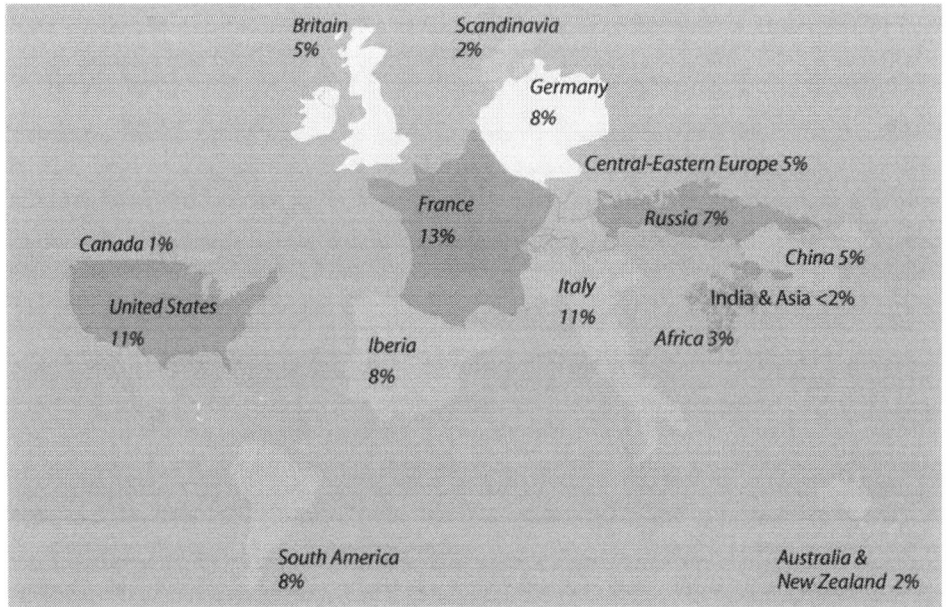

The world distorted according to wine consumption emphasizes the importance of the European and American continents, and diminishes India, Asia, and Australia.[4]

The modern era is caught between history and innovation. Many of the vineyards of Europe are planted according to historical imperatives; they are not necessarily where you would choose to plant vineyards today if you had quality wine production in mind. In the New World, modern technology has made it possible to plant vineyards in places where historically the vines would not have succeeded, especially where irrigation is necessary to avoid desert conditions. Today, transport is just another cost factor rather than determining where wine is produced.

There are huge geographical disparities in production and consumption. The countries of western Europe remain both the largest producers and consumers. France and Italy together account for a quarter of the world's production and consumption. The United States is rising to prominence as the largest single market, following the European model of being both producer and consumer. It is already the largest market by value, and is projected to become the largest by volume by 2012.[5] The small populations of Australia and New Zealand mean that although they are now important producers, they have little importance as consumers. Central Europe, Russia, and China are significant consumers; but Asia and India disappear to insignificance on the map in terms of consumption.

Choose your Tipple

In the context of the craving for alcohol, wine is only a small part of worldwide consumption. Beer has the lion's share of volume (80%), with wine representing

11%, and spirits making up the other 9%.[6] Economically beer remains the most important sector in the alcohol business, providing about half the value of the total market; wine is in second place with just over a quarter. Western Europe dominates the wine market, the most important countries within it being Italy, France, Germany, and Britain in terms of value.

The 32 billion bottles (or equivalents) of wine sold each year have a production value around $100 billion. So the average price is only just over $3 each. More than 75% of all wine sold is at a level of under $5 per bottle. The total value of the world wine market fluctuates widely according to whether it is assessed in terms of receipts by producers, retail sales, or all sales including restaurants, with estimates ranging up to about $250 million depending on the basis.[7]

Europe leads the world in alcohol consumption. France, Spain, Germany, and Britain all have around an overall consumption of 11-12 liters of pure alcohol per adult per year;[9] Italy is somewhat lower.[10] Consumption of alcohol has been declining steadily in Continental Europe, but increasing in Britain (and also in the United States). But the drink culture varies greatly between countries. Britain and France may never break out of their love-hate relationship so long as the French mainly drink wine while the British mainly drink beer. The difference may reflect the fact that in each case the predominant alcoholic drink is largely produced within the country. France imports relatively little wine, and most of the 400 million cases it drinks each year are produced in France. Britain imports all of the 200 million cases of wine it drinks each year, but produces virtually all of the 500 million cases of beer it consumes.[11]

But the culture gap is narrowing between traditional wine-producing countries, where wine consumption is falling, and the Anglophone world, where it is increasing at the expense of other forms of alcohol. In France, there has been a small decline in consumption of beer and spirits in the past fifty years, but a dramatic decrease in wine consumption (the present level is about a third of that in 1965). Similar but less severe declines have occurred in Italy and Spain. The

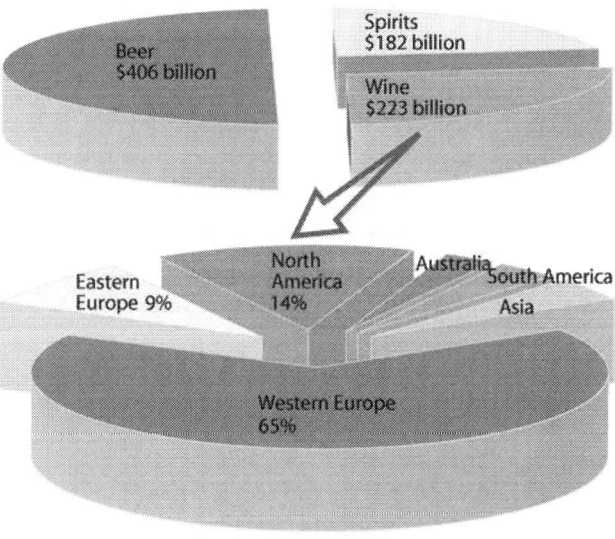

Western Europe is the most important wine market, followed by Eastern Europe and North America. Australia, South America, Asia and Africa have less than 5% share each.[8]

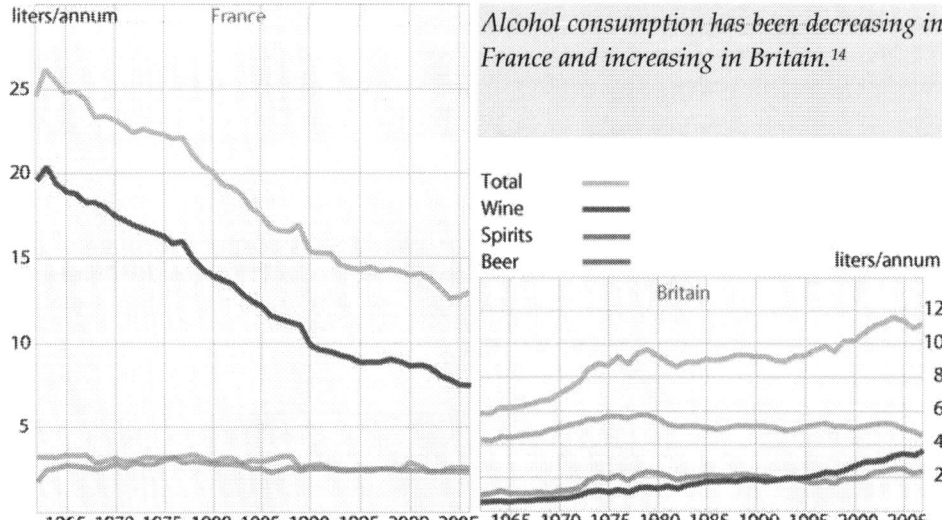

Alcohol consumption has been decreasing in France and increasing in Britain.[14]

decline in wine drinking is largely responsible for the overall fall in alcohol consumption. In Britain, beer has gone up and down again, spirits have increased somewhat, but wine consumption has increased about ten fold (albeit from a very small base in 1965). Wine consumption per person in Britain has now reached about half of the French level.[12] The increase in wine drinking is responsible for most of the overall increase in consumption.

There are some new markets, although their importance is hard to assess. China and India are the most rapidly growing markets, with the small proportion of drinkers compensated by large populations. China is growing as a producer as well as a consumer: some estimates place it as the world's sixth largest producer.[13] Its movement towards becoming an important worldwide player in wine is encouraged by the government, which believes that a switch to wine from rice spirits will reduce alcoholism. If production in China continues to grow at the present estimated rate of 30%, it could become the world's largest bulk exporter of wine within a decade.

Inequality of Supply And Demand

Looking at the variety of brands available in your local store, and their constantly changing nature, you would never think the wine industry was in crisis or decline. Yet worldwide consumption has shown little increase for years, there is a surplus of supply compared to demand, competition between new producers and old has created turmoil, and much of the change represents a desperate attempt to hold on to existing markets. The ramifications go all the way down to the diversity and pricing of the bottles available in each market.

There has been a worldwide glut of wine for more than three decades. Consumption declined steadily through the 1980s and 1990s before stabilizing, and although production has been reduced, it still remains typically about 15% in excess of consumption. If all of that surplus was bottled for sale, it would amount

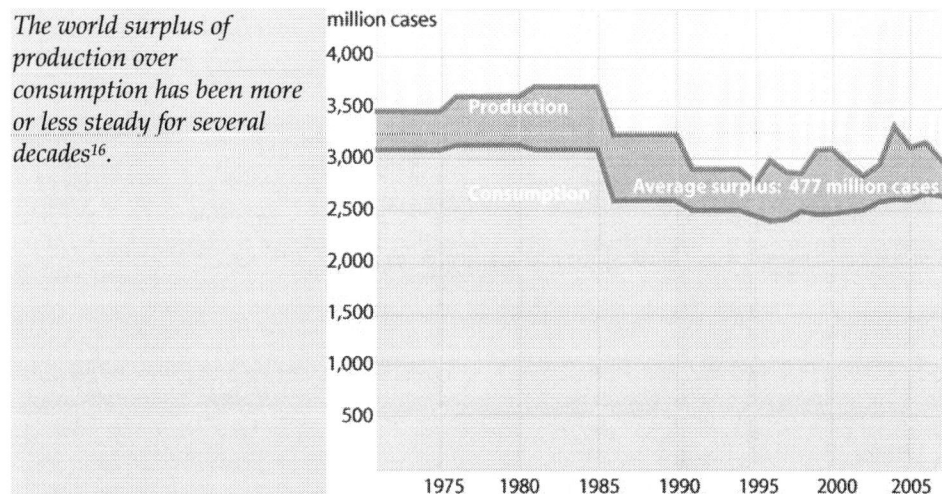

The world surplus of production over consumption has been more or less steady for several decades[16].

to about 500 million cases each year. However, a significant part of it is diverted to other uses, often by distillation to produce spirits or industrial alcohol.[15] But the glut places a pall over the whole industry, putting downward pressure on prices, especially at the highly competitive lower end of the market. The ill-advised policies of the European Union in subsidizing production suggest that this situation will not be easy to change.

Until relatively recently, most wine was consumed in the countries that produced it. There was a clear division between producing countries and consuming countries. The major producers, France, Italy, and Spain, imported little wine and consumed a major part of their own production. Most of the wine consumed in the United States was produced in California. Countries that did not produce wine, such as Britain, provided the major markets for those wines that were not consumed in the countries of origin. The major exception was Germany, which is an established producer, but which does not produce enough for its own consumption, and is therefore also a significant importer.

Today all that has changed. Overall, the proportion of wine that is exported has increased from 15% to almost 30% in twenty years. Almost 50% of the trade is accounted for by the three major importers: Britain, Germany, and the United States. The new producers, most notably Australia and New Zealand, consume little of their own wine; most is exported. In South America, there is a split between production from indigenous varieties for home consumption, and production from international varieties for export. The United States is the only New World producer to be a major importer; consumption of imported wine has reached more than 30%.

Some of the international exports are finished product, sent in bottles from the exporting country. Some is sent in bulk and bottled in the country where it is to be sold—England, not exactly renowned as a wine producer, can bottle the equivalent of 450 million bottles per year (about a quarter of the 1.7 billion imported each year).[17] Packaging close to the market is especially advantageous for wine that is sold in formats other than bottles, such as bag-in-box, which is

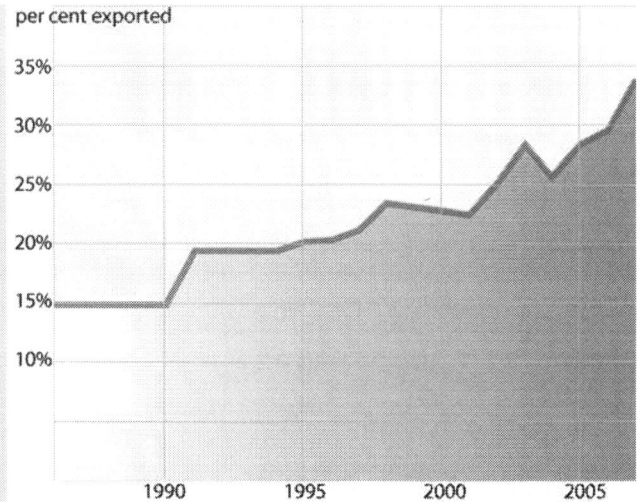

The world wine trade has become truly international in the past two decades[20].

difficult to transport and is intended for rapid consumption. Sometimes it's simply a financial calculation, based on the cost of bottling at source versus the cost of bottling at point of sale that determines what route is followed. On occasion, wine follows a circuitous route that isn't intuitively obvious; a major brand in Britain, Blossom Hill, is produced in California, shipped to Diageo's plant at Santa Vittoria d'Alba in Italy where it is bottled, and then exported to Britain.[18,] This accounts for a quarter of all Italy's wine exports to Britain, and a third of all its imports.[19]

Crisis in Europe: the Rise of the New World

Wine production was relatively stable in the nineteenth century. Just before phylloxera devastated the industry, France was the clear market leader with almost 40% of world production; Italy and Spain accounted for another 25% and 20% respectively. Even today these three remain the market leaders, but their combined proportion of world production has shrunk to about half. Production in France is about 50% greater than before phylloxera; Italy and Spain have roughly doubled. The largest decline in production may have been in Hungary, a major producer in 1880 but a struggling one today.[21]

Since the phylloxera epidemic, wine production has increased universally, but the pattern of production today is very different from a century ago. At the start of the twentieth century, wine production in Europe was the only game in town. At the start of the twenty-first century, having more or less doubled over a hundred years, Europe accounts for only about two thirds of world production.

The greatest change is the rise of the New World. Virtually insignificant in terms of quantity in 1900, and even less significant in terms of quality, the New World now accounts for almost 30% of world production, with a range from plonk to the very finest. The United States is its largest producer, with 90% coming from California; Australia and Argentina vie for second place.

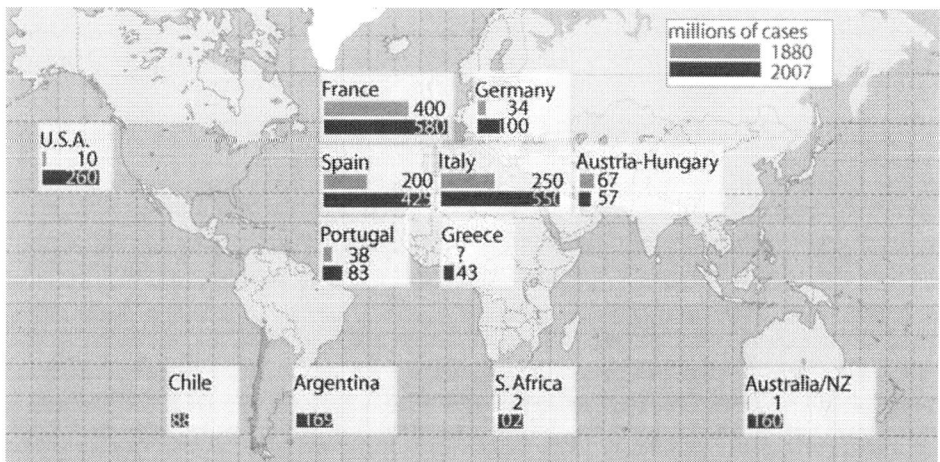

Europe has increased production since 1880, but the New World now accounts for almost a third of all production.[22]

The change has aroused outrage in Europe. "Until recent years, wine was with us," stated a report commissioned by the French Ministry of Agriculture in 2001. "We were the center, the unavoidable reference point. Today, the barbarians are at our gates: Australia, New Zealand, the United States, Chile, Argentina, South Africa."[23]

Production in Europe rose steadily during the twentieth century until peaking in the 1970s-1980s; after falling back about a quarter, it has been more or less stable for the past couple of decades. By contrast, production in the New World has continued its inexorable climb, from about 275 million cases in 1950 to 725 million cases today. This leaves the situation now with the big three of France, Italy, and Spain still dominating European and world production, but with the United States and Australia making important inroads from the New World. (Argentina is a larger producer than Australia overall, but not such an important exporter).

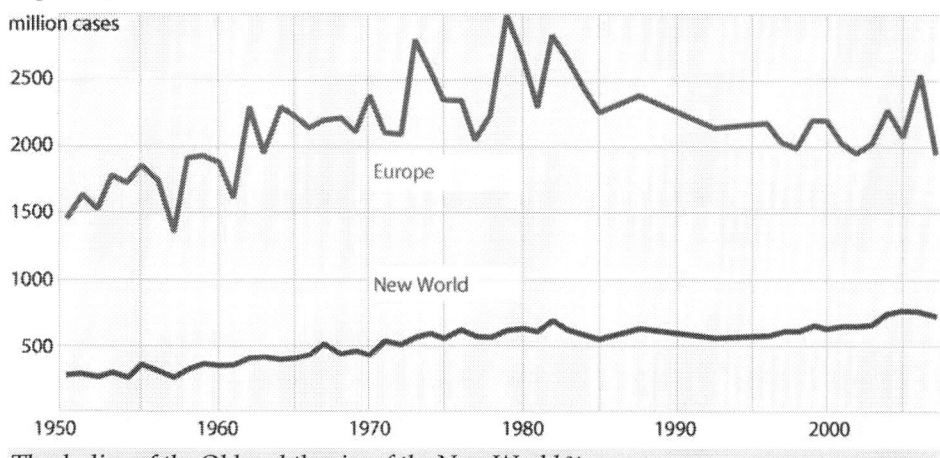

The decline of the Old and the rise of the New World.[24]

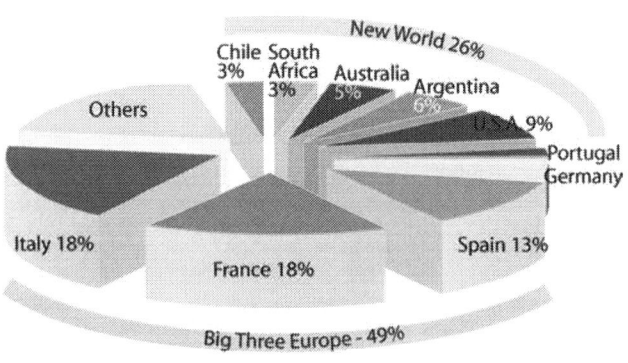

A few countries in the Old and New Worlds dominate wine production.[26]

One of the major changes in the wine industry has been the yield—the amount of wine produced from a vineyard area.[25] Advances in viticulture have led to yields increasing everywhere over the past century. Today, low yields are associated with higher quality. But for the first half of the twentieth century, low yields were generally due to the poor state of the vines and their inability to withstand pests and diseases. Increasing yield in the second part of the century resulted from the improved state of the vines and more productive viticulture.

Yields are not regulated in the New World, where they are limited simply by the intentions of the producer. With irrigation and fertilization, it's perfectly possibly to achieve 120 hl/ha—although the wine is unlikely to be very good. The figures for California and Australia include a mix of high yield production for bulk wine with production of quality wines at lower yields. The same is true in Europe, but yields are restrained in the AOC (or equivalents in other countries) by the regulations. In France for example, about half of production is within the Appellation Contrôlée system, where yields are usually restricted to 55 hl/ha or below.

But the trend to higher yields is pretty much parallel worldwide, and has evened off only in the past decade. So although the total area of vineyards worldwide declined from about 8.8 million hectares prior to 1990 to just under 8

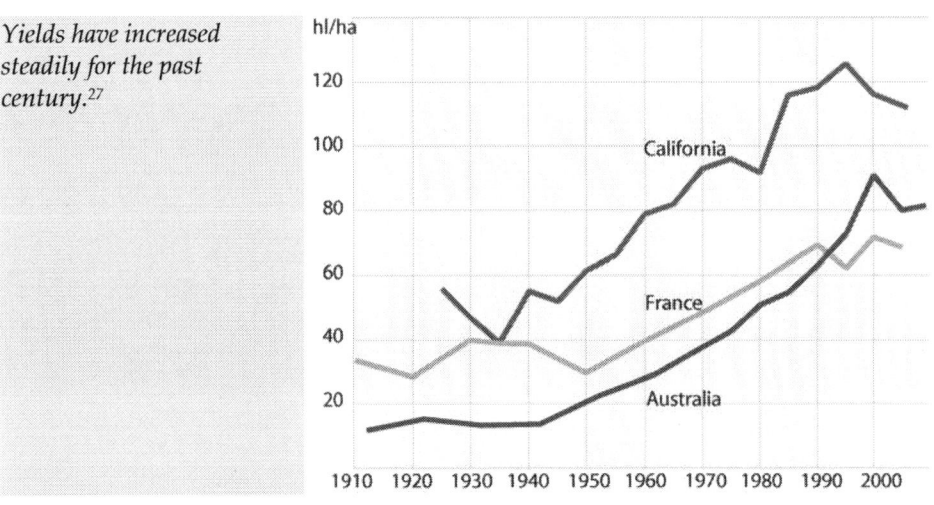

Yields have increased steadily for the past century.[27]

million hectares by 1995,[28] production has declined less, staying more or less around 2.5 billion cases annually. Control of yields has only had a real effect for the smaller part of the market represented by fine wines.

The New World became significant in exporting wine only in the past quarter century. Figures for the overall increase in production underestimate its importance. Certainly production has greatly increased, but a key factor has been a general trend to replace low quality varieties with high quality international varieties.[29] The change in quality was just as important as the change in quantity in becoming competitive in export markets.[30] Quality varietal plantings, producing wines suitable for export, have increased four fold in the New World since 1990.[31]

Rapidly falling consumption in Europe made it impossible to cut production enough to close the gap. And rapidly increasing production from the New World made it impossible for Europe to increase exports. The result has been a steady surplus of about half a million cases of wine produced every year by France, Italy, and Spain. This is actually not far from the total annual production of the New World. Increasing production in the New World has widened its surplus over consumption, but this became a major problem only recently with the worldwide financial crisis of 2009.

There's been a similar move to quality in Europe as in the New World. The trend is to replace poor varieties with better ones, especially in areas previously known for bulk production of wine, such as the south of France or Castille La Mancha to the south of Madrid. And as the total number of vineyards has contracted, it has been producers in the poorer locations who have gone to the wall. The surplus production is much larger with table wine than with quality wine. There is a clear trend to less production of table wine and more production of quality wine (as defined by the European Union).

Taken at face value, consumption of quality wine and table wine are at almost equivalent levels in Europe. However, the official figures have to be viewed with a certain amount of skepticism, because in some cases the change is simply that

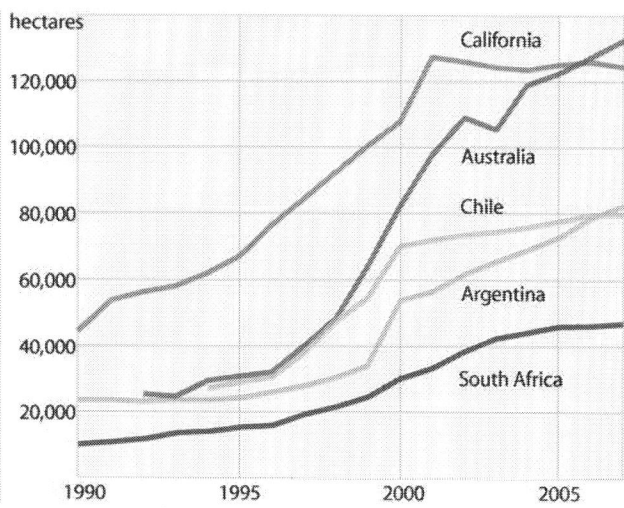

Quality varieties have expanded rapidly in the New World since the 1990s.

The graph for each country shows the total of international varieties.[32]

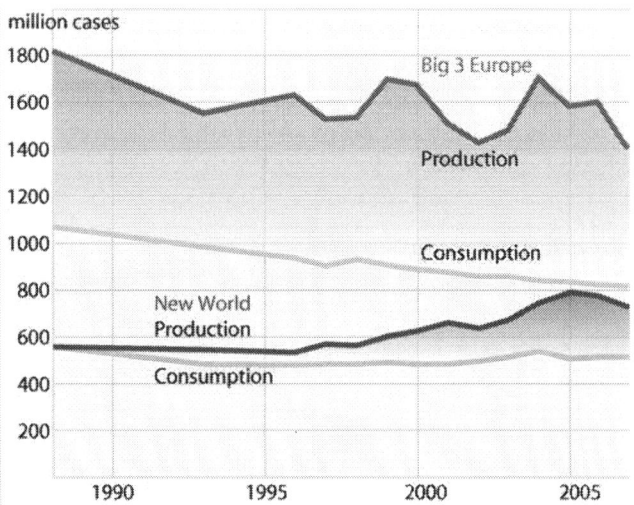

Production and consumption have fallen in France, Italy, and Spain, with a more or less constant surplus (red); production has increased in the New World, exacerbating the surplus (purple).[34]

reclassification has promoted vineyards from table wine to the level of quality wine. For example, appellation controlée vineyards are 99.8% of Bordeaux today, but were only 53% of the area in 1950;[33] but it's pretty much the same vineyards that are making the wine (albeit under the tighter conditions of the AOC).

What does Europe do with all its excess wine? Well, the European Union had a plan to handle the surplus. It consisted of two seemingly contradictory policies. (Fortunately contradiction never worried the bureaucrats.) First, subsidies were offered to grub up vineyards. Actually this was not completely unsuccessful: more than 500,000 hectares of vineyards were removed between 1988 and 1996, a reduction of more than 10%, albeit not enough to eliminate the wine lake.[36] The other half of the policy was to buy up the surplus wine and distill it to generate

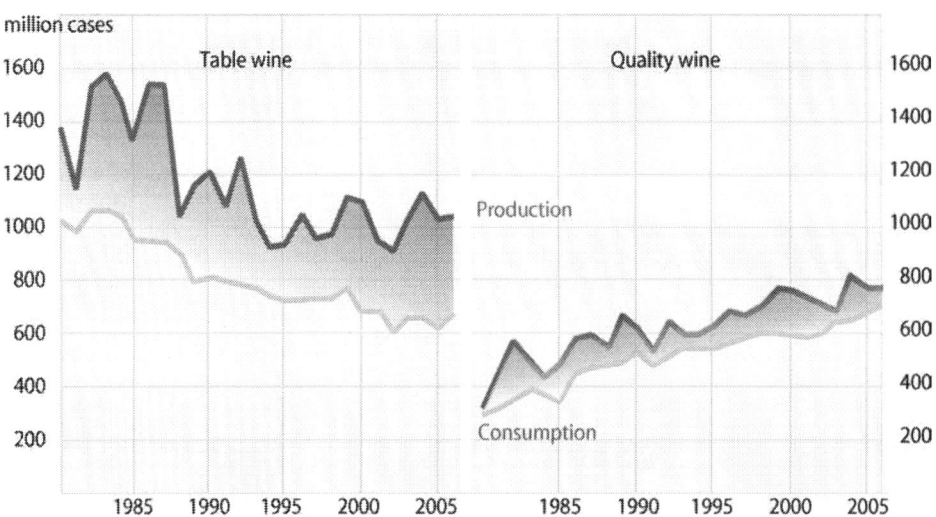

Table wine production has decreased steadily, while quality wine production has increased in Europe.[35]

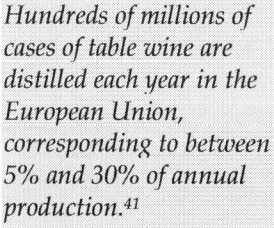

Hundreds of millions of cases of table wine are distilled each year in the European Union, corresponding to between 5% and 30% of annual production.[41]

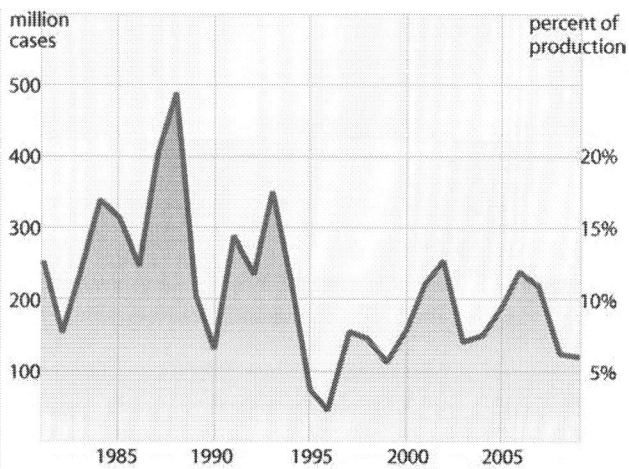

alcohol for industrial or other uses.[37] Whether this was successful depends on your criteria. On the one hand, the wine was removed from the marketplace. But since there was little diminution in the quantity of wine being distilled over the years, the policy had little permanent effect on the glut. Indeed, it created a dependency culture in which wine was produced solely for the purpose of being sold into the subsidy program. (History should have shown the futility of such interventions. A prime d'arrachage [payment for pulling out vines] was introduced in France in 1936, and payments were introduced for distilling excess wines,[38, 39] so the recipe seems to be to try more of the same old failed policies.) In a belated recognition of reality, the system is due to be reformed over the next few years, including phasing out the distillation subsidies.[40]

Boom and Bust in the Vineyards

Boom and bust cycles have been accompanied by attempts to regulate vineyard plantings since time immemorial. One basic problem is the time lag between deciding to plant vines and harvesting a crop, typically at least three years. High demand causes everyone to rush out and plant vines, no one know how many other vines are being planted, of course, until three or four years later they all produce wine. Suddenly shortage turns to glut. One of the earliest documented examples was the rush of planting in response to the eruption of Vesuvius in 79 C.E., which destroyed the local vineyards that were the main supply for wine for Rome. The result was a glut by the next decade.[42]

With some rare exceptions, attempts to direct plantings have not been very successful. Sometimes, of course, the regulations had ulterior motives. When the Roman Emperor Domitian banned new plantings and ordered half of the existing vineyards to be uprooted in the provinces in 92 C.E., his motives were probably mostly to protect producers in the home region near Rome.[43] In any case, it appears that no one paid much attention to the edict. Two hundred years later, Emperor Probus encouraged planting vines in Gaul, with more success.

The seventeenth century saw attempts to discourage plantings in unsuitable areas (the forerunner of the complex system controlling all vineyards in Europe today). Colbert, Minister of Finance under Louis XIV in 1682, noted the problem caused by "the excessive multiplication of vines in terrains that are not appropriate."[44] In Bordeaux, a "fureur de planter" (rush of planting) was triggered by the winter freeze of 1709 that killed many of the vines in the region, together with the end of the war with England that had suppressed trade. Planting became so excessive that it may have impacted production of other crops, and it sparked proposals to pull up many of the vines.[45] Expressing a characteristic free market view, Adam Smith commented that the real motive was "the anxiety of the proprietors of the old vineyards to prevent the planting of any new ones," rather than any genuine concern to promote production of corn rather than wine.[46]

Fast forward to Europe at the present, where the creation of vineyards is controlled by the arcane regulation of "planting rights." If you own a vineyard in the European Union, essentially you have the rights to that many hectares of vines. You cannot plant any more vines unless you can acquire additional planting rights. If you pull up the existing vineyard, you can replant it in the same place or plant the same number of hectares elsewhere. You can also pull up the vineyard and sell the planting rights to someone else. One producer in Tuscany told me that in order to plant a new vineyard, he had purchased planting rights from a producer who was relinquishing a vineyard in Sicily!

There is not much to be said in favor of this system. In an ideal world, it would work by encouraging producers in uneconomic areas to sell their planting rights to producers in areas better suited for viticulture. But like so many distortions of the free market, the law of unintended consequences triumphs. The negative effects of preventing good producers from expanding when they have identified good locations for new vineyards much outweigh any effects in limiting the wine glut. And it adds to the expense of innovation; at roughly €30,000 per hectare, planting rights in some areas almost double the cost of land for a new vineyard. The E.U. has announced plans to abolish the system in 2016 as part of an attempt to "phase out wasteful and expensive market intervention measures"[47]—but one wonders, if the deficiencies of the system are so obvious, why wait until then?

The Price of Everything

The price of land was never much of an issue before wine became a luxury item. Historically grapevines tended to be planted on land that could not grow other crops successfully, so land values were relatively low. But today the prices for top vineyard land have followed the prices of the wines into the stratosphere. Even the rise of garage wines in Bordeaux or cult wines in Napa Valley, often owing more to extreme measures for viticulture and vinification than to unique terroir, has not dented the inexorable rise of land prices.

Burgundy probably has the most expensive vineyard land in the world. The piecemeal nature of vineyard holdings means it is relatively rare for anything other than a tiny plot to change hands on the Côte d'Or, but the rate can put local housing prices quite to shame. Grand Cru Burgundy can sell at a rate of €4-6 million per hectare. Top châteaux in Bordeaux run at about half of that rate, although much larger sums of money are involved when a château with tens of hectares is sold.

Outside of France, the most expensive vineyards are in Barolo, where small parcels of the Cannubi vineyard (the local equivalent to a first growth) are reputed to change hands for around €1 million per hectare. The most expensive land in the New World is probably in the top-rated Rutherford region of Napa Valley, somewhere under $1 million per hectare.

The price of land becomes an expensive part of the cost of wine. Carrying costs on purchasing land alone could be the equivalent of $25 or more per bottle,

The surreal price of Le Montrachet floats in the stratosphere, even above other grand cru Burgundy. Pomerol is the most expensive area in Bordeaux, but the communes of the Médoc can come close. Although there is wide variation in each region depending on the reputation of the individual vineyard, land prices correlate approximately with the price of wine.[48]

Region	$/hectare
Le Montrachet	6 million
Grand Cru Burgundy	5 million
	4 million
Pomerol / Médoc Grand Cru Classé	3 million
	2 million
Champagne	
Barolo (Cannubi)	1 million
Napa Valley (Rutherford)	

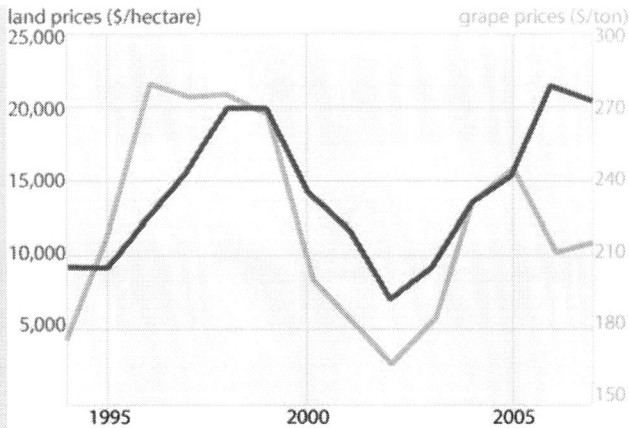

Land prices (red) adjust very rapidly to grape prices (green) in California. (The increase in land prices in the real estate bubble after 2005 disrupted the relationship temporarily.)[49]

so the wine has to sell at a very high price to justify such a purchase. Of course, the relationship is driven the other way, with high prices for wine encouraging purchasers to pay correspondingly higher prices for the land.

As a rough working rule, the price of land tends to be about 100 times the price of grapes per ton, which in turn is about 100 times the price of a bottle of wine. So if wine sells for $100 per bottle, you can expect the vineyard to be worth about $1 million a hectare.

The Supermarket Crunch

Supermarkets are the 600 pound gorilla in wine sales. Their penetration into wine is most evident at the consumer level in high-economy countries, where the majority of wines are now purchased in supermarkets,[50] whereas twenty years ago, specialist shops reigned supreme. But the effects go far beyond the visible stacks of bottles or piles of bag-in-boxes and are felt all the way down to the wine producer. Supermarkets naturally require to be supplied in larger bulk than small outlets, and this goes hand in hand with the consolidation among distributors and producers, since each requires a partner of appropriate (i.e., large) size.

The rise in supermarkets is largely responsible for the increased concentration in the retail market. In much of Europe, 50-60% of the retail market is in the hands of the five largest wine retailers. Monopoly situations, such as in Scandinavia, increase this to more than 80%; regulatory restrictions in the United States have the opposite effect, and restrain it to about 20% nationwide.[51]

Supermarkets are hated and feared by small specialist shops, and the usual reaction is epitomized by the owner of Young's Liquors on Long Island in New York State, where the fight to allow supermarkets to sell alcohol was intense in 2009.[52] "I've heard that if this bill passes a thousand licensed liquor stores will go under," said Edward Wassmer, adding that wine makes up 75 percent of his sales.[53] This parallels the popular impression of what has actually happened since supermarkets started to sell wine in Britain in the late 1970s; supermarkets have gone from a minor player to about 70% of the market.

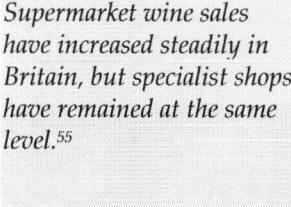

Supermarket wine sales have increased steadily in Britain, but specialist shops have remained at the same level.[55]

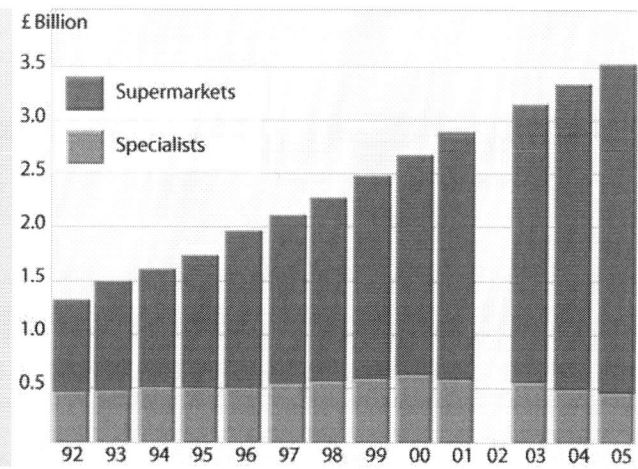

Has this been at the expense of other retailers? Well, yes and no. Supermarkets sell roughly three times as much wine today as they did at the start of the 1990s. But this is due more to the increase in the size of the market than to encroachment on the customers of other retailers. In fact, the total sales by small specialist shops have stayed more or less steady—not a great result against the background of inflation, but scarcely decimated as popular impression would have it. There's a good argument for saying that it is in fact the supermarkets that have expanded the market by making it possible for people to purchase wine in circumstances when they would not otherwise have done so.[54]

A common complaint against supermarkets is that the apparent choice offered to the consumer is deceptive— superficially there may be great variety, but actually all the wines fit the same, rather simple mold. There's more than a grain of truth in this. British supermarkets concentrate on wines in the fruit-forward New World style at the lower end of the price range, so that although a typical supermarket may have tens or even hundreds of different wines for sale, the focus on price makes it difficult to find distinctive wines.

More to the point may be the concern within the wine trade that the extreme price sensitivity of the supermarkets not only trains the consumer to regard wine as a cheap item, but also puts downward pressure on producers with regards to quality. Wines are commonly discounted. According to Jean-Manuel Spriet, the CEO of Pernod-Ricard in Britain, "[other wine suppliers] make the wines designed for sale at £3.99, introduce them at a higher price, and then bring the price down... they start at £7.99 and are discounted down to half price, which is crazy."[56] Indeed, according to Jon Moramarco, Constellation's former European chief executive, more than half of their wines are sold at discounts of 50% from the nominal price.[57] The attempt to create the impression of bargains just destroys any possibility of giving the consumer any sense of real value. (The favorite type of promotion is known as a "bogof"—buy one get one free.)

The contortions needed to sell wine at the "magic price point" of £3.99 in Britain[58] put huge pressure on producers. There are endless stories about supermarkets squeezing producers in order to sell wine at this price point;

Increased choice for the consumer in the serried ranks of bottles at the supermarket, or simply more of the same?

believing that a foot in the door will lead to better prices in the future, the producer may cut his price to an uneconomic level, but if so, he is operating under a sad illusion. Only the largest producers can afford to play the game, further emphasizing lack of diversity. For the supermarket, profit margin is everything, as captured by a story from Tim Atkin MW: "[A Tesco buying manager] was given a new wine to taste in Australia last year and was asked for his reaction. He swirled the contents of his glass, sniffed it, tasted it and replied: 'Not enough margin'."[59]

The Great Wine Agglomeration

There is continual moaning all across the world of wine about the effects of increasing concentration at all levels of the industry. The giants of the industry such as Constellation or Diageo are gobbling up wine producers worldwide. In the United States, the amalgamation of distributors makes it difficult for small wine producers to get to market. In France and Britain, supermarkets have an increasing share of the retail market. Yet wine remains the least concentrated of any part of the wider drinks industry. Constellation, the world's largest wine company, has sales of under $4 billion[60] out of the world's $220 billion spent on wine.[61] Yet large as Constellation seems to people in wine, it is dwarfed by companies in soft drinks, beer, and spirits.[62]

What a difference a decade makes! At the turn of the millennium, the top ten drinks companies in the world had a combined cash flow of $10 billion. At the end of the first decade of the new century, mergers and acquisitions brought the total cash flow of the top ten companies involved in alcoholic drinks close to $70 billion. About $16 billion came from sales of wine; not chump change, surely, but definitely taking second place in many cases to the other interests of the companies. During the decade, three of the top companies were swallowed by others in a continuing frenzy. Diageo acquired Seagrams, Fosters took over Southcorp, and Constellation bought Mondavi.

Wine is much less concentrated than any other sector of the drinks industry.

The histogram shows the worldwide per cent share of the largest three companies in each sector.[63]

The history of the world's largest drinks company, Diageo, started in the eighteenth century with whisky (J & B) and Guinness. It grew steadily by acquisition of spirits brands, including whisky, gin, vodka, and rum. Guinness, as it was known then, merged with another drinks company, Grand Met, in 1997 to form United Distillers & Vintners, which then became known as Diageo. Its holdings of beer and spirits remain far more important in revenue terms than wine, which accounts for only about 6% of total.

The world's top wine companies in 2008.

Company	Origins	Nature	Revenues ($billion)[64]	Wine ($billion)	Wine %	Principal Activities
Constellation	USA	public	$5,213	$3,842	74%	wine
Gallo	USA	private	$3,800	$3,200	84%	wine
Pernod-Ricard	France	public	$9,689	$2,240	23%	spirits, wine
LVMH	France	public	$24,098	$2,200	9%	luxury goods
Fosters	Australia	public	$3,642	$1,600	44%	beer, wine
Castel	France	private	$2,820	$1.297	46%	wine, beer, water
Diageo	Britain	public	$16,120	$967	6%	spirits, wine
Brown Foreman	USA	public	$3,282	$755	23%	spirits, wine
The Wine Group	USA	private	$735	$735	100%	wine
Freixenet	Spain	private	$730	$730	100%	sparkling wine

Pernod-Ricard was formed in 1975 by the merger of the two leading competitive producers of spirits in France—they had started with Absinthe, when it was legal. Wine was of little importance until 1989, when Pernod-Ricard purchased the Australian Company Orlando Wyndham, bringing them one of the world's largest brands, Jacob's Creek. When Seagrams was sold in 2001, Pernod-Ricard split the spoils with Diageo. Then in 2005 they split Allied Domecq (the British conglomerate) with Fortune Brands. This brought them Montana, making them the largest winemaker in New Zealand.[65] In little more than a decade, Pernod-Ricard went from insignificance to one of the top half dozen producers of wine.

No company may have achieved worldwide dominance, but several countries are dominated by their largest single producer. Gallo was for long the largest wine company in the world; still privately owned by the Gallo family, it is the dominant player in the United States market. Fosters has grown by gobbling up all of its former competitors in Australia, and now includes Southcorp, Rosemont, Mildara Blass, Beringer Blass, and Penfolds, giving it by far the most powerful position in Australian wine production.

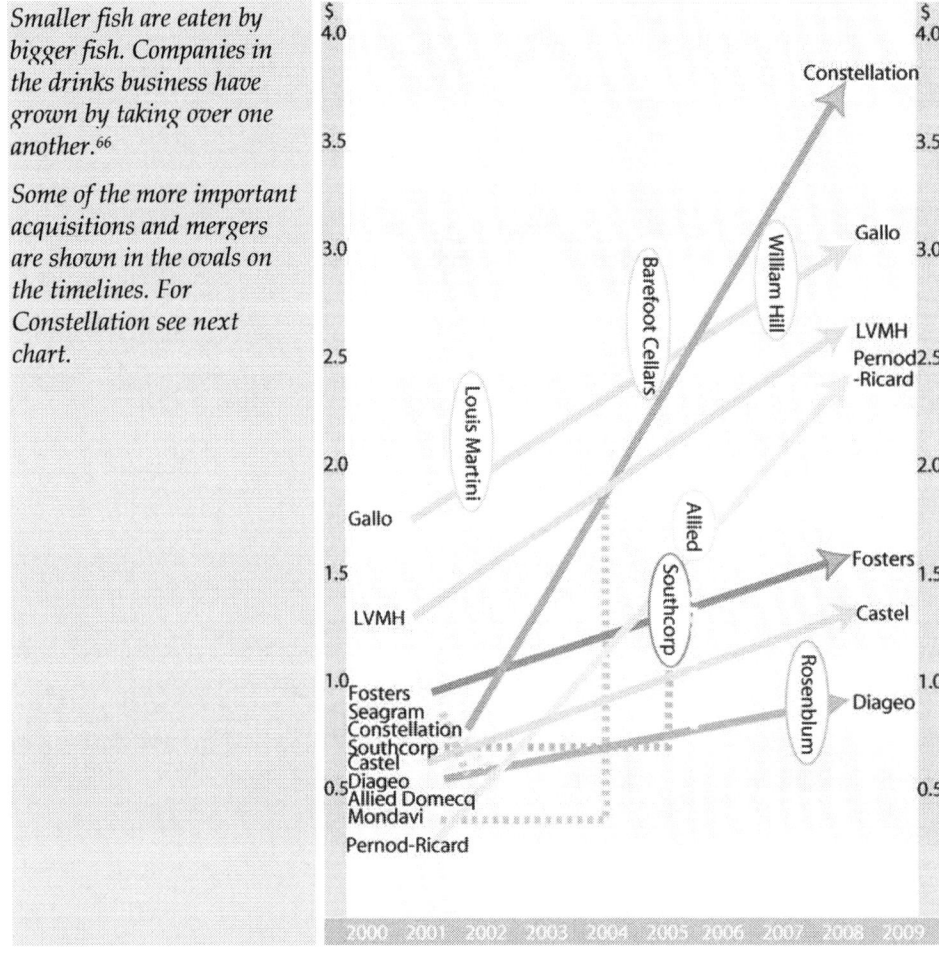

Smaller fish are eaten by bigger fish. Companies in the drinks business have grown by taking over one another.[66]

Some of the more important acquisitions and mergers are shown in the ovals on the timelines. For Constellation see next chart.

Often enough, these giant players trade divisions, somewhat like dealing out playing cards—or perhaps in the present climate of world recession, rearranging the deckchairs on the Titanic. Look at how the old Inglenook winery, once one of the top names in Napa Valley, has been run down. The brand was sold to United Vinters in 1964, became part of Heublein in 1969, Heublein sold it to Constellation in 1994, Constellation sold it to The Wine Group in 2008, and now The Wine Group has converted it from bottled wine to bag-in-box. None of this is apparent to the consumer, of course, indeed, you never see most of the über-company names on a label, but the Franzia brand is owned by The Wine Group, Mondavi by Constellation, Korbel by Brown-Foreman, Jacob's Creek by Pernod-Ricard, and Blossom Hill by Diageo.

Constellation is not the largest company involved in producing wine, but it is the largest company whose principal purpose is the production of wine. It has grown steadily by a series of acquisitions. It started out as the Canandaigua Wine Company in upstate New York in 1945, taking its name from the local town. Founded by Marvin Sands in 1945, its first year sales amounted to $150,000. Its initial products were not illustrious, consisting of wine made from indigenous varieties in the eastern United States, including the infamous Scuppernong.[68] Canandaigua moved into California wines only in the early 1990s, including its acquisition of Almaden and Inglenook when they were spun off after their disastrous period as part of Heublein. The move into more serious wines intensified with the acquisition of Franciscan (in Napa Valley) at the end of the nineties. In 2002 the name was changed to Constellation, and then a series of major purchases followed in Australia (BRL Hardy), California (Mondavi) and Canada (Vincor), the latter two each over the billion dollar level. With sales of $3.8 billion

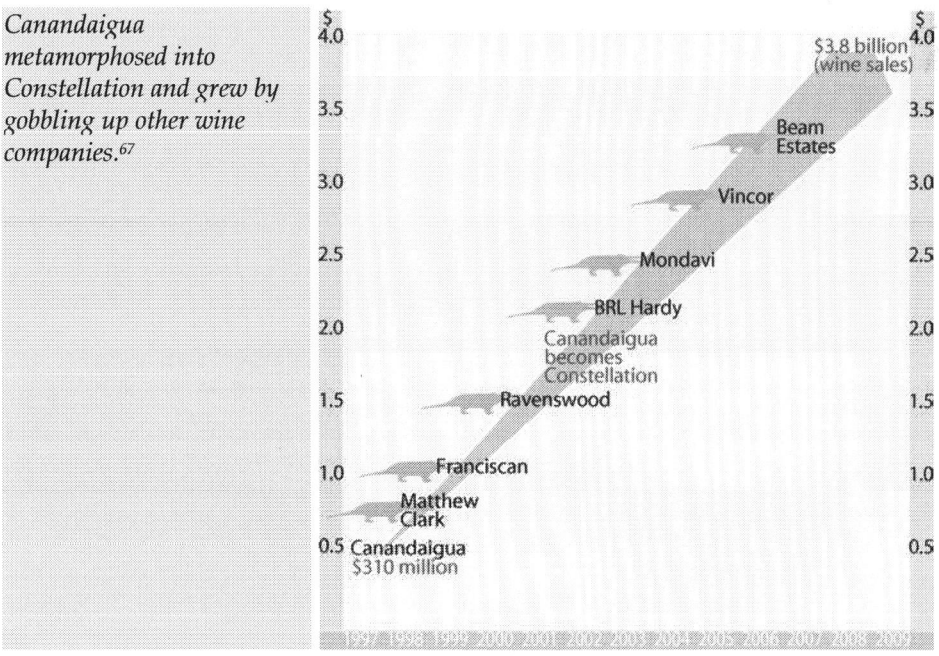

Canandaigua metamorphosed into Constellation and grew by gobbling up other wine companies.[67]

today in wine alone, the company is still run by the Sands family. True to its roots, it still produces Manischewitz kosher wine at its winery in Naples, New York. Made from Concord grapes in an old fashioned sweet style, Manischewitz remains consistent but—well, let's say idiosyncratic in order to avoid a snobbish value judgment.[69]

Certainly it seems easier to grow by buying someone else than by building your own business. But how much have all these acquisitions and mergers contributed to increased concentration in the industry? The wine revenues of the top ten companies have almost doubled in a decade during which wine revenues overall increased by perhaps 30% worldwide.[70] Like other industries, the big players are becoming more important.

If You Can't Beat 'Em, Join 'Em

There's a very long tradition of people or companies from outside wine-producing regions investing in wine. Perhaps the English takeover of Aquitaine was one of the first foreign investments, although from the perspective of the Bordelais maybe it was more of an invasion. Certainly the English—or the British as they had by then become—built the trade in Sherry and Port. The prestige of the Grand Cru Classés in Bordeaux has always made them particularly attractive to foreign investors, and at any given time there have usually been several foreign owners.[71] American investors have become important in France, starting at the top with banker Clarence Dillon's acquisition of Château Haut Brion in Bordeaux in 1935, followed in recent times by investments elsewhere, such as the takeover of the Burgundian producer Jadot in 1985 by their American distributor, Kobrand Corporation. Of course, some potential investments have been rebuffed, such as Robert Mondavi's attempt to establish wine production in the Languedoc, but for the most part foreign investment has been a welcome fillip to wine production in Europe, especially in France.

Wine production tends to be much more concentrated in the New World than the Old World, where it is especially fragmented. The major players have a large share of the market in New World countries, but a much smaller share in Europe, where there are far more producers, and individual vineyard holdings are far smaller. In Europe, no single company has more than 7% of total production in its home country, but in the New World, single companies can dominate production, as with Distell in South Africa, Concha y Toro in Chile, and Gallo in the United States. Of course, the actual level of production also varies widely, so the largest companies in France and Italy, although small in the context of their country's total production, each produce more than the total amount of New Zealand.[72] On the other hand, as in the case of Distell in South Africa, domestic dominance is nice for the company, but does not necessarily make it a major player on the world stage.

Concentration tends to go along with publicly owned conglomerates, and some of the same names appear in multiple places. Constellation is dominant in the United States and important in Australia, Fosters is dominant in Australia and owns Beringer in California, and Pernod-Ricard is French by origin but now more a global player. There are exceptions, most notably Gallo in the United States, Garcia Carrión in Spain, and Castel in France, all of which remain privately owned. Some of the most important companies, such as Constellation or Diageo, now have such widespread holdings that they can scarcely be identified any longer with their country of origin. Certainly there is a long-established trend for companies originating outside the major European wine-producing countries to buy up producers, most notably in France.

The largest wine producer's share of production in each country varies widely.[73]

Country	Largest Company	% share	Ownership
South Africa	DISTELL	45%	Public
Chile	Concha y Toro	29%	Public
United States	E&J Gallo Winery	26%	Private
New Zealand	Montana	22%	Pernod-Ricard
Australia	Foster's	22%	Public
Argentina	Grupo Peñaflor	17%	Private
Spain	Garcia Carrión	8%	Private
France	Castel	7%	Private
Italy	Riunite Lambrusco	4%	Cooperative

Concentration of wine production in major producing countries.[74]

Country	Average vineyard	Number of producers	Top-3 share	Top-5 share
New Zealand	50 ha	463	75%	80%
United States	100 ha	3,606	64%	80%
South Africa	25 ha	560	55%	
Australia	75 ha	2,320	48%	70%
Chile	1 ha	300	34%	51%
Argentina	5 ha	1,275	25%	41%
Spain	3.5 ha	6,355	12%	30%
Germany	1 ha	30,470	13%	
France	2 ha	36,440	13%	40%
Italy	1 ha	43,000	7%	10%

It's a more recent phenomenon for European wine producers to acquire subsidiaries in the New World. Sometimes the connection with the original producer is evident, more often it is obscure. The pioneers were the rich Champagne houses, whose subsidiaries are usually clearly identified. Among the first to realize the potential were Roederer, who established Roederer Estate in Anderson Valley in Sonoma in 1983, and Moët et Chandon, who set up their subsidiary Domaine Chandon in Napa Valley in 1986. The subsidiaries make sparkling wine—they are scrupulous about avoiding use of the term "Champagne." Champagne houses have also have set up subsidiaries in Australia or New Zealand. It's fair to say that, with rare exceptions, the warmer climates of the New World make a less refined product than Champagne itself, which is really a triumph in turning adversity of wine making in marginal climates into a luxury product. It's a bit too easy in the New World, the fruits are a little too ripe, the acidity is a little too low, but all the same, the wines can be good, even if lacking

Moët & Chandon have expanded out of Champagne to establish subsidiaries in Napa Valley and Australia. They use their own name in Napa, but use Greenpoint for exports from Australia, although the wine is available in the country as Domaine Chandon.

the finesse of Champagne. And now the trend has extended to other wines. Pernod-Ricard's subsidiaries dominate wine production in New Zealand. Major Spanish producer Torres first expanded around Spain and now is a major producer in Chile. Less obvious, because they don't necessarily operate under their own names, foreign companies own about 20% of Napa Valley vineyards. Globalization has definitely become a two way process.

The Bootleggers' Heritage

Most people who are interested in wine have some sense of which producers they like, whether it's a simple choice among leading brands or a sophisticated selection of artisan winemakers. They also are able to choose where they buy their wine, whether at supermarkets or specialist shops. But the pipeline from the producer to the shop is a black hole: there is little awareness of the extent to which the distributor in the middle affects the available choice and price.

Freedom of choice varies greatly, depending on where you live. In most of Europe, wine is a free market: in principle you can buy any wine you like, although of course choices are influenced by local conditions, such as preference for the local product over imports. Sweden is an exception, where monopoly rules: Systembolaget's 400 stores in Sweden have a monopoly on retail sales. You can buy anything you want, so long as Systembolaget decides to import it. Choice is inevitably more restricted than it would be in a free market, although not as much as in Canada, where the regional wine boards have a monopoly ensuring that 40% of sales are Canadian wine.

The contrast between the organization of the wine industry in Europe and the United States is ironic. In Europe, centuries of tradition now mean that producers (especially for quality wine) function under a wide range of legal constraints regulating what type of wine they can produce. Promotion is becoming impossible, but they can actually sell their wine to anyone, anywhere who wants it. But in the United States, where the experiment of Prohibition failed so ignobly, producers can make wine pretty much as they like, and there are relatively few restrictions on promoting it. Yet consumer choice is restricted by the mess in distribution resulting from ill-thought out features of the repeal process.

Distributors gained a stranglehold on the market during Prohibition. The illegality of distribution made it not only criminal but also highly lucrative. Inevitably the mob moved in. By the time Prohibition ended, they were well entrenched. Repeal forced the industry into the so-called three-tier system, designed to prevent concentration in the hands of the mob or anyone else. Producers are kept separate from distributors who are kept separate from retailers. Together with the ability of each State to impose its own regulations, the system is truly Balkanized.

We need producers: without them there would be no wine. We need retailers: without them it would be difficult to buy wine. But do we need distributors: are they the parasites of the system? You might argue that large producers are perfectly capable of undertaking their own distribution, but that for small producers, distributors provide the essential connection to market. Ironically, however, it is larger producers in whom distributors are interested; small producers often fall through the net.[75]

Whatever essential role distributors may have filled in the past in enabling producers to market their wines in spite of the confusing welter of state regulations, today they are the bottleneck in the system. Distribution tends to be the most concentrated part of the wine industry, and nowhere is this better illustrated than the United States. There are 2,800 wineries in California;[76] the national number of retailers is unknown, but even the largest (Costco) has less than 5% of the market—but there are only a few hundred distributors.

The number of distributors is declining while the number of wineries and brands is increasing. There were more than 10,000 wholesalers in the 1960s, but fewer than 300 at the turn of the century.[77] Mergers and acquisitions, increasing the market share of the giants at the top, have driven the decline. The top five distributors now have 43% of the market; the top 10 have 60%. Consolidation of distributors is driven mostly by consolidation in the distribution of spirits (affecting wine because the same distributors handle both wine and spirits). The higher profit margins in spirits place companies that handle only wine at a disadvantage, pushing the trend toward mergers. The better returns on spirits encourage investments there rather than in wine. The biggest distributor (Southern Wines and Spirits) has an annual cash flow of $7.0 billion, whereas the biggest retailer (Costco) weighs in at $0.8 billion.[78]

Southern started in a small enough way in 1968, with a $200,000 loan from Miami National Bank to a New York liquor executive, Walter Jahn. The bank was later reported to be a conduit for mob money. Its chairman, Samuel Cohen, was convicted of money-laundering charges, but became a business partner of Jay Weiss, who became a top executive of Southern. These connections were the basis for rumors that Southern was connected with the mob.[79]

Southern remains privately held, and handles its business secretively. By 1999, it was operating in 8 states, with an annual cash flow of $2.8 billion, representing close to 12% of all domestic wine and liquor consumption.[80] Growing by gobbling up smaller distributors, its most recent acquisition of another large distributor, Glazer, brought it to operating in 38 states. It has close to a quarter of the national market.

Together with other wholesalers, it is not afraid to exercise political influence. Southern contributed equally to Democrats and Republicans in recent elections, and the WSWA (Wine and Spirits Wholesalers Association) was one of the top donors to politicians.[81] A major objective is to uphold the restrictions of the three-tier system, which protects distributors' profits by restricting sales within a state to distributors licensed by that state. Preventing shipment across state lines is one of the main causes for inflating the cost of wine and depriving the consumer of choice.

When Prohibition was repealed by the 21st Amendment to the Constitution, states were given the authority to regulate sales of alcohol, in particular to regulate imports into the state. This was interpreted by many states as giving them the right to prevent producers from shipping wine directly to a consumer; instead the producer is supposed to sell only to a licensed distributor. Put simply, this conflicts with the provision of the Constitution that states shall not have the power to interfere with inter-state commerce.

The clash was finally tested in a case that reached the Supreme Court on the rights of wineries to sell directly to consumers in states with restrictive laws. The immediate commercial interest is relatively small, since direct sales are only about 2% of the whole market, but the implications are almost unlimited, since opening up direct shipping from wineries would almost inevitably release the other restrictions enabling the distributor to strangle the consumer. The Supreme Court decided in 2005 that restrictions on direct shipping were unconstitutional.[82]

The point was hammered home by another case, in which Costco fought the Washington State Liquor Control Board on the grounds that its limitations on the distribution of wine and beer violated federal antitrust law. Basically Washington State had in place a whole set of restrictions, ranging from minimum markups to bans on volume discounts and central warehousing—all designed to protect the distributors who no doubt had been hand in glove with the state legislators. Costco, which comes close to a national retailer of wines, won its case in April 2006.

Together the two cases opened up the market, and it became possible for consumers in many states to purchase wine directly from wineries or from retailers in other states. There has been a vigorous rearguard action from distributors desperate to protect their monopoly. Southern's attitude is best summarized by a note that was produced in a court case in 1995; scrawled on an advertising flier from a California wine retailer, offering to ship wines directly, was a note from Mel Dick, a senior Vice President of Southern, to the president, Wayne Chaplin: "Is there any way to stop this?"[83] Southern used its influence to make it a criminal offense for a consumer in its home state of Florida to ship wine from a winery in California; the penalty was the same as for burglary—five years in prison![84] This gives you some sense of the forces behind the scenes and the pressure to prevent choice for the consumer.

As a private company, Southern does not have to publish its accounts, so no one knows how much it spends on "lobbying," but it is thought to be the single largest source of funds for opposing liberalization of the wine laws. So every time an American consumer buys a bottle of wine distributed by Southern, part of the costs goes to efforts to deny freedom of choice. You might have thought that the growing power of Southern, which is now by far the largest wine distributor in the United States, would attract the attention of the anti-monopolies unit of Justice Department; one can only marvel at its immunity, especially since one of the stated purposes of the repeal of Prohibition was to prevent monopolies in wine and spirits distribution.

What public interest could be served by preventing consumers from having the same freedom of choice in purchasing wine as for other commodities? The excuses presented to preserve the remnants of the old system grow steadily feebler. "Social responsibility plays an integral role at Southern Wine & Spirits of America," said Lee Schrager, a Vice President of Southern.[85] But Southern and the other distributors are no doubt maneuvering even as you read this to prevent you from having free access to the market. State by state, legislators who put the interests of the distributors ahead of those of their constituents have been struggling to put the genie back in the bottle; let's hope they don't succeed.

The Unequal Equation of Supply and Demand

It's enough to make an economist despair. Not only is wine an inefficient market, but the imbalance of supply and demand has been perpetuated for decades; the worldwide surplus has really hardly shifted since 1970. Production has declined in parallel with the decline in demand, but never enough to close the gap. On top of this, wine remains an agricultural product, so there is unpredictable fluctuation in supply from year to year.

The basic problem in demand is the transition in Europe away from wine being a daily beverage, consumed in large quantities at cheap price. This has vastly reduced the total market. Growing consumption in new markets, such as the United States and Asia, has not been enough to compensate for the loss; and anyway, the new consumption is at a different level. There is little prospect that demand will be restored to the overall level of twenty years ago.

Europe will never solve the problem of its wine surplus so long as it subsidizes production that has become uneconomic. With a shifting world economy, other industries have moved out of Europe; why should wine be different? But having peaked in the 1970s-1980s, wine has merely gone back to where it was in the 1960s. It's not an easy problem to resolve, because there is no often no obvious alternative usage of the land; the fact that you can't even make decent wine often means that no other crop will be successful. Whether Europe will really allow another few hundred thousand hectares to be ploughed under remains to be seen, but nothing much else will restore balance.

While the surplus in the big three—Spain, Italy, and France—remains the major problem, there has been a shift of who gets stuck with the parcel when the music stops. Europe's problems in disposing of its surplus were exacerbated by the growth of production in the New World, which at first had little problem in selling its wines. But the rapidity of growth in supply, especially from Australia, has finally outgrown demand, leading to a classic boom and bust cycle in which wine cannot be sold, prices are dropping, grapes are unpicked, and finally some vineyards are being pulled out.[86] There are similar problems in South America, albeit lesser in magnitude.

The wine market is almost never in balance. Supply fluctuates with the vintage; and it's rarely practical to stockpile large vintages to even out the supply in small vintages. The transition from a cheap beverage to a drink which, if not a luxury item, is at least dispensable, makes wine more susceptible to general fluctuations in the economy.[87] The combination of the general worldwide surplus, annual fluctuations in supply, and unpredictable fluctuation in demand depending on the economy, makes for a roller coaster.

10

Fraud and Scandal

FRAUD IS THE INEVITABLE COMPANION OF REGULATION AND TAXATION. And regulation and taxation are as old as wine itself. By 2500 B.C., the "Inspector of the Wine Test" was required to approve wine for sale in Egypt.[1] By 400 B.C., laws in Greece prevented watering down wine and required it to be sold in airtight amphorae. Fines were imposed for selling wine on futures.[2] The major problem has always been adulteration in one form or another; Pliny the Elder complained in 77 C.E. that "genuine, unadulterated wine is not to be had now, not even by the nobility."[3] The most famous wine of the time, Falernian, made on the slopes of Mount Falernus near Naples, was apparently so ubiquitous as to arouse suspicions of authenticity.[4] Just before the lava came down over Pompeii, Falernian was available in bars for the unbelievable price of only four times that of the house wine.[5] Galen, the famous Roman physician of the second century, who had some experience of the real thing and thought it was at its best after 15 years or so, commented that "other wines like it are prepared by those who are skilled in such knavery."[6]

Adulteration varies from harmless dilution with water to addition of lethal concoctions. Mediaeval laws commonly forbade the watering of wine. An English law of 1327 required innkeepers to draw wine from casks in the view of their customers. The law provided not only that new and old wine could not be blended, but they could not even be kept in the same cellar. Wines from different sources could not be sold by the same merchant.[7] Punishments were public. In 1364, John Penrose, a vintner in the city of London, was found guilty of selling bad wine, and condemned to drink a draught of his own wine, before having the rest poured over his head, and being banned from selling wine.

Passing off inferior wine as better wine is a more subtle form of adulteration than watering down. This is particularly difficult to prevent in a context in which wines are being blended anyway. Although the history of wine is replete with regulations to prevent dilution, adulteration, or inappropriate blending, until the present century, concern was more about making sure the wine was sellable than protecting its authenticity of origin. In Carthage, around the sixth century B.C., Mago described how to produce high quality wine and what additives should be used to disguise wines of lower quality.[8]

During the nineteenth century in Bordeaux, wines were commonly blended with imports that were a bit stronger, brought in from Spain or from the Rhône valley in France. "Hermitager" became a verb describing use of the wines of Hermitage (in the northern Rhône) to strengthen those of Bordeaux or Burgundy. In fact, a major part of the skill set of the negociants who shipped the wine from Bordeaux was to adjust it to suit the tastes of their customers.[9] This blending was so important that arguments continued from the seventeenth through the nineteenth century about who should have the right to perform it. During the nineteenth century, Bordeaux shippers purchased vineyards in Hermitage in order to assure their supply, and as much as 80% of the production was shipped to Bordeaux.[10]

Blending with foreign wine was regarded as normal practice in Bordeaux, even for the top wines. It was regarded with skepticism only by outsiders. Cyrus Redding, an English commentator on wine, remarked in 1833 that, "Bordeaux wine in England and in Bordeaux scarcely resemble each other. The merchants are obliged to 'work' the wines before they are shipped, or, in other words, to mingle stronger wines with them, such as Hermitage, or Cahors, which is destructive almost wholly of the bouquet, color, and aroma of the original wine."[11] Thomas Jefferson was highly skeptical of the negociants' activities: "The vigneron never adulterates his wine, but on the contrary gives it the most perfect

Vignerons protested in Montpellier in 1907. The slogan on the barrel says "war on fraud, keep wine natural."

and pure care possible. But when once a wine has been into a merchant's hands, it never comes out unmixed. This being the basis of their trade, no degree of honesty, of personal friendship or of kindred prevents it."[12]

It was not until the twentieth century that authenticity of origin became an important issue. When the phylloxera epidemic devastated wine production, first in France and then in the rest of Europe, the market was opened to competition by cheap imports (from Algeria) or with synthetic products (basically made from sugar). Vignerons rioted in the Languedoc in 1907, setting a tradition for protest that continues to the present day. In Bordeaux, the negociants struggled to protect their vested interest in blending wines, and succeeded in delaying the implementation of laws protecting origin until 1912.[13] Finally, it became true that a bottle stating "Bordeaux" actually contained nothing but wine from the region.

Authenticity became of increasing importance and was the basis for the system of Appellation Contrôlée that was formally introduced in 1935. Initially this covered a relatively small proportion of vineyards, restricted to the top areas, representing about 10% of wine production. Since then it has spread to include more than half of the vineyards of France. It was the forerunner for the European Union system of QWPSR (Quality Wine Produced in a Specific Region); every country in Europe has its own system, but wines in the top category always have a label saying where they come from. Similar systems, although somewhat less well defined and less effective, are now spreading through the New World.

Authenticity of origin is a major characteristic for defining a quality wine. Usually it goes hand in hand with procedures to ensure that a certain standard is maintained, at a minimum that the wine has not been adulterated with non vinous components. The famous frauds alternate between passing off inferior wine as coming from a better location and actually adulterating the wine in order to "improve" it.

Plumbing the Depths

A variety of motives are responsible for adulterating wine, mostly to make it look better (typically more darkly colored) or taste better (most often to compensate for the results of a poor vintage). All involve an amount of deception in making the wine appear as something it is not. But the most lethal form of adulteration started more as a means of protecting the wine.

Needing preservatives to conserve their wine, the Romans often added a preparation called *sapa*. Columella, author of a famous series of books on agriculture in the first century, detailed how much sapa should be added to preserve the wine until the next vintage without letting the flavor become noticeable enough to discourage purchasers.[14] Sapa was a sweet syrup, prepared by boiling acidic wine in lead-lined vessels, and its active component was lead acetate. From Columella's recipe, it's possible to calculate that the lead content of the wines would have been about 20 mg/l, so consumption of a liter would give more than 40 times the level of 0.5 mg/day that produces chronic lead poisoning.[15] Indeed, there is a school of thought that lead poisoning may have

City officials escorting a wagon of confiscated wine casks for dumping in the river at Nuremberg, probably about 1630.[18]

contributed to the fall of the Roman Empire.[16] Since Columella's books continued to be available through the mediaeval period, lead poisoning did not stop with the Roman Empire.

The Romans had no idea that sapa contained a lethal dose of lead, but a millennium later, lead was added intentionally because it had been discovered that it improved wine flavor. In particular, it corrected the problem with sour wines by making them taste sweet. Once it was realized that the addition of lead was toxic, attempts were made to ban it. One of the very first edicts concerning adulteration is attributed to Charlemagne in 802, banning the use of leaded wines.[17] In Ulm, the center of the German wine trade, an edict of 1487 required all innkeepers to testify to the purity of their wine; and a list of banned ingredients included lead oxide. Fifteenth century edicts in both France and Spain banned the use of sapa to sweeten wine. A seventeenth century etching from Nuremberg shows a wagon of confiscated wine being taken to the river for dumping.

But the attraction for the wine merchant of correcting unsellable wine overcame any concern for the consumer. In the late seventeenth century, a recipe similar to Columella's was used in southern Germany, involving addition of litharge (a powder of lead oxide) to wine vats. Increased use probably resulted from a series of poor vintages that produced sour wines. In 1695, Eberhard Gockel, a physician in Ulm, pinned down outbreaks of chronic colic to lead poisoning caused by the use of litharge.[19] By 1696, the Duke of Württemberg issued another decree on adulteration of wine, banning the addition of litharge.

By the mid eighteenth century, such laws were common, and penalties included death.[20]

This was by no means the end of epidemics of lead poisoning. Subsequent outbreaks occurred in England at the end of the eighteenth century (due to contaminated cider, rather than wine), and a British physician complained in 1820 that the use of lead "adds the crime of murder to that of fraud."[21] There's a theory that the ill-health (and bad temper) of the composer Handel was due to lead poisoning.[22]

Lead in wine has continued to be a sensitive issue. Lead can get into wine from the environment, although the sources have effectively been eliminated in recent decades. In the early part of the century, vineyards were sprayed with lead arsenate, and lead paints were common in wineries.[23] Capsules on bottles used to be made of tin, and this seems to have been a source of lead in wine; apparently wine became contaminated during pouring, from lead residues deposited on the bottle.[24] Lead capsules were banned in 1996 in the United States, and capsules are now made of plastic.

The most recent excitement was the discovery that lead could leach from crystal decanters into wine.[25] Port kept in a decanter for several months achieved dangerously high levels (whether aside from that it was still drinkable after such a period is another question), but later studies showed that under normal conditions of consumer use, any level of lead in the wine was far below dangerous levels.

Red, Red Wine

You can make wine from elderberries. In fact, it's popular with home winemakers. But what does that have to do with the product of the grape? Well, there's a very long history of elderberries being used to improve the color of wine.

Elderberries grow on bushes that can become large, up to 4 meters high. They are relatively small, deeply colored berries. The color is due to a high concentration of anthocyanins, and they also contain tannins at levels comparable to the less pigmented red grape varieties. Sugar levels are much lower than grapes, typically about 75 g/l (a Brix of about 8, equivalent to 5% potential alcohol). Citric acid is the most abundant acid, and a lot of sugar is used to counteract the acidity when making elderberry wine. It's important to use ripe berries, and to avoid contamination, because the unripe fruit, leaves, shoots and bark are all harmful if not entirely poisonous.

So elderberry wine is no threat to the established order, but winemakers have been known to look enviously at the high anthocyanin concentrations in the dark blue skins of the small berries.

Elderberries have been employed from Champagne to Port. During the nineteenth century, the town of Fismes (in the Marne) was famous for providing elderberries for tinting rosé Champagne.[26] The Teinte de Fismes was made by "digesting 250 to 500 parts of elderberries, and 30 to 60 parts of alum [aluminium

Elderberries have a long but not very distinguished history in wine production. They are small and very deeply colored, and have been used widely for increasing color in wine.

potassium sulfate] with 800 to 600 of water, and then submitting the mixture to pressure."[27]

Its use was even more pronounced in Port. "It is my belief that the peculiar color of nearly all Port wines hitherto drunk in England... can only be produced by artificial means and is effected by an infusion of elderberry juice," commented the British representative in Lisbon in 1867.[28] The situation was so bad that in 1756 the Portuguese government had required that all elderberry trees in the region should be destroyed,[29] but the edict evidently had little effect.

Why Is Antifreeze Delicious?

Many noxious substances smell or taste bad, a clear warning to avoid them. But ethylene glycol, a syrupy derivative of alcohol, which lowers the freezing point and is widely used as engine antifreeze, actually tastes sweet and pleasant. A fair number of people are hurt by accidentally consuming it each year; and there've even been murder cases where it's been fed to victims by spiking their drinks.[30] The so-called antifreeze scandal in Austria in 1985 was actually somewhat misnamed; winemakers had been adding diethylene glycol to make their wine appear richer, but this is not the same as ethylene glycol. It is, of course, related, and it does have a slight antifreeze effect, but it's not as toxic. The sweet taste means it's relatively easy to ingest large amounts and reach a toxic level, however, so it is banned for use in foods and drugs.

Diethylene glycol owes its infamy in wine to the chemist Otto Nadrasky. He had been working on a means to produce "wine" simply from chemicals, without the inconvenience of needing to ferment grapes. During his research, he discovered that diethylene glycol masks the presence of additional sugar, with the result that sugar could be added to wine without being detected during analysis.[31] In the context of regulations rating wines according to grape sugar levels, this was a profitable discovery. One story has the fraud discovered in December 1984 when a wine producer tried to reclaim the VAT that he had paid on purchases of diethylene glycol.[32] Another places the discovery later, in March 1985 when a tax inspector queried purchases of large quantities of diethylene glycol by an obscure wine merchant in a village on the Hungarian border.[33]

The affair was covered up, but came to light in Germany (where much of the treated wine had been sold) in July; and by August all Austrian wine for sale in Britain was withdrawn. The scandal affected everyone, even impeccable producers, who had unknowingly purchased treated wine from others. More than a thousand different wines were found to have been treated, amounting to several millions of bottles. This could have accounted for as much as 10% of the wines produced in Austria over the period.[34]

With their usual irrelevance, the authorities finally announced that the regulations would be tightened, but current law was in fact adequate: addition of glycol was completely illegal, taking place against a background of general disregard for regulations. A warning sign had been sounded previously when the annual sales of the red Hirondelle brand (popular in Britain in the 1970s), which was labeled as Austrian red wine, were reported to exceed the entire production of red wine in the country.[36]

The events of 1985 are still referred to in Austria as "the scandal"—the word antifreeze is never mentioned. It was a drastic wake-up call. By the year following the scandal, exports of Austrian wine, which previously had accounted for a half to a third of production, collapsed to almost nothing. It took more than a decade before recovery even began.

In spite of press hysteria, there was no hazard to human health from the tainted wines. By far the worst case affecting health was the 1986 wine scandal in northern Italy when four large producers added methanol to their wines.[37] Twenty-six people died and many more were hospitalized. It emerged from the investigation that this was the extreme manifestation of a general disregard for regulations regarding blending of wine from different sources.

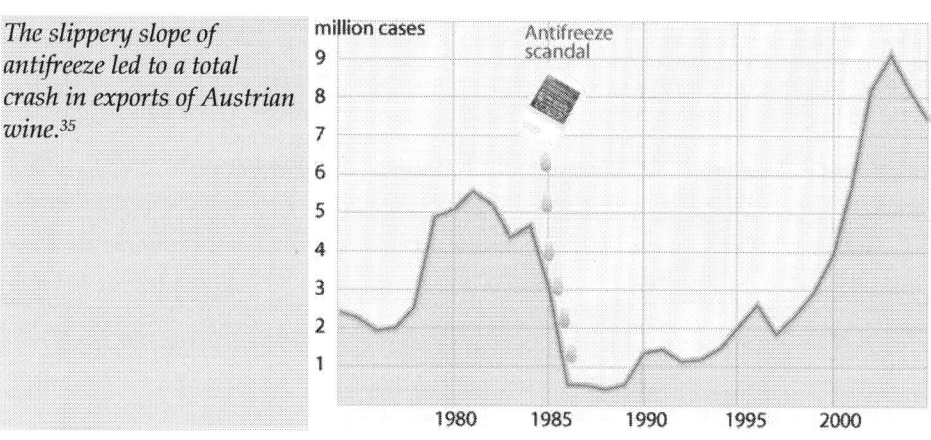

The slippery slope of antifreeze led to a total crash in exports of Austrian wine.[35]

A Spoonful of Sugar

You can't make wine without sugar, in fact you can't make any alcoholic beverage without it since alcohol comes from fermentation of sugar, but that very fact makes it extremely simple to abuse the process. Not only can the alcohol level be bumped up by adding sugar before fermentation occurs, but by using dried raisins and sugar, or even just by making a solution of sugar in water, fermentation followed by addition of some flavoring compounds will produce "wine." A recipe was published in a scientific encyclopedia in the 1760s: "Take 250 pounds of sugar; put in a cuve of 2 muids; fill within 16 pints of the top; put in a warm place; add 3 or 4 pounds of yeast from fresh beer... Color with sunflower extract to make red wine and add a little oil for aroma."[38]

At the peak of the crisis caused by the loss of production resulting from the phylloxera devastation (1885-1890), there were substantial sales of "sugar wines" consisting of industrial fabrications from alcohol, tartaric acid, flavoring compounds, and so on. During this period as much as 10-20% of total wine production in France[39] may have come from fermenting dried raisins that had been mixed with water and a little sugar (a large part was produced in industrial establishments in the Parisian region; if you weren't going to grow grapes, why not eliminate the costs of transport to the consumers).[40]

Today, addition of sugar is legal in the cooler parts of Europe; probably up to 20% of French wines have their alcohol level increased by this chaptalization.[41]

Wine scandals involving sugar are endemic. The stakes are highest in Germany and Austria, where the classification system grades wine according to the level of sugar in the grape must. By adding sugar to the must, the wine achieves a higher, and more valuable, grade. A similar, if less pronounced, effect is created whenever a wine is classified by alcohol level, for example, Beaujolais requires more than 9% alcohol, but Beaujolais Superieure must be above 10%.

It's really a scandal that sugar can be added legally in Germany so long as it is in the form of RCGM (rectified concentrated grape must, which is a sugar preparation made from grapes), although it's restricted to wines below the quality grade of QmP. It's not legal to add sugar from other sources, but it emerged in 1980 that addition of liquid sugar (a solution of fructose and glucose known as invert sugar) was common. Two hundred sugar merchants had illegally supplied 1,800 wine producers, who had artificially sweetened 300 million bottles of wine between 1977 and 1979.[42] Sugar had been added to wines in regions extending from the Mosel to the Nahe and the Pfalz; overall up to a ton of sugar was added per thousand hectoliters of wine.[43] (Proportionately, the most sugar was added in the most northernmost region, the Mosel.) A scandal involving people in high places erupted in the Mosel, where the President of the German Winegrowers' Association turned out to have illegally sweetened several million bottles of wine.[44] One wonders how much German wine was authentic before the authorities clamped down.

For whatever reason, Beaujolais seems to attract more scandal than most. As recently as the 1950s, when Beaujolais was producing less than 60 million bottles per year, it was estimated that the Paris region alone consumed more than 250 million bottles annually.[45] More recently, large purchases of sugar from supermarkets during the 2004 season led to the discovery that alcohol levels had been increased more than the legal limit of 2%.[46] The motive wasn't so much the classification of the wine as simply to reach a high enough alcohol level to be competitive in the modern world.

With sugar scandals continuing right up to the present day, perhaps the only solution to guarantee authenticity would be to ban chaptalization in any form and to make it illegal to have sugar in a winery. This would prevent accidents such as Christopher Fielden was encouraged to precipitate in the Médoc: "I was asked to stumble when I passed a certain problem vat and, just by chance, empty the open sack of sugar, that I happened to be carrying, into it."[47]

You Pays Your Money and You Takes Your Choice

Nominally a quality wine in Europe should be at least 85% of what is stated on the label, since in theory it's permitted to include up to 15% of wine from another vintage. Similarly, in cases where a grape variety is stated, 15% of another varietal can be included. But the place name has been sacrosanct since the enforcement of appellation rules throughout the European Community.

Nowhere was the impact of the regulations felt more keenly than in Britain, where for years appellation names had been used as folkloric descriptions of wines rather than referring to actual origins. Christopher Fielden quotes the complaint of the manager at the bottling plant of the giant Societé de Vins de France in England: "You English are such individualists. Each one wants a different blend for a different wine... As a result I have to keep halting my bottling line, pumping wines from tank to tank... just to satisfy old-fashioned quirks."[48] The plant, which became known as Château Ipswich, was stocking eight base wines, three white, three rosé, and two red, which were blended as necessary to make a series of different wines for sale. The two red base wines had alcohol levels of 12% and 11.5%, respectively. "Châteauneuf-du-Pape" was produced from the twelve percent; "Nuits St. Georges" was made by mixing in a little eleven-five; the mix was lightened a little more for "Beaujolais" by increasing the eleven-five a bit further; while the eleven-five alone was used when "Médoc" was required.[49] The operation was a great success until exposed by journalist Nicholas Tomalin in the Sunday Times in November 1966.

While this may have been an extreme case, the traditional practices of wine merchants in Britain were certainly threatened when the country joined the European Union. Nuits St. Georges, for example, was used as a generic name for Burgundy with a good body. Often enough the same wine would be labeled as Volnay, Nuits St. Georges, or Gevrey Chambertin, depending on the client.[50] There was enough wine in the pipeline that Britain needed to be given a three year derogation from joining in 1973 to requiring full compliance in 1976.

And certainly it is not unknown for Burgundies to be mislabeled at source. (I once inadvertently caused great offense in the cellars of a Burgundian producer, when looking at cage after cage of bottles whose contents were identified only by half-legible marks on chalkboards, I innocently asked if mistakes were ever made at labeling.) The Grivelet scandal in 1979 was stated by its protagonist, in the time hallowed way, to be nothing extraordinary because everyone was doing it. Faced with rapidly increasing demand for fine Burgundy in the United States, Bernard-Noël Grivelet took out full page advertisements offering individually numbered bottles of Burgundy from such prestigious appellations as Chambertin, Bonnes Mares, and various vineyards in Chambolle Musigny and Morey St. Denis. Five thousand cases were shipped (and consumed!) before it was discovered that M. Grivelet had in fact filled the bottles with non appellation wine.[51] Despite his claims that the practice "was widespread throughout the district," bankruptcy followed.

Sometimes the fraudsters are caught up by simple discrepancies in the numbers. Export figures showed that between 2005 and 2008, the Aude region of the Languedoc sold 1.3 million cases of Pinot Noir to the United States each year. The problem is that the whole Languedoc produces only 500,000 cases of Pinot each year! Winemakers and cooperatives sold the wine to the negociant firm Ducasse in Carcassone, which sold it to the huge producer Sieur d'Arques.[52] Sieur d'Arques then sold the wine to Gallo, for their Red Bicyclette brand. In the best French tradition, it remains unknown exactly who perpetuated the scam, but the profits must have been huge, since Pinot Noir sells for about twice the price of other black grapes. Everyone along the chain was prosecuted;[53] the defendants were found guilty in February 2010 and given suspended jail sentences and fines ranging from €,500 to €180,000,[54] rather piddling compared to the millions made in the fraud.[55] The defense was the same as usual: "There is no prejudice. Not a single American consumer complained," said the lawyer for Sieur d'Arques. Others defended themselves by arguing that they delivered a wine that had "Pinot Noir characteristics." Indeed, this doesn't say much for the ability of those farther along the chain to distinguish Pinot Noir from generic red wine! What's the point in paying a premium for a varietal if even the producer can't tell the difference?

The Scandal of the Century

Bordeaux had about ten vintages of the century between 1900 and 2000. But there was surely only one scandal of the century. Winegate had everything: a protagonist larger than life, Pierre Bert, who when he lost the case turned to the tax inspectors and said, "You've won, let me buy you a glass of champagne;" a judge at the Court in Bordeaux who palpably knew absolutely nothing about wine; the dogged tax inspector Destrau who pursued Bert for months while he untangled the threads of an extraordinarily ingenious fraud; inspectors whose bungled attempts to raid the headquarters of a suspect negociant made Inspector Clouseau look supremely competent; and the old-line major negociant, Cruse, who made no distinction between Vin de Table and top quality Bordeaux or Burgundy, and who went bust a year later.

The authorities thought they had an infallible system for control. "Our system of control has been perfected so that [fraud] is impossible. All these stories of coupages [blending], of wines from the Midi that are sold as Beaujolais or Bordeaux, are nothing but a tissue of ridiculous lies," said Pierre Perromat, the President of INAO[56] in 1973.[57] But there was a fatal flaw in the system.

Bert's system was so cunning that even after the tax inspectors knew there was a fraud, it took months for them to figure it out. But it would never have been successful but for the Cruses' cupidity and willingness to cooperate. They should have known better since Pierre Bert was a broker with a history of wine frauds.

The fraud occurred in the context of an overheated, speculative market. Prices rocketed in 1972 to 1973 and then collapsed in 1974. Early in 1973, Bert set up a small negociant business that he called Balan et cie (after the name of his driver, Serge Balan). Like many others, he was under financial pressure because in 1972 he had sold wine that he did not actually possess, expecting prices to fall before he needed to deliver. Confounded by a continued rise in the market, he was faced with a ruinous situation in the form of a deficit of 300,000 francs.

The "infallible" system for controlling wine in France provided a certificate of origin with every lot of wine. AOC wines had an acquit vert (green certificate), while table wines had a white certificate. The certificate was issued by the producer's local tax office, where the original remained. A copy of the certificate with detachable coupons traveled with every lot of wine. When the wine was moved from one location to another, for example from a grower to a negociant, an approved shipper could stamp a coupon, detach it, and return the copies to his local tax office and to INAO.

Balan et cie obtained a franking machine from the local tax office. (Machines were routinely available to reliable negociants.) The secret of their success was that they simultaneously purchased red table wine and white AOC Bordeaux. The red wine came with an acquit blanc, and the white wine came with an acquit vert. By swapping the acquits, that is by stamping the acquit vert when the red wine was sold and by using the acquit blanc for the white wine, Bert could sell the red wine as AOC Bordeaux and the white wine as table wine. The system fooled the authorities because the AOC of the wine is noted on the coupons, but the color of the wine was stated only on the original that remained in the originating tax office.

The price differential between white AOC Bordeaux and white table wine was small, about 10%, and Bert took a corresponding loss on that transaction. But the differential on the red wines was much larger, with AOC Bordeaux selling for about 3 times the table wine. So Bert trebled his money on that side of the transaction. A single tanker trundling from warehouse to warehouse where the switches were made was sufficient to move the equivalent of 4 million bottles and make several million francs of profits in a period of four months.

The stakes increased when Bert recruited Cruse as a client. They set up a trade in which Cruse purchased the fake red AOC wine at a price some 15% below market, while simultaneously selling the same amount of vin de table (of which they had an excess) to Bert. "We will deal with you," the Cruses said to

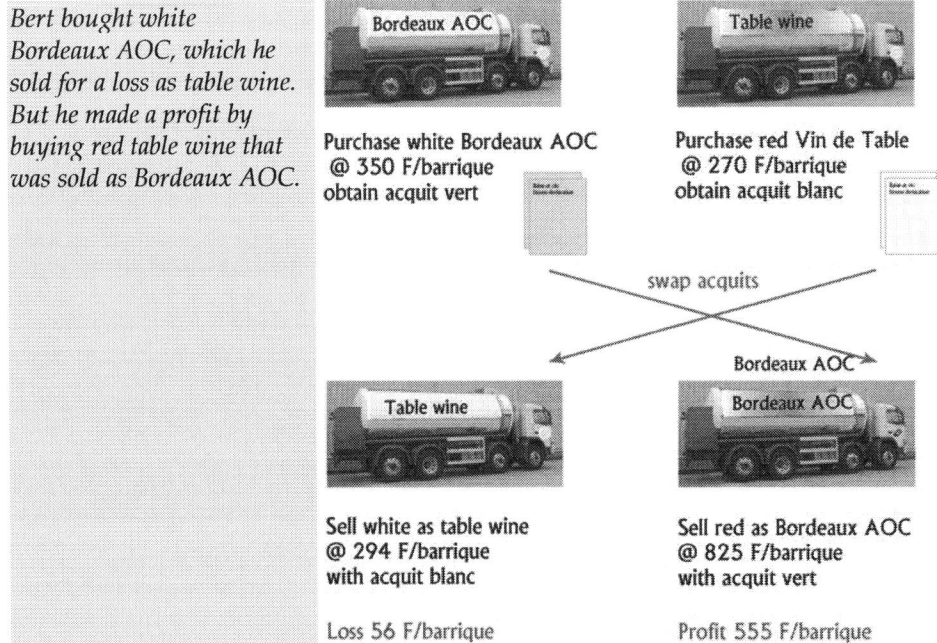

Bert bought white Bordeaux AOC, which he sold for a loss as table wine. But he made a profit by buying red table wine that was sold as Bordeaux AOC.

Bert, "on condition that we can exchange wines for current consumption [table wines] for the appellation wines that you deliver to us."[58] In due course, the system was simplified to the extent in which no wine actually changed hands, although for the sake of appearances a single tanker load of wine made the rounds from Balan to Cruse and back again. Essentially, Cruse received an acquit vert from Bert in exchange for an acquit blanc, but the wine stayed in the tanker. This enabled Cruse directly to sell their excess of vin de table as AOC Bordeaux.

The situation descended into farce when the tax inspectors appeared at Cruse headquarters on June 28 and demanded to take an inventory. There had for years been a gentleman's agreement between the negociants and the tax authorities that due notice would be given of inspections, and on these grounds, Cruse refused to allow the inspectors entry to the cellars. It took another two months before the inspectors were able to check the records, starting on August 28, when it soon became apparent that the fraud practiced by Bert was only a small part of the problem, and that Cruse had habitually sold the wine of one appellation as coming from another, labeled the same wine as coming from different appellations, sold the same wine under different château names, or had changed vintages, as well as promoting vin de table to AOC.[59] Only one wine, and from the Midi at that, apparently was used to compensate for ullage of the casks of the various AOC wines.[60] There were also accusations of chemical adulteration. Descriptions of vats were give-aways, such as "could be Beaujolais for the American market."

The trial started in October 1974, with Bert and the Cruses as the principal targets. Bert was accused of adulterating wine as well as changing its appellation. He defended himself vigorously on the grounds that, whether his actions were legal or not, they were no more than accustomed practice in improving the wine—"baptizing" was the term he used. He took the classic defense that he had never received any complaints from any of his customers. In one exchange that became famous, Bert conceded that he had mixed white wines with red, because "a little white wine does not harm the quality when there is too much tannin in the red." "Yes, but it's not legal," said the judge. "No, but it's good," Bert answered. He claimed that much of the wine labeled as AOC Bordeaux was in fact so poor in quality that it could be sold only after improvement.[61] When the verdict came in December, only Bert received a jail sentence jail; the Cruses were given suspended sentences.

The postscript was a mixture of farce and tragedy. Pierre Bert emerged after a short period in jail to write a humorous book about his experiences and became a minor celebrity. Unable to stand the disgrace, Herman Cruse committed suicide by jumping off a bridge into the Gironde. The house of Cruse went bust the following year, although more as a result of misjudgments in the market than because of the scandal.

Thomas Jefferson Was Here

It's not that Thomas Jefferson was omnipresent in wine regions when he was United States Minister to France from 1785 to 1789, but he left such a detailed record of his travels, and such perspicacious notes on wines and producers, that you feel he was a major authority of the late eighteenth century. He was an avid wine collector, known to have purchased the first growths of the Médoc and Graves as well as Château d'Yquem, not to mention later being involved in efforts (inevitably unsuccessful because of phylloxera) to grow Vitis vinifera at his home, Monticello, in Virginia. So it was a major event to find preserved bottles of Château Lafite, labeled 1787 and engraved with the initials Th. J. It was a pity that the engraving was later found to have been done with twentieth century power tools.

When Michael Broadbent brought the hammer down on lot 337, the first item in the afternoon session at Christie's wine auction in London on December 5, 1985, it was the most expensive bottle of wine in the world. Sold for a bid of £105,000 to the son of billionaire Malcolm Forbes, it was hand-blown in dark green glass; there was no label, but etched into the glass was "1787, Lafitte, Th. J.". This was one of a cache of bottles supposedly discovered in a bricked-up cellar in Paris that had been bottled for Thomas Jefferson.

Several of these bottles were later purchased by Bill Koch, an American tycoon. Koch became suspicious about their authenticity when the Thomas Jefferson Foundation cast doubt on the provenance of the bottles. Investigations of the wine itself, using techniques such as carbon dating, were inconclusive in most cases (although they did suggest that at least some of the bottles contained wine one or two centuries younger than claimed), but an examination of the bottles suggested that they had been engraved using twentieth century power tools.[62]

The seller of these, and many other old wines, was Hardy Rodenstock, a German living in Munich, who was originally a manager of pop music groups. Interested in wine as an amateur, he was a regular contributor to one of Germany's wine magazines (Alles über Wein) and a regular buyer at the London wine auctions. He acquired an almost mystical reputation for his ability to sniff out caves of old bottles. The Jefferson collection, supposed to have been revealed when a hidden cellar was exposed during the destruction of an eighteenth century house in Paris, was only one of these. Others included a supply of Pétrus in large format bottles, reported to be from an English cellar, a cache of old Bordeaux in Venezuela, and a cellar in Russia of first growth Bordeaux that was claimed to have belonged to the Tsar. By the 1980s, Rodenstock had become a professional wine trader, and hosted a series of high-end tastings at which a seemingly endless supply of extraordinary old bottles appeared. One of these tastings went through 125 vintages of Château d'Yquem.

The Jefferson cellar supposedly contained about a hundred bottles, including many of the first growths, and a couple of dozen bottles engraved with the initials "Th. J." Rodenstock has never revealed the source of the bottles, in spite of considerable pressure after the problems emerged. Believing that the bottles were fakes, Koch started an extensive investigation, not only to analyze the bottles, but also to search into Rodenstock's background. The investigation discovered that Rodenstock had changed his name, revealed various legal problems in Rodenstock's past, and culminated in a lawsuit in New York. There was of course an argument as to whether this was the appropriate jurisdiction, and to date the lawsuit has not brought any final resolution to the question of authenticity.

Several collectors have been burned by buying very expensive old bottles that could be traced back to Rodenstock and which now have dubious value. Bottles from Rodenstock were sold by Farr Wine Merchants in London, The Wine Li-

A bottle supposedly of Château Lafite from 1787 that was engraved for Thomas Jefferson. (Artist's impression.)

The affair remains so sensitive that Christie's refused permission to reproduce an original photograph of the bottle, as did its owner, Bill Koch.

brary in California, and various auction houses in London and New York. Finally this has led to sensitivity on the question of fraud, and the auction houses are refusing to accept suspect bottles. Is the apparent increase in the number of fakes due to fraud becoming more profitable with the rise in prices or has it been going on all along and only now is anyone paying attention?

With the very old wines, more is at stake than the authenticity of the particular bottles. Over the years, Rodenstock's supply of rare bottles included a significant number from the eighteenth and nineteenth centuries. Indeed, one writer pointed out that much of our knowledge about the supposed taste of these rare old wines depends on bottles provided by Rodenstock.[63] It now seems that, at the very least, the basis for all this knowledge is highly questionable. Is it a myth that we really know anything about the taste of nineteenth century wines?

Bibliography

Beeston, John, *The Wine Regions of Australia* (Unwin and Allen, Australia, 1999).

Belfrage, Nicholas, *Barolo to Valpolicella: the Wines of Northern Italy* (Faber & Faber, London, 1999).

Belfrage, Nicholas, *Brunello to Zibibbo: the Wines of Tuscany, Central and Southern Italy* (Faber & Faber, London, 2001).

Bert, Pierre, *In Vino Veritas. L'Affaire des Vins de Bordeaux* (Albin Michel, Paris, 1975).

Bird, Owen, *Rheingold: the German Wine Renaissance* (Arima Publishing, London, 2005).

Blom, Philippe, *The Wines of Austria* (Faber & Faber, London, 2000).

Brook, Stephen, *The Complete Bordeaux* (Mitchell Beazley, London, 2007).

Coates, Clive, *The Wines of Burgundy* (University of California Press, Berkeley, 2008).

Cooper, Michael, *Wine Atlas of New Zealand* (Hodder Moa Beckett, 2002).

Dion, Roger, *Histoire de la Vigne et du Vin en France des Origines au XIX Siècle* (Paris, 1959).

Faith, Nicholas, *Australia's Liquid Gold* (Mitchell Beazley, London, 2002).

Fielden, Christopher, *Is This the Wine You Ordered, Sir?: The Dark Side of the Wine Trade* (Christopher Helm, London, 1989).

Garner, Michael & Paul Merritt, *Barolo. Tar and Roses* (Wine Appreciation Guild, San Francisco, 1991).

Goode, Jamie, *The Science of Wine. From Vine to Glass* (Mitchell Beazley, London, 2005).

Hallgarten, Fritz, *Wine Scandal* (Sphere Books, 1987).

Halliday, James, *Wine Atlas of Australia and New Zealand* (HarperCollins, Australia, 1999).

Jackson, Ron. S., *Wine Science: Principles, Practice, Perception* (Academic Press, New York, 2000).

Jeffs, Julian, *Sherry, 4th edition* (Little Brown, New York, 1992).

Kramer, Matt, *New California Wine* (Running Press, Philadelphia, 2004).

Lapsley, James T, *Bottled Poetry: Napa Winemaking from Prohibition to the Modern Era* (University of California Press, Berkeley, 1997).

Lewin, Benjamin, *What Price Bordeaux?* (Vendange Press, Dover, 2009).

Livingstone-Learmonth, John, *The Wines of the Northern Rhône* (University of California Press, Berkeley, 2005).

Livingstone-Learmonth, John, *The Wines of the Rhône*, 3rd edition (Faber & Faber, London, 1992).

Mayson, Richard, *Port and the Douro* (Faber and Faber, London, 1999).

Mayson, Richard, *The Wines and Vineyards of Portugal* (Mitchell Beazley, London, 2003).

McGovern, Patrick E, *Ancient Wine: The Search for the Origins of Viniculture* (Princeton University Press, Princeton, 2003).

Penning-Rowsell, Edmund, *The Wines of Bordeaux, 6th edition* (Penguin Books, London, 1989).

Petrini, Carlo & Victtorio Mangnelli, *A Wine Atlas of the Langhe: The Greatest Barolo and Barbaresco Vineyards* (Slow Food Editors, 2003).

Pinney, Thomas, *A History of Wine in America : From Prohibition to the Present* (University of California Press, Berkeley, 2005).

Radford, John, *The Wines of Rioja* (Mitchell Beazley, London, 2004).

Richards, Peter, *The Wines of Chile* (Mitchell Beazley, London, 2006).

Rosso, Maurizio and Chris Meier, *The Mystique of Barolo* (Omega Edizione, 2002).

Stevenson, Tom, *The Wines of Alsace* (Faber & Faber, London, 1993).

Stevenson, Tom, *The World Encyclopedia of Champagne and Sparkling Wine* (Wine Appreciation Guild, San Francisco, 1999).

Sullivan, Charles L, *Napa Wine: A History from Mission Days to Present* (Wine Appreciation Guild, San Francisco, 1995).

Sullivan, Charles L, *Zinfandel: A History of a Grape and Its Wine* (University of California Press, Berkeley, 2003).

Taber, George, *To Cork or Not to Cork* (Scribner, New York, 2007).

Unwin, Tim, *Wine and the Vine: An Historical Geography of Viticulture and the Wine Trade* (Routledge, London, 1996).

Waldin, Monty, *Wines of South America* (Mitchell Beazley, London, 2003).

Wilson, James, *Terroir* (Wine Appreciation Guild, San Francisco, 1998).

Notes

References cited in the Bibliography are given in the notes by author and short title. Other references are given in full the first time cited in each chapter, and by author and short title with the indication *op. cit.* for subsequent citations in that chapter.

Organizations abbreviated by acronyms are:
AWBC: Australian Wine and Brandy Corporation.
AWRI: Australian Wine Research Institute.
BIVB: Bureau Interprofessionnel des Vins de Bourgogne.
CIVB: Conseil Interprofessionnel du Vin de Bordeaux.
CIVC: Comité interprofessionnel du Vin de Champagne
INAO: Institut National des Appellations d'Origine.
OIV: International Organization of Vine and Wine.
ONIVINS: Office National Interprofessionnel Des Vins (now known as VINIFLHOR).
USDA NASS: United States Department of Agriculture, National Agricultural Statistics Service.
TTB: United States Department of the Treasury; Alcohol and Tobacco Tax and Trade Bureau.

Chapter 1: The Grapevine

[1] A species is often defined as a group of organisms capable of interbreeding and producing fertile offspring. By this definition, all Vitis members would be one species. Because of the ability to interbreed, the exact number of Vitis subspecies is hard to define. However, I shall follow conventional terminology and describe the different varieties as "species" in the text.

[2] One of the best known of the other species is Vitis labrusca, which accounts for 80% of grape juice production in the United States. The Concord variety has been used to make wine, but the wine is marred by a characteristic "foxy" flavor.

[3] Most Vitis species are described as Euvitis (true Vitis). All Euvitis species are interfertile. In addition, there is a group of three species called Muscadinia. These split off from the Euvitis about 2 million years ago, and are found only in North America. They cannot breed with Euvitis species.

[4] Mutations suppressed development of male stamens in female plants and suppressed development of ovaries in male plants.

[5] Wild grapevines technically are known as Vitis vinifera ssp. silvestris and cultured grapevines are called Vitis vinifera ssp. sativa (or vinifera).

[6] McGovern, *Ancient Wine*, p. 7.

[7] Ibid., p. 72.

[8] Ibid., p. 16.

[9] Patrice This et al., *Historical Origins And Genetic Diversity Of Wine Grapes* (Trends in Genetics, 22, No. 9, 2006).

[10] R. Arroyo-Garcia. et al., *Multiple Origins Of Cultivated Grapevine (Vitis Vinifera L. Ssp. Sativa) Based On Chloroplast DNA Polymorphisms* (Molecular Ecology, 15, 3707-3714, 2006).

[11] Unwin, *Wine and the Vine*, p. 64.

[12] McGovern, *Ancient Wine*, p. 85.

[13] Theophrastus, *Enquiry into Plants*, trans. A. F. Horton, Heinemann, London, 1916.

[14] Unwin, *Wine and the Vine*, p. 118.

[15] Richard C. Selley, *The Winelands Of Britain: Past, Present & Prospective*, 2nd Edition (Petravin, London, 2008), pp. 13-19.

[16] Dion, *Histoire de la Vigne et du Vin*. p. 128.

[17] N. G. Davies and A. H. Gardiner, *Ancient Egyptian Paintings* (University of Chicago Press, Chicago, 1936), plate XXVIII.

[18] Dion, *Histoire de la Vigne et du Vin*, p. 3.

[19] The first Cistercian monastery, and the headquarters of the Cistercian Order, was established at Citeaux, close to Nuits St. Georges in Burgundy, in 1098. Kloster Eberbach, in the Rheingau of Germany, was established in 1136. These were the two most prominent monasteries in wine-producing regions. Both were important wine producers and innovators. The rules of the order (the "Carta Caritatis") required all monasteries to follow uniformity of custom. They were supposed to be self sufficient agriculturally. It is therefore possible that even the northern monasteries beyond the normal limits for wine production attempted to grow vines and produce wine. See also note 26.

[20] Unwin, *Wine and the Vine*, p. 146.

[21] Locations for monasteries producing wine were identified by Desmond Seward, *Monks and Wine* (Mitchell Beazley, London, 1979). The map shows only the major monasteries of the major orders. Identification of monasteries not making wine is less certain, but in all cases shown there are at least references to the purchase of wine by the monastery, and there is no record for wine having been produced in situ. For example, wine is known to have been produced at Altzel (south of Leipzig) and transported along the Elbe to Cistercian abbeys in northern Germany.

[22] Unwin, *Wine and the Vine*, p. 157.

[23] There were roughly 55 ha of vineyards, making the average vineyard around 1 ha in size (Tim Unwin, *Saxon and Early Normal Viticulture in England*, J. Wine Research, 1, 61-76, 1990). For a list of vineyards, see Selley, *The Winelands of Britain*, op. cit., p. 24.

[24] Hugh Barty-King, *A Tradition of English Wine: the Story of Two Thousand Years of English Wine Made from English Grapes* (Oxford Illustrated Press, Oxford, 1977), p. 40.

[25] By 1609 there were 139 vineyards in England and Wales, but later in the century the dissolution of the monasteries and the cooling climate led to their decline (ibid, p. 57).

[26] The Abbot of the Cistercian monastery near Bergen (the first to be established in Scandinavia, by monks who came from the Fountains Abbey in England in 1146), complained in 1338 that wine no longer came from England, suggesting that in Scandinavia even the Cistercians met their limit and were forced to bring in wine from other monasteries (Henry Goddard Leach, *The Relations Of The Norwegian With The English Church, 1066-1399, And Their Importance To Comparative Literature*, Daedalus, Proceedings of the American Academy of Arts and Sciences, XLIV, No. 20., May, 1909, p. 558.)

[27] Norman John Greville Pounds, *An Historical Geography of Europe, 1500-1840* (Cambridge University Press Archive, Cambridge, 1949), pp. 41-42.

[28] Unwin, *Wine and the Vine*, p. 162.

[29] Gary L. Peters, *American Winescapes: The Cultural Landscapes of America's Wine Country* (Boulder, CO, Westview Press, Swinchatt, Jonathan and Howell, 1997), p. 17.

[30] Its official name is now *Daktulosphaira vitifoliae*.

[31] Jeffrey Granett et al., *Biology and Management of Grape Phylloxera* (Annual Reviews Entomology, 46, 387-412, San Francisco, 2001), p. 403.

[32] Ibid., p. 396.

[33] Christy Campbell, *Phylloxera. How Wine Was Saved For The World* (Harper Perennial, London, 2007).

[34] Gilbert Garrier, *Le Phylloxéra. Une Guerre De Trente Ans 1970-1900* (Editions Albin Michel, Paris, 1989).

[35] Ibid., p. 38.

[36] The Concord grape takes its name from its origins in Concord, Massachusetts, where it was developed by Ephraim Bull. It was selected from 20,000 seedlings developed from Vitis labrusca. Because it is a hermaphrodite, it has been suggested that it has some Vitis vinifera in its parentage. One possibility is that the male parent (pollen donor) may have been Catawba, which is probably derived from Vitis labrusca and Vitis vinifera.

[37] Campbell, *Le Phylloxera*, p. 147.

[38] Le Journal Illustré, September 28, 1878. The legend says "The official commission visiting vineyards suspected of having phylloxera." The personages are not named, but are recognizable.

[39] In fact, it was recommended well before phylloxera became a problem as a means for improving quality in grapevines (Armand d'Armailhacq, *De La Culture Des Vignes, De La Vinification Et Des Vins Dans Le Médoc*, Chaumas, Bordeaux, 1867, p. 287).

[40] Although it proved impossible to graft Vitis vinifera directly on to Vitis berlandieri, a cross between the Chasselas variety of Vitis vinifera and Vitis berlandieri generated the "41B" rootstock that did well enough on chalk and had sufficient resistance to phylloxera.

[41] According to this analysis, in 1862 there were 2.32 million ha and in 1929 there were 1.6 million ha of vineyards. Distribution by département according to Genevieve Gavignaud, *Aspects de l'Evolution du Vignoble Français d'Après les Enquêtes Statistiques Agricoles (1806-1929)*. In A. Huetz de Lemps et al. (Eds.), *Géographie Historique des Vignobles, Tome I Vignobles Francais* (CNRS, Paris, 1978), pp. 93-110.

[42] Author's discussion with Francesco Cinzano at Col d'Orcia, October 2009.

[43] A report issued by the University of California commented that AxR1 had "only moderate phylloxera resistance," but nonetheless recommended it as "the nearest approach to an all-purpose stock." (Lloyd A. Lider, *Phylloxera-resistant grape rootstocks for the Coastal Valleys of California*, Hillgardia, 27, 287-318, 1958). AxR1 then became the rootstock of choice. The University should have known better.

[44] Data source: Garrier, *Le Phylloxéra*, op. cit., p. 175.

[45] Granett, *Biology and Management of Grape Phylloxera*, op. cit., p. 401.

[46] A "biotype" is no more than a new variant of the species. Biotypes of phylloxera were first proposed in the 19th century, but could not be substantiated (Michael C. Smith, *Plant Resistance to Arthropods: Molecular and Conventional Approaches*, Springer Science & Business, 2005, pp. 347-352). Renewed claims in the late 1980s identified A and B biotypes, which supposedly differed in their ability to feed on AxR1. B multiples twice as rapidly as A on AxR1 (Jeffrey Granett et al., *Evaluation Of Grape Rootstocks For Resistance To Type A And Type B Grape Phylloxera*, Am. J. Enol. Vitic. 38, 293-300, 1987). However, it is not clear whether this is relevant to the final outcome: death of the plant irrespective of biotype. In fact, there appears to be a general lack of correlation between genetic variants of phylloxera and susceptibility of rootstock hosts (A. Fornceck, *Ecological And Genetic Aspects Of Grape Phylloxera Daktulosphaira Vitifoliae (Hemiptera: Phylloxeridae) Performance On Rootstock Hosts*, Bull. Entomol. Res. 91, 445-451, 201).

[47] Frank Prial, *Wine Talk* (New York Times, August 12, 1992).

[48] Discussion with author, August 2008.

[49] Penning-Rowsell, *The Wines of Bordeaux*, p. 192.

[50] This would not be an easy project, because resistance to phylloxera probably involves many genes. The properties of hybrids show that sensitivity is more or less correlated with the proportion of Vitis vinifera parentage.

[51] Vitis International Variety Catalog (2007). See www.vivc.bafz.de.

[52] This includes Thompson seedless, which accounts for the majority of the world's white table grapes.

[53] Most new cultivars are results of crosses between existing domesticated grapevines, but it is still possible for crosses to occur between domesticated grapevines and wild grapevines. One relatively recent example of the introduction of genes from the wild may have been Riesling, which was probably generated by a cross between a variety called Heunisch Weiss (which was at one time widely distributed in Eastern Europe) and either a wild grapevine or a grapevine that was itself a cross between the domestic Traminer and a wild grapevine (Ferdinand Regner et al., *Heunisch x Fränkisch, ein wichtiger Genpool Europäischer Rebsorten (Vitis vinifera L sativa)*, Viticultural and Enological Sciences, V. 53, p. 114-118, 1998).

[54] Charles Sullivan, *Zinfandel. A History Of The Grape And Its Wine* (University of California Press, Berkeley, 2003).

[55] Quoted in Jordan Ross, *Balancing Quality & Yield: Impact Of Vine Age, Clone, And Vine Density*, Practical Winery and Vineyard, November, 1999.

[56] The growing season is April-October in the northern hemisphere. In the southern hemisphere, it is October-April.

Chapter 2: The Vineyard

[1] This is not so odd as it sounds, since one aspect of the Lenz-Moser training system, which is widely used in Austria, is a high canopy, one reason for which was to make it easier to harvest the grapes.

[2] Figures calculated from the declared vineyard area and total production for 2005.

[3] Quoted in Jordan Ross, *Balancing Quality & Yield: Impact Of Vine Age, Clone, And Vine Density*, Practical Winery and Vineyard, November, 1999.

[4] Ibid.

[5] Richard Smart, *Higher Yields Cause Lower Wine Quality*, Wine Business Monthly, November 2005.

[6] Jordan Ross, *Balancing Quality*, op. cit.

[7] A. J. Winkler et al. (General Viticulture. University of California Press, Berkeley, 1974), pp. 140-153; Linda Bisson, *In Search Of Optimal Grape Maturity* (Practical Vineyard and Winery, July 2001).

[8] This can be formalized as the maturation index, which divides the must sugar concentration in g/l by the titratable acidity expressed as tartaric acid equivalents per liter. It provides a valid comparison only within a variety, since different varieties have different typical indices.

[9] Brix × 0.9 gives the grams of sugar per 100 gms of juice. Fermentation generates 1% alcohol from 16.83 g/l of sugar. So Brix × 0.9 / 16.83 = Brix × 0.55 gives the per cent potential alcohol.

[10] Its level goes down by about half in the two weeks after veraison, largely due to dilution as the berry expands with the synthesis of other compounds.

[11] Uli Fischer and Ann C. Noble, *The Effect of Ethanol, Catechin Concentration, and pH on Sourness and Bitterness of Wine* (Am. Soc. Enol. Viticult., 45, 6-10, 1994).

[12] Hugh Johnson, *The Story of Wine* (Mitchell Beazley, London, 2005), p. 150.

[13] Unwin, *Wine and the Vine*, p. 107.

[14] IPT is measured by the optical absorbance at 280 nm (multiplied by 100). A rough equivalent in milligram equivalents of gallic acid per liter is given by multiplying the IPT by 0.08.

[15] IPT was typically about 62 in Bordeaux in 1982, 70 in year 2000, and 78 in year 2005.

[16] Pascal Ribéreau-Gayon et al., *The Handbook of Enology, Volume 1, The Microbiology of Wine and Vinifications* (John Wiley & Sons, New York, 2000), p. 357.

[17] One issue is that the physiological processes governing sugar and malic acid accumulation are much more dependent on temperature than those governing the color, aroma, and tannin levels that result from phenolic development. In cooler climates, phenolic ripeness is achieved at lower sugar levels than in warmer climates, which is part of the reason why higher alcohol (resulting from higher sugar) is associated with phenolic ripeness in warm climates.

[18] Helga Willer, *Organic Viticulture In Europe: Development And Current Statistics* (16th IFOAM Organic World Congress, Modena, Italy, June 16-20, 2008); Tom Stevenson, *Wine Report 2009* (Dorling Kindersley Publishing, London, p. 341).

[19] Official figures underestimate the extent of organic viticulture, because the expenses of certification are an impediment for small growers.

[20] Some growers in Germany's Rheingau, for example, who would like to be organic, feel that it's just too risky because their entire vineyards are devoted exclusively to Riesling, and an infection could spread too rapidly to be treated by organic methods.

[21] Copper accumulates in the top layer of soil and does not dissipate.

[22] Personal communication, Jean-Michel Comme, March 2009.

[23] This is now published annually (Maria Thun & Matthias Thun, *The Biodynamic Sowing and Planting Calendar*, Floris Books, Edinburgh, 2009).

[24] The movement is most highly developed in France, where biodynamic wine producers include Domaine d'Auvenay and Domaine Leflaive in Burgundy, Nicolas Joly and Didier Dagueneau in the Loire, Marcel Deiss and Marc Kreydenweiss in Alsace, Chapoutier in the Rhône, Domaine Gauby in Languedoc.

[25] Monty Waldin, *Biodynamic Wines* (Mitchell Beazley, London, 2004), p4.
[26] Guy Renvoisé, *Le Monde du Vin. Art ou Bluff* (Editions du Rouergue, Parc St Joseph, 1994), p. 156.
[27] On the occasion of a tasting of Château Musar in New York, October 2009.
[28] The certifying organization is Demeter, except in Australia where there is a government standard. See www.demeter.net.
[29] According to Demeter International, as of 2008 there were only 107,200 ha of certified biodynamic farms (including all types of agriculture) worldwide.
[30] The cost of certification is significant. The fee is 2% of net sales plus a charge for an annual inspection. See www.demeter.net.
[31] Claude Bourguignon, *Le Sol, La Terre Et Les Champs* (Sang de la terre, Auxerre, 1996).
[32] But note that this was an extremely brief report made at a Congress and that there appears to have been no detailed follow up or subsequent supporting study (Claude Bourguignon & Lydia Gabucci, *Comparisons Of Chemical Analysis And Biological Activity Of Soils Cultivated By Organic And Biodynamic Methods*, In H. Willer & U. Meier (Eds.), Proceedings 6th Annual Congress on Organic Viticulture, Basel, 2000, pp. 92-94).
[33] With permission from Maria and Matthias Thun, *The Biodynamic Sowing and Planting Calendar 2008*, Floris Books, Edinburgh.
[34] Jennifer Reeve et al., *Soil and Wine Grape Quality in Biodynamically and Organically Managed Vineyards* (Am. J. Enol. Vitic., 56, 367-376, 2005).
[35] Maria and Matthias Thun, *When Wine Tastes Best 2010* (Floris Books, Edinburgh, 2009).
[36] The Guardian, *Why Good Wine May Taste Like Moonshine Today*, April 18, 2009.
[37] Discussion with author, February 2010.
[38] Unfortunately, biodynamics has such an aura of mysticism that serious scientists are frightened to investigate the issues because they are concerned they will lose face with their peers (and, more practically, have difficulty getting grants).
[39] Interview with a winemaker in Napa Valley, February 2010.

Chapter 3: Terroir

[1] John Locke, The Works of John Locke, vol. 9 (Letters and Misc. Works, 1685) paragraph 1073.
[2] Dictionnaire de l'Académie Françoise, Nouvelle Edition, tome II, Paris, 1777, p. 542.
[3] It is mentioned by William Douglass, *A Summary, Historical And Political, Of The First Planting, Progressive Improvements And Present State Of The British Settlements In North America* (R. & J. Dodsley, London, 1760).
[4] Denis Morélot, *Statistique De La Vigne Dans Le Département De La Côte-D'Or* (Huzard, Paris, 1831), p. 4.
[5] Jake Hancock, *Terroir: The Role of Geology, Climate, and Culture in the Making of French Wines* (J. Wine Research, 10, 43-49, 1999).
[6] James Wilson, *Terroir* (Wine Appreciation Guild, San Francisco, 1998).
[7] Quoted in Michael Veseth, *Globaloney: Unraveling the Myths of Globalization* (Rowman & Littlefield, New York, 2005), p. 146.
[8] Matt Kramer, *The Notion Of Terroir*, in *Wine and Philosophy: A Symposium on Thinking and Drinking*, ed. Fritz Allhof, Wiley-Blackwell, Oxford, 2007, p. 228.
[9] The average size of vineyard holdings in Europe is around 2 ha, whereas in California or Australia it is 75-100 ha.
[10] "The answer lies in the soil" was the famous catch phrase in a British comedy radio program in the 1960s; the deep profundity of this expression, however, was far beyond their ken.
[11] Cornelius Van Leeuwen & Gerard Seguin, *The Concept of Terroir in Viticulture* (J. Wine Research, 17, 1-10, 2006).
[12] Marcus Vitruvius Pollio (27 B.C.), book VIII. In Vitruvius: The Ten Books on Architecture, by Morris H. Morgan, Harvard University Press, Cambridge, 1914. p. 236.
[13] Gerard Seguin, *Terroirs And Pedology Of Wine Growing* (Experientia, 42, 861-873, 1986).

[14] Author's discussion with Stefano Carpeneto at Tignanello, October 2009.

[15] Alex Maltman, *The Role of Vineyard Geology in Wine Typicity* (J. Wine Research, 19, 1-17, 2008), p. 5.

[16] Uptake of minerals is affected by the pH (acidity) of the soil, but uptake of potassium (most directly connected with lack of acidity in the plant) shows no effect over the pH range that grapevines can grow under (Jackson, *Wine Science*, p. 162).

[17] One study purporting to establish a relationship grew grapevines hydroponically. Increasing calcium carbonate in the hydroponic medium caused a 30% decrease in potassium concentration in the leaves of the plant, with a corresponding increase in acidity (Garcia et al., *Effect of various potassium-calcium ratios on cation nutrition of grape grown hydroponically*, J. Plant Nutrition, 22, 417-425, 1999). But no one has the faintest idea how the concentration of calcium carbonate in solution relates to effective concentration in soil, although this makes it plausible that increased available calcium in the soil could increase acidity in the grapes.

[18] Jennifer M. Huggett, *Geology and Wine: a review* (Proc. Geologists' Assoc., 117, 239-247, 2006), p. 240.

[19] The only difference between black and white grapes is that the former produce anthocyanins. These colored pigments do not contain iron; perhaps people have confused them with the blood pigment, hemoglobin, which requires iron! There appears to be no relationship between grape variety and iron content (Bruce W. Zoecklin et al., *Wine Analysis And Production*, Springer, 1995, p. 202).

[20] Soil areas based on Wilson, *Terroir,* p. 248. Topographic map from Google Earth.

[21] See décret in Journal Officiel, January 8, 1967, p. 412-413.

[22] See décret 78-238 of February 27, 1978.

[23] Jennifer M. Huggett, *Geology and Wine: a review* (Proc. Geologists' Assoc., 117, 239-247, 2006).

[24] Jake M. Hancock and Jennifer Huggett, *The Geological Controls in Coonawarra* (J. Wine Res., 15, 115-122, 2004).

[25] Maltman, op. cit., p. 10.

[26] Iron, Manganese, Boron, Molybdenum, Copper, Zinc, Chlorine, Cobalt.

[27] Alex E. Martin & R. John Watling, *Determining The Geographical Origin Of Wine* (Government of Western Australia, DAF, *Wine Industry Newsletter*, 89, 6-7, 2008).

[28] Maltman, op. cit., p.8.

[29] Taste thresholds for some metals are: Copper - 3 ppm; Iron - 0.1 ppm; Manganese - 1 ppm; Zinc - 4 ppm. Some comparable legal limits for concentrations in wine are: copper in wine in the E.U. is 1 ppm; zinc in wine in Australia is 0.005 ppm.

[30] For example, copper was ~1 ppm in must but ten-fold less in wine (C. M. Almeida and M. T. Vasconcelolos, *Multielement Composition Of Wines And Their Precursors, Including Provenance Soil And Their Potentialities As Fingerprints Of Wine Origin*, J. Agricult. Food Chem., 51, 4788-4799, 2003). Another study, attempting to demonstrate a reproducible relationship between concentrations of elements in soil and wine, showed widely variable levels influenced to some degree by berry ripeness (as seen in sugar levels and titratable acidity) (D. E. Mackenzie and A. G. Christy, *The Role Of Soil Chemistry In Wine Grape Quality And Sustainable Soil Management In Vineyards*, IWA Publishing: Water Science and Technology, 51, 27–37, 2005).

[31] Ron S. Jackson, *Wine Science*, p. 50.

[32] Takatoshi Tominaga et al., *Contribution of Benzenemethanethiol to Smoky Aroma of Certain Vitis vinifera L. Wines* (J. Agric. Food Chem., 51, 1373–1376, 2003).

[33] In the first edition of his book, *Burgundy*, in 1982, Anthony Hanson offended some people by writing "Great Burgundy smells of shit." In the second edition of 1995, he acknowledged an oversimplification, and implied that the odor might be due to microbial action (Anthony Hanson, *Burgundy, 1st edition,* Faber & Faber, London, 1982, p. 147; Anthony Hanson, *Burgundy, 2nd edition,* Faber & Faber, London, 1995, p. 151).

[34] ETS Laboratories, *Technical Bulletin - Eucalyptol*, February 8, 2009.

[35] Glynn Ward et al., *Smoke Taint in Western Australia*, Wine Business Monthly, September 15, 2008.

[36] Pliny the Elder (70 C.E.). The XIIII book of the history of nature. Containing the Treatise of Trees bearing fruit. Chapter VI.

[37] Unwin, *Wine and the Vine*, p. 111.

[38] James Busby, *A Treatise On The Culture Of The Vine And The Art Of Making Wine, Compiled From The Works Of Chaptal And Other French Writers ; And From The Notes Of The Compiler During A Residence In Some Of The Wine Provinces Of France* (R. Howe, Government Printer, Australia, 1825), p. 14.

[39] Ibid., p. 11.

[40] Jennifer M. Huggett, *Geology and Wine: a review* (Proc. Geologists' Assoc., 117, 239-247, 2006), p. 243.

[41] Ibid., p. 241; Alex Maltman, *Wine, Beer and Whisky: the Role of Geology* (Geology Today, 19, 22-29, Blackwell, Oxford, 2003).

[42] Adam, Smith, *An Inquiry into the Nature and Causes of the Wealth of Nations*, 1776, Book 1, Chapter 11, p. 41.

[43] Joseph Capus, *Proposition De La Loi Sur La Protection Des Appellations Contrôlées*, Revue du vin de France, July 25, 1935, cited in Philip Whalen, *'Insofar as the Ruby Wine Seduces Them': Cultural Strategies for Selling Wine in Inter-war Burgundy* (Contemporary European History, 18, 67-98, Cambridge University Press, Cambridge, 2009), p. 71.

[44] Lewin, *What Price Bordeaux?*

[45] Philip Whalen, *'Insofar as the Ruby Wine Seduces Them'*, op cit., p. 71.

[46] "The majority of wines sold behind respectable labels are more often the product of the chemist's laboratory rather than the vintner's cellar" (Gaston Roupnel, *La Crise Du Vin*, Dépêche de Toulouse, November 2, 1922).

[47] The protagonists in favor of terroir were the producers Gaston Roupnel, Albert Noirot, Georges Gouges, and the Marquis d'Angerville, and the legal cases were fought between 1924 and 1936 (Whalen, op. cit., p. 81).

[48] J. Lavalle, *Histoire et Statistique de la Vigne et des Grands Vins de la Cote d'Or* (Picard, Dijon, 1855), appendix.

[49] Walter Moran, *The Wine Appellation as Territory in France and California* (Annals Association American Geographers, 83, 694-717, Blackwell, Cambridge, Massachusetts, 1993), pp. 702, 714.

[50] Walter Moran, *Crafting Terroir: People In Cool Climates, Soils, And Markets* (Sixth International Cool Climate Symposium for Viticulture and Oenology, Christchurch, New Zealand, 2006).

[51] Ibid.

[52] Dion, *Histoire de la Vigne et du Vin*, p. 108.

[53] According to the Gimblett Gravels Winegrowers Association history of the region. See www.gimblettgravels.com.

[54] Ibid.

[55] Topographic map from Google Earth.

[56] John Schreiner, *Icewine. The Complete Story* (Warwick Publishing, Toronto, 2001), p. 36.

[57] Publicity brochure for J. L. Wolf.

[58] Personal communication from Christoph Graf (November 2008).

[59] Lewin, *What Price Bordeaux?*, p. 71.

[60] In 1710, when a ban was imposed on new plantings because there had been a surge of over-planting, gravel-based lands were excluded because of their known superiority (René Pijassou, *Le Médoc: Un Grand Vignoble De Qualité. Tomes I & II*, Tallandier, Paris, 1978, p. 421.)

[61] A little farther inland, roughly 10 km from the river, soils are also gravel-based, but here the mix also includes more sand and clay on a limestone plateau.

[62] Gérard Seguin, *Influence Des Facteurs Naturels Sur Les Caractères Des Vins. In Traité D'ampélologie*, (Sciences et Technique de la vigne, Bordas, Paris, 1980); Wilson, *Terroir*, p. 188.

[63] www.atlaspeakappellation.com/elan.html

[64] Topographic background from Google Maps.

[65] Quoted in James Conway, *Napa. The Story of an American Eden* (Houghton Mifflin, New York, 2002), p. 363.

[66] The subsequent story was not entirely happy; most of the original partners in the deal bailed out during the 1990s, the vineyards finally came under the control of Antinori, there were unsuccessful attempts to make a Sangiovese wine, then the brand name became the property of Beam vintners (who own nearby William Hill Vineyards), and now the vineyards themselves have reverted to Antinori, although the brand name remains the property of Beam.

[67] Conway, *Napa*. op. cit., p. 130.

[68] Wine Business Monthly, *Wine Business Insider, Sierra Club Lawsuit Triggers Hillside Moratorium: CEQA Applies, Napa County Says*, January 29, 2000.

[69] Conway, *Napa,* op. cit., p. 58.

[70] www.winespectator.com/Wine/Daily/News/0,1145,1664,00.html

[71] Topographic background from Google Earth.

[72] Richard Smart, *Terroir Unmasked* (Wine Business Monthly, June 15, 2004).

[73] Randall Grahm, *The Phenomenology of Terroir: A Meditation by Randall Grahm* (University of California, Davis, Terroir Conference, March, 2006).

[74] A variation called partial root drying was introduced by two Australian scientists in the early 1990s. Two separate irrigation lines are placed on either side of the vine. Water is shut off from one side, and the root zone is permitted to dry while the other side gets irrigation. Then the situation is reversed. Each side is used 2-3 times per week. Drying out causes the root system to generate a signal that it is under stress. This causes the vine to close its stomata (pores) under the leaves where most of the water evaporates from the vine, in order to minimize water loss. The net result is to mimic the effects of a water deficit stress, but without the harmful consequences of water loss (P. R. Dry et al., *Partial Rootzone Drying - An Update*. The Australian Grapegrower and Winemaker, Annual Technical Issue, 2000, pp. 35-39). The technique is controversial because it's not entirely clear whether it really offers advantages over simply reducing the amount of water provided during deficit irrigation.

[75] See page 355.

[76] Until the 1989 vintage it was labeled Grange Hermitage, in reference to the great Syrah-based wines of Hermitage in the Rhône, but since then it has stood on its own as just Grange.

[77] Max Schubert, *The Story of Grange* (Paper delivered at the first Australian National University Wine Symposium, Canberra, 1979).

[78] Data source: Langton's auctioneers, Melbourne, Australia; see www.langtons.com.au/images/pdfs/grange_guide.pdf

[79] Topographic background from Google Earth.

[80] The range is from 100% to 86% Shiraz.

[81] Bureau National Interprofessionel du Cognac (www.cognac.fr).

[82] Jake Hancock & Richard Selley, *Coquand's joke*, Geoscientist, 13, 17, 2003.

[83] Kyle Jarrad, *Cognac. The Seductive Saga of the World's Most Coveted Spirit* (John Wiley, New York, 2005), p. 89.

[84] Richard C. Selley, *The Winelands of Britain: Past, Present & Prospective* (Petravin, London, 2008), p. 50.

[85] Location of chalk-based soils from Richard C. Selley, *The Winelands of Britain*, op cit., p. 51. Topographic background from Google Earth.

[86] Wilson, *Terroir*, pp. 211-213.

[87] One study tried to assess terroir in terms of describing features such as soil types and the presence of slopes. But the wines were all from the Médoc in Bordeaux, damning the study with a basic misunderstanding of the nature of wine production in Bordeaux, where the châteaux have large landholdings, showing diversity of terroir that is not susceptible to simple description. Critics' ratings or prices were used to assess quality, which encounters the difficulty discussed in the text. The authors concluded that winemaking features show a better correlation with critics' ratings than does terroir; but in fact the only strong correlations with putative quality were manual picking and use of new

oak, both of which could be consequences of the château's ability to make better wine rather than the cause of it (Olivier Gergaud and Victor Ginsburgh, *Natural Endowments, Production Technology, and the Quality of Wines in Bordeaux. Does Terroir Matter*, The Economic Journal, 118, F142–F157, 2008). Any study of this type may be futile, but better results might be obtained with Burgundy, where my analysis shows a correlation between price and level in the AOC hierarchy, supposedly determined by terroir (see pp. 380-384 in Chapter 14 of this book).

Chapter 4: Vintage & Global Warming

[1] Dion, *Histoire de la Vigne*, p. 120.

[2] Following a detailed discussion of different pitch and resins, Pliny commented that "the pitch most highly esteemed in Italy for preparing vessels for storing wine is that which comes from Bruttium. It is made from the resin that distils from the pitch-tree; that which is used in Spain is held in but little esteem, being the product of the wild pine." (*The Natural History Of Pliny*, Volume 3, edited John Bostock and H. T. Riley, Kessinger Publishing, p. 267).

[3] A transition to storage in barrels took place in Roman times, but increased the risk of spoilage by exposure to air. And as soon as the wine was transferred from the barrel to a smaller container, its life was measured in days if not hours.

[4] This depended on the introduction of sulfur as a preservative, allowing wine to be kept in barrels for 3-4 years before bottling, and the development of bottles that could be sealed with corks so the wine could be kept by the consumer.

[5] The proverb came to mean: there is no drawing back. It was famously used to stiffen Louis XIV's courage at a battle in 1710 (Alphonse Mariette, *French and English Idioms and Proverbs with Critical and Historical Notes*, Hachette, Paris, 1896, p. 43).

[6] A contemporary view in 1751 of the merits of wine of different ages noted, "wine begins to degenerate as it enters its second year." (L'Encyclopédie de Diderot et d'Alembert, 1751, tome 17, p. 290.)

[7] At first it was used by individuals for wine (or cider or beer) bottled at home, but by the end of the century it came into use by wine merchants (John Worlidge, *Vinetum Britannicum, Or, A Treatise Of Cider And Other Wines And Drinks From Fruits Growing In This Kingdom*, Thomas Dring, London, 1678).

[8] Tim Unwin, *Wine and the Vine*, p. 266.

[9] René Pijassou, *Le Médoc: Un Grand Vignoble De Qualité*, Tallandier, Paris, 1978, p. 597.

[10] Ibid., p 537.

[11] There were some occasional reports early in the century that wines forgotten in a cellar might taste better than the current vintage; but this was clearly contrary to expectation (Asa Briggs, *Haut-Brion*, Faber & Faber, London, 1994, p. 5).

[12] The Writings of Thomas Jefferson (1905). Issued under the auspices of the Thomas Jefferson Memorial Association of the United States.

[13] The proprietors of the first growths believed Jefferson may have been drinking his wines too young (James M. Gabler, *Passions: The Wines and Travels of Thomas Jefferson*, Bacchus Press, 1995, pp. 118-119).

[14] George Saintsbury, *Notes on a Cellar Book*, MacMillan, London, 1931, p. 51.

[15] For example, the average price of wine in the Médoc varied over a 4-fold range in the period from 1741 to 1774, according to data shown in Pijassou, *Le Médoc*, op. cit., p. 1408.

[16] For example, prices at Château Latour showed as much as 4-5-fold variation from year to year in the second half of the 19th century (Lewin, *What Price Bordeaux?*, p. 97).

[17] Range for Cabernet Sauvignon taken from Gregory Jones, *Climate and Terroir: Impacts of Climate Variability and Change on Wine*, in *Fine Wine and Terroir - The Geoscience Perspective*, Macqueen, R.W., and Meinert, L.D., (eds.), Geoscience Canada Reprint Series Number 9, Geological Association of Canada, St. John's, Newfoundland, 2006.) This was based on relationships between phenological requirements and climate for high to premium quality wine production in the world's benchmark regions for the variety over the period prior to 1999.

[18] Orley Ashenfelter, David Ashmore, and Robert LaLonde, *Bordeaux Wine Vintage Quality and the Weather* (Harris School Working Paper Series 04.13, 1995); Orley Ashenfelter, *Predicting the Quality and Prices of Bordeaux Wines* (American Association of Wine Economics, Working Paper #4., 2007).

[19] More precisely, the formula explains auction prices in terms of age of the wine and quality of the vintage. Wines become more valuable as they become older (if the vintage was good), but I have adjusted the formula to assign a rating to each vintage by omitting the age factor.

[20] The main deficiency in the formula is that it does not allow for a transition when increase in temperature becomes too much (as in 2003, which is vastly overrated on Ashenfelter's scale) or when there is too much rain earlier in the season. Another major mistake is 1997, rated very highly by Ashenfelter: "the 1997 vintage... is probably the only seriously under-priced vintage currently available." I hope he did not buy too much of it.

[21] Of the 25 leading brands in the United States, 17 have no vintage.

[22] Sales data from Adams Wine Handbook, Norwalk, CT, 2008.

[23] Data from Instituto dos Vinhos do Douro e Porto.

[24] Global warming is attributed to the excessive accumulation of greenhouse gases such as carbon dioxide, methane, nitrous oxide, sulfur hexafluoride, perfluorocarbons, and hydrofluorocarbons, which are mostly produced by human activities. Fluorocarbons are being phased out in industrialized countries, but because they persist in the atmosphere for ~200 years, they will continue to contribute to global warming for some time. It may be impossible to reverse the trend in the next 20-30 years.

[25] Carbon dioxide was probably 270 ppm pre industrial age. It began to increase with the industrial revolution, rising from 310 ppm to 370 ppm over the period 1961-1997; the trend extrapolates to 700 ppm by 2050. Increases for methane and nitrous oxide show similar proportions (J. R. Ehleringer and T. E. Cerling, *Atmospheric CO2 and the Ratio of Intercellular to Ambient CO2 Concentrations in Plants*, Tree Physiol. 15, 105-111, 1995; Wuebbles et al, *Global Change: State of the Science*, Environmental Pollution, 100, 57-86, 1999).

[26] Projections for temperature increase out to 2080 have been used to suggest that by then the north of England might grow Pinot Noir and Chardonnay, while the south might grow Merlot (Selley, *The Winelands of Britain*, op cit., p. 97).

[27] The chalk subsoil of the South Downs, for example, is not unlike the underlying structure in Champagne.

[28] Martin Hickman, *Top Champagne House May Buy English Vineyards*, The Independent, November 17, 2007.

[29] See for example extensive differences between J. Esper et al., *Low-Frequency Signals in Long Tree-Ring Chronologies for Reconstructing Past Temperature Variability*, Science, 295, 2250-2253, 2002, and A. Moberg et al., *Highly Variable Northern Hemisphere Temperatures Reconstructed From Low- And High-Resolution Proxy Data*, Nature, 443, 613-617, 2005.

[30] Jean Ribéreau-Gayon and Emile Peynaud, *Traité d'Oenologie*, Tome I, Librairie Polytechnique, Paris, 1960, p. 122.

[31] According to the Australian Bureau of Statistics, Australian Wine and Grape Industry Report 1329.0, 50% of current vineyards were planted between 1998 (total 78,709 ha) and 2008 (total 172,676 ha).

[32] According to New Zealand Winegrowers Vineyard Surveys, 50% of current vineyards have been planted in the past six years, bringing the total from 13,787 ha in 2002 to 29,310 ha in 2008.

[33] Temperatures are rolling five year averages from P. D. Jones and M. E. Mann, *Climate Over Past Millennia*, Reviews of Geophysics, 42, RG2002, 2004. They are generally in the middle of range when comparing other temperature estimates (which actually vary considerably). For details of the origins of particular varieties, see Chapter 7.

[34] Albert Julius Winkler et al., *General Viticulture* (University of California Press, 1962), p. 61.

[35] Degree days were originally defined in Fahrenheit, but you can also calculate them in Centigrade using a base of 10 °C.

[36] Winkler et al., *General Viticulture*, op. cit., pp. 64-65.

[37] Other, more sophisticated systems for assessing climate also include the effects of moisture (rainfall and relative humidity), sunlight, cloud cover, soil characteristics, difference between maximum and minimum daily temperatures, wind conditions, air pollution, and solar radiation. One heat summation method is the Huglin index, which puts more weight on maximum temperature and adds a parameter for latitude to reflect the effect of increasing hours of sunlight. The formula sums average temperature minus 10°C plus maximum temperature minus 10°C, multiplied by a coefficient for latitude that increases from 1.02 at 40° to 1.06 at 50°. It has been used to establish limits for the minimum values required to ripen each variety successfully. It includes days from April 1 to September 30 (P. Huglin, *Biologie Et Ecologie De La Vigne*, Payot, Lausanne, Switzerland, 1986).

[38] More recent analyses would place them close to a zone apart.

[39] The most accurate way to do this is to take the average of daily temperatures during the growing season. It can be done with less accuracy by using monthly averages. The difference between average temperature and degree days is only significant if the calculation is done on a daily basis (in which case days at the beginning and end of the season where average temperatures do not reach 10 °C count as zero for degree days, but do contribute to average temperature).

[40] See note 44.

[41] The average difference in temperature during the growing season (April-October) was calculated for the two periods 1945-1990 and 1991-2009 for weather stations operating during both periods. Data source: National Climatic Data Center, US Department of Commerce, GHCN (Global Historical Climatology Network)-Monthly Version 2.

[42] Gregory Jones, *Climate and Terroir: Impacts of Climate Variability and Change on Wine*. In Fine Wine and Terroir - The Geoscience Perspective. R. W. Macqueen & L. D. Meinert (eds.), Geoscience Canada Reprint Series Number 9, 2006, Geological Association of Canada, St. John's, Newfoundland.

[43] Data from the Goddard Institute database of weather stations.

[44] Optimum growing season temperature for each variety was calculated as the average of growing season temperature in its classic region for the best vintages (taken as those rated 90 points or more in the Wine Advocate). Projected optima were 14.3 °C for Riesling (the Mosel), 15.8 °C for Pinot Noir (Burgundy), 15.9 °C for Chardonnay (Burgundy) 16.2 °C for Sauvignon Blanc (the Loire), 17.3 °C for Cabernet Sauvignon (Bordeaux), 18.6 °C for Nebbiolo (Barolo), 18.9°C for Grenache (Southern Rhône), and 19.3 °C for Sangiovese (Tuscany). Similar growing season optima have also been calculated on the basis of a regression analysis by Gregory Jones et al, *Climate Change and Global Wine Quality* (Climatic Change, 73, 319–343, 2005).

[45] The temperature projected for 2025 assumes the same average annual increase after 2005 as occurred between the periods 1986-1995 and 1996-2005. This gives 15.2 °C for the Mosel, 16.5 °C for Burgundy, 16.8 °C for the Loire, 18.6 °C for Bordeaux, 19.2 °C Ribera del Duero, and 19.3 °C for Tuscany. Temperatures for wine regions in 2049 have been projected previously by Gregory Jones et al, *Climate Change and Global Wine Quality* (Climatic Change, 73, 319–343, 2005).

[46] Isotherms show average growing season (Apr-Oct) temperatures for the period 1945-1990 based on weather station data from National Climatic Data Center, US Department of Commerce, GHCN (Global Historical Climatology Network)-Monthly Version 2.

[47] Burgundy for 1996-2005 shows the same average growing season temperature as Bordeaux from 1961-1970; based on analysis of monthly data from the weather stations at Dijon and Merignac as available on the Goddard Institute database.

[48] Locations of isotherms based on data in National Climatic Data Center, US Department of Commerce, GHCN (Global Historical Climatology Network)-Monthly Version 1. Topographic background from Google Earth..

[49] B. Ganichot, *Evolution De La Date Des Vendanges Dans Les Côtes Du Rhône Méridionales* (Proceedings of the 6th Rencontres Rhodaniennes, Institut Rhodanien, pp. 38- 41, Orange, France, 2002).

[50] Harvest dates became later during the mini-ice age around 1500, and then stayed stable, with the exception of a warmer period in the 17 century, until the past half-century (I. Chuine et al., *Grape Ripening As A Past Climate Indicator*, Nature, 432, 289-290, 2004).

[51] Data from the cliflo database of New Zealand weather stations. The change is from about 15.3 °C to about 16.3 °C.

[52] Increase from 17.7 °C to 18.7 °C at the weather station at Nuriootpa in Barossa Valley between 1953 and 2008 (Australian Government Bureau of Meteorology).

[53] Weather data: Goddard Institute; Harvest dates: Fédération des Grands Vins de Bordeaux.

[54] Data from Roger Dubrion, *Trois Siècles de Vendanges Bourguignon* (Editions Féret, Bordeaux, 2006).

55 Based on data of Gregory V. Jones, *Climate Change in the Western United States Grape Growing Regions* (Acta Horticulturae (ISHS), 689, 41-60, 2005) and M. A. White et al., *Extreme Heat Reduces And Shifts United States Premium Wine Production In The 21st Century* (Proc. Nat. Acad. Sci. USA, 103, 11217-11222, 2006). Topographic background from Google Earth.

[56] AWRI 2003 Annual Report, p. 44.

[57] Hans Schultz, *Climate Change In Viticulture: A European Perspective On Climatology, Carbon Dioxide And UV Effects* (Austr. J. Grape and Wine Research, 6, 2-12, 2000).

[58] The grapes for QmP wine must have a minimum sugar level equivalent to 9.1-10.0% alcohol, depending on the German wine region.

[59] Results obtained at the University of Bordeaux from a test plot of Cabernet Sauvignon grapes harvested in the Médoc. Merlot would have a higher level of potential alcohol. Actual wine would be a blend of varieties and very likely be chaptalized to increase the alcohol level. See www.oenologie.u-bordeaux2.fr..

[60] Data for sugar levels at harvest from the Grape Crush Report, California Department of Food and Agriculture, Sacramento. Data for seasonal growing temperatures from the Goddard Institute.

[61] At the Grandes Pagos tasting in London, March 12, 2010.

[62] Data from the Goddard Institute database of weather stations.

[63] Jonathan Leake, *The Great Climate Change Science Scandal*, The Sunday Times, London, November 29, 2009.

[64] Based on this type of assumption, estimates forecast a further increase of 1.8-2.5 °C warming by the middle of the century (Intergovernmental panels on climate change (IPCC), 1992, 1994, 1998, 2001).

Chapter 5: Grape Juice into Wine

[1] The best known teinturier is Alicante Bouschet, sometimes used in blends to add extra color. It was popular during Prohibition in the United States because the grapes transported well and gave deeply colored wine.

[2] Olivier de Serres, *Le Théâtre D'agriculture Et Mesnage Des Champs*, 1600.

[3] This became common in Bordeaux only after the 1970s, but the advantages have in fact long been known. A book published in California in 1911 advocated temperature control for fermentation, and several wineries in Napa Valley introduced cooling systems in the 1930s (Lapsley, *Bottled Poetry*, pp. 53, 59). By the late 1940s it was common in Napa (Wines and Vines, February, 1949).

[4] This happened in the 1945 vintage in Bordeaux.

[5] Yeast convert vanillin extracted from the oak into the odorless vanillin alcohol, giving a more subtle balance to the wine.

[6] Pasteur's involvement started when the father of one of his students asked him to resolve some problems he was having in manufacturing alcohol from beetroot. The fermentations often went sour, producing lactic acid (Patrice Debré et al., *Louis Pasteur*, Johns Hopkins University Press, Baltimore, 2000, pp. 82-114.)

[7] Photograph under common license from flickr.com.

[8] When alcohol was produced, the fermenting mixture contained cells that appeared round under the microscope; but when lactic acid was produced, the cells were elongated like rods (Debré et al., *Louis Pasteur,* op. cit.).

[9] Although this is true, fermentation usually gets off to a better start with a kick of oxygen to provoke the yeasts. Oxygen exposure also helps to avoid the development of reduced aromas, which can happen during fermentation.

[10] Debré et al., *Louis Pasteur,* op. cit., pp. 232-233.

[11] Cultured yeasts have been used since the 1960s. Cakes of compressed yeast became commercially available in the United States in 1963 (Lapsley, *Bottled Poetry,* p. 168).

[12] Pascal Ribéreau-Gayon et al., *The Handbook of Enology, Volume 1, The Microbiology of Wine and Vinifications,* 2nd edition (John Wiley & Sons, New York, 2000), p. 46.

[13] Winemakers who practice fermentation with indigenous yeast argue that if they get into trouble, they can always overwhelm the must by inoculating with cultured yeast.

[14] Personal communication from Sebastiano Rosa (winemaker at Sassicaia), October 2007.

[15] Once Brettanomyces has infected a winery, it is impossible to remove. It can be eliminated from wine by filtration or prevented by using compounds that are toxic to yeast.

[16] Two types of compounds are responsible for Brett. Low concentrations of tetrahydropyridines may show as bread, popcorn or cracker aromas, but at high concentrations they turn to mousy aromas. Tetrahydropyridines are not volatile and so are not detected on the aroma, but only as a result of tasting, usually on the aftertaste. The major cause of barnyard aromas is the production of volatile phenols, including 4-ethyl phenol (band-aid aroma) and 4-ethyl guaiacol (wet burnt wood aroma). These compounds are only produced by Brettanomyces, and the presence of 4-ethyl phenol is used as a quantitative marker for the level of Brettanomyces infection.

[17] This usually occurs with red wine, because of the higher polyphenol levels (which form substrates for Brettanomyces to form its typical phenols) and because pH is higher (that is, acidity is lower, forming better conditions for bacterial growth).

[18] Sam Harrop MW, *Production of High Quality Syrah-based Wines,* Institute of Masters of Wine Dissertation, 2003.

[19] See note 33 in Chapter 3.

[20] The amount of alcohol generated per unit of sugar is called the conversion ratio. For unknown reasons, it seems to have increased slightly in recent decades.

[21] Jean-Antoine Chaptal, *L'Art de Faire le Vin* (Bouchard-Huzard, Paris, 1801, 1807, 1839).

[22] It is possible that the technique was used previously. The chemist Pierre Joseph Macquer proposed that cassonade (brown sugar) should be used rather than honey or molasses to increase alcoholic strength, so as not to affect flavor (Jean-François Gautier, *Le Vin Et Ses Fraudes,* Presses Universitaires De France, 1995, p. 16). Addition of sugar may have been practiced regularly at Clos Vougeot before 1790 (Hallgarten, *Wine Scandal,* p. 64).

[23] The recommended dose was 15-20 livres of sugar per muid (456 liters).

[24] Denis Morélot, *Statistique de la Vigne dans le Département de la Cote-d'Or* (Ch. Brugnot, Dijon, 1831), p. 250.

[25] Harry W. Paul, *Science, Vine, and Wine in Modern France* (Cambridge University Press, Cambridge, 1996), p. 130.

[26] Christopher Fielden, *Is This the Wine You Ordered, Sir?: The Dark Side of the Wine Trade* (Christopher Helm, London, 1989), pp. 67-68.

[27] Paul, *Science, Vine, and Wine,* op. cit., p, 128.

[28] Fortification was sometimes practiced with the wines of Bordeaux in the mid nineteenth century (Lewin, *What Price Bordeaux?,* p. 59).

[29] It is generally agreed that more than 1-1.5% increase creates an unbalanced wine.

[30] Consider a vineyard where the costs of production are €7 per kg of grapes (a typical price in Champagne), which will give about 0.75 liters of wine, corresponding to €9/liter. You can buy a kilo of sugar for €0.85; this will increase the volume of the wine by 0.66

liters, corresponding to a cost of €1.25/liter. The legal limits allow 3.6 kg of sugar to be added to a hectoliter of red wine, or 3.4 kg to a hectoliter of white wine, basically diluting the wine by 2-3% of volume at the low production cost of the sugar.

[31] One measure of the profitability of chaptalization was contained in an official report of the Institut des Vins de Consommation Courante (the old name for Vin de Table) in 1974, stating that the cost of wine per degree-hectoliter was 2.90F, compared with an average sale price of 9F.

[32] Pierre-Marie Doutrelant, *Les Bons Vins et les Autres* (Editions du Seuil, Paris, 1976), p. 197.

[33] Decanter on line, December 13, 2007 and March 18, 2009; see www.decanter.com/news/169103.html; www.decanter.com/news/news.php?id=278929.

[34] A bit below the use of sugar for ice cream. Data from the statistics memo of CEDUS LeSucre at www.lesucre.com.

[35] The sugar producers report usage of sugar for chaptalization over the period 2002-2006 varied from a low of 11,180 tonnes in the hot year of 2003 to a high of 30,359 tonnes in 2002. Assuming that chaptalization was performed at the legal limit of 3.5 kg/hl, the amount of treated wine would be 6.7% in 2003 and 16.7% in 2002. If chaptalization was performed at the more reasonable limit of 2.5 kg/hl (this is about the limit for avoiding change in the organoleptic quality), the corresponding proportions would be higher, at 9.4% and 23.2%. Data from the statistics memo of CEDUS LeSucre at www.lesucre.com.

[36] Bacteria that perform malolactic fermentation had actually been identified long previously by H. Müller-Thurgau and A. Osterwalder in 1913 (Ian Spencer Hornsey, *The Chemistry and Biology of Winemaking*, Royal Society of Chemistry, London, 2007, p. 224.)

[37] Peynaud published a paper in 1959 reporting successful induction of MLF (CR Seances Acad. Agric, France, 45, p. 355.)

[38] Malolactic fermentation removes one of the two acidic groups from malic acid by converting it into lactic acid with the release of carbon dioxide.

[39] Champagne houses have varying views on whether to perform MLF, but there's a tendency to use it to make the wine more drinkable for nonvintage (which will be consumed young), but not for vintage (where it may detract from aging potential).

[40] Robert Parker, *Bordeaux, 4th edition* (Simon & Schuster, New York, 2003), p. XVII.

[41] Lewin, *What Price Bordeaux?*, pp. 192-193.

[42] The name, carbonic maceration, reflects the fact that carbon dioxide dissolves in water to form a (very weak) solution called carbonic acid.

[43] Jan Read, *Wines of the Rioja* (Sotheby Publications, London, 1984), p.35.

[44] John Radford, *The Wines of Rioja* (Mitchell Beazley, London, 2004), p. 41.

[45] As exemplified in several thousand hits on google for "wine is a living thing."

[46] The suspended compounds are negatively charged, and many fining agents are proteins with positive charges that bind by electrostatic interaction to the compounds in the wine. The clay bentonite is used for the opposite case when a wine has too much protein in it.

[47] "Oxygen penetration...has been measured as 2-5 ml/l per year. It depends on the thickness and type of wood...In tuns where the staves are 5 cm thick, it is virtually nil." (Emile Peynaud, *Knowing and Making Wine*, 2nd edition, Wiley-Interscience New York, 1984, p. 245).

[48] Discussion with author, June 2009.

[49] Chilling is the traditional method. More recent methods include crystallization, when potassium bitartrate is added to nucleate the formation of crystals, or electrodialysis when tartrate ions pass specifically across an ion-exchange membrane. Removal of tartrate by any method reduces acidity by the amount of tartaric acid that has been extracted.

[50] Sterile filtration uses membranes with a pore size <0.45 μm. (This is usually not possible with sweet wines, where the viscosity blocks the filter, and slightly larger sizes must be used.) Filtration at < 0.8 μm removes all yeast, and filtration at <1.2 μm removes most yeast. Alternatives to membrane filtration include depth filtration, when the wine is pushed through sheets that trap solid particles.

[51] Pascal Ribéreau-Gayon et al., *The Handbook of Enology, Volume 2, The Chemistry of Wine Stabilisation and Treatments*, 2nd edition (John Wiley & Sons, New York, 2000), p. 362.

[52] Ibid., p. 364.

[53] Robert Parker, *Parker's Wine Buyer's Guide*, 5th Edition, 1999, p. 29.

[54] Tannins take their name from their use in tanning animal hides into leather. Technically they are polyphenols formed by plants, falling into several different classes, but all sharing the feature that they have multiple phenol rings with hydroxyl and other groups that are negatively charged and can bind to proteins. Their binding to animal proteins is the basis for the tanning reaction.

[55] Because the stalks contain water, but not sugar, and absorb alcohol, destemming also increased alcoholic strength by up to 0.5%. It was advocated by Peynaud in his book of 1970 (later translated as Emile Peynaud, *Knowing and Making Wine*, Wiley-Interscience, New York, 1984, p. 146).

[56] The reason tannins in stalks and seeds are more bitter is that they are smaller than those found in the skin. Larger tannins are less astringent.

[57] Some methods measure ability to bind to proteins, some measure oxidative capacity, and so on, so the various methods for measuring total polyphenols can differ as to exactly which set of compounds is included in each assay. Total phenols are usually measured in grams/liter, with a typical level (depending on the black variety) in the range of 4-6 g/l.

[58] Variations on pump-over include délestage (rack-and-return) in which the juice is pumped through a screen to remove the seeds and then sprayed on to the cap (to ensure oxidative exposure), the auto-fermenter (which uses the pressure generated by carbon dioxide released during fermentation to drive the pumping-over), and rotary fermenters (which lie on their sides and rotate to keep the juice in contact with the skins).

[59] Enzymes used in extraction include pectinase, cellulase, hemicellulase, and protease activities. Breakdown of cell walls encourages extraction of skin tannins, giving the wine a more full-bodied nature.

[60] A high concentration of sulfur dioxide together with low temperature (10 °C) is used to prevent fermentation.

[61] Leonard Barkan, *Time, Space, And Burgundy* (The Yale Review, 92, 109-127, 2008).

[62] Free anthocyanin content can vary in young wines from 100 mg/l in Pinot Noir to 1500 mg/l in varieties such as Shiraz and Cabernet Sauvignon, to a minimum of 50 mg/l or less during aging.

[63] Stable color results from interactions between anthocyanins and tannins to form polymeric color pigments that are stable. Tannin levels can therefore influence color by stabilizing the anthocyanins.

[64] Copigmentation is due to an association of components, not a chemical reaction.

[65] Roger Boulton, *The Copigmentation of Anthocyanins and Its Role in the Color of Red Wine: A Critical Review* (Am. J. Enol. Vitic., 52, 67-87, 2001).

[66] Because the effect depends on extraction of cofactors from the skins during fermentation, it is not achieved by blending wines.

[67] Author's discussion with Roger Boulton, UC Davis, December 2009.

[68] This was common in Rioja, Chianti, and at Côte-Rôtie and Hermitage in the northern Rhône. It no longer occurs in Rioja or Chianti, but it is still legal to include up to 15% of permitted white varieties with Syrah (the only permitted black grape) in Côte-Rôtie and Hermitage.

[69] Flavonoids are found in most plants. The most important with regards to white wine are quercetin and kaempferol.

[70] Terms used to describe rosé wine in various countries are: Italy - Rosata, Chiaretto; Spain - Rosado; Portugal - Branco; Germany - Bleichert, Rotling.

[71] Acidity is reduced because potassium is extracted from the skins.

[72] Author's discussion with Jorge Muga, May 2009.

[73] Suzannah Ramsdale, *Fury At E.U. Rosé Wine Plans*, Decanter magazine on line, March 16, 2009.

[74] John Lichfield, *E.U. Abandons Plan To Allow Blended Rosé Wine*, The Independent, June 8, 2009.

[75] Edward Cody, *French Vintners Find E.U. Concoction Unpalatable*, Washington Post, May 4, 2009.

[76] The introduction of sulfur as a preservative made it possible to keep wine in barriques for 2-4 years without spoilage. The technique was invented by the Dutch, in the form of burning a sulfur candle in a barrel before it was filled with wine, and became known as the "allumettes hollandaises." It was used when barriques were initially filled and when wine was racked (moved) from one barrique to another. By the mid eighteenth century it was in common use. (René Pijassou, *Le Médoc: Un Grand Vignoble De Qualité: Tomes I & II*, Tallandier, Paris, 1978, p. 494.)

[77] Jackson, *Wine Science*, p. 312.

[78] In the United States, it is a requirement that no sulfur dioxide is used before a wine can be labeled "organic," although it can be described as "made from organic grapes" if the vineyard is certified as organic but sulfur dioxide is used at low levels (<100 ppm). In other countries, low levels of sulfur dioxide addition are allowed in production of organic wine.

[79] A study at Hallcrest Vineyards in Santa Cruz, California, during the 1991 harvest showed that wines fermented without any added sulfur dioxide had levels varying from 0 to 41 ppm after fermentation. While it is a myth that fermentation *always* produces some SO2, it certainly can produce low levels, depending on the conditions of fermentation.

[80] The major problem is for the 0.1% of people who lack the enzyme sulfite oxidase and therefore cannot metabolize sulfites.

[81] Sulfur dioxide is measured in ppm (parts per million). Legal limits in the European Union are 160 ppm for dry red wine, 210 ppm for dry white wine and rosé, and 300-400 ppm for various classes of sweet wines. In the United States it is 350 ppm for all wines. In Australia it is 250 ppm for dry wines and 350 ppm for sweet wines.

[82] Harry W. Paul, *Science, Vine, and Wine in Modern France* (Cambridge University Press, Cambridge, 1996), pp. 197-198.

[83] Ibid., pp. 189-190; Anthony Hanson, *Burgundy*, 2nd edition (Faber & Faber, London, 1995), p. 417; Frank Prial, *Wine Talk*, New York Times, November 26, 1997.

[84] Levels of allergens including sulfur dioxide and histamines are much lower in wine than many other foods, but alcohol may enhance the effects of histamine, so that its effect becomes significant for sensitive people.

[85] I tasted both wines from the 2007 vintage at Sepp Moser in August 2009. They were the Grüner Veltliner Kremstal Schnabel 2007 and Kremstal Schnabel MINIMAL 2007, both trocken with virtually no residual sugar (1.2 g/l) and 13.5% alcohol.

[86] Certainly there are different views as to what constitutes minimalist winemaking. Rowald Hepp at Schloss Vollrads in the Rheingau says that their winemaking attempts to achieve minimal intervention focus on going straight from fermentation in stainless steel into the glass bottle with minimal exposure to outside influences including oxygen (Author's discussion with Rowald Hepp, August, 2008).

Chapter 6: The Alchemist's Delight

[1] In the United States tolerance in labeling is reduced to 1% for wines above 14% alcohol.

[2] Michelle Waterman of Brochelle Vineyards, Paso Robles, discussion with author, January 2010.

[3] Troy Bunnell of Coyote Canyon Wines in the Santa Lucia Highlands, discussion with author, January 2010.

[4] 16% of winemakers use it routinely, 33% use it occasionally, 48% never use it, 2% do not know what it is (survey of winemakers in California conducted by the author in January 2010).

[5] Kathleen Inman of Inman Family Wines in Russian River Valley, discussion with author, January 2010.

[6] Douglas Braun of Presidio Winery in Santa Barbara County, discussion with author, January 2010.

[7] www.vinovation.com/alcadjustment.htm.
[8] Clark Smith, *Some Like It Hot*, Appellation America, September 2007.
[9] Felicity Lawrence, *Blanc Check For Wine Purity*, The Guardian, January 24, 2004, London.
[10] Michael Fridjhon, *Wine column*, Business Day, February 19, 2004.
[11] Charlotte Matthews, *KWW Fires Cheating Wine Makers Over Fruity Sauvignon*, Business Day, December 7, 2004.
[12] Acidity in g/l determines the taste of the wine, but another measure used by winemakers is the pH. This is a logarithmic scale indicating the concentration of hydrogen ion. pH varies from 0 to 14; pH of 7 is neutral, and lower pH means more acidity. pH is important because it determines the effectiveness of sulfur dioxide and the inhibition of bacterial growth. pH and acidity in g/l are not exactly correlated, which is why both are used.
[13] If grapes start with 9 g/l, after alcoholic fermentation the wine will have about 8 g/l (due to conversion of some malic acid to alcohol), and after malolactic fermentation acidity will be down to about 6 g/l (due to conversion of the rest of the malic acid to lactic acid).
[14] See p. 99.
[15] Double salt deacidification uses ACIDEX (calcium carbonate double seeded with small amounts of calcium tartrate-malate). This removes both tartaric acid and malic acid by forming crystals of the insoluble calcium tartrate-malate, but it is expensive.
[16] Per-Henrik Mansson, *Vive Le Vin Nature!* (Wine Spectator, February 3, 2000).
[17] The International Riesling Foundation has a scale based on the ratio of sugar to acid, where wines <1.0 are described as dry, ratios of 1.0-2.0 are called medium dry, ratios of 2.1-4.0 are medium sweet, and >4.1 is sweet.
See www.drinkriesling.com/tastescale/thescale/
[18] Quoted in Jamie Goode, *Residual Sugar*, Wine Business, April 2007.
[19] This is called back-blending, and the technique was developed in Germany after the second world war. In fact, it was more a rediscovery of an old technique, since the Romans knew that lowering the temperature would prevent fermentation, and they used this to preserve some unfermented grape juice that they could use later for sweetening wine they considered too dry.
[20] RCGM is also somewhat more expensive than using raw sugar.
[21] Grape juice contains two sugars, glucose and fructose, in roughly equal amounts. Yeasts ferment glucose first, so when sweetness is achieved by stopping fermentation, it is usually due to unfermented fructose. Fructose is usually reckoned to be almost twice as sweet as glucose. When süssreserve is added, it consists of both glucose and fructose, and the balance is different, because more sugar must be added to reach the same sweetness level, and the sweetness integrates less well.
[22] Quoted in Dan Berger, *Mega Purple* (Wines & Vines, March, 2006).
[23] There are several hybrids resulting from crosses of Aramon and Rupestris, the best known being AxR1 (infamously used as a rootstock in California), which is Aramon Rupestris Ganzin #1.
[24] Nick Dokoozlian, *Rubired*, in *Wine Grape Varieties in California* (University of California Agricultural and Natural Resources Publication 3419, Oakland, 2003). pp. 126-129.
[25] It is in seventh place in the list of leading varieties (Grape Crush Report, California Department of Food and Agriculture, 2009).
[26] Alternatively if it is added to the must rather than to the wine, the sugar will ferment to give alcohol.
[27] Berger, *Mega Purple*, op. cit.
[28] Ibid.
[29] Concentrate represents almost 20% of all crushed grapes in California, with 80% of the concentrate produced from white varieties, largely Thompson seedless, and 20% from red varieties, primarily Rubired, Royalty, and Salvador.
[30] Corie Brown, *What's Really In That Wine?*, Los Angeles Times, March 28, 2007.
[31] The latest idea is to try polyethylene which has "breathing capabilities."

[32] Some producers who punch-down the cap find that the conical shape is important because it allows better submersion of the cap.

[33] Technically the defining feature is the presence of a sulfur-hydrogen moiety.

[34] This is produced when yeast do not have enough nutrients during fermentation.

[35] It's usually reckoned this gives up to 0.5% less alcohol in the wine.

[36] Sometimes it is used with wine being matured in barrel as an alternative to racking, since it has the same effect in counteracting the reductive effect of the lees. This is called clicage and is popular on the right bank of Bordeaux, where it has been legal since 1997.

[37] He produces wines from Coonawarra, Clare Valley, and Adelaide Hills at Petaluma Wines.

[38] Although the top producers, such as the first growths in Bordeaux, have usually replaced all their oak every year given their greater resources.

[39] Light toasting might be 10 minutes duration at 120-180°C, medium is 10 minutes at 200°C, and heavy is >15 minutes at 230°C.

[40] Altogether about 100 volatile compounds have been reported to come from exposing wine to oak (Pascal Chatonnet, *Incidence Du Bois De Chêne Sur La Composition Chimique Et Les Qualités Organoleptiques Des Vins. Applications Technologiques*, Thesis, Université de Bordeaux II, 1991).

[41] Flavors derived from oak:

Compound	Effects on wine	Effect of toasting
Lactones	Coconut aromas; responsible for much of the "oaky" aromas in wine.	Levels reduced.
Vanillin	Extraction depends on the stage at which the wine is exposed. Barrel fermentation reduces concentration.	Derived from lignins, levels are greatest at medium toast.
Furfural, 5-methylfurfural	Butterscotch and caramel aromas.	Generated from sugars during toasting.
Eugene	Clove-like aromas.	A volatile phenol, increased by seasoning and toasting.
Coumarone	Cinnamon-like aromas.	Cinnamon acid derivatives extracted from oak.
Guaiacol, 4-methylguaiacol	Smoky aromas.	Formed by degradation of lignins during toasting.
Ellagitannins	More astringent than grape tannins.	Heavy toasting decreases concentration.

[42] Two types of oak trees are mixed in French forests (Quercus robur and Q. pedunculata), but it is mostly Q. robur that is used for barrel-making. The major forests in France are Limousin, Tronçais, Nevers, Allier, Jupilles, Vosges. Each has its own characteristics. Oak in Limousin grows fast and forms wide rings; it is mostly used for aging cognac. Allier oak from central France grows slowly, with tight rings. Tronçais is a small forest within Allier, forming even tighter grain. Nevers is a medium grain. Jupilles is very tight grain. In the past, the forest of origin was emphasized, but the trend at coopers now is more to select by the grain of the wood (finer is better).

[43] Quercus alba.

[44] Based on an analysis reported by ETS Laboratories, Technical Bulletin, February 8, 2009.

[45] StaVin Inc, Sausalito. see www.stavin.com/tanksystems/oakbeans.htm.

[46] Aurélia Rivier, *The Alchemy of Oak Add Ins* (Nadalie, USA, 2004); see www.nadalie-usa.com /pdf/nadalie_add-ins_alchemy.pdf.

[47] The Vines & Wines listing of oak alternatives suppliers has 4 providers for oak extract, 10 for oak dust or granules, 14 for chips, 5 for cubes, 12 for segments, 13 for tank inserts, 15 for staves to give a rough idea of relative popularity (Vines & Wines, April, 2008).

[48] Oak chips have been allowed in Vin de Pays but not at higher quality levels. The ex-

tension was recommended in a report commissioned to improve the competitiveness of French wines and will apply to all wines in France except for individual AOCs that ban the procedure (Bernard Pommel, *Réussir l'Avenir De La Viticulture Française. Plan National De Restructuration De La Filière Viti-Vinicole Française*, Ministry of Agriculture, Paris, 2006).

[49] As reported by Panos Kakaviatos, Decanter, March 30, 2006.

[50] TCA is estimated to be responsible for about 85% of corked wines, but the taint can also be produced by other, related compounds. Of course, sometimes there is a tendency to ascribe any problem with mustiness to the cork, and it can also be produced in other ways. See Mark A. Sefton & Robert F. Simpson, *Compounds Causing Cork Taint And The Factors Affecting Their Transfer From Natural Cork Closures To Wine - A Review* (Australian J. Grapes Wine Research, 11, 226-240, 2005).

[51] The value of cork exports was €850 million in 2007 according to the Portuguese National Institute of Statistics), representing 0.7% of Portugal's GDP. The total value of all wine exports was €575 million according to the IVV (*Vinha e do Vinho*: Vine and Wine Institute).

[52] The cork starts out with an average diameter of 24 mm (just under 1"), is compressed to 16 mm to fit it into the bottleneck, and expands to 18 mm after insertion.

[53] Those also implicated in wine include TeCA (2,3,4,6-tetrachloroanisole) and TBA (2,4,6-tribromoanisole).

[54] George Taber, *To Cork or Not to Cork*, pp. 71-79.

[55] Pascal Chatonnet, *Nature et Origin des Odeurs de "Moisi" dans les Caves, Incidences sur la Contamination des Vins* (J. Int. Sci. Vigne Vin, 28, 131-151, 1994).

[56] George Taber, *To Cork or Not to Cork*, pp. 31-35.

[57] According to John Kolasa of Château Canon, one of the few producers to be open about the problem, as reported in Conan, *L'Inavouable Maladie du Vin*, see note 58.

[58] Eric Conan & Jean-Paul Géné, *L'Inavouable Maladie du Vin* (L'Express, December 24, Paris, 1998).

[59] Ibid.

[60] Taber, *To Cork or Not to Cork*, pp. 181-191.

[61] H. R. Buser et al., *Identification of 2,4,6-Trichloroanisole as a Potent Compound Causing Cork Taint in Wine*, J. Agricultural and Food Chemistry 30, 359–38, 1982.

[62] Taber, *To Cork or Not to Cork*, p. 35.

[63] The Diamond process developed by Sabaté (now known as Oeneo) consists of treating corks with CO2 in a "supercritical state," in which it is at the interface between gaseous and liquid conditions. As gas, it extracts TCA from the cork; as liquid it solubilizes it. It is much more efficient than previous techniques for washing corks, although more costly. The ROSA (Rate of Optimal Steam Extraction) process developed by Amorim uses steam treatment to extract volatile compounds; this reduces the level of TCA by 70-80%. However, it deforms the cork, but is useful with technical corks (corks made from agglomerated particles.

[64] This analogy was suggested to me by Paolo di Marchi.

[65] Jeffrey Grosset, famous for his Polish Hill Riesling, took the lead, and recruited 13 of the 25 winemakers in Clare Valley who produced Riesling.

[66] Taber, *To Cork or Not to Cork*, p. 49.

[67] The figures in the original study superficially suggest a difference of 1000-fold between the tightest and loosest corks. This may be misleading, and the real variation in corks is probably a few fold (Alan Limmer, *The Chemistry of Post–bottling Sulfides in Wine* (Chemistry in New Zealand, 69, 2-5, 2005).

[68] A. Hart and A. Kleinig, *The Role of Oxygen in the Aging of Bottled Wine* (Aust. N.Z. Wine Ind. J. 20, 46-50, 2005).

[69] Richard Alleyne, *Screwcaps Blamed for Tainting Wine*, Daily Telegraph, London, September 20, 2006.

[70] 1,1,6-trimethyl-1,2-dihydronaphthalene.

[71] Peter Godden et al, *Towards Offering Wine To The Consumer In Optimal Condition - The Wine, The Closures And Other Packaging Variables, Part II* (Infowine, Internet J. Viticul. Enol.,

Enoforum, Piacenza, March 2005).

[72] Pascal Ribéreau-Gayon et al., *The Handbook of Enology, Volume 2, The Chemistry of Wine Stabilisation and Treatments*, 2nd edition (John Wiley & Sons, New York, 2000), p. 405.

[73] Emile Peynaud, *Knowing and Making Wine* (Interscience, 1984), p. 254.

[74] packagingnews.co.uk, May 6, 2009.

[75] Victor Hugo, *Les Contemplations, La Fête Chez Thérèse*, I, 22.

Chapter 7: Thousand Cultivars

[1] This figure is biased by the fact the Airén is planted at an unusually low density, typically about 1500 vines per hectare. If the numbers were calculated in terms of number of vines planted rather than area planted, Airén would come out somewhat lower in the list.

[2] It's enormously difficult to get accurate figures on a worldwide basis. Data sources: for 1990 - Patrick Fegan, The Vineyard Handbook: Appellations, Maps and Statistics, 2nd edition, Chicago Wine School, Chicago, 2003; for 2004 - Jancis Robinson, Oxford Companion to Wine, 3rd edition, 2006, p. 746. The main difficulty is to keep up with the pace of change, which can outrun the official statistics. The trends shown in the figure are undoubtedly correct, but the exact numbers should be regarded as an approximation.

[3] Data based on the latest census for grape variety plantings in each country. There are some inconsistencies because data are more timely for the New World than for Europe.

[4] Data sources for plantings of varietals in individual countries are: Argentine Instituto Nacional de Vitivinicultura (Registro de Vinedos y Superficie), Australian Bureau of Statistics (Annual Reports 1329.0), California Department of Food and Agriculture, Sacramento (California Grape Acreage Reports), Catastro Viticola Nacional, Chile; SAWIS (South Africa Wine Industry Information and Systems; Statistics of Wine Grapes); ONIVINS (Les Principaux Cépages De Cuve / Departements Principaux : Blancs, Noirs); New Zealand winegrowers statistical annual, 2008; Moldova WineGuild MoldovaWein Dossier.

[5] The mutations are not in the genes actually coding for the enzymes that produce anthocyanins, but in regulatory genes that control expression of the anthocyanin genes. There are two (very similar) regulator genes, either of which can turn on anthocyanin synthesis. Both of them are inactivated in white grapevines. The two mutations (a different one in each regulator gene) are identical in 55 different cultivars that were examined (Amanda R. Walker, *White Grapes Arose Through The Mutation Of Two Similar And Adjacent Regulatory Genes*, The Plant Journal, 49, 772-785, 2007).

[6] Relationships were determined by DNA mapping of 222 cultivars and 22 wild grapevines (Mallikarjuna K. Aradhya et al., *Genetic structure and differentiation in cultivated grape, Vitis vinifera L*, (Genet. Res., 81, 179-92, 2003).

[7] This does not necessarily mean they were the first to be cultivated, but does indicate that they have been better preserved since their cultivation; many original cultivars from Greece and Italy, for example, may have been lost.

[8] Rosso, *Mystique of Barolo*, p. 18.

[9] According to the Unione Produttori Vini Albesi (Alba).

[10] Giovanni Battista Croce, *Della Eccellenza E Diversità Dei Vini Che Nella Montagna Di Torino Si Fanno E Del Modo Di Farli*.

[11] Dion, *Histoire de la Vigne*, p. 297.

[12] The origins of one such clone were analyzed by H. Yakushiji et al., *A Skin Color Mutation Of Grapevine, From Black-Skinned Pinot Noir To White-Skinned Pinot Blanc, Is Caused By Deletion Of The Functional Vvmyba1 Allele* (Biosci. Biotech. Biochem., 70, 1506-1508, 2006). Another is referred to by Amanda R. Walker et al., *Two New Grape Cultivars, Bud Sports Of Cabernet Sauvignon Bearing Pale-Coloured Berries, Are The Result Of Deletion Of Two Regulatory Genes Of The Berry Colour Locus* (Plant Mol. Biol., 62, 623-635, 2006).

[13] Pierre Gouges says that a white mutant was discovered in 1936 in the Clos des Porrets vineyard in Nuits St. Georges by his grandfather. Some cuttings were propagated in

1938, but it was not until 1947 that the major planting, 400 vines in the Perrières vineyard, was made. In 1997 a larger area was planted just outside Nuits St. Georges and is used to produce a Bourgogne Pinot Blanc. The cultivar was called Pinot Gouges at the oenological school at Montpellier (personal communication, Pierre Gouges, October 2009).

[14] Freddie Price, *Riesling Renaissance* (Mitchell Beazley, London, 2004).

[15] Jean-Alexandre Cavoleau, *Oenologie Française, Ou Statistique De Tous Les Vignobles Et De Toutes Les Boissons Vineuses Et Spiriteuses De La France, Suivie De Considérations Générales Sur La Culture De La Vigne* (Huzard, Paris, 1827).

[16] John Bowers et al., *A Single Pair Of Parents Proposed For A Group Of Grapevine Varieties In Northeastern France* (Acta Hort., 528, 129–132, 2000).

[17] Widespread genetic variety is consistent with the idea that it originated in the region. As a working rule, the greatest genetic variation in grape variety is found closest to its point of origin.

[18] Giovan Vettorio Soderini, *Trattato Della Coltivazione Delle Viti*, Firenze, 1590.

[19] Di Cosimo Trinci Pistojese, *Agricoltore Sperimentato*, Venezia, 1738; Gallesio, Pomona Italiana, Niccolò Capurro, Pisa, 1830.

[20] José F. Vouillamoz et al., *The Parentage Of 'Sangiovese', The Most Important Italian Wine Grape* (Vitis 46, 19-22, 2007).

[21] George M. Taber, *Judgment of Paris: California vs. France and the Historic 1976 Paris Tasting That Revolutionized Wine* (Scribner, New York, 2006).

[22] Is it a sign of progress that the estimate for aroma complexity does not come from direct measurement of ability to smell, but from genetic analysis of the human genome, which shows several hundred genes coding for odorant receptors? By contrast, there are only five types of taste receptor genes, and the largest family (for bitter taste) has only 25 members.

[23] A. F. Blakeslee, *Unlike Reaction Of Different Individuals To Fragrance In Verbena Flowers*, Science, 48, 298-299, 1918.

[24] Andreas Keller and Leslie B. Vosshall, *Better Smelling Through Genetics: Mammalian Odor Perception*, Curr. Opin. Neurobiol., 18, 364-369, 2008.

[25] The range is from 10 to 10,000 depending on the odor (Yehudit Hasin-Brumshtein et al., *Human Olfaction: From Genomic Variation To Phenotypic Diversity*, Trends Genetics, 25, 178-184).

[26] Different combinations of the proteins coded by these genes are used to detect sweet and unami.

[27] Dennis Drayna, *Human Taste Genetics* (Ann. Rev. Genomics Human Genetics, 6, 217-235, 2005).

[28] Beverly J. Tepper, *Nutritional Implications of Genetic Taste Variation: The Role of PROP Sensitivity and Other Taste Phenotypes* (Annu. Rev. Nutr. 2008., 28, 14.1–14.22, 2008).

[29] Stephen Wooding, *Phenylthiocarbamide: A 75-Year Adventure in Genetics and Natural Selection* (Genetics, 172, 2015-2023, 2006).

[30] The gene is called TAS2R38. Inactive variants are recessive. There is one major inactive variant in the human population, and several minor variants, one of which causes intermediate sensitivity to bitterness. Although the inactive variants do not react with PTC, it is possible they are active with some other (unidentified) bitter compound (U. K. Kim and Denis Drayna, *Genetics Of Individual Differences In Bitter Taste Perception: Lessons From The PTC Gene*, Clin. Genet., 67, 276-280, 2004).

[31] 6-n-propylthiouracil.

[32] Linda M. Bartoshuk et al., *PTC/PROP Tasting: Anatomy, Psychophysics, And Sex Effects* (Physiol. Behav., 56, 1165-1171, 1994).

[33] I have been unable to find any published scientific support for the connection with morning sickness (obviously more difficult to prove than the others since it rests on anecdotal evidence). One study that tested for a connection in pregnant women themselves found no increase in morning sickness for super-tasters (Sipiora et al., *Bitter Taste Perception And Severe Vomiting In Pregnancy*, Physiol Behav., 69, 259-267, 2000). Another showed a preference for high salt intake in infants whose mothers had morning sickness (Susan R. Crystal and Ilene L. Bernstein, *Infant Salt Preference and Mother's Morning Sick-

ness, Appetite, 30, 297–307, 1998). However, unpublished results obtained by consumer research of the Napa Seasoning Company are reported to show directly a correlation between morning sickness and bitter sensitivity in offspring (personal communication, Tim Hanni MW, February 2010).

[34] PTC and PROP are thiols (sulfur-containing) substances, and it has been thought that the receptor recognizes compounds containing the thiocyanate (N-C=S) structure. This is not found in tannins or caffeine. The range of compounds to which PTC/PROP tasters have increased sensitivity also includes saccharin, salt, potassium benzoate.

[35] Super-tasters have greater sensitivity to a wide range of features in red wine, including acidity, saltiness, textural factors, and astringency (Gary J. Pickering and Gordon Robert, *Perception Of Mouthfeel Sensations Elicited By Red Wine Are Associated With Sensitivity To 6-N-Propylthiouracil*, J. Sensory Studies, 21, 249–265, 2006).

[36] Based on data of Dennis Drayna et al., *A Model System for Identifying Genes Underlying Complex Traits* (Cold Spring Harbor Symp. Quant. Biol., 68, 365-371, 2003).

[37] Super-tasters are not reliably predicted by threshold tests. Instead, methods called suprathreshold testing are used. These basically rely on the tasters' reported reactions to a given dose (see note 32). If super-tasters detected a lower absolute threshold, they would occupy the far right part of the curve, but in fact they appear to be distributed among the entire taster population. Their reported response is strong whatever their threshold levels. This is shown by the fact that people can be divided into the same groups of nontasters, tasters, super-tasters when tested with PROP over a 100-fold concentration scale (Gary J. Pickering, Katerina Simunkova, and David DiBattista, *Intensity of taste and astringency sensations elicited by red wines is associated with sensitivity to PROP (6-n-propylthiouracil)*, Food Qual. Pref. 15, 147–54, 2004, table 1).

[38] Gregory K. Essick, et al., *Lingual tactile acuity, taste perception, and the density and diameter of fungiform papillae in female subjects* (Physiol. Behav., 80, 289-302, 2003).

[39] Juyun Lim, Lenka Urban, and Barry G. Green, *Measures of Individual Differences in Taste and Creaminess Perception* (Chemical Senses, 33, 493- 501, 2008).

[40] The association of super-tasters with bitter perception may simply be due to a historical accident: that diagnosis has been performed with PTC/PROP. This has the consequence that nontasters for PTC/PROP cannot be assessed. It might be that with a different test, super-tasters would also be present in the PTC-nontaster population, which would give a broader perspective on the phenomenon. A real understanding of the super-taster phenomenon requires a more objective measurement for supertasting than is presently available.

[41] Alexey A. Fushan et al., *Allelic Polymorphism within the TAS1R3 Promoter Is Associated with Human Taste Sensitivity to Sucrose* (Current Biol., 19, 1-6, 2009).

[42] Martha R. Bajec and Gary J. Pickering, *Astringency: Mechanisms and Perception* (Crit. Rev. Food Science Nutrition, 48, 858–875, 2008).

[43] Incidentally, it is not only the senses of taste and smell that differ among individuals, but also vision. There are two different red eye pigments in the human population, with the result that different individuals do in fact see slightly different red color spectrums, so presumably will have slightly different views of red wines (Benjamin Lewin, *On Neuronal Specificity and the Molecular Basis of Perception*, Cell, 79, 935-943, 1994).

[44] Pavla Polásková et al., *Wine flavor: chemistry in a glass* (Chem Soc. Rev., 37, 2478-2489, 2008).

[45] Christian Lindinger, *When Machine Tastes Coffee: Instrumental Approach To Predict the Sensory Profile of Espresso Coffee* (Anal. Chem. 2008, 80, 1574-1581).

[46] John E. Bowers & Carole P. Meredith, *The parentage of a classic wine grape, Cabernet Sauvignon* (Nature Genetics, 16, 84-86, 1997).

[47] J.-M. Boursiquot et al., *Parentage of Merlot and related winegrape cultivars of southwestern France: discovery of the missing link* (Australian J. Grape and Wine Research, 15, 144-155, 2008).

[48] Ibid.

[49] France 60,800 ha (including 30,382 ha in Bordeaux and 19,299 ha in Languedoc), Chile 40,765 ha, United States 30,769 ha, Australia 27,309 ha, Spain 19,430 ha, Argentina

17,921 ha, Bulgaria 16,600 ha, South Africa 12,252 ha. Data sources; see note 4.

[50] Armailhacq comments in his book that Cabernet had been spreading rapidly in recent years (Armand d'Armailhacq, *De la culture des vignes, de la vinification et des vins dans le Médoc*, Chaumas, Bordeaux, 1867, p. 37).

[51] Lewin, *What Price Bordeaux?*, p. 60.

[52] Ibid., p. 161.

[53] John Livingstone-Learmonth, *The wines of the Northern Rhône*, p. 237.

[54] Serine d'Ampuis (from Côte-Rôtie) and Syrah de l'Hermitage were only recognized as being the same variety in the twentieth century.

[55] Not to be confused with the grape today sometimes called Petite Syrah in California, which is really Durif.

[56] John Livingstone-Learmonth, *The Wines Of The Northern Rhône*, p. 16.

[57] Ibid., p. 16.

[58] James Halliday, *The History of Shiraz in Australia* (World of Fine Wine, issue 20, 2008).

[59] France 67,800 ha; Australia 42,806 ha; Spain 16,586 ha; Argentina 12,772 ha; South Africa 9,754 ha; United States 6,896 ha; Chile 4,795 ha. Data sources: see note 4.

[60] Burgundy has 10,040 ha, including 5,800 ha on the Côte d'Or and 2,800 ha on the Côte Chalonnaise. California has almost 5,000 ha, with half in Sonoma and rest spread among Napa, Santa Barbara, and Monterey. Germany's main area is Baden, with 5,729 ha. New Zealand now has 4,650 ha. Data sources; see note 4.

[61] France 27,900 ha (11,650 ha in Champagne and 10,040 ha in Burgundy); Germany 11,371 ha; United States, 11,038 ha (3,268 ha in Oregon and 4,982 ha in California); New Zealand, 4,650 ha; Switzerland 4,659 ha; Australia, 4,208 ha; Italy, 3,287 ha; Moldova accounts for most of the other plantings in Europe, with 8,200 ha. Data sources; see note 4.

[62] Jackson, *Wine Science*, p. 50.

[63] The genetic map is shared with two other varieties, Pinot Moure and Pinot fin teinturier (which has colored juice).

[64] Paul K. Boss & Mark R. Thomas, *Association of dwarfism and floral induction with a grape 'green revolution' mutation* (Nature, 416, 847-850, 2002).

[65] S. Hocquigny, *Diversification within grapevine cultivars goes through chimeric states* (Genome 47, 579–589, 2004).

[66] France, 43,887 ha (13,500 in Burgundy; 9,000 ha in Languedoc); United States, 39,728 ha; Australia, 30,820 ha; Italy, 11,686 ha; Chile, 8,753 ha; South Africa, 8,327 ha; Argentina, 6,613 ha; Spain, 5,423 ha; New Zealand, 3,861 ha. Data sources; see note 4.

[67] There is one prominent exception. The Chardonnay Musqué clone has strong aromatics with some grapey, Muscat-like features. This is ENTAV-INRA clone 809. The comparison with Muscat is based solely on gustatory experience; there appears to have been no direct analysis of volatile compounds. There's a little grown in Macon, and some in northeastern Italy; otherwise it's favored by some New World producers who want to make a more aromatic wine than you usually get from Chardonnay's neutral profile.

[68] One vineyard block was given over to the experiment. There were six rows of each clone, giving 5-10 barrels of wine per clone.

[69] The number of clusters per vine varied from 20 to 28, the number of berries from 68 to 125, the weight per berry from 1.0 to 1.4 g, total range of yields varied from 1.7 to 4 tons per acre, the Brix at harvest varied from 23.4 to 25, acidity varied from 8.1 to 9.7 g/l tartaric (personal communication from Mark Lingenfelder).

[70] Comments on properties of individual clones from the author's tasting notes.

[71] France, 22,062 ha (divided between the Loire, Bordeaux, and the Languedoc); New Zealand, 13,988 ha (two thirds in Marlborough); Chile, 8,862 ha; South Africa, 7,753 ha; United States, 5,697 ha; Australia, 5,327 ha. Data sources: see note 4.

[72] IBMP levels were measured in Cabernet Sauvignon grown in Tarragona by Christina Sala et al., *Contents of 3-alkyl-2-methoxypyrazines in musts and wines from Vitis vinifera variety Cabernet Sauvignon: influence of irrigation and plantation density* (J. Science Food Agric., 85,1131-1136, 2005).

[73] The intensity of each aroma on the spider chart is indicated by its distance from the center. Red shows fermentation with a yeast that has increased carbon sulfur lyase activity

compared to the yeast used for the blue fermentation (Jan H. Swiegers et al., *Enhancement of Sauvignon blanc wine aroma through yeast combinations,* Wynboer, South Africa, 2000).

[74] The detection threshold is 2 ppm; levels in wine vary from 2 ppm to 40 ppm (Jan H. Swiegers et al., *Meeting consumer expectations through management in vineyard and winery,* AWRI Report, 2005).

[75] 4-MMP is 4-mercapto-4-methylpentan-2-one. The others are 3-MH (3-mercapto-hexan-1-ol) and 3-MHA (3-mercaptohexyl-acetate).

[76] The perception threshold is only 0.8 ppb. Typical levels in wine are 4-24 ppb (Denis Dubourdieu et al., *The role of yeasts in grape flavor development during fermentation: the example of Sauvignon Blanc,* Am. J. Enol. Vitic., 57, 81-88, 2006).

[77] Threshold levels give impression of broom, tropical fruits before the 25 ppm level, first signs of cat's pee by 50 ppm. 3-MH and 3-MHA require much higher levels relative to threshold before they turn to cat's pee (personal communication from Sakkie Pretorious).

[78] The inactive form is bound to the amino acid cysteine. The enzyme that releases the volatile compound is called a carbon-sulfur lyase. Both 4-MMP and 3-MH are formed by this mechanism. 3-MHA is not present at all in the berry and is synthesized by yeast enzymes by modifying 3-mercaptohexanol (Jan H. Swiegers et al., *The Influence of Yeast on the Aroma of Sauvignon Blanc Wine* (Food Microbiology, 26, 204–211, 2009).

[79] Ibid.

[80] W. R. Sponholz and T. Hühn, *Einflussfaktoren von Klonenmaterial und verwendetem Hefestamm auf die Alterung von Riesling Weinen (Factors influencing the ageing of Riesling wines : Clonal material and used yeast strain),* Wein-Wissenschaft, 52, 103-108, 1997.

[81] Although it is fair to say we don't fully understand all the factors determining when and how much develops, it can reach levels of 200 µg/l in aged wines, some ten times greater than the threshold for detection (Uli Fischer, *Wine Aroma,* Wine Aroma – Flavours and Fragrances. Chemistry, Bioprocessing and Sustainability. Ed. R.G. Berger, Springer Verlag, 241-267., Berlin, 2007).

[82] Tom Cannavan's wine-pages.com; see www.wine-pages.com/guests/tom/riesling-petrol-2.htm.

[83] Germany, 20,627 ha; Australia, 4,270 ha; France, 3,480 ha (mostly in Alsace), United States, 1,802 ha; Austria, 1,642 ha; New Zealand, 917 ha. Data sources: see note 4.

[84] About 40 terpenes have been found in grapes. All terpenes are based on a five-carbon unit called isopentenyl pyrophosphate (IPP). They are named for the number of these 5-carbon units: hemiterpenes (one 5-carbon), monoterpenes (2), sesquiterpenes (3), etc. Terpenes can be simple hydrocarbons (endings in "ene"), aldehydes (endings in "al"), alcohols (endings in "ol"), ketones (endings in "one"), acids and esters.

[85] Albariño is an exception where the majority are free.

[86] Jan H. Swiegers et al., *Yeast and bacterial Modulation of Wine Aroma and Flavor* (Australian J. Grape and Wine Research 11, 139–173, 2005), p. 157; Uli Fischer, *Wine Aroma* (Wine Aroma. Flavours and Fragrances. Chemistry, Bioprocessing and Sustainability. Ed. R.G. Berger, Springer Verlag, 241-267., Berlin, 2007).

[87] Jancis Robinson, *The Oxford Companion to Wine* (Oxford University Press, Oxford, 1994), p. 649.

[88] Manna F. Crespan and N. Milani, *The Muscats: A molecular analysis of synonyms, homonyms and genetic relationships within a large family of grapevine cultivars* (Vitis 40, 23-30, 2001); Cecilia B. Agüero, *Identity and Parentage of Torrontés Cultivars in Argentina* (Am. J. Enol. Vitic., 54, 318-321, 2003).

[89] Robinson, *The Oxford Companion,* op. cit., p. 651.

[90] Unidentified "Muscat" represents 38% of plantings, Muscat d'Alexandrie is 29%, Muscat Blanc à Petits Grains is 14%, Muscat Ottonel and Hamburg are 9% each. Data sources; see note 4.

[91] Christian Lindinger, *When Machine Tastes Coffee: Instrumental Approach To Predict the Sensory Profile of Espresso Coffee* (Anal. Chem. 2008, 80, 1574-1581.)

[92] Based on the original aroma wheel of Ann Noble of the University of California.

[93] This was the highest proportion for a genetically modified crop. Cotton was 47%, maize 23%, and rapeseed 21% (Clive James, *Global Status of Commercialized Biotech/GM*

Crops: 2008. ISAAA Brief No. 39., ISAAA, International Service for the Acquisition of Agri-Biotech Applications, Ithaca, NY; see also GMO Compass, www.gmo-compass.org).

[94] The sequence of the grapevine genome has 30,434 genes (Olivier Jaillon et al., *The grapevine genome sequence suggests ancestral hexaploidization in major angiosperm phyla,* Nature, 449, 463-467, 2007).

[95] C. L. Barker et al., *Genetic and physical mapping of the grapevine powdery mildew resistance gene, Run1, using a bacterial artificial chromosome library* (Theor. Appl. Genet., 111, 370-377, 2005).

[96] Actually, special techniques are required because Muscadinia has a different number of chromosomes from Vitis, so it would not be possible simply to breed the gene into a cultivar.

[97] Institut National des Appellations d'Origine.

[98] These vines actually are 41B rootstocks modified to resist the nematode that carries fanleaf virus. They come from an experiment started by Moët and Chandon in Champagne in 1996, but the vines were pulled up there in 1999 as a result of public protests.

[99] Two examples would be the widespread use of the Pinot Droit clone of Pinot Noir in Burgundy in the 1960s, and the more recent use of clones based on the over-productive Grosse Syrah strain in the northern Rhône.

[100] 124 samples of table grapes were purchased in supermarkets in Germany, France, Holland, Hungary, and Italy in 2008. 123 contained detectable pesticide residues, with an average content of 0.65 mg/kg. The study was reported by MDRGF (Mouvement pour le droit et le respect des générations futures) in France; see www.mdrgf.org.

[101] Melané A.Vivier and Isak S. Pretorius, *Genetically tailored grapevines for the wine industry* (Trends Biotechnology, 20, 472-478, 2002); Isak S. Pretorius & Peter B. Hoj, *Grape and Wine Biotechnology: Challenges, Opportunities and Potential Benefits* (Australian J. Grape and Wine Research, 11, 83–108, 2005).

[102] Isak S Pretorius & Florian F Bauer, *Meeting the consumer challenge through genetically customized wine-yeast strains* (Trends Biotechnology, 20, 426-432, 2002).

[103] ML01 is basically the same as the parental strain Prise de Mousse S92, one of the standard cultured yeast strains for wine fermentation, except that it can also perform malolactic fermentation. It was created by the insertion of two genes. One is the malate permease gene, obtained from another yeast strain, S. pombe; this allows the yeast to take up malic acid. The second is the malolactic gene, obtained from Oenococcus oeni (the bacterium usually responsible for malolactic fermentation), which causes the yeast to convert malic acid to lactic acid (John I. Husnik et al., *Metabolic engineering of malolactic wine yeast,* Metabolic Engineering, 8, 315-323, 2006).

[104] The authors claim that the wine has lower content of histamine (reducing risk of migraines), because biogenic amines are usually produced by bacteria during MLF. It also has lower volatile acidity (less acetic acid) (John I. Husnik et al., *Functional Analyses of the Malolactic Wine Yeast ML01,* Am. J. Enol. Vitic., 58, 42-52, 2007).

[105] It was approved by the FDA and has been available on the United States market since 2005. It was initially distributed by Springer Oenologie, but now does not have a commercial distributor, although it is available directly from its creator, Hennie van Vuuren, in the United States and Canada. It is not known how many wineries are using it, because none is presently prepared to admit publicly to its use.

[106] It was ordered to be pulled out in Lorraine in 1598 and in Besançon in 1731 (Pierre Galet, *Cépages et Vignobles de France: L'Ampelographie Française,* Paul Dehan, 1956, p. 146).

[107] Grape varieties arising from crosses between Gouais Blanc and Pinot include Aligoté, Aubin Vert, Auxerrois, Bachet noir, Beaunoir, Chardonnay, Dameron, Franc Noir de la-Haute-Saône, Gamay Blanc Gloriod, Gamay noir, Knipperlé, Melon (Muscadet), Peurion, Romorantin, Roublot, and Sacy (John Bowers et al., *Historical Genetics: The Parentage of Chardonnay, Gamay, and Other Wine Grapes of NorthEastern France,* Science, 285, 1562-1565, 1999).

[108] Müller-Thurgau was created by Dr. Hermann Müller (who was born in the Swiss canton of Thurgau) at the Geisenheim Institute in Germany. It was originally thought to

be a cross between Riesling and Sylvaner, but recently it was discovered that Sylvaner is not the other parent. After confusion arising from the fact that several cultivars in the reference grapevine collections were misclassified, which led to the misidentification of Chasselas as the other parent, DNA mapping showed that the second parent was the Madeleine Royale cultivar from the collection in Montpellier (Büscher et al., *On the origin of the grapevine variety Müller-Thurgau as investigated by the inheritance of random amplified polymorphic DNA (RAPD)*, Vitis, 33, 15-17, 1994; Erika Dettweiler et al., *Grapevine cultivar Muller-Thurgau and its true to type descent,* Vitis, 39, 63-65, 2000).

[109] Currently most new grapevine plantings in France are clones.

Chapter 8: Global Wine Trends

[1] Unwin, *Wine and the Vine*, p. 128.

[1] Quoted in *Wine War. Savvy New World marketers are devastating the French wine industry*, Business week cover story, September 3, 2001.

[1] Phil Davies and Dermot Walsh, Alcohol problems and alcohol control in Europe, Gardner, 1990. p. 74.

[2] DGDDI (Direction Générale des Douanes et Droits Indirects); INSEE (National Institute for Statistics and Economic Studies).

[3] The Wine Institute (California) figures for U.S. consumption, 1937-2007.

[4] "Plonk" may have originated as a generic term for cheap wine as a transmogrification of "vin blanc" by British soldiers in the first world war (Ian Gately, *Drink. A Cultural History of Alcohol,* Gotham Books, New York, 2008, p. 361).

[5] Lewin, *What Price Bordeaux?*, p. 67.

[6] Data from the vines.org auction database of prices for auctions at Christie's, Sotheby's and Acker Merrall in London and New York for wines of vintages after 2000 sold at auctions through 2009. Numbers refer to different types of wines reaching a price over $100 per bottle.

[7] In terms of total sales of wines at more than $100 per bottle at the auctions during the first decade of the 21st century, France accounts for 90% of revenue, with Bordeaux twice as important as Burgundy. See note 6.

[8] The numbers of wines in individual regions are: Burgundy, 144; Bordeaux, 61; Rhône, 36; Napa, 47; Sonoma, 41; Piedmont, 12; Tuscany, 12; Rioja, 8; Barossa, 15; McLaren Vale, 7. See note 6.

[9] Brands from the USA: Gallo, Mondavi, Beringer, Blossom Hill, Sutter Home, Inglenook, Kendall Jackson; Australia: Hardy's, Jacob's Creek, Lindemans, Yellow Tail, Banrock Station, Wolf Blass, Penfolds; Chile: Concho y Toro; Spain: Torres; South Africa: Kumala (Intangible Business, *The Power 100. The World's most powerful spirits and wine brands*, London, 2008).

[10] Jean-Bernard Marquette, *La Vinification dans les Domaines de l'Archeveque de Bordeaux a la fin du Moyen Age* (In A. Huetz de Lemps et al. (Eds.), Géographie Historique des Vignobles, Tome I Vignobles Français, CNRS, Paris, 1978).

[11] Some sample prices from a Christies' auction in April 1820 (recalculated per dozen bottles) are: Port, £3.15; East India Madeira, £4.24; White Creaming Champagne, £3.54; Hock (Mannheim), £4.05.

[12] It has been claimed that in the early nineteenth century, Riesling from Germany's Rheingau became the most expensive wine in England, at 50s per bottle representing twice the price of any other wine (John Hurley, *A Matter of Taste: The History of Wine Drinking in Britain,* The History Press, 2005, p. 84.) I am unable to substantiate this claim from Christies' auction records, which suggest to the contrary that Riesling (usually identified only as "Hock" or "Moselle") was generally priced close to claret.

[13] Samples prices from a Christies' auction in June 1860 (recalculated per dozen) were: Claret (Cos d'Estournel, 1848), £3.30; Sherry (1820 vintage), £3.45; Madeira (old Boal), £4.20; Port (Quarles Harris, 1840), £4.30.

[14] Christies auction records for the 1890s show sales mostly of three dozen lots, with prices (recalculated per dozen) for some typical lots as follows: Pommery 1874, £10.25-

12.00; Veuve Clicquot 1874, £6.24-7.00; Perrier-Jouet 1874, £7.75-12.50; Lafite 1870, £3.30-4.75; Lafite 1864, £5.36; Margaux 1870, £2.36; "Port" 1847, £6.25; Sandeman 1863, £4.67; Yquem 868, £5.00; Yquem 1870, £4.20; Steinberg Cabinet 1862, £6.75; Liebfraumilch 1874, £2.33; Romanée-Conti 1868, £6.50; Le Montrachet (Bouchard) 1870, £4.00.

[15] In 2009, boxes of Franzia Chablis could be bought on the U.S. market for $1.60 per 750 ml; the most expensive wine of the Bordeaux 2005 vintage, Château Ausone, came on the market for $2200 per bottle.

[16] Hugh Johnson, *The Story of Wine* (Mitchell Beazley, London, 2005), p.145.

[17] Prices for 1890 taken from Christies' auction results (see note 14). Prices for 2010 taken for current releases of the most expensive wine in each category (Red Burgundy – Romanée-Conti; Bordeaux – Château Ausone; Napa – Screaming Eagle Cabernet; Sauternes – Château d'Yquem; Rhône – Côte-Rôtie La Turque; White Burgundy – Le Montrachet; Champagne – Dom Pérignon, Roederer Cristal.

[18] See Chapter 1.

[19] James Conaway, *Napa* (Mariner Books, New York, 2002), p. 9.

[20] Tim Unwin, *Wine and the Vine*, pp. 102-104.

[21] Thomas Pellechia, *Wine. The 8000 year old story of the wine trade* (Running Press, Philadelphia, 2006), p. 48.

[22] Unwin, *Wine and the Vine*, pp. 108-109.

[23] By 1959, Peynaud published a scientific paper showing that malolactic fermentation could be induced by inoculating wine with the appropriate bacteria (CR Seances Acad. Agric, France, 45, p. 355).

[24] Quoted in Frank Ward (Connoisseur magazine, New York, May issue, 1987).

[25] According to châteaux identified on the web sites of the oenologists or oenologists identified on the web sites of the châteaux.

[26] Decanter magazine (U.K.) was founded in 1975, Finigan's Private Guide to Wines (U.S.) became national in 1977, The Wine Advocate (U.S.) was founded in 1978, and The Wine Spectator (U.S.) in its present form dates from 1979. Alles über Wein in Germany dates from 1982. Only in France does consumer criticism go back substantially earlier, to the Revue du Vin de France founded in 1927.

[27] The Private Guide finally ceased publication in 1990.

[28] Author's discussion with a château proprietor in Margaux, March 2009.

[29] Lewin, *What Price Bordeaux?*, pp. 145-148.

[30] David Darlington, *The chemistry of a 90+ wine*, New York Times, August 7, 2005.

[31] Michael Steinberger, *Grape Rot. The new Wine Spectator's distinct aroma of fishiness* (Slate, December 26, www.slate.com/id/2075720/, 2002).

[32] James Suckling, *Magnificent Wines From a Flawless Vintage*, Wine Spectator, July 31, 2004.

[33] Chateau St. Jean was founded in 1973, became known for the elegance of its Cabernet Sauvignon and Chardonnay, and was bought by Beringer Wine Estates in 1996.

[34] Michael Steinberger, *Grape Rot*, op. cit.

[35] Ibid.

[36] Ibid.

[37] Amanda Hessser, *A Wine Award that Seems Easy to Come By*, New York Times, July 9, 2003.

[38] Details are on Robin Goldstein's blog at blindtaste.com.

[39] Quoted in Jerry Hirsch, *Hoax leaves bitter taste for wine magazine*, Chicago Tribune, August 24, 2008.

[40] Omer Gokcekus and Andrew Fargnoli, *Is Globalization Good for Wine Drinkers in the United States?*, J. Wine Economics, 2, 187-195, 2007.

[41] Robert Joseph and Joel Payne, *Wines Without Frontiers*, Wine Business International, January 2007.

[42] Ibid.

[43] Examples of globally-sourced brands: Blue Nun has 20 wines from Germany, France, Chile, Australia, and the United States; Bernard Magrez has wines from France,

Italy, United States, Morocco, Spain, Uruguay; Mateus includes wines from Portugal and Spain; Torres has wines from Spain and Chile; Lindemans has wines from Australia. South Africa, and Chile; Ravenswood has wines from the United States and Australia. Ibid.

[44] A total of 5.73% from Gallo, Franzia, Carlo Rossi, Tavernello, Almaden, Sutter Home, Woodbridge, Beringer, JP Chenet, and Riunite in 2002 (Liz Thach & Tim Matz, *Wine: A Global Business, 1st edition*, Miranda Press, 2004, p. 7).

[45] Gallo, Hardy's, Concho y Toro, Mondavi, Beringer, Jacob's Creek, Lindemans, Blossom Hill, Yellow Tail, and Sutter Home were the top ten in 2008 according to Intangible Business, *The Power 100. The World's most powerful spirits and wine brands*, London, 2008.

[46] Ellen Hawkes, *Blood and Wine: The Unauthorized Story of the Gallo Wine Empire* (Simon & Schuster, New York, 1993), p. 167.

[47] Accurate numbers on a worldwide basis are difficult to obtain; these are approximations, especially given the rapidly of change. Total worldwide consumption is about 32 billion 750 ml-equivalents. Glass accounts for around 19.68 million, approaching two thirds. Of the glass bottles, about 13 billion are sealed with natural corks, 2.8 billion are technical corks, and 2.5 billion are synthetic (plastic) corks (Skalli & Rein, *Global Wine Closure Report*, 2006). The hardest number to assess is the proportion under screwcap, because it has been increasing so rapidly. In the 2006 report it was stated as 1.24 billion, but more recent estimates vary from 1.7 billion from cork producer Amorim to 2.5 billion from Italian screwcap producer Guala and synthetic cork producer Nomacorc (Jamie Goode, *Screwcaps take 15% of Global Market*, Decanter, March 9, 2009). No one knows the breakdown of the other types of packaging, but bag-in-box, tetrapak, and P.E.T. bottles are probably used in declining order of importance.

[48] Energy consumption measured in a study of a winery in Italy was 28.1 MJ/bottle of wine produced, but only 13.2 MJ/750 ml of bulk wine (Fulvio Ardente et al., *POEMS: A Case Study of an Italian Wine-Producing Firm*, Environmental Management 38, 350–364, 2006).

[49] Study performed for Nomacorc (producer of synthetic corks) using the Bilan Carbone method, April 2008. Similar results were reported previously in a study performed for Oeneo, reported by Jamie Goode, *The Carbon Trail of Closures* (Wine Business, April, 2007). Another study was performed for Amorim in October 2008 by PriceWaterhouseCoopers, *Evaluation of the environmental impacts of Cork Stoppers versus Aluminium and Plastic Closures* (Amorim, 2008).

[50] Unwin, *Wine and the Vine*, p. 132.

[51] Dion, *Histoire de la Vigne*, p. 31.

[52] Total revenue was Ff380 million, which was 15% of all revenue (Charles K. Warner, *The Winegrowers of France and the Government since 1875*, Columbia University Press, New York, 1960, p. 1).

[53] Unwin, *Wine and the Vine*, p. 242.

[54] For example, The World Health Organization's European Charter on Alcohol proposes that each Member State should: "Promote health by controlling the availability, for example for young people, and influencing the price of alcoholic beverages, for instance by taxation."

[55] Peter Anderson and Ben Baumberg, *Alcohol In Europe. A Public Health Perspective. A report for the European Commission*, Institute of Alcohol Studies, London, June 2006, p. 385.

[56] The effect of price increases is least for beer, in the middle for wine, but quite effective for spirits (Anderson and Baumberg, op cit., p. 259).

[57] The pattern is slightly different among young people, but the same principle holds. The high tax countries of Britain, Sweden, Norway are at the top; the low tax countries of France and Italy are at the bottom (Anderson and Baumberg, op cit., pp. 93, 105).

[58] Ibid.

[59] Consumption in liters of pure alcohol per person per year from European health for all database (HFA-DB) (data.euro.who.int/hfadb/). Data for tax on wine from individual countries.

[60] Data for U.K. market from Wine and Spirit Trade Association, London, September

2009; data for U.S. market from Wine Institute, California, *Proposed Excise Tax Surcharge on California Wine*, Stonebridge Research report, January 2009.

[61] l'Association Nationale de Prévention en Alcoologie et Addictologie (ANPAA)

[62] The fine was imposed by the Tribunal de Grand Instance de Paris on December 20, 2008.

[63] Quoted in The Times, London, September 19, 2008.

[64] The advice was apparently based on a claim by INCA, the French national cancer institute, claiming that any consumption of alcohol increases risk of mouth and throat cancer. Other authorities regard this as flawed (Decanter, February 20, 2009).

[65] Tyler Colman, *Wine Politics: How Governments, Environmentalists, Mobsters, and Critics Influence the Wines We Drink* (University of California Press, 2008), p. 57.

[66] www.heineken.fr now gives a message "Le site www.Heineken.fr est momentanément indisponible." Unfortunately, "momentanément" is a euphemism.

[67] Recent government guidelines in Britain recommend, entirely without any evidence, that children under 15 should not be allowed to consume alcohol even at meals with their parents. See www.direct.gov.uk/en/Nl1/Newsroom/DG_174464.

[68] Most countries fit the pattern, although there are some exceptions (Griffith Edwards and Marcus Grant, *Alcoholism: New Knowledge and New Responses*, Croom Helm, London, 1977, p. 25).

[69] This should be better evidence than the correlation between different countries because there are fewer variables. However, there is almost as good a correlation between the drop in alcohol consumption and a drop in accidental poisoning! (WHO Global Status Report on Alcohol, 2004.)

[70] As one measure of the contrast, moderate drinking is considered to be a couple of glasses of wine per day. Statistics show that 14% of alcoholics who drink the equivalent of 2 bottles of wine or half a bottle of spirits every day for 8 years will develop cirrhosis (Robert E. Mann, *The epidemiology of alcoholic liver disease*, Alcohol Research & Health, Fall, 2003).

[71] Roy Porter, *The Creation of the Modern World. The Untold Story of the British Enlightenment*, W. W. Norton, 2001, p. 81.

[72] Raymond Pearl, *Alcohol and Longevity* (Alfred Knopf, New York, 1926).

[73] One weakness in the study is lack of clear definition of the groups, with the moderate group extending from those who took only an occasional drink to those who drank regularly but in small amounts.

[74] Extrapolations from effects on other organisms, such as mice, suggest that people would require 20 mgm of resveratrol per day for any anti-aging effect to become noticeable (but note that such extrapolations are extremely unreliable). There are roughly 160 µg of resveratrol per fluid ounce of red wine. This means that roughly 5 bottles of red wine would be required for the daily dose.

[75] Aside from cirrhosis of the liver, there is increased risk for cancers of the pharynx and esophagus (M. Gronbaek, *The positive and negative health effects of alcohol and the public health implications*, J. Internal Medicine, 265, 407-420, 2009).

[76] Probably a function of the lower average body weight of women.

[77] It's not completely certain, but it seems that premenopause women have increased susceptibility; postmenopause there is no increased risk except for those on estrogen therapy (Gronbaek, op. cit.)

[78] Richard Doll et al., *Mortality in relation to consumption of alcohol: 13 years' observations on male British doctors* (British Medical Journal, 309, 911-918., 1994).

[79] It was first diagnosed in 1973 as a consequence of heavy drinking, defined as more than 4-5 drinks per day.

[80] A review of an international meeting on FAS says in the introduction "Wherever heavy drinking occurs, FAS can be detected," and then moves in its conclusion to the recommendation "no alcohol drinking during pregnancy is safe," without ever explaining the transition from heavy drinking to no alcohol (Edward P. Riley et al., *Prenatal Alcohol Exposure: Advancing Knowledge Through International Collaborations*, Alcohol Clin Exp Res, 27, 118–135, 2003).

[81] A summary of the reason for the new position refers to studies on exposing rat brain to alcohol, the review of a meeting discussing the syndrome (see note 80), and a study of behavioral changes in children whose mothers drank. There were no new data on exposure levels of pregnancy and their effects (Raja A S Mukherjee, *Low level alcohol consumption and the fetus. Abstinence from alcohol is the only safe message in pregnancy*, British Medical Journal, 330, 375–376, 2005).

[82] A typical piece of scare mongering from the BBC (July 19, 2004) reads "A mother drinking while pregnant will not necessarily have a child with FAS, although there is no known safe level of alcohol consumption during pregnancy." A study of 400,000 women in 1997 who consumed less than 8.5 drinks per week did not report any cases of FAS (S. Wilkie, *Global overview of drinking recommendations and guidelines*, AIM Digest (Supplement), June, 1997, 2-4).

[83] Ernest L. Abel, *Fetal Alcohol Syndrome: A Cautionary Note* (Current Pharm. Design, 12, 1521-1528, 2006).

[84] Quoted in Iain Gately, *Drink. A cultural history of alcohol* (Gotham Books, New York, 2008), p. 468.

[85] House of Commons, Public Accounts Committee - Forty-Seventh Report, *Reducing alcohol harm: health services in England for alcohol abuse*, July 2009..

[86] Unfortunately there is a common trend to diagnose a medical problem among chronic alcohol abusers (who are relatively easy to identify) and to commit the error of assuming that a low level of alcohol will be associated with the disease at proportionately reduced frequency. This is not necessarily true. Another example of such a mistaken extrapolation is with osteoporosis (which is clearly associated with alcohol abuse). But advice to post-menopausal women to avoid alcohol could be ill-advised because in fact the response curve may be J-shaped, so that a small amount of consumption could even be beneficial (Karina M. Berg et al., *Association between alcohol consumption and both oesteoporotic fracture and bone density*, Am. J. Med., 121, 406-418, 2008).

Chapter 9: International Wine Trade

[1] Unwin, *Wine and the Vine*, pp. 99, 131.

[2] Gaston Roupnel, Histoire de la campagne française, Éditions Bernard Grasset, Paris, 1932, p. 194

[3] Ibid., p. 231.

[4] The OIV gives a total world consumption of 2.6 billion cases in 2007, of which France accounted for 360 million, Italy for 300 million, the United States for 295 million, Germany for 220 million, China for 145 million, Spain for 140 million, United Kingdom for 135 million, Argentina for 120 million, and Russia for 115 million (6th General Assembly of the OIV, Verone, 2008). Another report suggested that Italy overtook France as the largest consumer in 2007 (source: see note 5).

[5] A report commissioned by Vinexpo from International Wine and Spirit Record in January 2009 projects United States as world's largest consumer by 2012. Total spent by consumers on wine in 2007 was $22 billion, which would make the USA the largest market by value.

[6] Latest figures show beer production at 1.7 billion hl (equivalent to 226 billion 750 ml bottles), wine at 240 million hl (32 billion 750 ml containers), and spirits at 26 billion bottles. Sources: Beer Institute (Washington DC), Brewers Almanac; VinExpo-IWSR (International Wine and Spirit Record, 2009).

[7] $100 billion is a conservative estimate for receipts by producers. Total market value was estimated at $152 billion in the Vinexpo/IWSR study of 2010 (without stating which basis was used). Comparative figures for markets for different forms of alcohol usually use figures nearer $250 billion.

[8] Data sources: Datamonitor, *Drinks: Global Industry Guide*, April 2009; and industry guides for individual countries, March and April 2009. See text for explanation of discrepancies in total wine market value.

[9] Because beer, wine, and spirits have different levels of alcohol, total alcohol consumption is usually expressed in terms of the amount of pure alcohol consumed, assuming beer at 4.6%, wine at 12%, and spirits at 40%.

[10] Germany, 11.99 liters, Britain 11.75 liters, Spain 11.68 liters, France 11.43 liters, Italy 8.02 liters per adult per year (WHO, *World Health Statistics 2008*).

[11] Cases of 12 bottles of 750 ml of wine; cases of 24 bottles of 500 ml of beer.

[12] In fact, there has been a general convergence of wine-drinking patterns in the past half century; a survey of 36 countries shows that wine consumption has declined in many traditional consuming countries and has increased in many traditional beer-drinking countries (Joshua Aizenman and Eileen Brooks, *Globalization and Taste Convergence: the Cases of Wine and Beer*, Review of International Economics, 16, 217–233, 2008).

[13] OIV figures for 2008 report 500,00 ha of vineyards with production of 12 million hl, a level between Argentina and South Africa.

[14] Data sources: France - IREB (Institute de Recherches Scientifiques sur les Boissons), Paris, *Mémento Alcool Edition 2008*; Britain - Institute of Alcohol Studies, London, *Drinking in Great Britain, factsheet 2008*.

[15] OIV State of the vitiviniculture world report, 2007, claims that up to 35 million hl is absorbed in this way.

[16] Data sources: OIV statistical report, 2005; OIV State of the vitiviniculture world report, 2007.

[17] Bottling capacity in the UK has increased sharply, from 130 million bottle equivalents in year 2000, to 240 million in 2006, and to 450 million by 2009 (Wine and Spirits Trade Association, U.K.). Part of the recent increase is due to Constellation's new packaging and bottling plant, with a capacity for 120 million bottles each year (Packaging News, U.K., March 15, 2007).

[18] In 2006 and 2007, the equivalent of approximately 6 million cases of Blossom Hill was shipped from Santa Vittoria, according to Diageo's Corporate Citizenship Report, 2007.

[19] This has a collateral effect in distorting trade figures, since the same wine shows up as imported into Italy from the United States, but also is included in Italy's export figures to Britain. Italy's total reported exports to Britain were 25 million cases in 2007, according to the Global Trade Atlas. The inclusion of Blossom Hill therefore inflates the figure significantly. Italy's total imports of wine are about 20 million cases annually (OIV statistical report, 2005), having increased sharply when Blossom Hill began bottling at Santa Vittoria.

[20] Data sources: OIV statistical report, 2005; OIV State of the vitiviniculture world report, 2007.

[21] In the early nineteenth century, Hungary had 572,000 hectares of vineyards, making it Europe's third largest wine producer (David Copp, *Hungary: its fine wines and winemakers*, András Wiszkidensky, Budapest, 2006, p. 25).

[22] Data for 1880 from George Goudie Chisholm, *Handbook of Commercial Geography* (Longmans, Green & Co., London, 1913), p. 88. Data for 2007 from Euromonitor.

[23] Quoted by Kym Anderson, *Wine's New World* (Foreign Policy, 136, 46-54, 2003), p. 47.

[24] Production figures from the FAOstat database for 1950-85; for subsequent years from OIV annual statistical reports, 1999-2005.

[25] Yield in Europe is usually expressed in terms of wine volume per area as hl/ha. In the New World it is more often expressed in grapes harvested per area, as tonnes/acre. (Very) roughly, 1 hl/ha = 16 tons/acre.

[26] Production figures from OIV (latest available 2006).

[27] Sources. *France*: Gilbert Carrier, *Le Phylloxéra* (Albin Michel, Paris, 1989), p.175; Marcel Lachiver, *Vins, Vignes et Vignerons* (Fayard, Paris, 1988), pp. 616-619; ONIVINS. *California*: U.S. Dept Agriculture, National Agricultural Statistics Service. *Australia*: James Halliday, *Wine Atlas of Australia and New Zealand* (Harper Collins, New York, 1998), p. 26; Australian Bureau of Statistics, Australian Wine and Grape Industry Report #1329.0, 1994-2008. Some figures have been converted from tons/acre to hl/ha, so may be approximate.

[28] OIV World Statistics, 6th General Assembly, Verona 2008.

[29] The most extreme example is that total plantings in Argentina stayed between 200,000 and 220,000 ha from 1990 to 2007, but plantings of quality varietals increased from 20,000 to 80,000 hectares over the period (Argentine Instituto Nacional de Vitivinicultura, Registro de Vinedos y Superficie).

[30] In California, international varieties increased from 15% to 65% of production between 1982 and 2009. In Australia, quality varieties increased from 30% in 1978 to 75% in 2008 (annual statistical report 1329.0 from Australian Bureau of Statistics). In Chile, Cabernet Sauvignon overtook País (an indigenous, low quality, grape) as the principal black variety in 1997.

[31] Total hectares increased from 760,000 in 1990 to 1,200,000 in 2007; quality varietals (defined as in note 32) increased from 100,000 ha to 450,000 ha, that is from 13% to 37%.

[32] The plantings for each country include: Cabernet Sauvignon, Merlot, Pinot Noir, Syrah, Chardonnay, Riesling, Sauvignon Blanc, and Sémillon comprise the vast majority; Cabernet Franc, Mourvèdre, Nebbiolo, Petit Verdot, Sangiovese, and Tempranillo are also included. Data sources: Argentine Instituto Nacional de Vitivinicultura (Registro de Vinedos y Superficie), Australian Bureau of Statistics (Annual Reports 1329.0), California Department of Food and Agriculture, Sacramento (California Grape Acreage Reports), Catastro Viticola Nacional, Chile; SAWIS (South Africa Wine Industry Information and Systems; Statistics of Wine Grapes).

[33] Lewin, *What Price Bordeaux?*, p. 224.

[34] Data source: annual reports of OIV.

[35] Data sources: E.U. report AGRI/EVALUATION/2002/6, and AGRIVIEW, Wine History Survey, 2008.

[36] The major reduction was 216,000 ha in Spain; other reductions were 137,000 ha in Italy, 101,000 ha in France, 37,000 ha in Greece, and 14,000 ha in Portugal. Data source: E.U. commission reports.

[37] Distillation was regarded as an "exceptional" measure until 1982, when it became the main means of regulation (Unwin, *Wine & Vine*, p. 322).

[38] Philip Whalen, *'Insofar as the Ruby Wine Seduces Them': Cultural Strategies for Selling Wine in Inter-war Burgundy* (Contemporary European History, 18, 67-98, Cambridge University Press, Cambridge, 2009), p. 69.

[39] The system has continued unabated ever since the 1930s. From 1935 to the mid 1950s, the average amount of distilled wine was about 65 million cases each year, corresponding to about 10% of production (Charles K. Warner, *The Winegrowers of France and the Government since 1875*, Columbia University Press, New York, 1960, p. 191). Distillation reached a peak in 1961-1962 when one third of all table wine production was distilled (Leo A. Loubère, *The Wine Revolution in France* (Princeton University Press, Princeton, 1990, p. 132).

[40] Proposals adopted by the Council of Ministers in April 2008 (Regulation 479/2008).

[41] Data source: European Commission DG AGRI and AGRIVIEW Wine History Survey. Numbers apply only to table wine. In addition, a small amount of Quality Wine is distilled.

[42] Unwin, *Wine & Vine*, p. 115.

[43] The ostensible reason was that the land was needed to produce grain (Dion, *Histoire de la Vigne*, p. 128).

[44] Ibid., p. 133.

[45] It is disputed whether the trigger was concern about excessive wine production, possible disruption to production of corn, or simple protectionism (Société Académique d'Agen, *Recueil des Travaux*, 1908, pp. 342-344; Alan I. Forrest, *The Revolution in Provincial France: Aquitaine, 1789-1799*, Oxford University Press, Oxford, 1996, p. 125).

[46] Adam, Smith, *An Inquiry into the Nature and Causes of the Wealth of Nations*, 1776, Book 1, Chapter 11, p. 37.

[47] European Union directive EU/NR 40/08, *Adoption of wine reform to balance markets, preserve rural areas and simply rules for producers and consumers*, April 29, 2008.

[48] Details: one small plot of land in the Rutherford area of Napa was sold for $350,000/acre (personal communication) although the quoted top rate is $250,000/acre (Dan Levy, *Slump takes hold of Napa Valley*, International Herald Tribune, March 9, 2010), giving a rate around $700,000/ha; producers in Barolo say that Cannubi sells at about €1 million/ha if available; the top rate for land in Champagne is quoted as €1.1 million/ha in the Valeur Venale; a Médoc Grand Cru Classé sold for €2 million/ha; land in Pomerol is quoted as €2-3 million/hectare; the top rate for Grand Cru Burgundy is quoted as €4 million/ha in the Valeur Venale (and premier cru is quoted as €800,000), but other figures place it as up to €6 million/ha (Business Week, April 23, 2009); and it is reported that a very small parcel of Le Montrachet sold for a rate of $20,000,000/ha (Decanter, November 2009).

[49] Based on grape and land prices in the San Joaquin Valley as reported in a study by Tony Correia, *Valuing Vineyards* (Royal Institution of Chartered Surveyors, New York, 2008).

[50] Overall sales in supermarkets are USA - 25%; Japan - 40%; Italy - 50%; France - 62%; Britain - 80%; Denmark - 80%; Netherlands - 80%; Germany - 82%. The United States is bimodal because individual states regulate whether or not supermarkets can sell wine (it is permitted in 35 states), so the level is high in Florida but zero in New York.

[51] Market share of the top five retailers: more than 75%, Norway, Sweden, Finland, Denmark; 60-75%, Belgium, Poland, Switzerland; 50-60%, Germany, France, Austria, Britain, Netherlands, Spain.

[52] The proposal failed. Large distributors, such as Diageo, campaigned furiously against it, although not openly (their efforts were channeled under the guise of protecting small stores).

[53] Quoted in Long Island Business News, February 5, 2009.

[54] Women purchase more wine than men, a significant part in the context of the weekly household shopping at supermarkets (Wine Intelligence Seminar, March 2006).

[55] Data source: A. C. Nielsen.

[56] Quoted in Simon Bowers, *Wine world soured as half-price offers are labelled misleading*, The Guardian (U.K.), August 14, 2006.

[57] Bowers, *Wine world*, op. cit.

[58] Roughly 60% of wine is sold below the £3.99 price point in Britain.

[59] Tim Atkin, *Super Mark-Ups*, The Observer, October 5, 2003.

[60] According to the 2007 annual report, Constellation Wines had $3.8 billion of sales, comprising $2.7 billion of branded wine and $1.1 billion of other wine sales.

[61] Since Constellation's figures refer to retail sales, the best total for comparison is probably the $220-250 billion range for total value of all sales worldwide.

[62] Coca Cola has annual sales of $32 billion (and accounts for 50% of cola sales), beer company Annheuser-Busch has annual sales of $22 billion, and the largest spirits company, Diageo, has sales of $16 billion (which includes some wine) (Forbes Global 2000 report, March 2009).

[63] The three largest wine companies probably have wine sales of around $7 billion. For other sectors see: coffee (Jelle Bruinsma, *World agriculture: towards 2015/2030*, Food and Agriculture Organization of the United Nations, 2005, p. 277; coffee and chocolate (Jagjit Plahe, *The global commodity chain (GCC) approach and the organizational transformation of agriculture*, working paper 63/05, Monash University Department of Management, 2005); beer (Peter Swinburn, *Global beer brewing industry and the Coors Molson merger*, Global Executive Forum, University of Colorado, 2005).

[64] Data from annual reports for 2008 for public companies; private companies estimated from public information (for Gallo see Chapter 11).

[65] Joel B. Payne, *Pernod-Ricard's Wine Empire* (Wine Business International, January, 2006).

[66] Annual cash turnover in 2000 according to Kym Anderson, *The World's Wine Markets: Globalization at Work* (Edward Elgar Pub, 2005), p.67; see also Raúl Green et al., *Global market changes and business behavior in the wine sector* (LORIA (Laboratoire d'Organisation Industrielle Agro-alimentaire, INRA), cahier 2003-02, 2003). For current data see note 74.

All figures are adjusted to show cash turnover from wine only, excluding beer and spirits, when information is available.

[67] The largest acquisitions were BRL Hardy in 2003 for $1.4 billion, Robert Mondavi in 2004 for $1.03 billion, Vincor in 2006 for $1.3 billion, and Beam Estates in 2007 for $885 million.

[68] See Pinney, *A History of Wine*, p. 256.

[69] The brand name is in fact licensed from R.A.B. Foods, which markets several brands of kosher food including Manischewitz matzo. The wine is sweetened with fructose from corn syrup, except for a special Passover bottling which is sweetened with cane sugar.

[70] At an annual rate of increase of 2.6% according to *Wine: Global Industry Almanac* (Datamonitor, May 2009).

[71] Lewin, *What Price Bordeaux?*, p. 107.

[72] Actual production volumes (millions of cases per year) are:

Country	Company	Company Production	Country Total
South Africa	Distell	41.0	92
Chile	Concho y Toro	26.6	92
United States	Gallo	67.0	260
New Zealand	Montana	3.5	16
Argentina	Peñaflor	26.9	155
Australia	Constellation	17.5	136
Spain	Garcia Carrion	30.0	377
France	Castel Frères	37.5	560
Italy	Riunite	20.8	545

[73] Share is measured by volume. Sources: Wine Business Monthly, Top 30 Report, February 2009; New Zealand Wine Industry, PriceWaterhouseCoopers report, 2007; Australia Bureau of Statistics reported by winebiz.com.au; Jane Anson, *The Place de Bordeaux* (Wine Business International, February, 2007); Castel Freres company web site; Michéle Shah, *Up by the boot hell. Doing the Italian job* (Wine Business, January, 2007); Gary Greenfield, managing director, Distell Europe, Just-drinks.com, November 27, 2006; Chile, Concho y Toro company web site; Argentina, Peñaflor company web site; personal communication from Food and Wines from Spain, Spanish Embassy, London, November 2009. For actual production levels see note 72.

[74] Discrepancies between the top-3 and top-5 shares shown in this table and those for the top companies in the previous chart are probably due to differences in measuring market share by volume versus value and to whether only table wine is included. There are also difficulties in obtaining accurate data when the companies are privately held. Where possible, share is calculated by volume. For Australia, there was a large drop in market share of the leading companies in 2009; Fosters market share by value was 28.5% in 2005 but 21.2% in 2009, while Constellation (Australia) moved from 22% to 13.5% (Nigel Austin, *Wine families strike back*, Herald Sun, Melbourne, December 8, 2009). Producer number refers to the number of wineries that make wine; the number of growers is usually larger. Data sources: Rabobank Global Focus, *Australian wine – the easiest growth comes first*, winter 2007; Victor de la Serna, *Spanish eyes seeing red* (Wine Business International, March, 2007); Argentine Instituto Nacional de Vitivinicultura (Registro de Vinedos y Superficie); Australian Bureau of Statistics (Annual Reports 1329.0); California Department of Food and Agriculture, Sacramento (California Grape Acreage Reports); *The Top 30 U.S. Wine Company profiles,* Wine Business Monthly, February 2008; Catastro Viticola Nacional, Chile; SAWIS (South Africa Wine Industry Information and Systems; Statistics of Wine Grapes).

[75] According to the Wine Institute (an association of Californian producers) only 17% of its members currently had complete national distribution as of 2005.

[76] In 2008 there were 2,843 bonded wineries in California and 6,368 in the United States as a whole according to the Wine Institute.

⁷⁷ Thomas Pinney, *A History of Wine in America : From Prohibition to the Present*, p. 347.

⁷⁸ Costco is a buying club, with an annual membership fee of $50. It offers a relatively small selection of wines (fewer than 150 different wines in each store compared with 1000 or more at a typical supermarket), but the wines change frequently, are different in each store, and pricing is very keen, driven by a maximum markup of 14% above wholesale. Wine sales in 2007 were $800 million. Sources: Kevin McCallum, *Costco: The high quality, mass market retailer*, Wine Business International, October 20, 2007; The Wine Economist, November 7, 2009.

⁷⁹ John R. Emshwiller & Alix M. Freedman, *Early Relationships Help Shape Southern Wine & Spirits' Image* (Wall Street Journal, October 4, 1999).

⁸⁰ Alix M. Freedman & John R. Emshwiller, *Vintage System: Big Liquor Wholesaler Finds Change Stalking Its Very Private World --- Southern Wine & Spirits Is A Mandated Middleman Under Increasing Attack --- A Vineyard Breaks the Mold* (Wall Street Journal, October 4, 1999).

⁸¹ Tyler Colman, *Wine Politics: How Governments, Environmentalists, Mobsters, and Critics Influence the Wines We Drink* (University of California Press, 2008), p. 97.

⁸² The case was Granholm versus Heald. Technically it argued that it was unconstitutional for a state to ban shipment to consumers from wineries out of state if it allowed shipment from wineries within the state. The 5-4 decision on May 16, 2005 agreed that this was an unconstitutional protection of the in-state wineries. This left states the option of allowing all shipments or banning all shipments; as a practical matter, banning shipments within the state would often simply kill the local industry.

⁸³ Freedman & Emshwiller, *Vintage System*, op. cit.

⁸⁴ Freedman & Emshwiller, *Vintage System*, op. cit.

⁸⁵ Business Wire on line, January 26, 2010.

⁸⁶ It's really quite remarkable that in the context of an overall worldwide surplus of 450 million cases annually, Australia was able to double its production since 1995 to its present level of 130 million cases without running into trouble sooner. But supply has now really outrun demand, and probably close to 20% of the vineyards are uneconomic.

⁸⁷ This was seen at its most dramatic in the high end of the New York wine auctions, where prices collapsed by more than 50% in matter of a few weeks during November 2008.

Chapter 10: Fraud

¹ Thomas Pellechia, *Wine. The 8000 year old story of the wine trade* (Running Press, Philadelphia, 2006), p. 30.

² Ibid., p. 35.

³ Pliny XXIII.1.

⁴ Andrew Dalby, *Empire of pleasures: luxury and indulgence in the Roman world* (Routledge, London, 2000), p. 49.

⁵ Hugh Johnson, *The Story of Wine* (Mitchell Beazley, London, 2005), p. 36.

⁶ Lynn Thorndike, *A history of magic and experimental science*, Columbia University Press, New York, 1923, p. 132.

⁷ Bee Wilson, *Swindled: the dark history of food fraud, from poisoned candy to counterfeit coffee*, Princeton University Press, 2008, p. 57.

⁸ Fielden, *Is This the Wine You Ordered, Sir*, p. 169.

⁹ Lewin, *What Price Bordeaux?*, p. 211.

¹⁰ Jean-Alexandre Cavoleau, *Oenologie Française, ou statistique de tous les vignobles et de toutes les boissons vineuses et spiritueuses de la France, suivie de considérations générales sur la culture de la vigne* (Huzard, Paris, 1827).

¹¹ Cyrus Redding, *A History and Description of Modern Wines* (Henry Bohn, London, 1833).

¹² James M. Gabler, *Passions: The Wines and Travels of Thomas Jefferson* (Bacchus Press, Lutherville, Maryland, 1995), p. 133.

¹³ René Pijassou, *Le Médoc: Un Grand Vignoble De Qualité. Tomes I & II*, Tallandier, Paris, 1978, p. 845.

[14] Josef Eisinger, *Lead and Wine. Eberhard Gockel and the Colica Pictonum* (Medical History, 26, 279-302, 1982).

[15] Ibid., p. 288.

[16] S. C. Gilfillan, *Lead poisoning and the fall of Rome*, J. Occup. Med., 7, 53-60, 1965.

[17] Christian Warren, *Brush with death: a social history of lead poisoning*, Johns Hopkins University Press, Baltimore, 2001, p. 23.

[18] Ibid.

[19] Eisinger, *Lead and Wine*, op. cit., p. 295.

[20] Ibid., p. 298

[21] Warren, *Brush with death*, op. cit., p.24.

[22] David Hunter, *Handel's Ill Health: Documents and Diagnoses*, RMA Research Chronicle, 41, 69, 2008.

[23] Maynard Amerine, Composition of Wines II Inorganic Constituents, In Advances in Food Research, Emil Mark, Mrak (Ed.), John Wiley, New York, 1958, p. 191.

[24] Study by the U.S. Bureau of Alcohol, Tobacco, and Firearms.

[25] J. H. Graziano & C. Blum, *Lead exposure from lead crystal* (Lancet, 337, 141-2, 1991); E. Guadagnino et al., *Estimation of lead intake from crystalware under conditions of consumer use*, (Food Addit. Contam., 17, 205-218, 2000).

[26] Fielden, *Is This the Wine You Ordered, Sir*, p. 67.

[27] Arm. Gautier, *On the Fraudulent Coloration of Wines*, J. Chem. Soc., 30, 426-446, 1876.

[28] Quoted in Fielden, *Is This the Wine You Ordered, Sir?*, p. 101.

[29] Ibid., p. 97.

[30] Iver Peterson, *Plea of Not Guilty in Tainted-Drink Death*, New York Times, July 13, 2004.

[31] Fielden, *Is This the Wine You Ordered, Sir?*, p. 86.

[32] Fritz Hallgarten, *Wine Scandal*, p. 29.

[33] Fielden, *Is This the Wine You Ordered, Sir?*, p. 87.

[34] Total production in Austria in 1984 was a bit over 2 million hectoliters, or 250 million bottles. 15 million liters (20 million bottles) were stated to have been confiscated by August 10. Ibid., p. 89.

[35] Data source: Austrian Wine Marketing Board, *Austrian Wine*, December 2008 edition.

[36] Fielden, *Is This the Wine You Ordered, Sir?*, p. 84.

[37] Roberto Suro, *Italy acting to end sale of methanol-tainted wine*, New York Times, April 9, 1986.

[38] In the *Encyclopédie, ou dictionnaire raisonné des sciences, des arts et des métiers*, published in France between 1751 and 1772, article by Chevalier Louis de Jaucourt. See Jean-François Gautier, *Le Vin Et Ses Fraudes* (Presses Universitaires De France, 1995), p. 14.

[39] Based on calculations of the gap between wine consumption minus production plus imports, first made by Armand Gautier, *La sophistication des vins: méthodes analytiques et procédés pour reconnaitre les fraudes* (Baillière, 1898), p. 3.

[40] Alessandro Stanziani, *La Falsification Du Vin En France, 1880-1905: Un Cas De Fraude Agro-Aliminetaire* (Revue d'Histoire Moderne et Contemporaine, v. 50, 2003), p. 154.

[41] See note 35 in Chapter 5.

[42] Fritz Hallgarten, *Wine Scandal*, p. 68.

[43] According to the chief prosecutor, 6,270 tons of liquid sugar were used in the Pfalz, 4,070 tons in the Mosel, 1,150 in Rheinhessen, and 550 in the Nahe over a three year period (Ibid). Annual production in these regions totaled about 5 million hl, making the usage of sugar close to 1 ton/thousand hl/year. One ton of sugar will convert 300 hl of table wine to the high grade of Auslese, so this "improvement" of quality may have affected a major part of production.

[44] Fielden, *Is This the Wine You Ordered, Sir?*, p. 78.

[45] P. E. Schneider, *France's wine casks are in the red* (New York Times magazine, December 8, 1957).

[46] Decanter on line, December 13, 2007 and March 18, 2009; see www.decanter.com/news/169103.html; www.decanter.com/news/news.php?id=278929.

[47] Fielden, *Is This the Wine You Ordered, Sir?*, p. 72.
[48] Ibid., p. 47.
[49] Hallgarten, *Wine Scandal*, pp. 176-177.
[50] Fielden, *Is This the Wine You Ordered, Sir?*, p. 46.
[51] Ibid., pp. 49-51.
[52] Oliver Styles, Vin de Pays d'Oc in massive US fraud scandal. Decanter online, February 9, 2009.
[53] The case came to court in January 2010 (*Carcassonne. Faux pinot : prison et amendes*, La Depeche, January 26, 2010).
[54] Decanter online, February 18, 2010.
[55] The wine merchant Ducasse, who sold the wine to Sieur d'Arques was purchasing wine for €58 /hl compared with the price of Pinot Noir at €97/hl. The difference on 110,000 hl (1.3 million cases) would be several million euros per year. It was stated in court that overall the illicit profits amounted to €7 million, with Ducasse taking €3.7 million and Sieur d'Arques making €1.3 million (Rory Mulholland and Suzanne Mustacich, French plonk scam spreads to world's top wine group, AFP News, February 18, 2010).
[56] Institut National des Appellations d'Origine.
[57] Le Figaro, May 23, 1973, p. 4.
[58] Bert, *In Vino Veritas*, p. 128.
[59] Faith, *The Winemasters*, p. 266.
[60] Hallgarten, *Wine Scandal*, p. 141.
[61] Ibid., p. 134.
[62] Benjamin Wallace, *The Billionaire's Vinegar* (Crown Publishing, New York, 2008).
[63] Patrick Keefe, *The Jefferson Bottles*. New Yorker, September 3, 2007.

Index

1959 vintage, 334
1973 vintage, 195
1978 vintage, 107
1982 vintage, 196
1985 vintage, 318
1996 vintage, 198
1997 vintage, 122
1999 vintage, 135, 198
2000 vintage, 198
2001 vintage, 198
2002 vintage, 491
2003 vintage, 122, 466
2005 vintage, 348, 349, 374
2006 vintage, 348
2007 vintage, 71, 348
2008 vintage, 197
Abadia Retuerta, 92, 469, 470
Accad, Guy, 107
acetaldehyde, 112, 517
acetic acid, 93, 95, 112, 120, 122, 534
Acetobacter, 93, 104
acetone, 334
acid whip, 119
acidification, 29, 122
acidity, 12, 24, 28, 29, 30, 45, 50, 77, 81, 82, 83, 87, 89, 96, 99, 101, 109, 113, 115, 116, 121- 122, 123, 153, 162, 163, 164, 169, 170, 172, 173, 174, 175, 178, 179, 196, 234, 243, 260, 273, 275, 326, 327, 329, 361, 371, 372, 395, 396, 398, 399, 402, 409, 427, 438, 444, 447, 458, 461, 465, 473, 478, 479, 484, 490, 501, 508, 532, 539, 543, 545, 546
Aconcagua, 330, 331, 332
acquit, 249, 250
Adelaide, 62, 63, 192, 297, 300, 303, 304, 306, 307
adjustments, 25, 49, 61, 492, 521
adulteration, 239, 241, 242, 250, 506, 525
Aglianico, 420, 421, 448
agrément, 393, 401
Ahr, 163, 483
Airén, 143, 144, 452, 453
alambic, 65
Albariño, 174, 453, 473
albariza, 64, 519
Albillo, 467
albumin, 103, 105
Alcan, 140
alcohol, 28, 29, 30, 31, 49, 81, 82, 83, 84, 87, 89, 93, 95, 96, 97, 98, 99, 100, 102, 106, 112, 113, 115, 116-121, 122, 123, 128, 141, 151, 156, 162, 164, 167, 169, 170, 173, 178, 182, 190, 194, 196, 202, 204, 205, 206, 207, 208, 209, 210, 211, 214, 215, 217, 223, 226, 236, 243, 244, 246, 247, 260, 261, 262, 263, 273, 274, 283, 285, 288, 292, 293, 300, 306, 307, 311, 320, 327, 371, 372, 375, 386, 394, 397, 398, 402, 409, 427, 445, 449, 451, 452, 461, 476, 479, 490, 491, 492, 496, 499, 501, 506, 513, 517, 526, 531, 536, 540, 542, 546
Alentejo, 472
Alicante, 261, 269, 277, 457
Alicante Bouschet, 124
Aligoté, 361, 362
Alion, 468
Allegrini, 450
allergen, 111, 112
Allobroges, 69, 360
almacenista, 521, 522
Almaden, 231
Almaviva, 332
Aloxe Corton, 364
Alsace, 112, 148, 163, 172-175, 181, 189, 308, 387, 388, 390, 393, 395, 399-405 414, 476, 486, 534, 536
Altare, Elio, 425, 426
Altentejo, 451
Altesino, 434, 438, 537
Alvarinho, 473
Amarone, 444, 445
Amerine, Maynard, 258
amontillado, 516, 517, 518, 522
Amorim, 134, 136
AMPAA, 207, 208
ampelography, 16, 329
amphora, 1, 6, 69, 87, 185, 204, 239, 447, 448
Ampuis, 408
anaerobic, 128, 189
Anbaugebiete, 477, 483, 487
Andalucia, 451, 460
androstenone, 151
Aniane, 193, 416
Anschluss, 489
Ansonica, 420
anthocyanin, 108, 147, 165, 243, 326
antifreeze, 244, 245, 487, 489
antimicrobial agents, 111, 182
Antinori, 441
anti-oxidant, 111, 210
AOC, 46, 52, 53, 66, 98, 99, 187, 220, 222, 249, 250, 251, 341, 342, 343, 351, 352, 353, 358, 363, 364, 365, 367, 368, 370, 371, 373, 374, 382, 385, 387, 388, 389-395, 397, 399, 400, 401, 403, 405, 406, 409, 414, 415, 416, 417, 418, 503, 504, 533

Appassimento, 445
Aquitaine, 232, 345
Aramon, 124, 414, 415
Archaval-Ferrer, 325
Ardèche, 148
Argentina, 18, 161, 162, 177, 218, 219, 234, 255, 256, 260, 321, 322-327, 328
Armagnac, 397
Arneis, 427
Arsac, 353
Ashenfelter, Orley, 72
asparagus, 155, 161, 171, 498
assemblage, 67, 369, 405
Assenlogi, 449
Asti Spumante, 178, 422
astringency, 105, 106, 119, 153, 334, 414, 424, 426, 473
astrology, 38
Aszú, 540, 541, 542, 543
Atkin, Tim, 228
Auckland, 316, 318
Aude, 248
Ausbruch, 490
Auslese, 172, 476, 478, 481, 482, 490
Ausone, Château, 44, 352, 375
Australia, 8, 13, 18, 27, 33, 47, 49, 50, 51, 60, 62, 76, 80, 82, 105, 117, 121, 122, 123, 126, 129, 137, 138, 140, 146, 150, 161, 162, 164, 166, 167, 168, 172, 173, 174, 175, 177, 188, 189, 191, 192, 201, 202, 208, 214, 215, 217, 218, 219, 220, 228, 229, 230, 231, 232, 234, 238, 255, 256, 272, 275, 283, 295-315, 318, 320, 321, 322, 323, 325, 328, 370, 388, 408, 409, 412, 418, 535, 547, 549
Austria, 46, 112, 114, 173, 175, 205, 244, 245, 246, 475, 487-498, 534, 540, 547
autovinification, 528
AVAs, 263-266, 268, 276, 285, 291, 292
AWRI, 138, 139, 140, 192, 549
Bacchus, bricks of, 262
back-blending, 124, 126
Baden, 163, 483, 484
baga, 473, 525
bag-in-box, 87, 203, 217, 226, 231
Baixo corgo, 523
banana, 94, 101
Banfi, 128, 434, 435
Banyuls, 538
Barbaresco, 149, 421, 422, 423, 424, 427, 428, 430, 447, 548
Barbera, 270, 420, 422, 427, 430
Barca Velha, 473, 474
Barcelona, 455
barnyard, 97, 425
Barolo, 19, 67, 146, 149, 198, 225, 337, 421-430, 450, 462, 547, 548
Baron de Oña, 463

Barossa, 63, 150, 161, 162, 188, 255, 256, 301, 303, 304, 305, 306, 307, 308, 315
Barraida, 473
barrels, 87, 89, 97, 99, 100, 102, 103, 106, 110, 111, 114, 115, 116, 129-133, 155, 166, 170, 172, 189, 194, 298, 311, 347, 359, 365, 417, 463, 468, 506, 514, 515, 516, 517, 521, 534, 545, 546
barrique, 130, 132, 170, 425, 426, 428, 434, 438, 439, 443, 447
Barsac, 532, 533, 534
Bartles & Jaymes, 288
Bas Médoc, 353
basalt, 54
Basilicata, 448
Batàr, 447
Bâtard Montrachet, 51, 447
BATF, 263, 264
battonage, 102
Beaucastel, Château, 97, 409, 411
Beaujolais, 80, 98, 101, 157, 246, 247, 249, 250, 361, 362, 363, 375, 384-386, 387, 388, 405, 445, 473
Beaulieu, 8, 135, 278, 281
Beaumes de Venise, 177, 410, 538
Beaune, 53, 79, 122, 163, 320, 360, 362, 363, 364, 365, 384
Beckstoffer, Andy, 274, 281
beer, 4, 140, 191, 202, 204, 208, 209, 213, 215, 228, 229, 237, 246, 262, 452, 532
Beerenauslese, 112, 175, 476, 482, 490, 536, 539
Beiras, 472
Benedictine, 490
beneficio, 529
bentonite, 49, 102
benzene-methanethiol, 50
Bereich, 477, 479
Bergerac, 533
Beringer, 230, 233, 265, 278, 535
Bernkastel, 79, 477, 478, 485
Bernkasteler Doctor, 15, 48, 477, 478, 479
Bernkasteler Kurfürstlay, 477, 479
Berry Bros, 371
Bert, Pierre, 248, 249, 250, 251, 547
Berthomeau, Jacques, 313, 418
Bettane, Michel, 200, 392
Beyer, Leon, 404
Bienaymé, Madame, 313
bilan hydrique, 44
biodynamic viticulture, 35, 36, 37, 38, 398, 496, 546
Biondi-Santi, 431, 432, 438
bisulphide, 10
bitter, 105, 106, 132, 150, 151, 152, 153, 175, 409, 424, 448
bitterness, 29, 105, 129, 151, 152, 153, 178, 334

Index

BIVB, 361, 549
black grapes, 30, 45, 108, 110, 118, 146, 165, 176, 189, 248, 278, 286, 299, 307, 323, 334, 337, 342, 360, 384, 410, 421, 448, 453, 454, 461, 483, 484, 500
blackcurrant, 150, 159, 160, 161
Blanchots, 382
Blanquette de Limoux, 506
Blauer Portugieser, 498
Blaufränkisch, 491, 498
blending, 30, 63, 64, 67, 73, 74, 110, 122, 124, 126, 206, 239, 240, 241, 245, 249, 269, 301, 302, 307, 339, 367, 390, 399, 405, 407, 409, 427, 430, 433, 434, 435, 438, 439, 440, 454, 460, 461, 462, 467, 499, 502, 509, 510, 513
Blossom Hill, 202, 218, 231
blush wine, 110
Bobal, 453, 454
Bodenstein, Toni, 492, 493, 494
bogof, 227
Boissenot, 194
Bolgheri, 96, 428, 431, 437, 440, 441, 442, 443
Bollinger, 15, 509, 512
Bombino, 445
Bommes, 533
Bonarda, 323, 422
Bonnes Mares, 248
boom and bust, 238, 295, 322, 348, 514, 520
bootleggers, 261, 262
Bordeaux, 6, 9, 13, 16, 17, 19, 20, 26, 27, 35, 41, 43, 44, 45, 52, 53, 55, 56, 62, 63, 67, 70, 71, 72, 74, 75, 76, 79, 81, 82, 83, 84, 100, 104, 105, 118, 122, 130, 131, 135, 145, 146, 149, 150, 157, 158, 159, 160, 161, 162, 169, 171, 188, 190, 191, 192, 193, 194, 195, 196, 197, 198, 222, 224, 225, 232, 240, 241, 248, 249, 250, 251, 252, 255, 257, 259, 266, 267, 273, 274, 275, 277, 279, 281, 283, 284, 291, 293, 294, 295, 296, 301, 307, 309, 310, 315, 320, 321, 323, 327, 328, 329, 331, 332, 336, 337, 339-360, 368, 369-379, 380, 381, 382, 384, 387, 388, 390, 391, 392, 393, 394, 399, 407, 416, 417, 418, 422, 423, 426, 440, 441, 442, 443, 444, 449, 456, 457, 467, 468, 471, 473, 476, 482, 486, 487, 532, 534, 536, 547, 548, 549
Bordeaux, blend, 157, 198, 310, 320, 329, 336, 343, 416, 440, 443, 449
Bordeaux, left bank, 44, 80, 157, 159, 160, 341, 342, 343, 344, 345, 346, 350, 353, 354, 357, 359, 375, 384, 532, 533
Bordeaux, right bank, 9, 44, 62, 63, 80, 157, 159, 160, 194, 341, 342, 343, 344, 345, 346, 350, 358, 359, 375, 384, 417, 443
Bordeaux, Supérieur, 371, 374, 394
botrytis, 64, 112, 156, 157, 170, 175, 398, 402, 448, 476, 489, 490, 491, 492, 499, 532-537, 539, 540, 541, 542, 543
botti, 424, 425, 426, 438, 439, 448
bottling, 36, 73, 111, 123, 137, 138, 202, 218, 247, 258, 263, 265, 284, 340, 347, 367, 369, 397, 411, 412, 427, 428, 432, 457, 473, 487, 494, 496, 501, 506, 507, 515, 520, 521, 526, 527, 528, 542
Bouchard, 367
Bourgogne, AOC, 42, 360, 361, 362, 363, 364, 367, 368, 369, 373, 396, 549
Bourgogne, Passe-Tout-Grains, 361
Bourgueil, 399
Bourguignon, Claude, 37
Boursiquot, Jean-Michel, 329
Bouzy, 93
Brand Australia, 201, 301, 312, 313
brands, 73, 123, 189, 201, 216, 229, 230, 235, 236, 265, 301, 302, 312, 313, 314, 318, 340, 349, 355, 358, 369, 404, 441, 487
Brettanomyces, 50, 97, 125, 162, 319
Brix, 28, 29, 30, 82, 118, 119, 168, 243, 540
Broadbent, Michael, 132, 251
Brunello di Montalcino, 146, 149, 337, 421, 431-436, 442, 444, 450
Brunellopoli, 435
bubblegum, 94, 101
Burgenland, 488, 489, 490, 497, 498
Burgundy, 6, 8, 13, 17, 19, 20, 42, 46, 51, 52, 53, 59, 67, 74, 76, 77, 79, 80, 81, 97, 100, 107, 114, 122, 145, 148, 149, 163, 165, 167, 168, 188, 190, 192, 193, 224, 225, 240, 247, 248, 255, 258, 266, 267, 286, 288, 294, 307, 310, 315, 317, 320, 337, 339-340, 360-369, 373, 374, 380-384, 387, 388, 390, 391, 397, 399, 405, 407, 417, 418, 425, 430, 454, 465, 475, 480, 482, 483, 487, 492, 496, 498, 500, 501, 510, 547
butterscotch, 130
cabbage, 127
Cabernet Franc, 14, 110, 146, 157, 158, 160, 182, 281, 334, 342, 343, 344, 396, 399, 440, 441, 443
Cabernet Sauvignon, 3, 14, 17, 19, 20, 44, 47, 53, 55, 56, 62, 63, 71, 72, 76, 79, 83, 105, 106, 107, 139, 143, 144, 145, 146, 148, 149, 150, 154, 155, 156, 157-161, 162, 171, 182, 198, 255, 256, 259, 265, 267, 269, 273, 279, 281, 282, 284, 285, 286, 297, 299, 306, 307, 308, 309, 315, 320, 321, 323, 325, 326, 327, 328, 329, 331, 334, 337, 342, 343, 344, 359, 387,

399, 414, 415, 416, 418, 420, 421, 426, 428, 431, 435, 438, 440, 441, 442, 443, 454, 456, 461, 465, 467, 469, 471
Cabernet-Shiraz, 308
Cadillac, 532
Cafayate, 327
Cahors, 240, 323
Calabria, 448, 449
calcium 44, 49, 122
California, 8, 13-14, 17, 50, 82, 84, 105, 110, 118, 119, 120, 124, 125, 126, 150, 161, 163, 164, 165, 167, 168, 177, 196, 197, 217, 218, 220, 226, 231, 236, 257-292, 293, 300, 312, 320, 321, 322, 327, 371, 409, 449, 535
Campania, 448
Canada, 18, 231, 235, 292, 294, 540
Canaiolo, 437, 438
Canandaigua, 231
Cannonau, 421, 448
Cannubi, 225
Canon, Château, 135
canopy management, 61
Cantábrica, 456, 458, 460
Cap Classique, 335
Cape Blend, 335
Cape Mentelle, 318
Cape Riesling, 334
Capus, Joseph, 52
carbonic maceration, 100-101, 156, 157, 414, 456
Carignan, 110, 143, 144, 146, 261, 269, 410, 414, 415, 460, 471
Carmenère, 16, 157, 158, 256, 321, 328, 329
Carneros, 164, 167, 276
Carthage, 240
Casa Lapostolle, 332
Casella Wines, 302, 311, 313, 314
Castelão Frances, 473
Castiglione Falletto, 423
Castile-Léon, 454
Castilla-La Mancha, 454
Catarratto, 420, 421, 448
Catawba, 259
Cathiard, Daniel, 379
Caucuses (Georgia), 21, 447
Cava, 455, 508, 513
Cazes, Jean-Michel, 27
Cazetiers, Gevrey Chambertin, 53
Central Otago, 163, 164, 316, 318, 320
Central Valley, 80, 125, 264, 265, 269, 273, 286-290
cépage, 45, 51, 59, 63, 79, 144, 149, 166, 198, 343, 356, 369, 390, 394, 405, 414, 415, 461
Cepparello, 442, 450
Ceretto, 425

Chablis, 47, 48, 67, 123, 150, 166, 167, 258, 316, 361, 362, 363, 399, 503
Chalone, 135
Chalonnaise, 362, 363
Chambertin, 53, 248, 363, 368, 381, 382
Chambolle Musigny, 248, 364, 368, 384
Champagne, 7, 15, 18, 19, 64, 66, 73, 74, 75, 110, 123, 135, 140, 163, 189, 190, 207, 234, 243, 248, 335, 337, 370, 387, 388, 390, 398, 401, 418, 500-513, 548, 549
Champagne, brut, 501
Champagne, extra-brut, 509
Chaptal, Jean-Antoine, 87, 97
chaptalization, 82, 97-99, 115, 117, 122, 124, 141, 173, 246, 247, 315, 394, 403, 475, 490, 536, 545, 546
Chardonnay, 3, 19, 29, 46, 50, 59, 82, 94, 99, 100, 135, 143, 144, 145, 146, 148, 149, 150, 164, 166-168, 176, 180, 182, 193, 255, 268, 269, 270, 273, 279, 286, 291, 292, 293, 297, 299, 300, 301, 308, 309, 310, 319, 320, 321, 323, 325, 326, 328, 331, 333, 337, 339, 360, 361, 362, 363, 399, 414, 416, 420, 421, 446, 447, 449, 461, 497, 498, 500, 501, 502, 509
Charente, 158
Charlemagne, 6, 185, 242, 490, 496
Chartronnais, 346
Chassagne Montrachet, 167, 364, 382
Chasselas, 177, 398
château bottling, 340, 347, 348
Château Grillet, 390, 406, 407, 409
Château Margaux, 17, 27, 132, 195
Chatonnet, Pascal, 135
Chave, Jean-Louis, 407
Chenin Blanc, 19, 146, 193, 258, 270, 321, 333, 334, 336, 387, 396, 397, 398, 534
Cheval Blanc, Château, 44, 352, 375
Chevalier Montrachet, 51
Chianti Rufina, 436
Chile, 13, 16, 18, 161, 162, 164, 168, 201, 219, 232, 234, 235, 255, 256, 260, 321, 322, 323, 325, 327-332, 548
Chinon, 395, 399
Chiroubles, 386
chloroanisoles, 135
chlorophenols, 134
chlorophyll, 23
chlorosis, 12, 45
Christies, 190, 251, 298, 486
Ciliegiolo, 148
Cima corgo, 523
cinnamate, 156
Cinsault, 110, 322, 334, 410, 411, 414, 415
Cistercian, 6, 366, 483, 490
Citronellol, 175
CIVB, 135, 370, 549

Cladosporium, 541
claret, 190, 209, 257, 258, 261, 307, 308, 375, 407
classed growths, 355, 370, 377
classification, 52, 64, 67, 123, 185, 190, 246, 247, 309, 315, 341, 350, 351, 352, 353-355, 374, 375-384, 389, 392, 393, 394, 402, 403, 427, 430, 434, 441, 450, 469, 475, 480, 489, 490, 491, 496, 498, 503, 504, 517, 529, 539, 541
classification, *the 1855*, 56, 315, 339, 349-352, 351, 352, 376, 377, 378, 379, 382, 417
clay, 12, 44, 46, 49, 51, 56, 57, 65, 102, 342, 361, 409, 433, 441, 503, 532
Clerico, Domenico, 425
climate, 16, 19, 20, 21, 24, 39, 47, 54, 61, 64, 67, 72, 74-85, 118, 121, 122, 123, 143, 163, 164, 166, 169, 170, 172, 174, 183, 231, 275, 276, 290, 293, 294, 300, 301, 303, 304, 306, 307, 308, 309, 310, 316, 317, 319, 320, 325, 326, 327, 330, 336, 371, 387, 396, 399, 400, 405, 409, 413, 414, 415, 416, 418, 421, 433, 440, 444, 445, 452, 455, 458, 466, 471, 475, 481, 487, 491, 493, 498, 501, 513, 518, 528, 535, 541
clones, 16-17, 20, 148, 161, 164, 166, 168, 180, 181, 183, 274, 311, 315, 319, 361, 409, 421, 423, 432, 434, 436, 438, 454, 494
Clos Apalta, 331, 332
Clos du Marquis, 356, 377
Clos St. Hune, 404
Clos Vougeot, 6, 30, 51, 59, 366, 368, 382, 510
Cockburn, 527
Codorníu, 465, 508
Colchagua, 331, 332
cold stabilization, 103, 122
Colheita, 527
Colombard, 193, 258, 269, 270
Colorino, 437, 438
Columella, 1, 5, 30, 164, 193, 241, 242
complantation, 405, 524
concentrator, 117
Concha y Toro, 232, 328, 331, 332
Concord, 11, 232, 259, 270, 271, 292, 293
Condrieu, 406, 407, 409
conglomerates, 125, 230, 232, 282, 283, 531
Consejo Regulador, 455, 459, 519, 521
Constantia, 336
Constellation, 125, 126, 227, 228, 229, 230, 231, 232, 282, 292, 313, 318, 441
Conterno, Giacomo, 425, 426
Contino, 462
Coonawarra, 47, 63, 161, 301, 303, 306, 307, 308, 309, 315
cooperative, 248, 287, 333, 401, 408, 410, 413, 416, 417, 444, 459, 471, 495, 511, 520
copigmentation, 108, 409
copper, 34, 49, 108, 127
Coppola, Francis Ford, 282
Corbières, 415
cordon, 22
cork, 69, 70, 87, 91, 95, 112, 114, 133-136, 137, 138, 139, 140, 141, 192, 202, 203, 204, 271, 308, 450, 468, 506, 508, 526, 548
corked, 133, 135, 136
corkscrew, 133, 137, 139
Cornas, 406, 407
coronary disease, 209-210
Cortés, 8
Cortese, 445, 447
Corton, 167, 382, 510
Corton Charlemagne, 167
Corvina, 444
Cos d'Estournel, Château, 57, 377
Cosecha, 455
Costa Russi, 428
Costco, 236, 237
Côte d'Or, 46, 67, 78, 150, 167, 225, 339, 360, 362-367, 368, 374, 380-384, 418
Coteaux du Tricastin, 410
Côte-de-Nuits, 52
Côte-Rôtie, 161, 199, 406, 408, 409
Côtes de Luberon, 410
Côtes du Ventoux, 410
Coulée de Serrant, 398, 534
coulure, 23
Counoise, 411
coupage, 249
courtier, 346
CRAV, 412
Crémant, 361, 401, 402, 513
criadera, 515, 516, 517
Crianza, 456, 462, 463, 464, 468
Criolla, 177, 260, 321, 322, 323
critics, 38, 67, 100, 153, 194, 195, 196, 197, 198, 311, 335, 349, 371, 402
critter brands, 312
Crljenak, 17
Croatia, 17
Croser, Brian, 129, 300, 313
cross-fertilization, 16
Crouchen, 334
Crozes-Hermitage, 54, 405, 406, 407, 408, 409
Cru Bourgeois, 351, 352, 374, 379
Cruse, 248, 249, 250, 251
cryoextraction, 540
cult wines, 57, 159, 188, 224, 283 284, 321, 358

cultivar, 16-17, 75, 124, 147, 149, 158, 161, 180, 181, 183, 192, 259
Curicó Valley, 332
cuvée, 284, 359, 411, 412, 459, 461, 463, 502, 509, 511
CVBG, 349, 371
CVNE, 463
DAC, 491, 492
Dão, 473
Darmagi, 428
deacidification, 122
dealcoholized, 120
débourbage, 102
Decanter, 132, 195, 197, 200
declassification, 435
degree day, 76, 77, 458
dehydration, 112, 124
Deiss, 405
dèja, 450
Delegat, 318
Denominación de Origen, 329, 452, 455, 464
Derenoncourt, 194
deserpia, 519
desiccation, 29, 311, 537, 538
Desseauve, Thierry, 200
destemming, 91, 105
diacetyl, 100
Diageo, 218, 228, 229, 230, 231, 233
Diehl, Armin, 481
diethylene, 244
Dijon clones, 165, 168
Dijon, institute, 192
dioecious, 4
disgorgement, 508, 509, 510
Distell, 232, 333
distillation, 28, 34, 64, 65, 66, 120, 144, 217, 222, 223, 287, 333, 386, 392, 396, 413, 451
distributors, 197, 206, 226, 228, 232, 235-238, 261, 293, 347, 348, 464, 486
Districtus Austriae Controllatus, 491
diurnal variation, 57, 77, 317, 318, 325, 326, 416, 448, 458, 466, 493
DOC, 419, 420, 422, 423, 428, 430, 431, 432, 433, 435, 437, 439, 440, 441, 443, 444, 446, 448, 449, 450, 455, 471, 472, 518, 519
DOCa, 455, 459
DOCG, 419, 420, 422, 423, 427, 428, 430, 431, 432, 433, 436, 439, 440, 448, 449, 450
Dolcetto, 420, 422, 427
Dom Pérignon, 499, 500, 501, 502, 505, 507, 509
Domecq, 230
Domesday book, 7, 345
Dominio de Valdepusa, 454, 455

Dominio de Pingus, 465
Domitian, Emperor, 6, 185, 223
Don Melchor, 331
Dordogne, 341
Dornfelder, 484
Douro, 10, 15, 53, 64, 451, 452, 473, 474, 522-525, 528, 529, 530, 548
Dourthe, 349, 371
drainage, 34, 41, 43, 44, 45, 47, 48, 51, 54, 55, 56, 57, 59, 60, 61, 67, 78, 109, 135, 158, 285, 353, 440
drought, 61, 81, 300, 448, 453, 519
Drouhin, Joseph, 367
Duboeuf, Georges, 385
Dubourdieu, Denis, 194
Ducru Beaucaillou, Château, 27
Dugat-Py, Bernard, 384
Duhart Milon, Château, 57
Dureza, 148
Durif, 258, 261
Dutch influence, 55, 110, 332, 396
Duval-Leroy, 140
Ebro, 456, 458
échelle des crus, 64, 505
eclipse, 424
Egypt, 1, 4, 20, 176, 185, 213, 239
Einzellage, 477, 478, 479
Eiswein, 54, 476, 490, 539, 540
Elan Vineyards, 58
elderberry, 126, 243, 244, 525
en foule, 12
en primeur, 347, 348, 349, 385
Enologix, 197
enrichment, 98, 540
Entre-deux-Mers, 341
Epernay, 502, 507
Errázuriz, 330, 332
Erstes Gewächs, 480, 481
Est! Est!! Est!!!, 445
Estremadura, 472
Eszencia, 542, 543
ethylene, 26, 244
Etna, 448
eucalyptus, 50, 164, 175
Eurasia, 4, 5
European Union, 110, 111, 117, 123, 124, 185, 208, 217, 221, 222, 223, 224, 241, 247, 390, 395, 412
Euvitis, 549
Faiveley, Maison, 367
Falernian, 51, 69, 187, 189, 239
fanleaf, 181
Fargues, 533
Federspiel, 491
Feinherb, 479
Felsina, Fattoria di, 430, 439
fermentation, 5, 28, 49, 50, 64, 87, 89, 91, 92, 93-97, 99, 100, 101, 102, 105, 106,

107, 108, 111, 112, 113, 114, 115, 116,
117, 118, 119, 122, 123, 124, 126, 127,
128, 129, 132, 155, 156, 157, 166, 168,
170, 171, 174, 177, 182, 190, 193, 246,
260, 309, 311, 319, 332, 334, 335, 347,
356, 382, 385, 402, 408, 426, 428, 445,
446, 447, 473, 499, 500, 501, 506, 507,
510, 513, 514, 516, 517, 518, 520, 522,
525, 527, 536, 537, 538, 540, 542
fermentation, barrel, 133, 447
fermentation, stuck, 30, 93, 114, 118
fermenter, 100, 101
fermenters, 128
Fernández, Alejandro, 468
Ferñao Pires, 473
Fiano, 449
fifth growth, 350, 378, 379
Filhot, Château, 536
filtration, 101, 102, 103, 104, 124, 189, 526
Finigan, Robert, 196
fining, 49, 102, 103, 104, 456, 545
first growth, 41, 57, 190, 195, 225, 251,
252, 347, 348, 350, 351, 352, 354, 357,
368, 375, 377, 378, 379, 381, 384, 407,
480
Flaccianello, 442
flavonoid, 108
Fleurie, 386
flor, 516, 517, 518, 519, 522, 534, 543
flowering, 18, 23, 24, 25, 29, 81, 84
Folle Blanche, 396
Fonseca, 474
Fontodi, 432, 442
foreign owners, 232, 318, 531
formate, 156
fortification, 113, 298, 299, 525
Fosters, 123, 201, 228, 229, 230, 232, 313,
314, 318
foudres, 425
fourth growth, 57, 357, 378
foxy, 11, 125, 259, 315
Franciacorta, 513
Franschhoek, 336
Franzia, 123, 231, 265, 266
Frascati, 445
fraud, 98, 110, 240, 243, 245, 248, 249,
250, 253, 389, 435, 459
freeze, 224, 537
Freixenet, 229
Frescobaldi, 441
Friulano, 421, 446
Friuli-Venezia-Giulia, 446
Fromonteau, 500
Frontignac, 176, 177
fructose, 93, 98, 124, 246
Fumé Blanc, 170, 399
Furmint, 534, 542, 543
Gaglioppo, 421, 448, 449

Gaia, 447, 528
Gaja, Angelo, 425, 426, 427, 428, 430, 444, 447
galets, 44, 411, 412
Gallo, 202, 229, 230, 232, 233, 248, 258, 286-290
Gamay, 156, 360, 361, 362, 384, 399
garage wine, 61, 62, 194, 224, 358-360, 379, 444, 542
Garcia Carrión, 233
Garganega, 420, 421, 445, 446
garlic, 127
Garnacha, 451
Garonne, 341, 532, 533, 534
Garramiola, Txomin, 467
garrigue, 416
Gascony, 345
Gattinara, 422
Gault-Millau, 481
Gaussen, 55
Gavi, 422, 445, 446, 447
Geisenheim, 17, 82, 192
geraniol, 156, 174, 175, 177
Gevrey Chambertin, 53, 247, 364, 381, 382, 510
Gewürztraminer, 108, 146, 154, 156, 169, 174, 175, 177, 400, 401, 402, 403, 404
Geyserville, 286
Giacosa, Bruno, 425
giberellic acid, 165
Gigondas, 410, 411
Gimblett Gravels, 53
Gironde, 251, 341, 348, 350, 351, 353, 354, 372, 392, 412
Gisbourne, 317, 318
Gladstones, John, 309
global warming, 74-85, 117, 118, 317, 327, 337, 382, 423, 481, 539
globalization, 20, 193, 194, 235, 425
glucose, 93, 98, 124, 246
glycerol, 123, 517, 534
Gönci, 542
gooseberries, 171, 318
Gouais Blanc, 182, 497
Gouges, Henri, 148, 183
gout, 42, 49, 531
Graciano, 460, 461, 462
grafting, 11, 12, 20, 49, 181
Grahm, Randall, 60
Gran Reserva, 456, 462, 463, 464, 465, 468
Grand Cru Classé, 232, 347, 350, 352, 354, 355, 359, 368, 370, 371, 374, 379
Grand Enclos, 356
grand vin, 354, 355, 356, 357, 358, 374
Grange, 62, 63, 162, 297, 302, 308, 416
Gratallops, 471
gravel, 41, 44, 53, 56, 57, 158, 160, 342, 353, 354, 411, 521

gravel mound, 56, 57, 353, 354
Graves, 251, 341, 342, 343, 352, 354, 377, 378, 532, 535
gravity, 92, 118, 281, 469
Gravner, Josko, 447, 448
Grecanico dorato, 420
Greenpoint, 234
Grenache, 19, 110, 143, 261, 270, 388, 390, 409, 410, 411, 414, 415, 421, 448, 451, 454, 460, 461, 462, 470, 471, 538
Grivelet, 248
Gros Plant, 397
Grosses Gewächs, 480, 481
Grosslage, 477, 480
Grosslagen, 477, 478
growing season, 18, 19, 23, 25, 61, 71, 72, 74, 75, 76, 77, 78, 79, 80, 82, 84, 117, 165, 174, 267, 276, 300, 307, 309, 422, 423, 448, 481, 493
growing temperature, 83, 84, 275
Grüner Veltliner, 46, 114, 489, 491, 493, 494, 496-498
Guado al Tasso, 440
Guigal, 199, 408
Guinness, 229
Gültig Corks, 136
gunflint, 48, 399, 439
Gutiérrez Colosía, 519
Guyot, 494
gyropalette, 507, 508
Hajii Firuz, 4
halbtrocken, 175, 475, 476, 479, 482, 487, 490
Hanepoot, 333
Hanzell, 135
Haraszthy, Agoston, 260
Haro, 457
Hárslevelü, 542, 543
harvest, 14, 22, 24, 26, 28, 30, 31, 32, 33, 35, 45, 61, 72, 74, 80, 81, 83, 84, 93, 97, 98, 109, 112, 117, 118, 119, 161, 168, 171, 172, 182, 193, 196, 281, 285, 310, 326, 333, 347, 359, 371, 385, 398, 402, 423, 445, 448, 455, 458, 463, 475, 476, 489, 491, 510, 526, 533, 534, 535, 539, 540, 543
Haut Brion, Château, 41, 232, 350, 354, 377
Haut Médoc, 55, 342, 343, 353, 358, 374
Haut-Marbuzet, Château, 379
Hautvillers, Abbey of, 499, 507
Heiligenstein, 496
Heineken, 208
Henschke, 304
Hepp, Rowald, 477
Hérault, Vin de Pays de l', 416
herbaceousness, 50, 150, 154, 157, 159, 160, 161, 162, 164, 169, 170, 171, 172, 306, 307, 318, 371, 372
herbicides, 33, 34, 37
hermaphrodite, 4
Hermitage, 9, 53, 54, 148, 150, 161, 162, 240, 306, 334, 337, 388, 405, 406, 407, 408, 409
Hermitager, 240, 407
Heublein, 125, 231, 282
Heunisch Wasser, 497
Heurigen, 490
hexanoate, 156
Hirondelle, 245
histamines, 112
hotrienol, 174, 175
Humboldt current, 266, 330
Hume, David, 209
hydric balance, 44
hyperoxidation, 129
ice-wine, 175
import, 235, 463
INAO, 27, 52, 53, 99, 181, 249, 352, 371, 374, 377, 389, 393, 394, 395, 403, 415, 417, 503, 504, 549
Indication Géographique Protegée, 395
Iniskillin, 292, 293, 540
investment, 232, 332, 416, 431, 471, 510
IPT, 30
irrigation, 1, 4, 38, 54, 60, 61, 71, 81, 214, 220, 286, 290, 291, 300, 304, 317, 322, 325, 327, 330, 331, 418, 434, 453, 466, 493, 519
Isole e Olena, 439, 442
isotherm, 18, 79
Itata, 330
IVDP, 529
Jancis Robinson, 146, 296, 445
Janus, 468
Jefferson, Thomas, 70, 240, 251, 252
Jerez, 64, 337, 455, 513, 514, 515, 517, 518, 519, 520, 538
Joly, Nicolas, 398, 534
Joven, 455
Judgment of Paris, 149, 294
jug wine, 271, 272, 282, 288, 311
Jura, 522, 538
Jurassic, 46
Kabinett, 172, 476, 478, 481, 482
Kalimna, 63
Kamptal, 489, 491, 492, 493, 495, 496, 497
Kerner, 487
kerosene, 173
Kesselstatt, von, 14
Kimmeridgian, 45, 46, 47, 361, 399, 503
Kirchenstück, 54, 55
Kloster Eberbach, 6, 483, 485
Kobrand, 232
Koch, Bill, 251, 252
Korbel, 231

kosher, 102, 232
Kremstal, 114, 489, 491, 492, 493, 496, 497
KWV, 333
La Morra, 423
La Tache, 384
La Turque, 408
lactone, 156
Lafite Rothschild, Château, 15, 55, 57, 190, 332, 377, 486
lagares, 101, 456, 468, 469, 473, 527, 528
Lambrusco, 434
Lancers, 474
Landwein, 475, 490
Landweingebiete, 475
Langhe, 422, 423, 427, 428, 430, 548
Languedoc, 98, 162, 177, 193, 232, 241, 248, 306, 371, 387, 388, 391, 409, 412-417, 506, 538
late harvest, 33, 112, 141, 274, 311, 336, 401, 402, 403, 414, 533, 534, 535, 541, 543
Latour, Château, 57, 356
Laurent-Perrier, 511
LBV, 526, 530
lees, 102, 104, 114, 397, 445, 509
Leeuwin, 310
Lenz-Moser, 494
Léoville Las Cases, Château, 56, 356, 377
Leroy, Domaine, 384
Les Forts de Latour, 356
Libournais, 341, 342, 343, 346
Libourne, 341
Liebfraumilch, 183, 201, 475, 482, 486-487
lignins, 109
limestone, 12, 44, 45, 46, 47, 64, 307, 316, 361, 363, 399, 409, 532
Limoux, 506
Lindemans, 201, 202, 313
Lirac, 410
Lisini, 15
Listrac, 55
litharge, 242
Locke, John, 41
Logroño, 456, 457
Loi Evin, 207
Lopez de Heredia, 103, 457, 462, 465
Louis Jadot, 367
Louis Latour, 53, 111, 367
Loupiac, 532
Loureiro, 473
Luján de Cuyo, 325, 326
Lustau, 521
luxury items, 224, 238, 381
LVMH, 229, 318, 504, 511, 512
lychees, 154, 156, 174, 175
Lynch Bages, Château, 27

Lynch, Kermit, 389
Macabeo, 453
Mâconnais, 362, 363
Madiran, 128
Magdelaine, Château, 158, 182
Magill, 62, 63, 297
Maipo, 331, 332
Maipú, 325
Malbec, 62, 157, 158, 159, 255, 321, 322, 323, 325, 326, 327, 344, 417, 467
malic acid, 29, 89, 96, 99, 101, 121, 122, 534
malolactic fermentation, 87, 89, 99-100, 113, 114, 115, 122, 128, 157, 166, 182, 193, 309, 319
Maltus, Jonathan, 359
Malvasia, 146, 148, 437, 438, 460, 461
Manischewitz, 232
Manzanilla, 516, 517, 519
marais, 55, 56
Maremma, 431, 443
Margaret River, 49, 301, 303, 309
Margaux, 55, 343, 353, 354, 377, 422
Maria Gomes, 473
Marlborough, 50, 80, 164, 169, 170, 172, 193, 256, 316, 317, 319, 320
marque, 52, 356, 358
Marqués de Murrieta, 457
Marqués de Riscal, 456, 457, 460, 461
Marsanne, 407, 408, 409, 410
marshes, 55, 56, 59
Martinborough, 164, 320
Mas de Daumas Gassac, 193, 413, 416
Masi, 445
Masseto, 441
Mastroberardino, 448
Mateus, 201, 474
Maule, 14, 331, 332
Maury, 538
Mayacamas, 275, 276, 284, 285
Mazuela, 460, 461
Mazzocolin, Guiseppe, 430, 439
McCloskey, Leo, 197
McCrae, winery, 193
McLaren Vale, 161, 188, 301, 303, 306
Médoc, 55, 56, 59, 160, 190, 225, 247, 251, 307, 339, 341, 342, 343, 344, 345, 346, 347, 350, 351, 352, 353-355, 359, 368, 370, 374, 375, 377, 378, 379, 418, 441
Mega Purple, 124, 125, 546
Mendocino, 264, 272, 323
Mendoza, 256, 324, 325, 326, 327
menthol, 164
mercaptans, 127
Merlot, 16, 17, 19, 44, 62, 76, 82, 143, 145, 148, 157, 158, 160, 182, 259, 269, 281, 299, 307, 328, 329, 334, 337, 342, 343, 344, 357, 359, 414, 415, 417, 418, 420,

421, 440, 441, 442, 443, 445, 449, 467
Merlot Chileno, 329
Mesnil-sur-Oger, 31
Mesopotamia, 1, 4
metabisulfite, 111
methanol, 245, 262
Méthode Champenoise, 335, 513
Méthode Traditionelle, 513
methoxypyrazine, 50, 161, 171, 172
methylanthranilate, 259
método rural, 101
Meursault, 150, 167, 364
micro-oxygenation, 127, 128, 132
micropore, 105
Mildara Blass, 230, 305, 313
mildew, 34, 35, 71, 159, 180, 457
millerandage, 23
minerality, 50, 54, 167, 173, 174, 498
minerals, 49, 60, 172
Minervois, 415, 538
Minho, 472
Mission grape, 177, 260-261, 321
Mittelburgenland, 491
Mittelrhein, 480, 483
modernist, 425, 426-428, 434, 462, 542
Modesto, 286, 287, 288, 289
moelleux, 398
Moët & Chandon, 31, 93, 234, 281, 310, 326, 506, 512
Molinara, 444
Monastrell, 454
Moncão, 473
Mondavi, Robert, 170, 187, 228, 231, 232, 265, 279, 416, 441
Mondeuse, 148
Mondovino, 194
Mongeard-Mugneret, 122
monovarietal, 146, 159, 161, 323, 329, 344, 399, 430, 438, 439, 442, 463, 473
Mont St. Luisants, 361
Montepulciano, 420, 431, 432, 436, 437
Monterey, 290
Montosoli, 438
Montpellier, Oenology Institute, 10, 192
Morélot, Denis, 42, 97, 98
Morgon, 386
Moscadello, 432
Moscato, 177, 422
Mosel, 7, 14, 15, 48, 54, 79, 173, 174, 176, 246, 337, 477, 478, 479, 480, 481, 483, 484, 485, 486
Moselle, 190, 258
Mosel-Saar-Ruwer, 485
Mount Veeder, 277
Mourvèdre, 110, 261, 388, 390, 410, 411, 414, 415, 416, 454
Mouton Cadet, 349, 369
Mouton Rothschild, Château, 55, 57,

158, 332, 349, 377, 379
Muga, Jorge, 109, 461, 462
Müller-Thurgau, 183, 315, 316, 317, 484, 487
Muscadelle, 174, 311
Muscadello, 432
Muscadet, 395, 396, 397
Muscadinia, 180, 549
Muscardin, 411
Muscat, 108, 154, 155, 156, 174, 175, 176-178, 311, 322, 323, 333, 336, 400, 403, 404, 420, 421, 422, 534, 538, 542, 543
Muscat Hamburg, 176
Muscat Ottonel, 176
Musigny, 381
Muskateller, 497
mycorrhizal, 37, 48
Nadrasky, Otto, 244
Nahe, 246, 477, 480, 484, 486
Nantais, 395, 396, 397
Napa, 14, 27, 57-59, 71-72, 80-84, 135, 149, 150, 161, 164, 166, 167, 169, 170, 171, 187, 189, 190, 193, 224, 225, 231, 234, 235, 255, 258, 260, 264-266, 267, 270, 273, 274, 275-284, 285, 287, 288-294, 371, 399
Napoleon, 97, 350, 351, 417, 497
NAPPAS, 445
Navarra, 101
Nebbiolo, 19, 67, 76, 107, 146, 148, 149, 154, 337, 421, 422, 423, 424, 425, 426, 427, 428, 430, 444
Nebbiolo, Lampia, 423
negociant, 52, 196, 240, 241, 248, 249, 250, 340, 345, 346, 347, 348, 349, 358, 360, 365, 366, 367, 369, 371, 380, 381, 385, 390, 397, 407, 427, 457
Negroamaro, 420, 421, 448
nematode, 181
Neolithic, 4
nerol, 177
neurotoxin, 10
Neusiedlersee, 489, 492, 535
Neusiedlersee-Hugeland, 489
New French Claret, 70
New York state, 226, 231, 232, 259, 269
New Zealand, 18, 50, 53, 76, 80, 129, 140, 149, 163, 164, 168, 169, 170, 172, 173, 189, 193, 202, 214, 217, 219, 230, 232, 234, 255, 256, 295, 315-320, 387, 398, 547
Niagara, 292, 293, 540
Niederösterreich, 488, 489, 491, 497
Niersteiner Gutes Domtal, 478
Nikolaihof, 492, 493, 496
Nobilo, 318
Noiren, 148
Novartis, 469, 470

oak, 36, 62, 87, 89, 94, 108, 113, 114, 115, 116, 127, 128, 129-133, 141, 154, 155, 157, 166, 167, 169, 170, 172, 176, 189, 194, 196, 298, 311, 319, 334, 357, 397, 398, 417, 424, 425, 426, 428, 433, 434, 447, 448, 455, 463, 464, 467, 468, 469, 491, 514, 529, 542, 543, 545, 546
oak, Baltic, 131
oak, beans, 132, 178
oak, chips, 116, 131, 132, 133, 546
oak, new, 62, 67, 106, 113, 126, 130, 132, 133, 150, 166, 167, 169, 194, 357, 399, 425, 426, 447, 463, 542
oak, staves, 102, 130, 131, 132, 133, 463
oak, toasting, 113, 130, 131, 157
oenologist, 30, 45, 96, 97, 99, 104, 107, 192, 193, 194, 319, 327, 372, 386
oïdium, 34, 432, 457
Okanagan Valley, 292
Oloroso, 64, 516, 517, 518, 519, 521, 522
Oporto, 473, 522, 525, 528
Oregon, 13, 149, 163-165, 264, 267-271, 190-292, 294, 320
Oremus, 468, 543
Ornellaia, 440, 441, 442, 443
Orvieto, 445
Orzalesi, Guido, 434, 438
oxidation, 50, 69, 87, 92, 102, 103, 108, 111, 112, 114, 122, 126, 127, 128, 129, 130, 136, 137, 138, 139, 140, 141, 156, 172, 209, 328, 399, 426, 433, 445, 448, 465, 468, 509, 513, 516, 517, 527, 538, 542
oxygen, 48, 50, 89, 95, 100, 101, 102, 111, 112, 127, 128, 129, 130, 138, 139, 140, 141, 172, 189, 203, 439, 446, 517
P.E.T., 203
Paarl, 336
Pahlmeyer, Jayson, 58, 283
País, 260, 321, 327, 330, 331
Palacios, Alvaro, 471
Paleolithic, 4
Palmer, Château, 377
Palomino, 29, 146, 337, 453, 518, 521
palu, 55, 350
Pape-Clément, Château, 377
parasites, 235
Parker, Robert, 104, 194, 195, 196, 197, 274, 314
Paso Robles, 268, 273, 274
passerillage, 112, 533, 535, 541
Pasteur, Louis, 87, 95, 111, 139, 194
pasteurization, 95, 111
Patriarche, 367
Pauillac, 57, 343, 344, 351, 354, 368
Pavie, Château, 352
Pavie-Macquin, Château, 352
Pechstein, 54

Pedro Ximénez, 337, 518, 538
Peñafiel, 466
Penedès, 455
Penfolds, 62, 230, 297, 305, 308, 313
penicillin, 134
Peñin, José, 463
Periquita, 473
Pernod-Ricard, 208, 227, 229, 230, 231, 233, 235, 304, 313, 318
Perrier-Jouët, 501
Perromat, 249
Persia, 148
Pesquera, 465, 466, 467, 468, 469
Pessac-Léognan, 342, 350, 352, 376, 377, 379
pesticide, 33, 34, 38, 134, 135, 181, 182, 546
Petaluma, 285
petit château, 349, 392
Petit Verdot, 157, 343, 344, 469
Petite Sirah, 258, 277
petrol, 139, 154, 156, 157, 172, 173, 179
Pétrus, Château, 44, 159, 252, 375
Pewsey Vale, 308
Peynaud, Emile, 75, 87, 99, 102, 139, 193, 194, 319, 416
Pfalz, 54, 55, 246, 477, 483, 484, 486
phenolic ripeness, 30, 31, 82, 83, 106, 118, 439, 463
phenylthiourea, 151
pheromones, 34
Philipponnat, 500
phosphorus, 33, 48
photosynthesis, 24, 25, 48, 77
phylloxera, 8, 9-16, 17, 20, 31, 45, 159, 181, 192, 204, 218, 241, 246, 251, 259, 261, 274, 277, 321, 323, 325, 327, 329, 330, 337, 361, 369, 389, 395, 398, 413, 457, 458, 543
Pichler, Lucas, 492, 494, 495
Pichon Comtesse de Lalande, Château, 344, 377
Piedmont, 148, 149, 168, 188, 198, 323, 337, 421, 422, 428, 444, 446, 447
Piesporter Michelsberg, 478
Pieve Santa Restituta, 428
pigeage, 106
Pignoletto, 420
Pignolo, 448
Pingus, 465
Pinot Blanc, 148, 165, 382, 400, 401, 402, 447
Pinot Droit, 192, 361
Pinot Gouges, 183
Pinot Grigio, 420, 421, 445, 446
Pinot Gris, 108, 165, 292, 319, 382, 398, 400, 401, 402, 403, 404, 420, 421, 500
Pinot Meunier, 165, 166, 501, 502, 510

Pinot Noir, 8, 17, 19, 20, 46, 53, 59, 76, 79, 106, 107, 108, 110, 118, 125, 145, 146, 148, 149, 150, 154, 155, 156, 163-166, 183, 192, 248, 267, 268, 269, 285, 286, 292, 293, 301, 310, 319, 320, 322, 334, 336, 337, 339, 360, 361, 362, 366, 382, 387, 393, 396, 399, 401, 402, 404, 407, 423, 426, 427, 480, 481, 482, 483, 484, 485, 498, 500, 501, 502, 509, 510
Pinotage, 321, 334, 335, 336
Pintia, 466, 468, 470
Place de Bordeaux, 346-349, 353, 375, 377
Planchon, Jules-Émile, 10, 11
Planeta, 449
plonk, 218, 413
ploughing, 25, 32
polyculture, 290, 430, 495
polyphenol, 30, 105, 126
polyphenols, 105, 106, 107, 111, 209
Pombal, 528, 529
Pomerol, 194, 225, 341, 352, 375, 379, 418
Pommard, 165, 364, 367, 381
Pommery, 190
Ponsot, Laurent, 361
Pontac, 41
Pontallier, Paul, 17, 27
Pontet Canet, Château, 35
Port, 15, 53, 64, 73, 113, 124, 146, 189, 190, 232, 243, 244, 288, 297, 337, 345, 396, 451, 471, 472, 473, 474, 499, 522-532, 538, 548
Portlandian, 46, 47
Porto, 529
Portugal, 10, 15, 16, 133, 136, 177, 201, 205, 451, 471-474, 525, 526, 528, 530, 531, 535, 548
potassium, 33, 43, 48, 103, 111, 121, 244, 361
Pouilly Fuissé, 363
Pouilly Fumé, 169, 170, 395, 396, 398
Prädikat, 475, 480, 482, 484
Prädikatwein, 490, 491
Prager, Weingut, 492, 493, 494
pregnancy, 210
Preignac, 533
premium wine, 240, 271-272, 281, 286, 288, 296, 311, 315, 333
pressing, 5, 91, 92, 94, 105, 129, 293, 345, 356, 450, 500, 510, 517
press-run, 101
prime d'arrachage, 349
Primitivo, 17, 268, 420, 421, 448
Priorat, 48-49, 455, 470, 471
Probus, Emperor, 6, 223
Prohibition, 205, 207, 208, 209, 235, 236, 237, 255, 259, 260, 261-263, 269, 273, 277, 279, 281, 282, 286, 292, 293, 547, 548
PROP, 151, 152, 153
Prosecco, 420
Provence, 109, 387, 388, 412
pruning, 5, 21, 23, 24, 25, 27, 38, 423
PTC, 151, 152, 153
Puglia, 448
Puligny Montrachet, 108, 167, 364
pumping-over, 106
pumps, 92
punch-down, 106
pupitre, 506, 507
puttonyo, 542, 543
pyrazine, 121, 156, 161
QbA, 475, 477, 487, 490
QmP, 82, 246, 475, 476, 477, 478, 479, 481, 490
Quai des Chartrons, 346
Qualitätswein, 201, 475, 483, 487, 490
QueChosir, 393
Querciabella, 447
Quercus suber, 133
quinta, 15, 473, 526, 528
Quinta de Vargellas, 526
Quinta do Noval, 15
Quintano, Manuel, 456
QWPSR, 241
rainfall, 56, 60, 61, 71, 72, 78, 276, 300, 304, 309, 310, 317, 330, 331, 400, 409, 423, 466, 523
rancio, 538
Rasteau, 410
Ratti, Renato, 429, 430
RCGM, 124, 246
Real de Asua, 463
Recioto, 113, 445, 538
red wine, 3, 26, 70, 74, 89, 90, 91, 93, 94, 95, 99, 102, 103, 104, 105, 106, 108, 109, 110, 111, 113, 118, 123, 125, 132, 141, 146, 152, 153, 163, 178, 189, 201, 208, 209, 210, 245, 246, 248, 249, 267, 288, 298, 299, 303, 306, 307, 309, 310, 335, 339, 341, 342, 343, 344, 350, 352, 361, 363, 364, 383, 387, 388, 396, 398, 399, 407, 410, 411, 416, 421, 426, 431, 440, 444, 448, 449, 451, 452, 455, 461, 473, 474, 482, 483, 484, 487, 489, 501, 510, 527, 530, 533
reductive winemaking, 13, 25, 50, 102, 122, 126, 127, 128, 129, 138, 139, 140, 141, 156, 172, 181, 200, 209, 222, 314, 327, 393, 439, 446, 463, 492, 504
refermentation, 113, 445, 499
refractometer, 28, 29
Reh-Gartner, Annagret, 14
Reims, 500, 501, 502, 503
reinfection, 113
remuage, 506, 507, 508

rendement, 373, 374
Renvoisé, Guy, 36
Reserva, 13, 74, 456, 462, 464, 467, 468
residual sugar, 112-114, 123, 125, 172, 173, 178, 189, 311, 320, 402, 424, 476, 479, 481, 484, 487, 490, 491, 498, 517, 518, 536, 537, 540, 542
resins, 69, 87, 124
resveratrol, 182, 210
retsina, 69
reverse osmosis, 116, 117, 118, 119, 545
Rheingau, 7, 79, 148, 174, 190, 192, 337, 477, 480-481, 483, 484-485, 486, 535, 539
Rheinhessen, 201, 484, 486, 487, 539
Rhine, 8, 400, 484, 486
Rhône, 8, 9, 19, 53, 54, 79, 97, 146, 148, 149, 161, 162, 177, 188, 190, 199, 240, 255, 268, 273, 306, 360, 367, 387, 388, 390, 405-412, 413, 414, 538, 548
Ribatejo, 472
Ribera del Duero, 74, 454, 455, 465-469, 470
Ribéreau-Gayon, Jean, 75, 96, 104, 139
Ribolla, 448
Richebourg, 381
riddling, see remuage
Riesling, 19, 29, 46, 48, 79, 82, 99, 129, 139, 145, 146, 148, 154, 156, 157, 169, 172-176, 177, 178, 179, 183, 261, 268, 291, 293, 300, 308, 309, 319, 333, 337, 387, 400, 401, 402, 403, 404, 405, 438, 480, 481, 484, 485, 487, 491, 493, 496, 497, 498, 534, 535, 539
Riesling Italico, 173
Rioja, 13, 19, 101, 103, 109, 131, 146, 149, 189, 327, 337, 451, 454, 455, 456, 457, 458, 459, 460, 461, 462, 463, 464, 465, 466, 467, 548
Rioja Alavesa, 458, 460, 461, 462, 465, 466
Rioja Alta, 458, 460, 461, 463, 465, 466
Ripasso, 445
Riserva, 422, 433
Riverina, 302
Rivesaltes, 177
Roda, Bodega, 463
Rodenstock, Harvey, 252, 253
Roederer, 75, 135, 234, 505
Roero, 427
Rolland, Michel, 194, 327, 332
Romanée-Conti, 190, 381, 382, 384
Rondinella, 444
roots, 8, 9, 11, 13, 14, 15, 25, 31, 34, 36, 37, 43, 44, 48, 49, 56, 60, 61, 181, 232, 255, 259, 310, 330, 389
rootstock, 3, 12, 13, 14, 15, 16, 17, 20, 31, 45, 181, 192, 261, 274, 330, 494

Rosacker, 404
rosé, 109-110, 118, 152, 163, 177, 190, 201, 243, 247, 269, 375, 387, 393, 395, 396, 402, 410, 417, 455, 473, 474, 510
Rosemont, 230
Rosenmuskateller, 177
Rosso di Montalcino, 433
Rotundone, 156
Roupnel, Gaston, 367
Roussanne, 407, 408, 409, 410
Rubicon, 274, 281, 282
Rubired, 124, 125, 270
Rudesheim, 484
Rust, 489
Rutherford, 225, 264, 265, 276, 281
Rutherglen, 168, 177, 310, 311
Ruwer, 485
Ruwertal, 485
S. cerevisiae, 89, 95, 96
S. ellipsoideus, 516
Saahs, Nikolaus, 492, 496
Saar, 485
Saar-Ruwer, 485
saca, 515
saignée, 109, 118, 119
Saintsbury, 71
salivary, 105, 153
San Joaquin valley, 265, 273, 274, 286, 289
Sancerre, 135, 163, 169, 395-399
Sangiogheto, 148
Sangiovese, 15, 19, 107, 146, 148, 149, 154, 337, 420, 421, 431, 432-436, 437, 438, 439, 440, 441, 442, 443, 444
Sanlúcar, 518, 519
Santa Barbara, 164, 268, 273, 274, 290
sapa, 241, 242
Sardon del Duero, 455
Sassicaia, 96, 199, 431, 440, 441
Sauternes, 64, 112, 124, 146, 190, 258, 311, 341, 342, 350, 351, 376, 476, 532, 533, 535, 536, 541
Sauvignon Blanc, 19, 29, 50, 80, 99, 108, 114, 121, 129, 139, 145, 146, 154, 155, 156, 157, 158, 161, 169-172, 174, 182, 189, 193, 255, 256, 279, 300, 315, 317, 318, 319, 320, 328, 329, 331, 333, 336, 342, 387, 396, 398, 399, 414, 416, 461, 491, 497, 498, 534, 535
Sauvignonasse, 329
Savennières, 395, 398, 534
Schiopetto, Mario, 446
schist, 48, 53, 471, 522
Schloss Johannisberg, 535
Schloss Vollrads, 477
Schlossberg, 403, 404
Schnabel, 114
Schoonmaker, Frank, 257, 258, 259

Schram, Jacob, 258
Schramsberg, 258
screwcap, 87, 91, 112, 114, 136, 137-141, 192, 202, 203, 204, 271, 287, 308, 449, 450
Scuppernong, 231, 259
Seagrams, 228, 230, 317
second growth, 56, 351, 352, 357, 377, 378, 407
second wine, 340, 354, 355, 356, 357, 358, 359, 360, 374, 377, 378, 379, 433, 467, 468
Seguin, Gérard, 43
selection massale, 17, 454, 494
self-fertilization, 4, 16
Sémillon, 50, 146, 156, 169, 171, 300, 301, 303, 310, 333, 342, 399, 534, 535
Serralunga d'Alba, 422, 423
Setúbal, 177
SGN, 402, 403, 536
Sherry, 29, 73, 112, 146, 190, 232, 297, 337, 390, 451, 453, 499, 513-522, 531, 534, 543, 547
Sherry, cream, 516
Sherry, fino, 112, 456, 516, 517, 518, 519, 521, 522, 543
Sherry, sack, 247, 514
Shiraz, 47, 62, 63, 146, 148, 150, 161, 162, 201, 255, 256, 297, 299, 300, 306-308, 315, 334, 336, 388, 408
Shiraz-Cabernet, 315
Shiraz-Viognier, 408
Shrikhande, Anil, 125, 126
Sichel, 487
Sicilia, 74, 465, 466, 467, 468, 469, 470
Sieur d'Arques, 248
Sillery, 190
Sinskey, Robert, 283, 284
slate, 14, 46, 48, 174, 485
Smaragd, 491, 498
smell, 29, 41, 42, 48, 49, 100, 115, 122, 127, 133, 138, 141, 150, 151, 153, 154, 169, 174, 199, 244, 259, 425
smokiness, 50, 130
Soave, 421, 445, 446, 450
Sociando-Mallet, Château, 379
Sogrape, 473, 474, 531
soil, 11, 12, 27, 33, 34, 35, 36, 37, 38, 41, 42, 43, 44, 45, 46, 47, 48, 49, 51, 53, 54, 56, 57, 59, 60, 61, 64, 67, 167, 174, 181, 275, 301, 307, 310, 317, 325, 330, 363, 399, 405, 407, 409, 440, 485, 493, 496, 519, 523, 532
solera, 64, 73, 311, 499, 513, 514, 515, 516, 517, 518, 519, 520, 521, 522
Sonoma, 14, 119, 161, 163, 164, 167, 168, 188, 197, 198, 234, 260, 264, 266, 273, 274, 276, 277, 281, 284, 285, 286, 287, 288, 289, 290
Sorì San Lorenzo, 428
Sorì Tildìn, 428
sorting table, 92
Sotolon, 156, 534
Soussans, 353
South Africa, 332-336
Southcorp, 121, 228, 230, 314
sparger, 128
Spätburgunder, 484
Spätlese, 172, 476, 478, 480, 481, 482, 487, 490
Sperss, 428
Spurrier, Stephen, 149, 294
St. Emilion, 135, 341, 352, 359, 379, 418
St. Julien, 343, 354
staves, 129, 130
Steiermark, 488, 497
Steinberger, Michael, 197
Steinfeder, 490
Stellenbosch, 336
Stelvin, 137, 140, 141
sterilization, 60, 104, 105, 111, 189, 309
Stevenson, Tom, 172, 548
stickies, 310
Stimson Lane, 271
Stockkulture, 494
Strohwein, 490
stylet, 34
suberin, 134
sugar, 19, 24, 28, 29, 30, 31, 73, 77, 81, 82, 83, 87, 89, 93, 95, 96, 97, 98, 99, 100, 111, 112, 113, 116, 117, 119, 122, 123, 124, 125, 141, 152, 153, 156, 172, 173, 174, 178, 189, 194, 241, 243, 244, 246, 247, 260, 311, 327, 329, 334, 394, 402, 445, 475, 476, 477, 478, 479, 481, 490, 492, 498, 501, 506, 507, 509, 518, 524, 525, 533, 534, 535, 536, 537, 539, 540, 542, 545, 546
sulfate, 244
sulfide, 127, 128, 138
sulfites, 111
sulfur, 11, 34, 35, 48, 50, 87, 96, 100, 102, 110, 111, 112, 113, 114, 127, 129, 138, 155, 178, 180, 185, 335, 426, 447, 546
super-cuvée, 355, 359
supermarket, 38, 98, 114, 182, 202, 206, 226, 227, 228, 235, 247, 358, 487, 520
super-second, 377, 379
Super-tasters, 151, 152, 153
super-Tuscan, 44, 96, 419, 421, 431, 432, 437, 439, 440, 441, 442, 443, 444
süssreserve, 124, 126, 475, 490
sweeteners, 152
sweetness, 29, 113, 116, 123, 126, 141, 151, 153, 164, 172, 177, 178, 179, 398, 402, 476, 477, 478, 479, 487, 491, 498,

509, 513, 527, 532, 536, 538, 539, 542, 546
Sylvaner, 401, 402, 404, 480, 484, 487
Symington, 527, 528, 531
Syndicat, 363, 371, 512
Syrah, 19, 46, 97, 107, 110, 125, 143, 146, 148, 149, 150, 154, 156, 161, 162, 255, 261, 269, 291, 297, 299, 306, 307, 323, 325, 326, 334, 337, 387, 388, 390, 407, 408, 409, 410, 411, 414, 415, 416, 440, 441, 442, 443, 449, 454, 465, 469
Systembolaget, 235
Szamorodni, 522, 543
Szepsi, Abbé, 535, 540
Szepsy, Ivan, 542
Tafelwein, 475, 490
Taittinger, 500
Tannat, 128, 327
tannin, 30-31, 91, 93, 94, 101, 102, 103, 105, 106, 107, 113, 116, 128, 129, 130, 152, 153, 162, 178, 180, 194, 196, 210, 243, 251, 326, 371, 372, 375, 418, 424, 426, 427, 433, 437, 438, 439, 456, 461, 463, 545, 546
tannins, ellagitannins, 130
tartaric acid, 1, 4, 29, 103, 121, 122, 246, 445
Tasmania, 301
Taurasi, 448
Tavel, 410
taxation, 185, 204, 205, 206, 211, 239, 369, 457, 496
Taylor, Fladgate, 526, 529, 531
TDN, 139, 156, 172, 178
teinturier, 30, 91, 124
Tempranillo, 19, 76, 146, 149, 154, 337, 451, 452, 453, 454, 460, 461, 462, 463, 465, 467, 468, 469, 470, 473, 524, 525
terpenes, 155, 156, 174, 175, 177, 534
Terra Rossa, 47-48, 301, 307
terraces, 43, 53, 54, 56, 58, 489, 492, 493, 495, 522, 524
Terrassen, 496
Terrazas de los Andes, 326
terroir, 17, 30, 33, 39, 41-68, 67, 75, 77, 79, 97, 104, 129, 149, 162, 166, 168, 173, 224, 264, 266, 272, 275, 276, 283, 284, 286, 301, 307, 318, 319, 339, 342, 352, 353, 354, 355, 356, 359, 364, 369, 371, 379, 380, 382, 384, 391, 403, 404, 405, 408, 411, 415, 416, 417, 418, 428, 433, 434, 438, 442, 454, 465, 471, 485, 492, 494, 496, 498, 505, 510, 518, 519, 522
Tesco, 228
Tesseron, Guy, 35
tetrapak, 203
Teyssier, Château, 359
Theophrastus, 1, 5, 549

Thienpont, Jacques, 352
thiol, 50, 127, 129, 155, 156, 171, 172
third growth, 367, 378
Thunderbird, 287-288
Thunevin, Jean-Luc, 359
Tignanello, 44, 441
Tinta Barroca, 473, 524
Tinta Cão, 124, 524
Tinta Roriz, 473, 524, 525
Tocai Friulano, 329
Tokaji, 400, 468, 522, 534, 535, 540, 541, 542, 543
tonneau, 70, 371
topsoil, 50, 56, 407, 493, 503
Toro, 328, 454, 468, 470
Torres, 235, 332
Torrontés, 154, 177, 322, 323, 327
Touraine, 395, 396, 397, 398, 399
Touriga Francesca, 473, 524
Touriga Nacional, 146, 452, 473, 524
traditionalist, 96, 114, 194, 425-426, 434, 462
Traisental, 489, 490, 491
tranche, 198, 348
tranches, 348
Transcaucasia, 4
Trás-os-Montes, 472
Trebbiano, 144, 148, 420, 421, 438, 445, 446
trellis, 4, 20, 22, 32
Trentino-Alto-Adige, 421
Trimbach, Hubert, 402, 404
trimethyl-dihydronaphthalene, 172
Trocard, 135
trocken, 123, 172, 173, 175, 309, 402, 475, 476, 478, 479, 481, 482, 490, 498
TTB, 263, 264
Tuscany, 14, 15, 148, 149, 168, 188, 224, 419, 421, 430, 431, 432, 434, 436, 437, 440, 442, 443, 444, 538, 547
typicity, 45, 113, 149, 150, 163, 164, 171, 181, 182, 302, 303, 329, 334, 360, 393, 394, 425, 439, 446, 459, 462, 463, 492, 497
Ugni Blanc, 144
ullage, 250
Umbria, 168
ungrafted, 13, 14, 15, 526
Unico, 74, 467, 468
University of California, Davis, 14, 124, 164, 192
unoaked, 150, 166, 167, 170
Vaccarèse, 411
Vacqueyras, 410, 411
Valandraud, Château, 359
Valbuena, 466, 467
Valckenberg, 486
Valentini, Eduardo, 445

Valpolicella, 444, 445, 450, 538, 547
Veneto, 421, 445, 446
Venezia-Friuli-Giulia, 421, 445
veraison, 23, 24, 28, 29, 44, 81, 84, 161, 170
verbena, 151
Verdejo, 453
Verdicchio dei Castelli di Jesi, 445
Vermentino di Sardegna, 522
Vernaccia, 445
Veronelli, Luigi, 430
vertical press, 92, 94, 510
Viader, 59
Vichon, 416
Vieilles Vignes, 15, 26
Vin de Paille, 113, 538
Vin de Pays, 389, 390, 391, 392, 395, 396, 414, 415, 416, 417, 419, 455, 475
vin de presse, 91, 356
Vin de Table, 110, 248, 373, 374, 389, 390, 391, 392, 395, 413, 414, 416
vin doux naturel, 538
Vin Jaune, 522
Vincor, 231, 292
vine density, 13, 27, 28, 107, 152, 153, 178, 281, 494, 495
VINIFLHOR, 389, 549
Vino da Tavola, 419, 420, 431, 440, 441, 445, 449
Vinos Finos, 456
Vinovation, 119
Vinsobres, 410
Viognier, 146, 407, 408, 409, 410
Vitis berlandieri, 12
Vitis labrusca, 11, 259, 260, 315
Vitis riparia, 12
Vitis rotundifolia, 259
Vitis rupestris, 12, 14, 124, 192
Vitis vinifera, 1-5, 8, 9, 11, 14, 15, 16, 124, 143, 180, 192, 251, 259, 260, 261, 267, 269, 270, 277, 293, 315, 549
Vitis vinifera silvestris, 21, 147
Vitis, interfertile, 549
Vitruvius, 43
Viura, 453, 460, 461
VLQPRD, 472
Voerzio, Roberto, 426
Vogüé, Comte de, 384
volatile acidity, 112, 120, 122, 424, 426
Volnay, 247, 364, 367, 381, 510
VORS, 521, 522
Vosges, 400
Vosne Romanée, 122, 364, 368, 384
Vouvray, 395, 396, 398
VQPRD, 472
Wachau, 46, 489, 490, 491, 492, 493, 495, 496, 497, 498
Wairarapa, 320

Wairau, 317, 318
Walla Walla, 267, 291
warming trend, 19, 71, 75, 77, 79, 84, 85, 173, 343, 398, 424
Washington, 168, 237, 264, 267-271, 290-292
water stress, 27, 334
Watervale, 173, 309
Weinbaugebiete, 475, 488
Weinbauregion, 488
Weinviertel, 489, 491, 497
Welschriesling, 173, 497
white grapes, 45, 108, 110, 144, 146, 147, 161, 165, 166, 175, 193, 270, 286, 299, 342, 343, 362, 382, 387, 408, 409, 410, 421, 437, 438, 439, 448, 450, 453, 461, 462, 467, 473, 482, 492, 497, 500, 502
white wine, 3, 26, 51, 64, 69, 82, 87, 89, 90, 91, 92, 93, 94, 99, 102, 103, 104, 108, 109, 110, 111, 113, 121, 129, 132, 143, 146, 148, 169, 179, 182, 183, 189, 190, 191, 193, 209, 249, 251, 258, 263, 268, 278, 297, 298, 299, 301, 308, 311, 315, 320, 321, 337, 341, 342, 361, 362, 363, 382, 387, 396, 398, 407, 409, 410, 411, 417, 421, 422, 435, 445, 446, 447, 448, 451, 462, 473, 483, 487, 489, 490, 514, 518, 521, 533, 534, 535
Wildman, 258
Willamette Valley, 164, 267, 271, 290, 291, 292
Williams-Selyem, 286
Wine Advocate, 195, 196, 197, 198, 200, 274, 314, 436
wine lake, 61, 110, 222, 314, 370, 412, 413, 415
Wine Spectator, 195, 196, 197, 198, 199, 200, 314
Winegate, 248
Winkel, 79, 484
Wynns, 307
Yakima Valley, 291
Yarra Valley, 164, 301, 303, 309, 310
yeast, indigenous, 96, 105, 114
yeast, cultured, 96, 174
YellowTail, 123, 201, 202
Ygrec, 535
yield, 13, 25, 26, 27, 164, 168, 220, 273, 354, 360, 373, 374, 392, 393, 397, 471, 492, 494, 504, 523, 536
young vines, 356
Yount, 277
Zéta, 543
Zinfandel, 17, 152, 201, 258, 261, 268, 269, 273, 277, 279, 285, 286, 420, 421, 449, 548
Zolzenberg, 404
Zweigelt, 498

Printed in Great Britain
by Amazon